W0091383

SAGE was founded in 1965 by Sara Miller McCune to support the dissemination of usable knowledge by publishing innovative and high-quality research and teaching content. Today, we publish over 900 journals, including those of more than 400 learned societies, more than 800 new books per year, a growing range of library products including archives, data, case studies, reports, and video. SAGE remains majority owned by our founder, and after her lifetime will become owned by a charitable trust that secures our continued independence.

Los Angeles | London | New Delhi | Singapore | Washington DC | Melbourne

Parmesh Shahani is an original. This beautifully written debut book, Gay Bombay, merges autobiographical, ethnographic, institutional, and historical perspectives to paint a vivid picture of the emergence of a gay community in modern India. This book will inspire and provoke many interested in understanding the intersections between sexuality, globalization, and new media.

Henry Jenkins
Provost Professor of Communication, Journalism, Cinematic Arts and
Education at the University of Southern California
Author of *Convergence Culture: Where Old and New Media Collide*

FINALLY! Finally we have the definitive gay historical document of the city we still lovingly call Bombay. Parmesh Shahani shows us in his quiet Indian way that being gay in India is no Stonewall revolution.

It comes from the heart of someone who has lived in Bombay and researched his city with love. Here is a work of academia infused with very touching personal experience. Did you know that the word homo-sexual was coined in 1869? Or when the Page 3 was launched by Times of India? *Read on to get the trivia, truth and factual history.*

Shahani's Gay Bombay *traces the modern and the old with charming first person. This book takes you to the television studios, the editing rooms, the dance floors, the chat rooms and the private parlours to discover gay Bombay in all its subtle victories, intimate vibrancy and surprising diversity.*

Late Wendell Rodricks
Fashion Designer, author and activist

Gay Bombay is a must-read! Shifting seamlessly through the personal, the Gay Bombay community, the national, and the transnational, the book gives the reader a unique understanding of what it means to be gay and Indian. Its contribution lies in giving middle-class urban gay identity a history and context. The chapters weave scholarly analysis with rich details and poignant accounts of gay life and identity. A courageous and compelling book.

Jyoti Puri
Professor of Sociology at Simmons University
Author of *Sexual States: Governance and the Struggle
against the Antisodomy Law in India's Present*

Parmesh Shahani's book is a gateway to new ideas, but also a way of seeing beyond the concept of `India Shining' in purely economic terms. It offers a wide range of approaches: part-memoir, part-thesis, part-ethnography—each part a starting point for a wider discussion. Gay Bombay comes highly recommended for anyone who is interested in how globalisation works, in India today, and Shahani's pioneering study provides a multifaceted and illuminating introduction to a brand new scene.

Charlie Henniker
Businessworld

Well researched and written in a frank and conversational style, the book manages to bridge the gap between being heavily academic and serious and being frivolous and mushy.

Taneesha Kulshetra
Mint

Shifting effortlessly from the personal to the theoretical, from the local to the global, Gay Bombay *is a pathbreaking study of homosexuality in modern Bombay/Mumbai that will be essential reading for students of gender and sexuality. Parmesh Shahani's analysis of gay, metropolitan India is one which will be welcomed among its subjects as well as by many other readers.*

Rachel Dwyer
Professor of Indian Cultures and Cinema
School of Oriental and African Studies, University of London
Author of *All you Want is Money, All you Need is Love: Sexuality and Romance in Modern India*

A chatty book by a new young voice on the block, combining autobiography, queer theory, interviews with gay male Bombayites, and descriptions of gay male life and activism in Mumbai. Easy to skim and fun to dip into.

Ruth Vanita
Professor, University of Montana
Author of *Love's Rite: Same-Sex Marriage in India and the West*

For someone like me who has been part of the queer community movement in Mumbai since 1999, Parmesh's Gay Bombay (the 2020 special anniversary edition) reads like a personal diary. The book does a laudable job of providing an engaging portrayal of queer lives in contemporary India. Since its first print in 2008, there have been huge developments impacting queer lives here, such as the decriminalization of homosexual relationships in 2018 with reading down of Section 377. Millions of young queer folks now have the courage to come out and express themselves at forums, an idea that seemed unthinkable two decades ago. Challenges remain of course, as the book points out, as regards the continuing struggle to gain further social acceptance and legal rights along with ensuring greater representation of the even more marginalized sections within the queer community.

Balachandran Ramiah
Core administrator of the Gay Bombay group
A petitioner in the Supreme Court against Section 377

SPECIAL ANNIVERSARY EDITION

GAY
BOMBAY

Globalization, Love and (Be)longing
in Contemporary India

PARMESH
SHAHANI

Los Angeles I London I New Delhi
Singapore I Washington DC I Melbourne

First published in 2008
This edition published in 2020 by

SAGE Publications India Pvt Ltd
B1/I-1 Mohan Cooperative Industrial Area
Mathura Road, New Delhi 110 044, India
www.sagepub.in

SAGE Publications Inc
2455 Teller Road
Thousand Oaks, California 91320, USA

SAGE Publications Ltd
1 Oliver's Yard, 55 City Road
London EC1Y 1SP, United Kingdom

SAGE Publications Asia-Pacific Pte Ltd
18 Cross Street #10-10/11/12
China Square Central
Singapore 048423

Published by Vivek Mehra for SAGE Publications India Pvt Ltd and typeset in 10/13 pt Amerigo BT by AG Infographics, Delhi.

Library of Congress Cataloging-in-Publication Data

Names: Shahani, Parmesh, author.
Title: Gay bombay : globalization, love and (be)longing in contemporary India / Parmesh Shahani.
Description: Special anniversary edition. | Thousand Oaks, California: SAGE, 2020. | Includes bibliographical references.
Identifiers: LCCN 2020016181 | ISBN 9789353884208 (paperback) | ISBN 9789353884215 (epub) | ISBN 9789353884222 (ebook)
Subjects: LCSH: Gays–India. | Gay culture–India. | Gays–India–Social conditions.
Classification: LCC HQ76.3.I4 S53 2020 | DDC 306.76/6–dc23
LC record available at https://lccn.loc.gov/2020016181

ISBN: 978-93-5388-420-8 (PB)

SAGE Team: Manisha Mathews, Sandhya Gola and Rajinder Kaur

To my gurus—Henry Jenkins, Tuli Banerjee and Edward Baron Turk.
And to Bombay: muse, nemesis, saviour, home.

Thank you for choosing a SAGE product!
If you have any comment, observation or feedback,
I would like to personally hear from you.

Please write to me at **contactceo@sagepub.in**

Vivek Mehra, Managing Director and CEO, SAGE India.

Contents

Acknowledgements

This book would not have been possible without the backing of my terrific MIT thesis committee. Henry Jenkins was the ideal thesis supervisor and also ideal boss. He, along with Edward Baron Turk and Tuli Banerjee, helped me conceive, mould and eventually pare down the manuscript to its current length. William Urrichio helped with the ini-tial push and (then freshly minted University of Michigan professor!) Aswin Punathambekar provided the motivational pull at the finish line.

I wanted to write this book in multiple voices. I am not sure that I have succeeded, but among the different academic voices that I had the pleasure of discovering while researching this book, were Kath Weston, John Campbell, Arjun Appadurai and closer home, Henry Jenkins, Grant McCracken and Robert Kozinets. These are the voices that have inspired me to continue to keep one foot in academia and if I can eventually manage to express myself with even a fraction of their lucidity and conviction, I will consider myself a success.

I am grateful to my family of classmates and co-workers at MIT Comparative Media Studies, my home during the three years that this book was being written.

I am obliged to the many advisors, experts and confidantes that helped me during my research, with follow-ups, reading drafts and making suggestions for this book. To the wonderful SAGE Publications team in New Delhi, a big big thanks.

To all my interviewees, I am overwhelmed by how you freely gave me your time and your stories and the several other random acts of kindness that made this journey so special.

I must express my gratitude to my family of friends spread all over the globe, who love me not in spite of my quirks, but because of them and whose affection provided vital nourishment during the process of writing. To my maternal grandparents, I owe an eternal debt for raising me like no parents ever could and to my parents, I am grateful for the space, the intellectual freedom, the understanding and the acceptance.

Finally, to my gay support systems—Gay Bombay for the subject matter of the book, for helping me rediscover my city and myself; Humsafar for their always accessible advice; the MASALA network in Boston for introducing me to fabulous *desi* queerdom; the incredible resources of LBGT@MIT and the MIT community at large, for being such a wonderful refuge while this book was being written.

Preface to the Special Anniversary Edition

If you'd told me in 2008 at the time of this book's release, that there would be a second edition, or that this book was important enough to even consider a second edition of, I'd have wondered what you'd been smoking. I was just so grateful for it to be published in the first place. Now, when I read the comments from professors I deeply admire like Ulka Anjaria, Kareem Khubchandani and Dhiren Borisa in this special anniversary edition, it feels slightly surreal that this small academic labour of love continues to have an afterlife. Over the years I have stumbled upon the book in the most unlikely of places – the library at the University of Auckland in May 2009, or as a part of artist Aditi Singh's exhibit installation at gallery Chemould in Mumbai in July 2019, to think of just two.

I wrote *Gay Bombay* between 2003 and 2005 as a memoir-ethnography. I heavily mined my own experiences of growing up gay, and my life between Bombay and Boston, which is where I was living at the time it was being written, and mixed them up with what I learned being part of the online forum Gay Bombay. When I re-read it now, I am overcome by multiple emotions.

In the chapter 'Up Close and Personal' I wrote about wanting to choose between living in India or the US based on considering what was important to my partner then. That relationship did not survive. In fact, it ended the very day I received the first copy of *Gay Bombay*. It was surreal that this book, which was dedicated to him, was being delivered to me by courier in Boston, literally right in the middle of our breaking up conversation. So filmy, *no*? The *"Kabhi Kabhie"* dedication to him is gone in this edition and my heart belongs to someone else now, as you will see in the poem that this foreword ends with. Still, each time I read the parts in which my ex appears, some wistfulness does happen, given that we haven't been in touch over the years.

Actually, the book makes me cringe in quite a few places when I re-read it. How naïve and self-assured I used to be! Why did I put in so *many* citations and why is there *so much* Appadurai love? The difference between writing something in one's 20s and now, in one's 40s, is stark. There are parts that I re-read and I am like, seriously, I don't remember this at all. Did I read all of this material? Did I write these words?

So much has changed over the years. One of the people I interviewed then has died; many others have gone off grid. Gay Bombay's online version during my research was mostly a mailing list on Yahoo groups – the Yahoo group service itself was discontinued at the end of 2019 – but by then the Gay Bombay online action had long shifted to Facebook. Yet so much remains the same. Sure, the tech is different, so instead of cybercafes or their own PCs, people are now messaging each other on their phones using WhatsApp or Instagram DMs or through dating apps like Grindr instead of Friendster which I'd written about then, but the urge to connect remains the same. Likewise, as I realized while researching *Queeristan*, my second book, we continue to negotiate and re-imagine very *desi* ways of being queer, whether in the workplace, the location that *Queeristan* is set in, or in our personal lives, which is what *Gay Bombay* is mostly about. This re-imagination continues to be *very* Bollywood inspired, and the construct of family continue to dominate our imaginations both work-wise as well as personally.

What *has* certainly changed a lot between the first and second editions of this book is the law. It has swung like a pendulum between criminalization and decriminalization of homosexuality. I remember the historic morning of July 2, 2009, the date when the Delhi High Court first decriminalized homosexuality in India, in its historic Naz judgement. The judgement spoke of the inclusively that was deeply ingrained in Indian society and protected by our country's constitution. What an amazing feeling it was for section 377 to finally go away just a year after my book release! This euphoria lasted for about four years until on December 11, 2013, it was like we had received one giant slap. Based on an appeal that opposed the 2009 Naz judgement, the Supreme court stated that queer community was a 'miniscule minority' in our country and therefore not deserving of constitutional protections. It put the onus on our country's Parliament and reversed the Delhi High Court judgment. Can you imagine? From criminal to not criminal to criminal again? Shudder!

Finally, after some more years of legal struggle, on September 6, 2018, a special five-judge constitution bench of the Supreme Court read down Section 377 as a law that violated the dignity and privacy of the LGBTQ community in our country. This progressive judgement, popularly called as the Navtej judgement, came on the heels of two other progressive Supreme Court judgments – one on Privacy (2017) and another on Trans rights (the NALSA judgement of 2014).

However, the rights that the progressive judgments like NALSA and Navtej have given us have been severely been curtailed by the new Transgender (Protection of) Rights Act 2019, which was passed without any debate in the Lok Sabha on August 5, 2019. This regressive act now mandates that India's transgender citizens submit themselves to a "certification process" involving a government official and doctor. Also, if transgender people are sexually attacked, their attackers face a maximum jail term of two years, against a minimum of seven years for women who are attacked.

So there's been a lot of back and forth and as things stand today, the situation is far from perfect. The regressive Trans Act certainly needs to be modified. We also need laws that recognize same sex marriage and enable same sex partners to inherit their spouse's property and also make decisions about the medical treatment of their spouses. We need anti-discrimination legislation, legislation that bans conversion therapy and protects intersex babies and minors from non-consensual conversion surgeries. I am enthused that there are many progressive states like Tamil Nadu, Kerala, Karnataka and Chhattisgarh, that are supporting their LGBTQ residents either with progressive policies, or with employment opportunities and I am hopeful that these acts of inclusion will percolate outward to other states in the country, as well as upwards, to a national level.

Another thing that has changed is that when *Gay Bombay* came out, it was one of a handful of projects that chronicled queer lives in our country. I'm thinking of the books that I referred to while writing it, like the Ashwini Sukhtankar edited *Facing the Mirror: Lesbian Writing from India* (1999), the Hoshang Merchant edited *Yaarana: Gay Writing from India* (1999), Saleem Kidwai and Ruth Vanita's *Same Sex Love in India* (2000), R Raj Rao's novels like *The Boyfriend* (2003), and Arvind Narrain and Gautam Bhan's wonderful *Because I Have A Voice: Queer Politics in India* (2005) and Gayatri Reddy's

With Respect to Sex: Negotiating Hijra Identity in South India (2005). I'm also thinking of the few landmark feature films like *Fire* (1996) and *My Brother Nikhil* (2005), or the documentaries like Riyad Wadia's *BOMgAY* (1996) or Nish Saran's *Summer in My Veins* (1999) that I saw during the course of researching this book.

Over the subsequent years there has been an explosion of queer content about our lives. The Queer Ink is a book publisher and film production company based in Mumbai and its founder Shobhna Kumar told me in January 2020 that she has catalogued about 250 books that deal specifically with queer and Indian themes, across both fiction and non-fiction. There is also an abundance of queer films now and showcases for them at festivals across the country. (For instance, the KASHISH queer film festival in Mumbai is now in its 11th year and growing bigger each year.) There are also more and more films being made in the mainstream with queer themes, whether in Hindi, like *Aligarh* (2015) or *Ek Ladki ko Dekha to Aisa Laga* (2019) or *Shubh Mangal Zyaada Saavdhaan* (2020) or other languages like the Tamil film *Super Deluxe* (2019) or the Malayalam film *Moothon* (2019).

The internet has been an incredible boon. There are now dedicated YouTube channels like Trans Vision that speak about trans lives, multimedia digital magazines like *Gaylaxy* and *Gaysi*, and hours and hours of queer content on apps like TikTok.

The rate of change has also increased. Each month or so now, I hear of a new town or city organizing a pride march or creating a support space or a queer festival, such as the Raipur Pride march in Chhattisgarh, or the Awadh Queer Literature Festival, that flourishes in Lucknow despite extremely challenging environment. Organizations like Xukia in Assam and Ya All in Manipur are doing exemplary work. My team at the Godrej India Culture Lab in Mumbai has been working on cataloguing queer organizations across the country and they have already listed 70 so far. Another difference between now and 15 years ago is that today, the queer movement is moving more and more towards intersectionality. There are groups being formed like the Dalit Queer Project, the Chinky Homo Project and the Queer Muslim Project all of which are addressing different intersectional queer identities and I am awestruck by their vision and passion of their founders.

There is much more visibility in the media today than there was in 2008. The different section 377 verdicts, the NALSA judgement and the journey of the subsequent transgender bill were widely reported across the country, in print as well as television media. To me, the key media moment of the past 15 years has been the *Satyamev Jayate* episode 3 from season 3 called "Accepting Alternative Sexualities", that first aired on 19 October, 2014. The show had Bollywood film star Aamir Khan interview queer people like trans scriptwriter Gazal Dhaliwal and her supportive parents, and also featured activists like Anjali Gopalan and Gautam Bhan who spoke about why section 377 needed to go (it had just come back at that time), and psychiatrist Dr Anjali Chhabria who patiently answered audience questions about whether homosexuality was a disease and if yoga could cure it. (The answers were no and no, obviously!) It was seen by millions of people in their homes across the country and continues to resonate, years later on Youtube, where this particular episode has 2.5 million views at the time of writing this preface. I can't tell you about how many of today's young queers have shown this particular episode to their family members during their coming out process.

The 2017 Vicks ad with the transgender activist Gauri Sawant, showcasing her real life story of mothering an abandoned girl child, was another key media disrupter, because of YouTube. It has more than 10 million views at the time of writing this foreword. What is common across both the Vicks ad as well as the *Satyamev Jayate* episode is the focus on family and the importance of parental support. Queer people needing support from their parents, and queer people being parents, to support others.

This is something I wrote about 15 years ago in this book and it continues to be paramount – being queer in India is all about negotiating family. The extraordinary Sweekar parent support group was formed in November 2017 in Mumbai. At the end of 2019, it had 60 members in Mumbai as well as on phone-chat groups, which included parents residing in Indian cities like Ahmedabad, Hyderabad, Bengaluru, Indore, and also from countries like Australia, USA, Oman and Thailand. So many more parents interact with the Sweekar group on social media. The parents hold regular get togethers. Learn new things. Understand, and accept their queer children. None of this was happening in 2008, when the first edition of Gay Bombay came out, and it is exciting to witness these new solidarities of love.

Personally too a lot has changed over the years. When *Gay Bombay* was first published, I had just finished a Master's degree and joined Mahindra. While there, I was satisfied with the special treatment I received from my bosses and didn't think it was important to stand up and ask for organisation-wide inclusion, but one of the first things I did when I joined Godrej to head the Godrej India Culture Lab, was advocate for changes in the company's policies to include LBGTQ people. It was personally important to me to secure my rights but it ended up with Godrej setting an example for companies across India who perhaps were too afraid to start this journey because of the shadow of Section 377.

While the legal battle was on, we continued to push for LGBTQ rights and visibility through the Godrej India Culture Lab's programming. We held numerous Mumbai pride and queer themed events that looking Indian queerness through various lenses – caste, protest and fashion, to list just three. In 2017, we collaborated with prestigious organizations like the United Nations to launch their UN Standards of Conduct for Business on our Godrej premises, and in 2018, I wrote the Godrej *Manifesto for Trans Inclusion in the Indian Workplace* along with my colleague Nayanika Nambiar that detailed a strong business case for LGBTQ inclusion. It has since been shared with more than 50 companies in the country. I have in a sense, become an ambassador for queer inclusion in corporate India!

When I talk to all these other companies, either at their own headquarters, or at forums organized by organizations like CII or FICCI, I use statistics and I use stories. The stats impress them – they are awestruck when they realise that the estimated size of India's LGBTQ economy could be US$ 200 billion, or that the cost of homophobia in our country is US$ 32 billion. But what moves them the most are the stories. Stories of queer people like Zainab Patel (KPMG), Aditya Batavia (Thoughtworks), Anubhuti Banerjee (TATA Steel) whose organizations have empowered them to flourish. Of the multiple job fairs taking place. Of initiatives like Periferry that trains and places transpeople or of Kochi metro that boldly goes out and recruits trans people en masse.

As I do these talks, I am reminded of how it all began – in a sense – with this book – *Gay Bombay*. While I have myself shifted, from academia to the business world, the personal stories that I heard 15 years ago while researching *Gay Bombay* were not that different from what I have been hearing recently. People continue to want love and respect, be treated decently by their families and workplace colleagues, and imagine a happy future. I am glad to see in today's India just how many families and workplaces are stepping up to create an ecosystem of change where this happy future looks more and more possible.

Another change personally over the years has been my own persona. From being someone who was rather shy 15 years ago, to being a flamboyant over the top fashionista who is regularly featured in our country's fashion magazine "best dressed" lists, it's been quite a ride! In fact, my fashionista journey began in 2008 with one of the first *Gay Bombay* book release events at the office of the fashion magazine *Verve* that I has just taken over as Editorial Director of. I wore a rather risqué rani pink silk kurta for that party with most of the top buttons open. I had also painfully waxed my chest – never again. (The risk-reward ratio just isn't worth it!) From there to being a regular at fashion weeks and parties over the years, even though I'm not directly involved with the glamour business any more – what can I say except that I'm loving every moment of it. Whether in fashion or in business, or as a blue tick holding micro influencer in the digital world, I am in a different place today than I was in 2008, and I consciously use my vantage point to push for queer visibility and inclusion, wherever and whenever I can.

I felt young when this book came out in 2008, but today, at age 44 I don't feel so young any more! At our Godrej India Culture Lab, I am surrounded by a team and interns that are all in their 20s and I can safely say that each one of my team members is much more talented and hardworking than me. I really think the world would be much better if we let the youth run it. It is now my endeavour to simply stay out of their way as much as I can, and come up with ways to pass my knowledge and experiences on to them and future generations. Time for legacy building!

One of the things my team members have taught me to do is to protest. As I march with them in the different student led protests in my city at the time of writing this foreword, I watch in awe, as my fellow citizens across the country brave so much more, and risk so much more. What inspires me today are the intersectional voices on the ground – the feminist, trans rights, anti-caste and environmental conservation movements are all coming together in solidarity, and this is so wonderful to witness. I was pretty ignorant of intersectionality when I wrote *Gay Bombay* and over the years, because of the exposure I have had, because of the kindness of friends and most of all because of my fab team, it has become the framework with which I view the world.

In the context of all of the above, what is the point of reading this old book about 15 years after it was first written? I think there are two points actually. The first is that queer lives matter. Our stories matter. The lives of people chronicled in *Gay Bombay* still continue to be relevant. The highlight of re-reading this book for me is in re-visiting the narratives of all my interviewees who shared their stories with me with so much trust. Just like dear old Rose when she gets back on the Titanic, I simply have to open this book to hear the voices of my interviewees and flashback to the time I spent doing the research for this project. (Cue for "My heart will go on…." to interrupt your line of thought, now!)

Point number two, the *modus vivendi* that I ended the book with then is as relevant now as ever. I had written about the conflict between the Gay Bombay group and the Humsafar Trust in the book, and also differences within the queer community over issues of class, language, straight acting-ness versus effeminacy, coming out versus being closeted, the different meanings of activism and attitudes towards HIV. I wrote in the book's initial introduction that within all these struggles, what was being negotiated was "the very stability of the idea of Indianness". My interviewees had fashioned a distinctly Indian gay identity for themselves, as opposed to a Western gay identity. I had hoped in the book's introduction that "as India re-imagines itself as a global superpower in the 21st century it is vital that this re-imagination includes the presence of its diverse and marginalized populations". I had extended this hope in the book's conclusion that the process of re-imagination should extend itself within the queer community towards marginalized queers, whose voices were often unheard in the larger conversations about Indian queerness. I had rather earnestly proposed a *modus vivendi* as the book's conclusion. I wanted to build a common ground for the queer community in which we came together to work through our differences. Parts of this *modus vivendi* are very idealistic when I read it now, but this is exactly why I feel it is so important to re-visit.

Today, as you read this special anniversary edition, our community continues to have conflicts. Conflicts around religion or caste, or terms we want to call ourselves. What kind of world are we going to create together now that section 377 is gone but we have a regressive trans act? How do we find the connectedness between trans rights, Dalit rights, Adivasi rights, and the rights of other minorities and move ahead together? I believe that we need the *modus vivendi* of this book's conclusion now, more than ever. Its components that include "strategic essentialism", pursuing equitable change, fighting for small as well as large changes, co-opting the media and emphasizing the rootedness of Indian queer histories, can be used to create a loose solidarity based, on what unites us, rather than our differences.

I haven't changed a lot of the text of the original book in this special anniversary edition – I want you to read it as it was then. I have, in a few places, added my thoughts or comments on the book, especially when what is being written about seems dated. To make it easier to read, these additional statements are in square brackets, to distinguish them from the original text. I do hope you will read it with kindness – as a slice of contemporary queer history, and also as a companion piece to my new book *Queeristan* – which in a sense takes off, where *Gay Bombay* ended. Speaking of connecting threads, I am going to leave you with this poem that I wrote for *Conde Nast Traveller*'s June 2018 queer love and travel edition. Too mush? What to do, we are like that only. This poem, just like my life now, is for my partner S.

Jannat
As we stopped at the top of Falaknuma Palace, the guide, appropriately named Faiz, recited in Urdu, a poem that said very simply – *Jannat* is where love lives.

Goa. Rose petals. A tub. Bubbles. Filled by a thoughtful room attendant, Who recognised intimacy in just one glance. Amritsar. The Golden Temple. Heads bowed. Grateful. Time. You.

Chhola-kulcha.

Tripping over a tree trunk. The sound of woodpeckers overhead. A fight all the way back. Landour. The lower Himalayas. Jabarkhet.

Our first Pride March. Your hand on my waist. Post pride party. Prosecco. Foolish smiling. A glimpse of your ankle at the departure gate. Oxidised silver *payal*, my bracelet. A cold Boylan soda, overlooking the High Line. You trickle down my throat, just one direct flight away. You. You. You. You.

You in bed, in Jaipur, freshly checked in, wearing three necklaces of welcome beads. Nothing else. Small fish. River fish, in the *Chao Phraya*, as our boat winds downstream. To Kumarakom where we argue over the biennale we have just left. Kissing.

Thyagaraja Swamy Temple. Restored murals. Sacred music. Silk. Soft. Jodhpur. A tent. Hot, passionate afternoon sex. *Lahariya* shopping. You, you, you. Everywhere. The presence of absence. The dripping desire of your touch.

Love is a thread
That travels between us.

January 2020
Mumbai

Preface to the First Edition

Gay Bombay is an online-offline community (comprising a website, a newsgroup and physical events in Bombay city), that was formed as a result of the intersection of certain historical conjectures with the disjunctures caused via the flows of the radically shifting ethnoscape, financescape, politiscape, mediascape, technoscape and ideoscape of urban India in the 1990s. Within this book, using a combination of multi-sited ethnography, textual analysis, historical documentation analysis and memoir writing, I attempt to provide various macro and micro perspectives on what it means to be a gay man located in Gay Bombay at a particular point of time. Specifically, exploring what being gay means to the members of Gay Bombay and how they negotiate locality and globalization, their sense of identity as well as a feeling of community within its online/offline world. On a broader level, I critically examine the formulation and reconfiguration of contemporary Indian gayness in the light of its emergent cultural, media and political alliances.

Gay Bombay is a community that is imagined and fluid; identity here is both fixed and negotiated, and to be gay in Gay Bombay signifies being 'glocal'—it is not just gayness but *Indianized* gayness. I realize that within the various struggles in and around Gay Bombay, what is being negotiated is the very stability of the idea of Indianness. The book concludes with a *modus vivendi*—my draft manifesto for the larger queer movement that I believe Gay Bombay is an integral part of, and a sincere hope that as the struggle for queer rights enters its exciting new phase, groups like Gay Bombay might be able to co-operate with other queer groups in the country, and march on the path to progress, together.

1

Gay Bombay and Queer Futures[*]

Ulka Anjaria[†]

Parmesh Shahani's book *Gay Bombay: Globalization, Love and (Be)Longing in Contemporary India* is a fascinating text that marks a contemporary moment of possibility for India's queer communities. Although originally published in 2008, 10 years before the repeal of Section 377 in September 2018, the book's optimism, playfulness and sense of experiment make it potentially even more relevant for today's moment, when long-standing activism and judicial petitioning have finally borne fruit, leaving time and energy for creative envisioning of India's queer futures. Like so much contemporary queer writing in India, *Gay Bombay* does not live in Section 377's shadow,[1] but probes the depths of queer experience in the city beyond the domains defined by the law, marking out spaces of pride, desire, 'love and (be)longing'.

The book crosses a number of genres, from a sociological study to an intimate coming-out narrative, a diary/memoir and a manifesto. This movement gives the book a productively excessive quality, which refuses to be definitive or demarcate a singular community or type of person that is its centre. By contrast, it registers, on a formal level, the heterogeneity of queer experiences in Mumbai. On every page, the book is dotted with narrative breaks, different fonts and asides, which makes the reading experience itself an experience in

[*] Some arguments of this chapter have been previously published in Ulka Anjaria, *Reading India Now: Contemporary Formations in Literature and Popular Culture* (Philadelphia, PA: Temple University Press, 2019; New Delhi: Orient BlackSwan, 2019).

[†] Ulka Anjaria is Professor of English at Brandeis University, Massachusetts. She is the author of *Realism in the Twentieth-Century Indian Novel: Colonial Difference and Literary Form* and *Reading India Now: Contemporary Formations in Literature and Popular Culture*.

heterogeneity. This refusal of singularity becomes the book's defining feature and characterizes the queer future that Shahani and so many of his informants seek to inhabit.

GAY BOMBAY

The heart of the book is a study of the Gay Bombay social network, both its online cultures and the events it has been organizing around Mumbai since its founding in 1998. Central to this discussion are important questions surrounding any kind of group mobilization: what binds a group? How can it be both meaningful to its members and broadly inclusive? What counts as political practice? And so on. Shahani addresses these questions through his own impressions and one-on-one interviews, both online and offline, that allow him to begin to discover 'the challenges and practical issues faced by gay men seeking long-term relationships in Bombay'. The best parts of these discussions are the long passages where Shahani combines thoughts from different people he interviewed, showing the sheer range of beliefs and views about queer futurity. These passages powerfully refute any sense of there being one singular gay community or of any homogeneity of viewpoint while also celebrating this multiplicity as part of the politically and socially rich nature of gay Bombay.

The brief discussion of Gay Bombay's role as a political organization is one of the most nuanced in the book; Shahani contrasts Gay Bombay to Humsafar, an organization much more involved in activism and health education. Some activists are critical of Gay Bombay because it focuses primarily on organizing social events rather than having a clear political agenda, but as Shahani points out, 'For many of my interviewees, Gay Bombay's appeal lay in the fact that it was not an activist organization.' One informant even said, 'that the parties that Gay Bombay organized at different venues all over the city were a kind of activism in their own way'—a view that raises important questions about the role of fun and pleasure in politics, especially in queer politics.[2]

The fact that most of the members of Gay Bombay are English-speaking and upper middle class is something that Shahani does not shy away from, and he frankly states that there are simply not very many studies of middle-class Indians, as researchers tend to be more interested in the poor. This allows him to dig deep into questions not only of sexuality but of desire and futurity in the post-liberalization era, questions that are often left out of current academic discussions which want to summarily dismiss all desire or aspiration as simply 'neoliberal'.

PROPERLY GAY

Interspersed throughout this academic study is Shahani's own coming-out story, which occupies much less of the book than his interviews and his reflections on gay cultures and politics but is nevertheless essential to it. This story sheds light on a significant concern for LGBTQ+ activism in India and across the Global South, which is how to imagine a specifically queer Indian identity even while acknowledging that queer people have something in common regardless of national borders. The normative coming-out story still tends to be white and middle-class, and the class split within the Indian LGBTQ+ population is still significant. Shahani's personal story beautifully illuminates the contours of this question. So while Shahani acknowledges that it was only when he travelled to the USA that he felt the complete freedom of living a gay life, he also refuses to reinforce binaries of Indian sexual backwardness, noting that his 'first gay relationship' after returning to India was with a man whose 'family was completely accepting of our relationship…it was that awesome!' and concluding that while appreciating America's sexual freedom, it wasn't enough for him:

> I had hoped that by coming to America I could finally become *properly* gay, but strangely enough and irrationally enough, I am missing and often craving for a notion of India that I had thought I had happily left behind. I realize that I need to understand my Indianness along with my gayness—they can't be two separate journeys.

The importance of this revelation should not be underestimated, as it offers one potential resolution to the question of embedded queer specificity as opposed to a supposed universalism whose centre is in the West. This appears in the work of the Gay Bombay organization as well, and within ongoing discussions among India's queer and LGBTQ+ communities around 'the use of terms like *gay*' as opposed to 'the more functional *men who have sex with men*'. Shahani aptly points out that to his informants, '*gay* does not mean what it does in America, or the West at large. They have creatively played with it, modified it, made it their own'.

We see this in the interviews as well. His informants are not content with a simplistic idea that equates freedom with coming out; while many of them are still not free to fully express their sexuality in India, most have no desire to simply pick up and leave for America. This comes from a subtle, rather than stereotypical, understanding of the nature of Indian homophobia, evident, for instance, in the words of Vidwan who says, 'There seems to be a lot more acceptance or at least tolerance of queerness in India as long as it does not come in the way of heterosexual procreative activity'. Two of Shahani's informants 'spoke of leaving India in search of their gay identity, but returning in disappointment—their experiences in foreign lands were an affirmation of their separateness from Western gay culture instead of the utopia they had hoped to find'.

These imaginings, in addition to Shahani's story, are not presented linearly but scattered throughout the book, reinforcing a sense of generic instability that is productive rather than distracting. Amidst the story of his coming out, we have persistent narrative asides that include personal anecdotes about a pickup or a first foray into gay porn, the description of a love affair and so on. Some of these are light and sentimental, and others incisive and summative. In their very formal heterogeneity, they index the importance of formal heterogeneity itself, as a necessary component of queer 'narrative'.

Thus, the book tells of Shahani's coming out not only as gay but as Indian, manifesting in his return to India from the USA. Shahani is privileged enough to have had the choice: to stay or to return, and by the end, he seems to have accepted the revelation that 'At heart, I guess I am a gay Indian and a gay Bombayite most of all.'

Bombay/Mumbai

Queering genre often means telling stories along non-normative or unexpected temporalities, and it is precisely this queering that allows alternative stories of Mumbai to emerge that break from the widely disseminated timeline of its decline from the cosmopolitan 19th-century metropolis to the communal and neoliberal city of the present. Indeed, most contemporary representations of Mumbai are mappable along this narrative of decline, which begins with the rise of the Shiv Sena and its communalist, xenophobic reimagining of the city, followed by the anti-Muslim riots in 1992–1993 and the city's name change a few years later. This narrative is also supplemented by two other narratives of decline, one based in economic liberalization and the rise of a consumer economy, and the second propagated by the diasporic subject, who returns to Mumbai (or Delhi, or Kolkata) only to find it a shell of its former self.[3] The writer's loss, based in the twin failures of secularism and socialism, permeates narratives of the Indian city.

It is notable, then, that Shahani refuses this cliché of Mumbai. Indeed, *Gay Bombay*'s aesthetic of narrative breaks and bricolage to tell the story of the city as a queer space also reveals an investment in synchronicity—the simultaneity of different kinds of queer lives—that offers an epistemological alternative to decline. Thus, when the book cuts, sometimes jarringly, from long excerpts of Bollywood songs to footnoted academic writing to scenes of sexual intimacy, and as the locales veer from Mumbai to Cambridge, Massachusetts, and back—with several liminal scenes in airports and airplanes—we can read these as a deliberate refutation of conventional urban writing in India.

Provocatively, Shahani uses the colonial name for the city in the book's title and throughout the text, seeming to do so as a statement against the renaming of the city in 1995. This use of 'Bombay' is common in writings that rely on the decline narrative, most notably Suketu Mehta's *Maximum City*, in which he rants:

> There was no good reason to change the name of Bombay.... The Gujaratis and Maharashtrians always called it Mumbai when speaking Gujarati or Marathi, and Bombay when speaking English. There was no need to choose. In 1995, the Sena demanded that we choose, in all our languages, Mumbai. This is how the ghatis took revenge on us.[4]

However, on closer inspection, Shahani's use seems quite different than Mehta's. Indeed, the title of the book has a second referent in addition to the city: the Gay Bombay group that has been a 'queer haven' for gay men in the city since its founding in 1998. And the use of the word Bombay in this double sense reconciles the decline narrative with a queer futurity.

For, in fact, the decline narrative appears largely unsustainable from a queer perspective, something clear in other queer Mumbai texts such as R. Raj Rao's *The Boyfriend* and Jerry Pinto's *Murder in Mahim* as well. For one, queer spaces have multiplied in the city recently, and economic liberalization has opened up possibilities for finding communities online and connecting with queer allies across the city, the country and the world, even as, Shahani reminds us, these build on a longer history of gay organizing from the pre-liberalization period. Any straightforward critique of economic liberalization must reconcile with these facts. Second, Shahani suggests that 'Gay Bombay' can also be seen as a queering of the city's name. In another article he wrote the same year as *Gay Bombay*, Shahani offers a different interpretation of the city's name change, through a reading of Riyad Wadia's film *BOMgAY*, considered to be 'the country's first "gay" film'[5] and based on a poem by queer writer and activist R. Raj Rao. Here, Shahani argues that the use of Bombay rather than Mumbai in the film's title represents a queering of the name: 'Insisting on Bombay, but queering it with a bold pink "g" and the pink triangle gay icon below it was Wadia's way of reclaiming a recently lost heritage as well as mapping an emerging new space.'[6] This repurposing of the old name is markedly different from the insistent use of 'Bombay' in a book like *Maximum City*; here, the term references the past *and* the future, where 'BOMgAY'—and perhaps also Gay Bombay—is an attempt to map out a more inclusive future by queering an antiquated name.

The refusal to abide by a linear decline narrative is also visible in Shahani's personal story of leaving India, which he scatters throughout the book. This story is not the typical one of exile and loss; in fact, the text ends on his *return* to Mumbai, where he (although this took place after the book was completed) is currently the director of the Godrej India Culture Lab in northern Mumbai. His relationship to the USA is thus a constant back and forth rather than a one-way immigration—a movement that is more representative of the contemporary moment than the old exilic imaginaries of a Salman Rushdie, an Amitav Ghosh or, indeed, a Suketu Mehta, where Bombay (never Mumbai) is *only* the city left behind, and any return, always temporary, must at its heart be a grappling with that loss.

We can go even further to say that Shahani seems to have a playful relationship with these oft-repeated clichés about decline and loss, as evinced in the experimental way he uses quotations in his scenes of transit. For instance, when he lands in the Mumbai airport, he writes: 'I have made this descent into Bombay airport so many times in the past, but this time when the plane taxies to a halt on the shantytown hugged runway, my emotions begin to swell.' Even readers who have never been to Mumbai will recognize this moment, so embedded in accounts of returning home in diasporic Indian writing. Yet Shahani immediately draws attention to the over-representation of this moment of arrival in his college, like the use of quotations from several books, including *Maximum City* and *The Boyfriend*. These quotations have no clear diegetic justification; he never says he was reading the books or explains why these quotes come to him at this particular time. They are set off from the narrative in italics and have only a metonymic relationship with Shahani's story. The result, therefore, is neither a criticism nor an endorsement of these earlier writings. Rather they point to the experience of the city as itself textually mediated. Shahani's 'Bombay' is thus presented as an oversignified city that can be encountered only through previous representations.

QUEER FUTURES

This experimental, mediated quality makes *Gay Bombay* inherently future oriented, and given the frustrations of so many activists in the early 2000s working to repeal Section 377, it reads as a surprisingly optimistic book. There are some touching stories of parents who have accepted their children's sexuality, and even Gay Bombay, far from a perfect organization, serves to many as a queer family. There is significant interest, from Shahani and his informants, on what he calls 'the imagined future' of gay life in India. This of course involves the repealing of the odious law, but also continuing to think about what an ideal future might actually look like, who will be included in its imagination, and the path to getting there. Shahani is honest that his research did not include 'lesbians, bisexuals, the transgender, *kothis*, *hijras* and the rest of the spectrum of sexual minorities in India', and clearly there is more work to do to think of Indian queerness inclusively, across class and community. He is also honest in naming occasional difficulties he faced in this project; for instance, when a Gay Bombay member 'wonder[ed] whether I am promoting the gay cause or my own self'. He is forthright about his own and other members' class privilege and describes class as a kind of spectre that affects so many interactions in the city, queer and straight alike. But despite the significant obstacles that lie ahead, Shahani and his informants are still able to dream, and it is these dreams that constitute the heart of this book: 'I think the coolest things would be to hold hands and walk on the roads of Bombay with my lover'; 'I want a lover. If not children, at least a dog or a cat. I want a home'; 'I will have a gay marriage. My family will come and dance.' The book's conclusion also offers concrete projects for queer advancement, including realizing 'that change is not just coming in from the west but also from other parts of the world' and the insistence that 'closeted gay men should not be shunned', emphasizing that there cannot be one model for coming out that applies unthinkingly to everyone.

In today's somewhat dismal moment, it is an especial pleasure to read a book that ends with hope and what feels like a genuine belief in a better future. 'I like Bollywood style happy endings,' Shahani claims, proudly, 'endings that fill one with hope and the possibility of something magical'. This sums up the tone of the book, which is optimistic but not naïve, hopeful but still clear-eyed. It is a book that does not look on the obstacles Indian queer people have to overcome as inherent signs of Indian backwardness, but rather pragmatically outlines what can be done for a better, more equitable and more *mazaa*-filled queer future.

NOTES

1. Ulka Anjaria, 'Indian Queer Futures', Review of *Murder in Mahim* by Jerry Pinto and *Mohanaswamy* by Vasudhendra *Public Books* (2 February 2018). Available at www. publicbooks.org/indian-queer-futures/ (accessed on 13 March 2020).
2. Jonathan Shapiro Anjaria and Ulka Anjaria, '*Mazaa*: Rethinking Fun, Pleasure and Play in South Asia', *South Asia: A Journal of South Asian Studies* 43, no. 2 (2020): 1–11.
3. Ragini Tharoor Srinivasan, 'Call Center Agents and Expatriate Writers: Twin Subjects of New Indian Capital', *Ariel: A Review of International English Literature* 49, no. 4 (2018): 77–107.
4. Suketu Mehta, *Maximum City: Bombay Lost and Found* (New York, NY: Vintage, 2009), 130.
5. Parmesh Shahani, 'The Mirror Has Many Faces: The Politics of Male Same-sex Desire in BOMgAY and *Gulabi Aaina*', in *Global Bollywood*, eds. Anandam P. Kavoori and Aswin Punathambekar (New York, NY: NYU Press, 2008), 146–163, 146.
6. Ibid., 151.

2

Gay Bombay to Boston to Bangalore and Back

*Kareem Khubchandani**

When *Gay Bombay* was released in 2008, my heart sank. My feelings were, of course, not about the book, but anxieties about my own research.[1] I was in my first year as a graduate student in the performance studies MA/PhD programme at Northwestern University. I entered the academy excited about the originality of my research project on LGBTQ performance, activism and nightlife in India and the South Asian diaspora. It was a novel project for the moment. But when *Gay Bombay* came out, it was as if Parmesh had done it all already. Moreover, he had done it more expansively, creatively and eloquently than I ever could. As a first-year student in graduate school, I had not yet come to the realization that more than one person can and should write about queerness in India. Studying with faculty who prized 'critical generosity',[2] I learned to embrace the possibilities of dialogue that come with scholarly writing and embodied research. Once my insecurity dissipated, I could engage with Shahani's work in depth, finding clarity in the contributions he was making and enjoying his wry playfulness. Soon, *Gay Bombay* became a foundation to my research.

This year, along with the re-release of *Gay Bombay*, my own book, *Ishtyle: Accenting Gay Indian Nightlife* will arrive in the world. *Ishtyle* follows Indian middle-class men to house parties, pubs and nightclubs, exploring how they perform in accordance with and against the expectations of

* Kareem Khubchandani is the Mellon Bridge Assistant Professor in the Department of Drama and Dance and the Program in Women's, Gender, and Sexuality Studies at Tufts University, Massachusetts.

these spaces. Based on research in both Bangalore and Chicago, my book argues that nightlife—particularly the social, sexual and aesthetic frictions on the dance floor—provides a valuable venue to understand global, national, regional and local politics in urban India and its diaspora. Caught in the slow but rigorous timeline of academic publication, my research has benefited from the growth in critical queer and trans studies over the past 12 years: many useful and influential essays and monographs on queerness in India have been published; the Annual Conference on South Asia has welcomed a Queer Preconference; and academic campuses, Pride celebrations and literary festivals in India have hosted many panels on queer and trans issues. *Gay Bombay* was one of only a handful of scholarly monographs on queer India when it was released. While there is no longer a dearth of scholarship—indeed, Brian Horton has marked this plenitude as an opportunity to reorient the methods and analytics that shape queer Indian research[3]—*Gay Bombay* remains a crucial pivot not only for my own research but for the field of queer Indian studies.

In this chapter, then, I use Shahani's *Gay Bombay* in three different ways. First, I explore how prescient this book was in staging research on queer Indian life. The book has the foresight to inscribe transnational methods, online research and personal experience into the doing of queer Indian studies. These methods and methodologies have become central to work that has emerged in the last decade. Ahead of its time, Shahani's shameless commitment to these risky methods, to seemingly 'nonserious modes of knowing',[4] sets a precedent for scholarship that is as much political economic critique as it is creative and activist world-making. Second, I think through the 'Bombay' in *Gay Bombay* to open up questions of geography, scale and migration in queer Indian studies. Bombay is very much a character in Shahani's book, and I'm interested in how the book's focus on place requires us to scrutinize the geopolitics of queer Indian research. Finally, I explain how 'nightlife' becomes an analytic for research in India—in many ways, *Gay Bombay* demonstrates how powerful this analytic can be. Nightlife is a framework used in cultural studies primarily to think through bars, parties, raves and clubs in Europe and North America. I'm interested in staging what nightlife studies can look like in India and can offer queer Indian studies. *Gay Bombay* is a gift, written not only with love, but theorizing love as central to its ethic. This chapter is my own love letter to the book, marking its major contributions and thinking expansively with them.

To Gay Bombay, with Love

Shahani's book offers many critical interventions: recrafting the timeline of queer activism and community in India so that gayness doesn't appear solely as emerging under economic liberalization, expanding Arjun Appadurai's ever-useful scapes of globalization to include politiscape and memoryscape,[5] refocusing queer studies to the global South and engaging in multimodal ethnographic research that moves between the digital and the embodied. Perhaps the book's most significant contribution is this last one, its insistence on the digital as a site of subject *and* community formation for queer Indians. I had not anticipated the continued importance of digital and media ethnography in queer Indian studies; Shahani both forecasts and lays the foundation for this work. In this section, I meditate on the importance of the online/offline analytic, as well as the other useful modes for queer Indian research he offers: mapping transnational itineraries of queer pleasure, identity and activism through his own travels, and centring pleasure, affect, sensation and desire by thinking through memoir.

I met Parmesh for the first time in 2018, when he was giving a talk at Brandeis University in Boston. I've only lived in Boston since 2016, so when I first read the book in 2008, the scenes in Boston did not resonate with me as much as they do now. Returning to the book this time around, his nights watching drag queens dance at Massachusetts Area South Asian Lambda Association (MASALA) parties jump out at me; *I* am now one of those drag queens performing at the parties. As we talked about his and my intimacies with this city, I registered the value of transnational movement in queer Indian scholarship, activism and creativity. It struck me also that Boston was where film-maker Nishit Saran made his landmark film *Summer in My Veins* (1999). Saran's documentary, in which he comes out to his mother during a visit to the USA, was formative to my own identity exploration and creative practice. Boston also appears amidst news clippings from my undergraduate days.

I found documentation of a play in Boston in the early aughts titled 'Two Men in a Shoulder Stand'; this small piece of paper set me on the path of studying queer South Asian performance. Meeting Parmesh *in* Boston suddenly reveals the ways that this city has incubated South Asian queer cultural production that moves across national borders.

I say all this not to privilege Boston as some kind of intellectual–cultural satellite to India; we might very well find these kinds of connections between Columbus and Calicut, Houston and Hyderabad. Boston just happens to the be node I'm working from right now. What is important, however, is the way that Shahani's movement between Maharashtra and Massachusetts, Bombay and Boston, stages systems of (be)longing. Sometimes the two places blend into each other as queens dance to the same songs across oceans, and in other cases Shahani must leave lovers, who can't travel with him behind, a piece of himself stuck thousands of miles away. The textures of globalization, so central to the book's argument, come into relief as we follow Shahani across national borders.

Shahani's writing makes clear the need for transnational perspectives in writing about art, activism and politics in queer India, dialoguing closely with other scholars. Monisha Das Gupta's *Unruly Immigrants* documents the successes and challenges of LGBTQ South Asian activism in North America. Through her interviews with diasporic activists, she traces the many migrations of queer South Asian people into the USA, via the Caribbean, Canada, the UK, the Middle East and subcontinent.[6] She accounts for the multiple political ruptures—economic liberalization, indenture, civil war, expulsion from East Africa, H1-B visas—that set South Asians into global motion. In my own research, moving between India and the USA has been especially valuable in dispelling the myth of US exceptionalism: that queerness thrives in the diaspora and is foreclosed in the subcontinent. I've written elsewhere about activist–film-maker Moses Tulasi, how his politics shift with migration between Hyderabad and Chicago such that his artistry and activism come into formation precisely *through* global circuits of travel.[7]

Queer Indian art is also formed through global circuits. For example, Canadian-born Sunil Gupta has paved the way for queer Indian artmaking through his photography. His series 'Mr Malhotra's Party' finds queer subjects in Delhi's urban landscapes, making queerness as public there as it is in his photographs taken in London, New York City, Toronto and Paris. US-based film-maker Sonali Gulati's feature-length documentary *I Am* (2011) tracks her travel to India to reckon with her mother's passing. This trip also times with Delhi's Pride march, at which she witnesses Indian mothers openly loving their queer children. The film is an important document of both India's queer movement and also the alienating conditions of migration; India's vibrant queer activism can make surviving diaspora more possible.

Queer activism in India, as Sandip Roy documents, also develops in transnational circuits. In particular, Roy names the legacies of diasporic community organizing and publishing by Trikone-Bay Area[8]; Trikone, Hindi for triangle, coined its name from the pink triangle used to mark queer people during the Holocaust. LGBT activism doesn't just flow from the USA to India; Rakesh Modi brought to Trikone his activist experiences in India, where he volunteered for the Humsafar Trust. In reverse, Bindumadhav Khire, who used to volunteer with Trikone, returned to India to help establish Pune's Samapathik Trust. Khire was at the centre of controversies around Pune Pride, when he tried to enforce 'decent' clothing and signage at the march. While these sentiments may reflect caste respectability in queer activism, if we follow Khire's global itinerary, we might also imagine how these tendencies are informed by ubiquitous homonormativity and homonationalism in the USA. Transnational approaches to studying queer India account more rigorously for the movement of morality, politics, aesthetics and people across national borders.

While a globalization framework encourages us to trace transnational itineraries of media, money, culture and politics, Shahani's own travels bring affective and embodied dimensions to queer globalization. In his bracketed vignettes, the author describes trysts, loves, longings and anxieties. He offers these moments as 'memoryscapes', auto-ethnographic windows that serve as 'warm data'[9] to enflesh his arguments. Shahani's use of memoryscapes takes up the charge offered by reflexive and queer ethnographers to not only resist colonial formations of ethnographic objectivity but to account for and stage the researcher's body and sexuality as formative to research, analysis and theorization.[10]

Given how small and close our circuits are (or feel) in queer India, researchers become part of 'the community'.[11] In Shahani's first iteration of *Gay Bombay*, he was a naïve youngster being seduced into the pleasures and challenges of gay life in India. But there is no doubt that in the years since the book's publication he has become an important auntie in queer Indian activism, creativity and research. As scholars, we are folded into community and must necessarily account for ourselves in our work, detailing from what sociopolitical position we write, what desires we bring to the field and how our presence creates frictions.[12] During my own fieldwork, performing in drag and putting up queer videos on YouTube gave me visibility and perhaps even notoriety. In fact, my video 'Shit Gay Desi Boys Say' incited a heated debate on the Gay Bombay listserv about the stakes of cultural representation for queer Indians. Being a performer and artist shaped my ethnography extensively. In Bangalore, I was asked to curate, perform and choreograph—which brought new people into my orbit who I might not have met otherwise.[13] Further, my own narrative, as a queer Sindhi growing up in Ghana, with family tracing ancestry to Pakistan, shapes my approach to writing about India. While I ground my analysis in the political economy of India on the global stage, my diasporic history and analytic steers me towards critiques of nationalism and imperialism rather an earnest investment in the idea of India. While we might have different attachments to India, Parmesh and I are both interested in articulating more inclusive and vibrant versions of South Asian life on and off the subcontinent, through our creative, professional and scholarly lives.

We find in other queer Indian scholarship how accounting for oneself in the field shapes research. For example, Naisargi Dave describes how, as she attempts to attend the legal hearings for the reading down of Section 377, the women officers at the court entrance try to make sense of her gender; this small and personal moment helps us understand the quotidian life of cis-heteronormativity that colludes with the state's legal arm.[14] Alok Gupta accounts for his social positions while doing research with hijras by discussing how they invite him in as *Englishpur Ki Kothi*.[15] This expression details the terms on which he is seen by his interlocutors, how they are seeing his class, gender and sexuality all at once. Taking account of the class and caste hierarchies we inhabit shapes what research looks like. For example, Dhiren Borisa's ethnography of Delhi's queer geographies not only brings caste analysis to his study but also uses his standpoint as a Dalit queer person to evidence the aspirational ethos of gay parties.[16] Through his experiences and feelings, Borisa details the performances he engages to traffic in shared aesthetics of gay desire, naming the *different* stakes for differently classed and casted people in those spaces. Shahani's research offers an important model for writing the personal into the intellectual in elegant and generative ways. He reminds us to take account of ourselves, inviting us to tell the story of why we do this research, and why it matters that *we* are the ones doing it.

I want to celebrate, as one of the book's major contributions, its staging of digital ethnography, and the centrality of the Internet in shaping community in queer India. *Gay Bombay* only scratches the surface of the many ways that queerness operates through online/offline modes in India, especially given rapidly changing and increasingly affordable interfaces. And yet it is so prescient in insisting on the importance of digital media to queer life. What is so excellent in Shahani's book is the reciprocity between the online and offline, how parties, e-mail lists, chat rooms, meetups and hook-ups become co-constitutive through 'virtual intimacies'.[17] *Gay Bombay* is a pioneering study that centres the digital without giving it credit for *everything*, but rather indexing the proximity of the digital to all facets of queer life.

Shaped by my training in performance studies, my work privileges people's bodies in research. I don't necessarily think *through* the digital. But Shahani's work has required me to revisit my own fieldwork to account for my online footprint on gay networking sites, location-based applications and social media. As I mentioned earlier, my YouTube posts shaped my visibility during fieldwork. Additionally, location-based platforms such as Grindr and PlanetRomeo offered a metric to imagine densities of gayness. They led me to ask why men were often so far away from the TamBram neighbourhood my parents live in. They helped me to understand how the city's geography was governed by heteronormativity, and why housing availability for single unmarried men was always better closer to tech parks. Central to my research on nightlife was the absence of print advertising for gay parties; all advertising was via PlanetRomeo,

Instagram, Facebook, Grindr and Gaydar. I've written about how these online promotions dictated an aspirational ethos for parties that neither party organizers nor party-goers could live up to in an anthology on *Queering Digital India,* edited by Debanuj DasGupta and Rohit Dasgupta.[18] The essays in that anthology extend the task Shahani set for us, to think and study across the digital and the embodied. *Queering Digital India* explores the class hierarchies produced by cell phones, how online music videos choreograph sexuality and how queer lives are made precarious through online blackmail and media reporting. Other exciting research on digital India has explored how profiles on gay networking sites stage expressions of desire and pleasure,[19] and how online platforms render hijra identities.[20]

The ways that queer Indians have made the use of the Internet to cultivate sexual subjectivities continues to amaze me. Diasporic artist Somnath Bhatt uses the frames of WhatsApp and Pornhub to offer witty takes on how South Asian bodies and desires circulate online. Also, Twitter, OnlyFans and Pornhub have made space for a bounty of South Asian amateur porn that is especially valuable when South Asian bodies are so illegible or absent in mainstream commercial gay porn. These ongoing innovations in queer Indian activism, artistry, sexual practice and cultural production mean that our methodological, analytic and interpretive tools must regularly be honed to meet the changing public sphere. In *Gay Bombay,* Parmesh has given us long-lasting tools for critical and efficacious research. In particular, I think his online/offline formation, transnational approach and privileging of the personal can keep queer Indian scholarship rigorous and captivating at the same time.

Bengaluru *Meri Jaan*

Community is built on Internet spaces such as the Gay.com India chatroom—one that Shahani describes as 'harder to get into than the tiniest South Bombay nightclub on a Saturday night'. These spaces facilitated virtual communities of queer South Asians who flirt across national borders. But these communities are also contingent on the physical, economic and political infrastructures of cities, regions and nation that craft the quality of queer life there. In *Gay Bombay,* Bombay comes to life as a central figure in the book. We walk with Shahani along the Queen's Necklace, and chug along on bumpy bus rides. We drop him off at Sahar Airport, and he holds our hand across the threshold into Humsafar Trust. Queerness' texture varies as we move across visible and invisible borders. Grounding his ethnography in the city, Shahani nuances generalizable data that might be produced by an online-only study. Moreover, Bombay is one of Shahani's several mercurial lovers that we meet in the book. Following my own trysts there as a teenager, Shahani's gorgeous crafting of the city, and its discursive staging as 'India's gay capital', I imagined Bombay as my own research site too.[21] However, my first research trip to India in 2010 took me to Bangalore, where my parents had retired.

I arrived knowing almost nothing about queer Bangalore, but it quickly proved to be a vibrant city for queer activism, community, nightlife and artmaking. Attending parties, film festivals, pride marches, social/support group meetings, protests and hangouts with queer friends kept my calendar full of faggotry. As Bombay does for Shahani, Bangalore offers me a love affair: the charm of sitting at Koshy's for hours on end; late nights at Empire eating egg dosa; the opulence of silver *bhartan*s (utensils) and tinsel decorations in Raja Market; reams of sequins, prints and chiffon begging to adorn my body on Commercial Street. Mythologies of queer Bangalore too kept me attached to the city: nostalgia for lost cruising grounds; hijra dances captured at birthday parties and illicitly watched in the midst of pride planning meetings; gay parties with Pink Passports that transported you beyond the city's limits; bars and cafes that were only queer if you knew when to go or where to sit; extended philosophical discussions about queer and trans life, justice and pleasure on the rooftop of the Alternative Law Forum. Over the last 10 years of fieldwork, I've had the opportunity to travel to other cities, observing how queerness interacts with the city, its geography and aesthetics. Inspired by Shahani's focus on Bombay, I show how I learned about the specificity of queer life in Bangalore. Also, I take stock of how queer Indian studies have importantly emerged as a located project, moving away from all-India frameworks to find specificity in place.

Discourse and literary analysis such as that of Ruth Vanita, Saleem Kidwai and Suparna Bhaskaran paved the way for queer Indian studies by using 'India' as their geographic framework, paying attention to how discourses of nationalism regulate who and what is queer.[22] Moving from *Impossible Desires* to *Unruly Visions*, Gayatri Gopinath rescales her geopolitical analytics away from critiques of the nation, to think about how region, Kerala in particular, can offer more particular insights into the quality of queerness in India.[23] One of the ways that region shapes queerness is the specificity of language. In Navaneetha Mokkil's *Unruly Figures*, a primarily Malayalam archive of sexuality opens up ways of thinking sex work and queerness together in India.[24] In Lawrence Cohen's research, we see how sexuality and masculinity are inscribed, sometimes to fatal ends, by competing visions of statehood and cosmopolitan citizenship in North India.[25] Aniruddha Dutta's research in Bengal demonstrates how political histories of leftist organizing in Eastern India shape queer and trans solidarities with other movements.[26] Harjant Gill's visual ethnographies of peri-urban Chandigarh help texture (and queer) Punjabi masculinity, and Paul Boyce and Rohit Dasgupta conducting ethnography in Siliguri and Barasat explore discourses of queer utopia—almost always theorized in relation to the urban—in rural and peri-urban contexts. [27] I have no interest in valourizing *or* dismissing the city as the cypher through which we think queer India; rather I'm interested in the value of using multiple geopolitical lenses to examine queer life. While cities are often imagined as the vanguard of queer modernity, it is also useful to think about the multiplicity of the city. For example, Maya Sharma's interviews with working class and poor queer women, and Gayatri Reddy's ethnography of hijras in Hyderabad, stage visions of the city that are quite far removed from stereotypes of the global gay.[28]

In my own research, I found Bangalore to have numerous queer ecologies, always tied to the rural and peri-urban. In public discourse, Bangalore is specifically set apart from the rest of Karnataka; it is the dangerous migrant city where too many strange languages and strange people converge.[29] Common in my interviews with gay men were narrations of migration from smaller towns, rural areas of Karnataka and other South Indian states to Bangalore. While in some cases it was the infrastructure of LGBTQ NGOs that attracted migrants, it was often education or labour opportunities that drove them into the city—queer migrations are not always motivated by sexuality.[30] Further, several migrant men discussed how their migration informed *how* they performed queerness, particularly through the framework of class. For example, one interlocutor didn't want to cruise in the park because it was too similar to the way he found sex in his small town. Another described a bar that many Bangaloreans thought of as divey or even dirty as 'upscale' when he first arrived. Whether parks, dive bars, lounges, nightclubs, dance bars, no place could tell a story of Bangalore's queer culture without taking into consideration *from where* my interlocutors had come and what they were looking for in those spaces.

Bangalore's changing economic, political and infrastructural specificities also shape how queerness is done there. In *Ishtyle*, I document how anxieties over rapid globalization, alongside worries about Karnataka's regional identity in relation to neighbouring states, produce a cultural conservatism that shows up as hypervigilant policing of nightlife. Further, the arrangement of the city, as shaped under British occupation, spiders outwards from a central core, placing affordable housing for migrants outside of the city centre. As such, even though the older and more expensive neighbourhoods of Bangalore are more fabulous to party in, suburbs and new developments bring 'bachelors' into proximity with each other. The dominance of engineering, software, business process outsourcing and adjacent industries as well as medical, law and engineering colleges in Bangalore shaped who I met in gay spaces. I recognized this specificity particularly when I travelled to Bombay and Delhi, where I met make-up artists, dancers, diplomats and entrepreneurs, folks who were not as ubiquitous in my Bangalore worlds.

Traveling to other cities during my research on nightlife helped me understand what was specific to Bangalore *and* how cities are in fact imbricated in each other. Friends I made in Bombay and Hyderabad showed up in Bangalore when they had to do trainings with head offices there. While I was impressed by the numerous queer parties that took place in Bombay—during my fieldwork, there was usually only one per week in Bangalore—I learned how deeply stratified they were by class and gender performance. In Hyderabad, I witnessed cops enter a party, shining flashlights in patrons' faces and ushering us all out; in Bangalore, cops entered the premises for bribes but didn't necessarily interrupt parties. These differences don't determine one city as more homophobic than the other, but rather remind us that situated norms of governance affect how we commune and find pleasure. *Gay Bombay* offers us a model to think about queer India through the rubric of one city, this specificity reminds us that queerness shifts with the contours of its locale.

DISCO *JALEBI* 2.0

While I was doing fieldwork in Bangalore, there was a backlash against nightlife, particularly the growth of pubs, bars and clubs, that brought upon restrictions on live music and social dancing, as well as early closing hours. These reactionary moves were responding to changing demographics in the city, the increasingly mobile global worker— whether software engineer bachelors or migrant women dancing in bars—whose sexualities could not be properly contained. In response to questions about nightlife restrictions, a police commissioner responded, 'Nighttime is for sleeping.'[31] But in *Gay Bombay* we see that night-time is in fact a vibrant and complex world that thrives in proximity to, in the interstices of, and in spite of heteronormativity. Shahani writes, 'I am a bright orange disco *jalebi*, hot and soft and syrupy, eaten after dancing for three hours non-stop at a Gay Bombay dance party, with random strangers who've suddenly become my new best friends.' In this vignette, the Bollywood sounds and brown bodies allow him to time travel between Gay Bombay parties and Sholay club nights in New York City. Nightlife has the capacity to drag people through spaces and time, to work one's body such that you feel sticky and sweet like a *jalebi*. Across his book, we see how nightlife becomes a site of desire, friendship and politics. We go cruising at the Walls by the Taj Hotel, and wander through Voodoo nightclub, which is only gay on Saturdays. We walk into glorious *mujra* (dance) performances at the Humsafar centre and learn about the privileging of foreign drag over hijra/*kothi* performance. We meet people who escort nervous newbies to Gay Bombay parties, and learn of the 'no drag' policy that keeps some people out. In *Gay Bombay,* nightlife is an important site through which Shahani comes to know his interlocutors and himself, to figure out who is and isn't in the Gay Bombay crowd, to centre desire, pleasure and the senses in this study, to think about community in less didactic ways than identity politics allows. While he doesn't explicitly foreground nightlife as critical to his project, he helps us see how nightlife becomes a valuable analytic through which to consider queer life in India.

Studying nightlife means attending to the relationships between space, time, gender and sexuality. It means listening to the rhythms of the city, so you know when the trains are full enough for fondling, or empty enough for cruising. It means finding out on which night Voodoo is queer, or on which days police presence is heavier by the Walls. Studying nightlife means understanding how the day and the week are tied up with hetero-capitalism. What TV programme are families assembled to watch each weeknight? Who is commuting *to* work at 7 p.m. instead of going home? Studying nightlife means thinking about bodies. Whose bodies are more policed at night-time because they are deemed more 'dangerous'? How do we account for the kinaesthesia, the sensation of movement, when dancing in the club? Researching with and through nightlife does not mean studying only bars, clubs, lounges and parties; rather it draws on the values and aesthetics of these spaces to ask how people convene in pursuit of pleasure and possibility. At the same time, it draws attention to the ways that we are governed by time, folded back into the logics of heteronormative family, of reproductive capitalism. Why are you out dancing when you could be resting so you are fresh for work the next day? It raises questions of *who* would want to be dancing on a weeknight, and *why* would someone risk a hangover, risk police surveillance and blackmail for a night of fun.

Other scholars working on sexuality in India have considered how time, space, aesthetics and desire weave into politics. The valuable studies of sex work across India remind us of how women are especially disciplined by time, expected to stay home, to not work at night, to not be out at night.[32] Taboos against women occupying public space,[33] especially at night, have meant that professional women labouring in India's global economy who must commute to work at night are subject to similar policing and violence as sex workers.[34] Like Shohini Ghosh in her documentary *Tales of the Night Fairies*, these scholars evidence the tactics that sex workers must engage to remain productive, to survive, for themselves and their families. The crackdown on dance bars is another venue in which women's sexualities, artistry and mobility are curtailed by both colonial laws and contemporary moral panics.[35] Hemangini Gupta has shown how the rise of pub culture in Bangalore is specifically tied to changing patterns of global labour and the enforcement of heteronormativity, and Arun Saldanha and Pavithra Prasad describe the racial formations that shape how time and space are navigated in Goa's rave scene.[36] Rohit Dasgupta brings class to bear in imagining queer nightlife in India, mapping the exploitation of young boys in Launda Naach, and detailing how gay parties in Kolkata re-inscribe class hierarchies.[37] It is perhaps Dhiren Borisa's research on Delhi's queer and caste-based geographies that most closely resembles my own, visiting parties, bathhouses, cruising spots and location-based apps—since he is included in this book, I will let you enjoy his brilliant contributions in his own words.

I want to briefly provide a snapshot of what nightlife research looked like for me. The first time my new gay friends in Bangalore took me out, it was to a fashion show, and then on to a house party. While I was anticipating a night out at the club, this interaction made clear that nightlife looks like a lot of things, not just dancing at the club—it looks like turning living rooms into *kothas*, feeding each other, and teaching friends how to walk the ramp. The first time I turned up at a gay party, there were but 10 people. This gave me an opportunity to befriend the lovely party organizer and gain more insight into the history of party planning in Bangalore. Ultimately, my fieldwork primarily consisted of visits to Saturday night parties at nightclubs that had DJs, bar service and packed dance floors. But these moments at house parties and my conversations with party organizers taught me how to scrutinize those club scenes for the meticulous labour that goes into organizing them, and the many kinds of kinship that form in the thick of dance.

During fieldwork, I danced, and sometimes I hooked up with people. Fieldwork has involved extended interviews with party-goers and planners, activists and friends who didn't feel like the nightclub was for them. It has meant clipping the very few news articles and op-eds that even acknowledged that queer nightlife exists. It included tracking the discourse around queer nightlife, from memes sent around on queer Facebook pages that joke that party gays and activist gays are different to watching and even acting in short films by lesbian film-makers who offered alternative visions of what fun can look like for them. It also involved performing, not just on the dance floor. As the drag scene in India's middle class and elite gay nightlife spaces has grown, I have had the opportunity to perform as my alter ego LaWhore Vagistan. Performing in drag in these spaces brought me in closer touch with party organizers, allowed me to see the audience from a different vantage point and brought people into my orbit who would not have seen me as an interlocutor before. As we see in *Gay Bombay,* in Dhiren's work, and in my own research, nightlife looks like a lot of things and can be approached in many different ways. It is a multi-modal analytic and method one can bring to thinking through queerness in India that points us to the multiplicity of strategies minoritarian subjects engage in to thrive.

Conclusion

Released *before* the Delhi High Court decriminalization of sodomy and re-released *after* the Supreme Court's final rejection of Section 377, it strikes me that *Gay Bombay* is not just a record of India's legal fight for queer and trans rights. This is one of the reasons I think it has such staying power. It is a book that attends to the complicated texture of queer world-making in a beloved city. It does not grant primacy to one event, or one episteme. Rather it gives us *many* tools to evaluate what queerness looks like in our bodies, our Internet usage, our nightlives and our geopolitical placements. In this chapter, I've offered some of the ways Shahani's work proves fruitful in imagining a dynamic version of queer studies in India by putting his scholarship in dialogue with others' and my own work. This re-release, particularly under a radically shifting politiscape in which the Indian government is severely restricting the mandates of citizenship, is a valuable opportunity to embrace all the tools we have at our disposal to think through the politics of inclusion and the work of justice through both global and local frameworks. Shahani has set an impressive precedent for theorizing minoritarian life, politics, community, pleasure and survival in India, and there is still more work for us all to do! I thought that *Gay Bombay* had already accomplished all the work there was to do when I first read it. Now, having written a book myself, it is obvious to me that there is *so much more* work to be done. I hope *Gay Bombay* inspires you, as it did me, to try on new methods, explore intimate archives and commit to the experimental scholar–activist work of imagining new and more just worlds in the present.

NOTES

1. I am grateful to Gowri Vijayakumar for her incisive and generous feedback on this chapter.
2. David Román, *Acts of Intervention: Performance, Gay Culture, and Aids*, Unnatural Acts (Bloomington: Indiana University Press, 1998).
3. Brian A. Horton, 'The Queer Turn in South Asian Studies? Or "That's over & Done Queen, on to the Next"', *QED: A Journal in GLBTQ Worldmaking* 5, no. 3 (2018).
4. Dwight Conquergood, *Cultural Struggles: Performance, Ethnography, Praxis*, ed. E. Patrick Johnson (Ann Arbor, MI: University of Michigan Press, 2013), 33.
5. Arjun Appadurai, 'Disjuncture and Difference in the Global Cultural Economy', *Theory, Culture & Society* 7, no. 2–3 (1990).
6. Monisha Das Gupta, *Unruly Immigrants: Rights, Activism, and Transnational South Asian Politics in the United States* (Durham: Duke University Press, 2006), 163.
7. Kareem Khubchandani, 'Caste, Queerness, Migration and the Erotics of Activism', *South Asia Multidisciplinary Academic Journal* 20, no. 20 (2019).
8. Sandip Roy, 'How Silicon Valley Fostered India's Lgbtq+ Movement', *LiveMint*. Available at https://www.livemint.com/mint-lounge/features/how-silicon-valley-fostered-india-s-lgbtq-movement-1567161918842.html (accessed on 13 March 2020).
9. Ronak K. Kapadia, *Insurgent Aesthetics: Security and the Queer Life of the Forever War* (Durham: Duke University Press, 2019).
10. Don Kulick and Margaret Willson, *Taboo: Sex, Identity, and Erotic Subjectivity in Anthropological Fieldwork* (New York, NY: Routledge, 1995); Ellen Lewin and William L. Leap, *Out in the Field: Reflections of Lesbian and Gay Anthropologists* (Champaign, IL: University of Illinois Press, 1996).
11. Gowri Vijayakumar, 'Collective Demands and Secret Codes: The Multiple Uses of "Community" in "Community Mobilization"', *World Development* 104 (2018).
12. Kareem Khubchandani, 'Dance Floor Divas: Fieldwork, Fabulating and Fathoming in Queer Bangalore', *South Asia: Journal of South Asian Studies* (2020).
13. Kareem Khubchandani, 'Voguing in Bangalore: Desire, Blackness, and Femininity in Globalized India', *Scholar and Feminist Online* 14, no. 3 (2018); Robert Ji-Song Ku, S. Heijin Lee, and Monika Mehta, eds., 'Between Screens and Bodies: New Queer Performance in India', in *Pop Empires: Transnational and Diasporic Flows of India and Korea* (Honolulu: University of Hawaii Press, 2019).
14. Naisargi N. Dave, *Queer Activism in India: A Story in the Anthropology of Ethics* (Durham: Duke University Press, 2012), 185.

15. Alok Gupta, '*Englishpur Ki Kothi*', in *Because I Have a Voice: Queer Politics in India*, ed. Gautam Bhan and Arvind Narrain (New Delhi: Yoda Press, 2005).
16. Dhiren Borisa, *Imagined Spaces of Freedom: Negotiating Queer Cartographies of Desires in Delhi* (Jawaharlal Nehru University, 2018).
17. Shaka McGlotten, *Virtual Intimacies: Media, Affect, and Queer Sociality* (Albany, NY: State University of New York Press, 2013).
18. Rohit K. Dasgupta and Debanuj DasGupta, *Queering Digital India: Activisms, Identities, Subjectivities* (Edinburgh: Edinburgh University Press, 2018).
19. Andil Gosine, 'Brown to Blonde at Gay.Com: Passing White in Queer Cyberspace', in *Queer Online: Media Technology and Sexuality*, ed. Kate O'Riordan and David J. Phillips (New York, NY: Peter Lang, 2007); Akhil Katyal, *The Doubleness of Sexuality: Idioms of Same-sex Desire in Modern India* (New Delhi: New Text, 2016).
20. Rahul Gairola, *Digital Hijras: Intersex/Tions of Postcolonial and Queer Digital Humanities with Rahul Gairola*. Available at https://youtu.be/Zk2Q6afbB4s (accessed on 13 March 2020).
21. NDTV, *Is Mumbai Emerging as India's Gay Capital*. Available at https://www.ndtv.com/cities/is-mumbai-emerging-as-indias-gay-capital-422355 (accessed on 13 March 2020).
22. Suparna Bhaskaran, *Made in India: Decolonizations, Queer Sexualities, Trans/National Projects* (New York, NY: Palgrave Macmillan, 2004); Ruth Vanita, *Queering India: Same-sex Love and Eroticism in Indian Culture and Society* (New York, NY: Routledge, 2002); Saleem Kidwai, Suparna Bhaskaran, and Ruth Vanita, *Same-sex Love in India: Readings from Literature* (New York, NY: St. Martin's Press, 2000); Brinda Bose and Subhabrata Bhattacharyya, *The Phobic and the Erotic: The Politics of Sexualities in Contemporary India* (Calcutta; New York, NY: Seagull Books, 2007).
23. Gayatri Gopinath, *Impossible Desires: Queer Diasporas and South Asian Public Cultures* (Durham: Duke University Press, 2005); *Unruly Visions: The Aesthetic Practices of Queer Diaspora* (Durham: Duke University Press, 2018).
24. Navaneetha Mokkil, *Unruly Figures: Queerness, Sex Work, and the Politics of Sexuality in Kerala* (Seattle, WA: University of Washington Press, 2019).
25. Lawrence Cohen, 'Song for Pushkin', *Daedalus* 136, no. 2 (2007).
26. Aniruddha Dutta, 'Dissenting Differently: Solidarities and Tensions between Student Organizing and Trans-Kothi-Hijra Activism in Eastern India', *South Asia Multidisciplinary Academic Journal* 20, no. 20 (2019).
27. Paul Boyce and Rohit K. Dasgupta, *Utopia or Elsewhere: Queer Modernities in Small Town West Bengal* (Basingstoke: Palgrave Macmillan, 2017); Harjant Gill, *Mardistan (Macholand)* (2014).
28. Maya Sharma, *Loving Women: Being Lesbian in Unprivileged India* (New Delhi: Yoda Press, 2006); Gayatri Reddy, *With Respect to Sex: Negotiating Hijra Identity in South India*, Worlds of Desire (Chicago, IL: University of Chicago Press, 2005).
29. M. K. Raghavendra, 'Local Resistance to Global Bangalore: Reading Minority Indian Cinema', in *Popular Culture in a Globalised India*, ed. K. Moti Gokulsing and Wimal Dissanayake (London: Routledge, 2009).
30. Lionel Cantú, Nancy A. Naples, and Salvador Vidal-Ortiz, *The Sexuality of Migration: Border Crossings and Mexican Immigrant Men* (New York, NY: New York University Press, 2009).
31. 'Bangalore Put on Mute at 10 pm', *Times of India*, 3 August 2013.

32. Svati Shah, *Street Corner Secrets: Sex, Work, and Migration in the City of Mumbai* (Durham: Duke University Press, 2014); Gowri Vijayakumar, 'Is Sex Work Sex or Work? Forming Collective Identity in Bangalore', *Qualitative Sociology* 41, no. 3 (2018); Kimberly Walters, 'The Stickiness of Sex Work: Pleasure, Habit, and Intersubstantiality in South India', *Signs: Journal of Women in Culture and Society* 42, no. 1 (2016).
33. Shilpa Phadke, Shilpa Ranade, and Sameera Khan, *Why Loiter?: Women and Risk on Mumbai Streets* (New Delhi: Penguin, 2011).
34. Reena Patel, *Working the Night Shift: Women in India's Call Center Industry* (Stanford, CA: Stanford University Press, 2010).
35. Jyoti Puri, *Sexual States: Governance and the Decriminalization of Sodomy in India's Present* (Durham: Duke University Press, 2016); Anna Morcom, *Illicit Worlds of Indian Dance: Cultures of Exclusion* (London: Hurst and Co., 2013); William Mazzarella, 'A Different Kind of Flesh: Public Obscenity, Globalisation and the Mumbai Dance Bar Ban', *South Asia: Journal of South Asian Studies* 38, no. 3 (2015).
36. Hemangini Gupta, 'No Sleep Till Ban-Galore!!!', Cityscape Digital. Available at https://www.cityscapesdigital.net/2013/05/08/no-sleep-till-ban-galore/ (accessed on 13 March 2020); Arun Saldanha, *Psychedelic White: Goa Trance and the Viscosity of Race* (Minneapolis, MN: University of Minnesota Press, 2007); Pavithra Prasad, 'The Baba and the Patrao: Negotiating Localness in the Tourist Village', *Critical Arts* 26, no. 3 (2012).
37. Rohit K. Dasgupta, 'Launda Dancers: The Dancing Boys of India', *Asian Affairs* 44, no. 3 (2013); 'Parties, Advocacy and Activism: Interrogating Community and Class in Digital Queer India', in *Queer Youth and Media Cultures*, ed. Christopher Pullen (London: Palgrave Macmillan, 2014).

3

The Heart Has Its Reasons

*Theoretical Domains, Exploratory Questions, Research
Schema, Topographic Terrain and Personal Motives*

And love
Is not the easy thing
The only baggage you can bring
Is all that you can't leave behind

QUEEN'S NECKLACE

*Walking down Marine Drive at seven in the evening. Hungry Eyes Chinese
Food truck is shut for the day. Every afternoon, it feeds the hordes that cannot
afford a table at the Oberoi and the grub's better too. Twilight, dusk. I am
surrounded by the Queen's Necklace. Very beautiful. High tide. The angry
sea rises above the breakers and hits passers-by. I've seen it much angrier.
Bombay has just had seven days of incessant rain. I have walked this route
for years. It is my catharsis. All the way from home, down Colaba Causeway
across Nariman Point and then along the seashore. I climb the rocks and
look at the vast sea, the eternity beyond.*

*The Queen's Necklace begins with the high rise buildings of Navy Nagar—
all similarly sized; then the tall Air India and Oberoi Hotel buildings at
Nariman Point and the new NCPA complex with flats more expensive than
Manhattan; the revolving restaurant of the Ambassador Hotel; the string
of art deco buildings, none of them more than six floors high; the flood-
light Wankhede Cricket Stadium, now dark, but when there is a match on,
all of Marine Drive is electrified and people climb up to the terraces of the
neighbouring buildings for a free aerial view. Walk past the flyover from
Metro cinema, which curls in a sweeping arc on to the sea front. The point
at which the flyover and Marine Drive intersect is the centre of the necklace.*

If you sit here, you can see the two ends in the periphery of your vision and the horizon beyond where the sky meets the ocean. I often pause at this point and wonder about life and being gay and finding happiness...rubbish like that. My yoga class is across the road at the 100 year-old Kaivalyadham Institute, but I've been skipping sessions.

Crowded traffic moving at 80 kilometres per hour. Crazy people running across at all the wrong places.

What you got, they can't steal it
No they can't even feel it
Walk on
Walk on
Stay safe tonight

A light drizzle. Now past the new renovated Police Gymkhana, the dilapidated Hindu and Parsi gymkhanas, the old Taraporewala Aquarium, where no one really goes anymore, except poor country-hick tourists. Chowpatty and its massage men; crowded bhel puri and falooda stalls, sanitized and contained into a concrete food plaza. The beach is cleaner than ever. Very different from the Ganpati festival with all the Plaster of Paris statue immersions, and the hundreds and thousands of tightly packed bodies, squeezed next to each other on the sands. Devotion mixed with rough fondling; sensations amplified by the noise, the smell, the spectacle and the release.

Nana-Nani park—a good idea for old people—but no parking, where I would take my grandparents when they were younger and I had car access. New Yorker's restaurant with the best Indianized nachos in the world outside—which there is always a line to get in, even on afternoons and weekdays. The glittering skyscrapers of Malabar Hill and oversized hoardings in the distance. Some like Binani and Raymonds have been there for decades; others like Reliance India Mobile are new. And then, the clasp of the necklace, a stretch of pristine land with its private beach—the governor's estate—Raj Bhavan.

And I know it aches
And your heart it breaks
You can only take so much
Walk on

Tall swaying palm trees, sea salt water spraying on my face, wind running through my hair, tears flowing down my cheeks. Nariyal pani *vendors huddled up under ineffectual beach umbrellas. Muscle men in their jogging suits, ladies in* salwar kurtas *and walking shoes, lots of people walking their dogs, lots of dogs walking their people; servants and children; beggars. Office-goers deciding to walk from Marine Lines to Charni Road station; the walk their only respite after a hard, hard day at work. The women will chop vegetables on the train ride home and men will play cards with their 'train friends' who will jump into fast moving trains before they stop at the station to claim a spot for them on the return journey. Trains filled with horror. Jayabala Asher thrown out, her legs cut off, for fighting a rapist while a compartment of men watches silently, not stepping in. The mayor gives her an award for bravery. Acid thrown on pregnant women from outside the train compartment. Aircraft engineer tossed out on to the tracks by rowdies. Killed. The city's trains devour 10 humans per day. Always hungry for more. Sometimes they are racked with bomb explosions. Sometimes, they are submerged under water due to floods.*

1996. Early morning train ride to Bombay University's Kalina campus. Someone gropes me in the jampacked compartment. No standing room even. Can't turn around and see who it is. Squatters are shitting on the railway tracks, their backs modestly turned towards us voyeurs on the trains. One should never board a running train, I hear my mother say. I am 14 years old and running after a bus I have just alighted from because I left my pencil box in it—but I am too slow. My mother screams at me when I reach home. Is your pencil box more important, or your life? Never run after a moving bus, train or anything, do you understand?

Leave it behind
You've got to leave it behind

I see myself in the school boys walking on the road today, their shoulders hunched over with their overloaded bags. They have finished their extra tuition class and will go home to do two sets of homework while the rest of the family watches Kyunki Saas Bhi Kabhi Bahu Thi *on television. They have to study hard and run, run, run, so that they can keep up in the rat race. But they have their arms draped comfortably around each other's waists and their friends will not taunt them with 'that's so gay'—this is India and physical contact between friends in normal; we are like that only. So they walk about, bodies comfortably touching, flip flops tossing up brown splotches of mud on their bare calves. Lovers sit down on the rocks amidst the crabs, holding hands—a brief moment of intimacy before the policeman comes and shoos them away. The drizzle turns into a downpour. I open my umbrella, adjust my iPod, walk on.*

All that you fashion
All that you make
All that you build
All that you break
All that you measure
All that you feel
All this you can leave behind.
(U2 'Walk On')[1]

This book was written during the course of my Master's programme in Comparative Media Studies at the Masschusetts Institute of Technology—where I spent three years between 2003–06. It began its life as my graduate thesis, which I completed in May 2005. I then left it alone for a year and returned to it for a few months towards the end of 2006, after I relocated back to Bombay from Boston. In some sense, its publication marks the end of my coming out journey as an Indian gay man, comfortable at last in his own skin. This comfort took several years to arrive at and the quest for this comfort was perhaps one of the reasons that I took this project upon myself.

I lived a pretty closeted gay life in Bombay for several years prior to my departure to the US. I was neither aware of nor did I seek to be a part of a greater gay community. Sure, I had some gay friends and socialized with them occasionally—but for the most part, my sexuality was something that I had compartmentalized as something that was surreptitious and all about the sexual act, not about an identity. In 2002, I visited the US to check out potential graduate schools and on my cross country trip, stayed with several gay individuals and couples, courtesy my friend and mentor in Bombay, the late Riyad Wadia. One of these included Riyad's brother Roy, who was living in Atlanta at that time, with his long-term partner, Alan. After experiencing the love and warmth that their household exuded, I became aware of the possibility of how wonderful gay coupledom might be.

Serendipitously, when I got back to India after my sojourn, I experienced my first gay relationship. It was crazy, because I had never imagined myself in such a context before, but now suddenly, I turned into a walkie-talkie Hallmark card, living out all the clichés of mushy-gushy love with another man. We texted each other a hundred times a day, went out on dates, long romantic walks, planned our dream house and argued over its décor, made love like in Hollywood movies, complete with slow-motion action and top 40 hits playing in the background... it was exhilarating. What was even more mind-blowing was that my boyfriend Z's family was completely accepting of our relationship. Our romance became everything that I had read about in comics and books and seen in movies—I mean, I would go to his house to pick him up for a date—and his parents would wave us goodbye—it was that awesome! How many straight couples in Bombay enjoyed that kind of equation with their partner's families?

One week, we got to know about a party being organized in the city by a group called Gay Bombay and I can still remember how we excitedly went shopping for new clothes for the big night and speculated wildly about what the experience would be like. It was magic. As we entered the portals of the nightclub, it seemed that we'd stumbled in on an episode of *Queer as Folk* or something, except that everyone here was brown. The dance floor was packed with male bodies swaying in tandem to Enrique, Cher and Madonna, the bar had more male flesh packed per square inch than we'd ever seen before in Bombay and it seemed that there were men everywhere...draped on the staircase, squeezed in dark corners, emerging out of the woodwork....

LEAVING ON A JET PLANE

Z takes my hand and leads me to the dance floor. I am surprised, he has never been the forward type before this...but the atmosphere is electrifying. We dance together—shyly at first and then as the music seeps into us, more confidently. After some time, we embrace and he kisses me. Tentatively, my instinctive reaction is to look around mortified. ('What if anyone sees us?!!!') Then I realize that we don't have to worry. Not here. Not for the present. As we dance, body to body, soul to soul, we feel the crowds spread apart... spreading open to celebrate our love. It is magic. I never want the night to end.

August 2003. I weep freely as my plane circles the Sahar Airport runway for its take-off. It has been three days since I visited the temple and prayed hesitantly for clarity, three months since I ended the relationship with Z that was supposed to go on forever. I look out of the rain-spattered window...

I see the pain and rejection that comes daily when classmates whisper 'pansy' as I pass them in the school hallway. I remember the thrill that comes with the first flush of longing, the transparency of desire, the innocence of newly discovered sex. I laugh at the preposterousness of trying to think for two people when thinking for one is hard enough and the stupidity of thinking that going away will give you all the answers.

I see myself in Nalanda—the bookshop at the posh Taj Mahal hotel, browsing through foreign magazines... looking at the beautiful men in GQ and their taut, sexy bodies, almost always white. The magazines are expensive. I hold them up to my nose and sniff with pleasure—it is the sweet smell of freedom—this is what Indian magazines will never have, I think... the reason why I need to go to America. For so many years and perhaps even now, America, to me, is the sweet smell in the folded perfume advertisements in GQ, Vogue and Bazaar that I read inside air-conditioned Nalanda, forgetting that I eventually have to walk out to the fly-buzzing, cockroach-crawling, shithole of a city that I call home. Inside, I belonged to the beautiful bodied, white, chiseled gods and within a few hours I will be among them.

When I reach MIT, I am astounded that through the grapevine, some students in the university already know of my sexual orientation. I am asked by the campus LBGT group to join them for a leadership retreat in the fabulous queer holiday destination of Provincetown. The event is an eye-opener and a perfect start to what turns out to be a very interesting year. Personally I decide to be completely *out* with regard to my sexual orientation as opposed to the 'don't ask, don't tell' policy I followed in India. This year is especially significant for the gay movement in the US, with the recognition of gay marriage in Massachusetts and the debates about it all over the rest of the country.

I enjoy myself thoroughly—the initial rush of freedom as an out gay man, living life in an environment that is supportive. At last, at last! I go to San Francisco and explore the Castro, wide-eyed, feeling proud of the rainbow flags fluttering high above. I go to Los Angeles and see beautiful boys at the Abbey bar, carefully poised with martini glass in hand, hair always perfect. I go on dates with semi-hot Harvard and Boston University guys that I have met online, through the social networking site Friendster. It is brilliant, but I realize soon, that it is not enough. I had hoped that by coming to America I could finally become *properly* gay, but strangely enough and irritatingly enough, I am missing and often craving for a notion of India that I had thought I had happily left behind. I realize that I need to understand my Indianness along with my gayness—they can't be two separate journeys. So I begin to study the different books and films touching upon Indian queer themes. This research as well as Riyad's untimely death provide the impetus for me to plan a film festival at MIT dealing with the negotiation of a South Asian LBGT identity across different contexts—amidst the diaspora in the West, as well as among the home countries.[2]

As a part of my learning process, I add myself to the Gay Bombay mailing list that I have come to know about and discover a whole new world in India—in my very own backyard—in Bombay. There is so much going on! Now, I am sheepish for having lived under a rock for all these years in Bombay and find it ironic that I have been so obsessed with nurturing and living in one kind of online-offline realm (my youth website *Freshlimesoda*[3]) that I have allowed this parallel gay universe to completely pass me by.

Begun in 1998, the Gay Bombay group is an example of what Campbell (2004) has termed as a 'queer haven'—a safe space for gay individuals to come together, 'affirm their identities and explore their sexuality'.[4] I find it very interesting that the space exists in different dimensions and these offer participants a multiple-choice introduction to a certain kind of gay life in and around Bombay city. These dimensions include—

(*a*) The Gay Bombay website—the web home of the Gay Bombay collective, with information, news and internal and external links to resources for the gay community. (http://www.gaybombay.org)

(b) The Gay Bombay mailing list—a Yahoo! Newsgroup. (http://groups. Yahoo.com/group/gaybombay/) [12 years later, the mailing list has morphed into an active Facebook group (https://www. facebook.com/groups/gaybombay/), which is where most of the conversations happen. There is also a Twitter account (@ GBGayBombay) but most of the community is now on Facebook.]

(c) Gay Bombay events held at different locations around Bombay, like dance parties, parents' meets, events to mark different Indian festivals, picnics and museum visits, New Year's Eve parties and film screenings.

(d) Fortnightly Sunday meetings, mostly with a pre-determined discussion topic.

I am intrigued by the possibility of the 'virtualization of real space and a realization of virtual space'[5] (Silver, 2003) that the group presents. I feel that in order to understand contemporary India, which I want to make the locus of my academic career, a group like GB even though it is ostensibly situated on the margins, reflects and in fact, symbolizes all the hopes and anxieties of the mainstream, and basing my research project around this world would serve as a perfect entry point into my quest for understanding myself, my sexuality and my Indianness. Sexuality would certainly make an interesting lens to examine the tremendous changes happening in India—the economic surge, the higher political profile, the cultural explosion on the world stage and a new and assert-ive confidence in its own capability as a major world power. Perhaps, the combination of my outing in the West, the distance and perspective I gain during my time abroad and my lived experiences also gay man in the rapidly changing urban India that I am seeking to catalogue, make me a good candidate to undertake such an effort. This acquired distance is valuable—it stimulates in me a desire to engage and understand and from this 'neither here, nor there' position, yields particular insights, which I have fashioned into this book.

Basing my study within this group would be important for the following reasons. First, the context of the study would be urban upper-middle class India, something that has not too often been explored in academia, which particularly in anthropological studies regarding India and South Asia, has a 'distinctly rural bias'[6] (Hansen, 2001).

Second, the Gay Bombay group is a symbol of the radical change that has swept across gay and lesbian Asia (especially India) due to the emergence of the Internet.[7] Third, while there have been some attempts in the past few years to catalogue a diversity of non-Western queer experiences,[8] most academic work on gay and lesbian or queer studies still tends to be American or Eurocentric. Jackson (2000) points out that there is especially, a sore lack of 'detailed historical studies of the transformations in Asian discourses which have incited the proliferation of new modes of eroticized subjectivity'.[9]

It is a pleasure to acknowledge recent work, which has tried to redress the balance with regard to both of the above issues. This includes the writings of individuals like Jyoti Puri[10] and Brinda Bose[11] and the collaborative readers *Because I Have a Voice* and *Sexuality Gender and Rights*.[12] Zia Jaffrey's *The Invisibles: A Tale of the Eunuchs of India* is quite well known and Serena Nanda is someone else who has written about the *hijras*.[13] Gayatri Reddy's *With Respect to Sex* covers *hijras, kothis* and other different sexualities and genders in India.[14] Academics like Jigna Desai, Gayatri Gopinath, Rajinder Dudrah, and Jasbir Puar cover sexuality, history, films and other media, identities and community in their work.[15]

Finally, there has been very little work done on online LBGT identity in any context;[16] the work that exists tend to focus exclusively on the *online*, leaving out the *offline* component of people's lives that I am deeply interested in; here I am in conjunction with Miller and Slater (2002) when they write that the Internet and its related technologies are 'continuous with and embedded in other social spaces' that 'happen within mundane social structures and relations that they may transform but cannot escape'.[17]

Altman (1996) has observed that 'sexuality, like other areas of life, is constantly being remade by the collision of existing practices and mythologies with new technologies and ideologies'.[18] I realize that a study of Gay Bombay, due to its timing, content and nature, would be the first academic account that would deal with the collision of gay male sexual identity and community, cyberculture, media and globalization in contemporary India. Studying this collision would (in a Bhaba-esque fashion) present me with an exciting opportunity to 'focus on those moments or processes that are produced in the articulation of cultural differences' (Bhabha, 1994).[19]

How do I resist? So, I begin my research by thinking that perhaps this book, just like my sexuality, is not a choice but my destiny.

SOME BIASES ARE GOOD?

Bombay: 25 August 2004. Channel surfing on one of those rare occasions that I come home before midnight, I chance upon Tonight at Ten, *a news programme on the finance channel CNBC India. Today's episode is a special debate on whether India's anti-gay laws need to be changed. The dapper news veteran Karan Thapar is the anchor and the guests are Vivek Divan of the Lawyer's Collective, Anjali Gopalan of the Naz Foundation, Father Dominic, a Christian priest and Jai Pandya, a member of the Indian parliament. I excitedly call my mom from the kitchen to come and watch the show with me.*

Thapar is manoeuvring the show adroitly—there is none of the 'balanced perspective' and 'giving both sides a fair view' pretence. It is clear that he is completely pro-gay, he talks about Persian poetry and Greek love; his agenda for the show is to passionately propound the gay-equality cause. I watch with delight as he constantly snubs Pandya and Father Dominic, never letting them complete their sentences, while at the same time, giving Divan and Gopalan more than enough time to make their case. Divan comes out on the show and Thapar gives him a lot of airtime to express the problems that he faces in his day-to-day life as a single gay man in India. Father Dominic is very flustered—he is simply not allowed to continue beyond stating that the church position on homosexuality is clear—it's a sin. Pandya is reluctant to stick his neck out—he opines that politics can only reflect the views of the masses—but Thapar counter-attacks him viciously, citing various laws, both in India and abroad that prove just the opposite. Thapar's partisanship is evident even in his concluding statement—'We haven't done the subject full justice, no single programme can, but perhaps this can be part of the process to start the change needed'.

19 September 2006. Another night in front of the television screen and Thapar has kept his promise. Homosexuality is back on his agenda; this time, his panel consists of former Attorney General of India Soli Sorabjee, actor-filmmaker Rahul Bose, and others. Same kind of feel good stuff, so I flip through the different news channels and every one of them is talking about homosexuality or Article 377. Earlier in the day, I visited the CNN India studios to observe a talk show on the same theme and it was quite a hilarious experience.

The host was a 20-something bundle of energy, with none of the gravitas of Thapar and the show format seemed to be more MTV than CNN. There were the same round of faces—Vivek Divan, check, Anjali the psychiatrist, check, Christian priest, check—supported by a motley bunch including a visiting gay Harvard student, a pedophilia victim, a fag hag, a token straight guy and a non-liberal lawyer. The show was chaotic. The host jumped from one topic to the other—and within half an hour show packed in everything from the perception of homosexuality as unnatural sex, to gay men being more promiscuous, to the laws on marital rape, to straight men being chased by gay guys, to gay marriage, to life of gay men in India, to why gay men make such good friends for straight women, to gay men in movies, and finally, a little bit of Article 377 too. I was slightly appalled because the host had sought my advice while researching the topic some days earlier, but none of what we discussed was brought up. It seemed that the intention was not really to understand the issue or present it fairly in the media—but rather to cash in on what was perceived to be the sensational topic of the week, following the other news channels' coverage of the subject.

THEORETICAL FRAMEWORK

At the onset, I would like to set the record *straight* and declare that I am primarily studying gay men in this book and not lesbians, bisexuals, the transgender, *kothis*, *hijras* and the rest of the spectrum of sexual minorities in India. These groups are quite stratified—there is little interaction between them and each of them has an entirely different ethos. Covering all of them would require a considerable amount of time and energy, much more than the three years that I spend on only working in the gay world. However, this does not mean that this book excludes these other groups completely—they make their appearance in several key debates, often surrounding pivotal issues, but it should be understood that the central characters here are gay identified, English speaking, middle class men, affiliated in some way or another to the different Gay Bombay spaces.

The questions that I am interested in exploring include—

(a) What are the factors responsible for the emergence of Gay Bombay within the 1990s? What has Gay Bombay's impact been on the pre-existing gay scene in the country?

(b) How have changes in the media over the last 15 years influenced the perceptions of gayness in India? How have Gay Bombay's participants responded to these changes?

(c) Do the participants of Gay Bombay envisage themselves as a community?

(d) How do they access and negotiate their gayness and their individual and collective identities in Gay Bombay's online-offline spaces?

(e) How do they imagine their personal futures as well as the future of Gay Bombay?

I am asking these questions first to locate *gayness* in Bombay and the world and second, to contextualize its public emergence as well as the private growth trajectories of a number of urban gay identified Indian individuals. Each of these questions seeks to reveal a different facet and together, I hope that they can add up and provide a complex, fractal view of what it means to be gay at this particular time in the history of contemporary India.

In my quest to answer these questions, I work with Appadurai's model for a general theory of global cultural processes or theory of rupture[20] (1996) as my overriding reference grid throughout this book. I am drawn to Appadurai because I find in him a willingness to confront complexity and an intellectual honesty that declares that there are no answers yet to the model that he is proposing; still it is vital to ask the questions that need to be asked and to shake things up. Appadurai's exploration of the effect of media and migration on the work of personal and collective imagination in modernity is the starting point for my own exploration within the context, history and character of Gay Bombay. I find his model to be broad-based enough to cover the scope of what I am trying to study and it offers me a way out of several conundrums that I find myself in constantly—global versus local, for example—by its insistence on heterogeneous viewpoints. I am also attracted by Appadurai's own background and experiences as an anthropologist often studying *home* from a distance and as a Bombay person, always taking Bombay with him wherever he travels. I find his model to be very *Bombay* in its reach, its ambition, its scope and ultimately, its ambivalence. I love it.

Appadurai's argument goes thus—

(a) The old models of studying centres and peripheries, push and pull (migration theory), or surpluses and deficits (balance of trade models) are inadequate to explore the complexity of the current global economy, at least from the cultural perspective. An alternative framework would be one that looks at 'fundamental disjunctures between economy, culture and politics'.[21] These disjunctures can be explored by examining five dimensions of global cultural flows or *scapes* such as ethnoscapes, financescapes, technoscapes, mediascapes and ideoscapes. (Scapes are perspectival constructs and the building blocks of what Appadurai deems *imagined worlds*, an extension of Benedict Anderson's concept of *imagined communities* (1983). These are 'multiple worlds...constituted by the historically situated imaginations of persons and groups spread around the globe', that 'contest and sometimes even subvert the imagined worlds of the official mind'.[22] Global flows today occur 'in and through the growing disjunctures among ethnoscapes, technoscapes, financescapes, mediascapes and ideoscapes'.[23]

(b) Although these disjunctures 'generate acute problems of social well-being', they also have positive aspects and 'encourage an emancipatory politics of globalization' through their effect on the reconstitution of imagination 'as a popular, social, collective fact'.[24]

In each of the subsequent chapters of this book, I work with the above framework to track and critically examine the imagination and reconfiguration of Indian gayness in the light of its emergent cultural, media and political alliances. I shift between methods and mode of inquiry, based on what I feel is best suited to the task at hand, aiming for not just thick description, but what Appadurai calls 'thickness with a difference',[25] that is constantly being aware of contexts and imagined possibilities in the lives of those that I seek to understand.

In Chapter 4, I contextualize and present the various *cultural dimensions* of this book through its intersecting network of scapes. Here, the *ethnoscape* denotes the landscape of persons who constitute my world of inquiry—the online or offline inhabitants of Gay Bombay. The *financescape* refers to the economic liberalization of India in 1991 that changed the fabric of the middle classes. The *mediascape* comprises the changing Indian urban media matrix, which witnessed a significant reconfiguration in the 1990s. The *technoscape* refers to the emergence of the Internet and the telecom and technology booms of the 1990s. The *ideoscape* refers to the local histories and global influences of the idea of homosexuality in India, as well as the contemporary circulation of ideologies like the struggle for human rights, the fight against Article 377 of the Indian Penal Code (colonial, anti-homosexual, outdated) and the different meanings of the word *gay*.

I add two more elements into Appadurai's mix—*politiscape* and *memoryscape*. I use the word *politiscape* in a narrow sense—to refer to the changing political spectrum in India between 1991–2007, especially the rise of the Hindu revivalist political party, the Bharatiya Janata Party (BJP—'Indian People's Party') and its conservative ideologies. My own location within Gay Bombay becomes a frame for me to look at issues from a deeply personal perspective—and I deem this perspective *memoryscape*. My memoryscape, which constitutes my thoughts, memories and lived experiences, both material and symbolic, is the self-activation of my own imagination at work—my personal narrative of being gay in Bombay—and it weaves itself in and out of the book, making it unabashedly subjective. I explore some aspects of this subjectivity in Chapter 5, when I discuss the joys and challenges of conducting ethnographic research *at home*. Following this, in Chapters 6 and 7, I attempt a sweeping study of the past, present and (imagined) future of Gay Bombay and the negotiation of identity, notions of community and the influences of globalization within its online and offline spaces. Finally, in the last chapter, I argue that it was the combination of Indian developments in the 1990s (economic liberalization, media proliferation, the advent of the Internet, expansion of the middle class and creation of a pan-Indian culture) together with the *pre-existing* social conditions (educated English speaking middle class, gay heritage and relative governmental non-interference), that offered gay identified men in Bombay (and India at large), 'new resources and new disciplines for the construction of imagined selves and imagined worlds' (Appadurai, 1996).[26]

With their frictions, overlaps and disjunctures, the scapes help me to contextualize the myriad online and offline circumstances that have made something like Gay Bombay as well as my own situated gay existence possible and sustainable. As Appadurai writes—'globalization…a cover term for a world of disjunctive flows—produces problems that manifest themselves in intensely local forms but have contexts that are anything but local' (Appadurai, 2000).[27]

Studying globalization and gayness for that matter, need not only be about problems and their contexts. It needs to also be about solutions and reimagination and thus, so as to take this book beyond the realm of a mere mapping exercise, I add a polemic edge and conclude with a *modus vivendi*, comprising suggestions and observations from my research and experiences in the field. I hope I might be able to engage my fellow Gay Bombayites with some of the issues that I raise in this section. Nothing would give me greater satisfaction than if this book were to ultimately serve not just as a chronicle of its times, but also as the impetus for a tangible action plan as the group imagines its road ahead.

In essence ultimately, this book is an attempt to map out the notion and locatedness of gayness in Bombay's (and on a larger level, India's) cultural geography. I am looking upon the online-offline Gay Bombay sphere as a 'counter public'[28] (Fraser, 1991) and studying its economic, institutional, cultural and social forces as a means of understanding core ideas about Indian citizenship at large. Counter publics like Gay Bombay serve as important sites of contestation—not just for their members, but also for the mainstream to work out some of their anxieties. I realize in this book, that within the various struggles in and around Gay Bombay, what is being negotiated is the very stability of the idea of Indianness. When one studies what it means to be *gay* in India at a particular point in time, one also studies what it means to be a gay *Indian* at that time. Thus at a macro level, beyond gayness, this is ultimately a book about Indianness—and how its core values are being constantly redefined and re-examined. As India re-imagines itself as a global superpower in the 21st century, it is vital that this re-imagination includes the presence of its diverse and marginalized populations—thus this book is an attempt to amplify the voices of one of these populations—its gay men.

LOVE, ACTUALLY

Happiness is waking up next to your partner in the morning in your Cambridge apartment, the blanket entangled between your four legs. Last night, before going to bed, he serenaded you with Bach fugues on his violin. Now, you hear his breath rise and fall, and see his face, serene and content, splayed across half of your pillow and you know that you will do anything (fight battles, climb mountains, watch as many episodes of Revolutionary Girl Utena *as needed) that needs to be done to protect this angel. You slowly tiptoe out of bed, put the kettle to boil and crawl back in for a cuddle. You smother your sweetheart with kisses, hugs and bites, urging him to get up in time for his early morning lecture. He yawns and stretches out his feline form; his crusty eyes open unhurriedly and then the sun comes out as a smile begins to form on his lips. I love you, he whispers and you feel unimaginably invincible, powerful…alive.*

You sing together to 106.7 Magic FM ('Boston's continuouuuuus soft rock') in the shower and subconsciously and silently, a harmonious routine begins to develop—you soap while he shampoos; you shave while he brushes his teeth; you smother on the body lotion while he applies lip balm. You observe the same synchronization while cooking together, shopping for groceries, or scouting for the good free food at the MIT graduate student Sunday brunches. You begin to recognize his moods and tastes, preempt his needs and give him his space when he needs it.

You come to know everyone well that is a part of his daily existence—the professors he likes, the classmates he doesn't, the homework that he can never seem to finish on time, and the financial success of his mother's clinic in Tokyo. You hold hands and walk through the Infinite Corridor and do not flinch when you see your crush from last year pass you by. You invite him to your departmental, community and other social engagements and go to all of his. You begin to plan a life together and argue over the holiday destinations you will go to, the colour of the house you plan to have, brand of the car that you will buy and the race of the children you will have. You even think of doing a PhD if that can keep you in Boston for the next few years that he will need to complete his. You introduce him to Prada and 'Kajra Re' and the pleasures of 3-hour song and dance Bollywood spectacles and in turn, learn about Cowboy Bebop, *Kawai pianos, and umami. When he* goes to visit his family in Japan for a month, you count the days, hours and then minutes until his return. When you are separated for months due to living apart, you wait every morning religiously for him to appear on Skype so that you can have your meals together—while video chatting. Now, all your previous failures at love seem to have been worth it; you acknowledge that happiness is really all that it's made out to be.

THEORETICAL DOMAINS

This book is situated at the intersection of Internet or cyberculture studies, gay and lesbian studies and globalization studies. All these theoretical domains are relatively new—gay and lesbian studies has been in existence for about 30 years, Internet or cyberculture studies is just over a decade old and globalization or global studies is an emergent field that is only now being articulated academically. Moreover, each of these domains is within itself constituted of several interdisciplinary and often overlapping sub-areas of study. The newness, connectedness and complexity of my domains means that there is no fixed path to take while navigating them—I have to figure out for myself, what it is in each of these domains that is relevant to this book and what can be left out or kept aside, to be used on some other occasion.

Cyberculture Studies

Cyberculture studies, also called new media, Internet and digital culture studies (Silver, 2004)[29] has over the past decade blossomed into a distinct and legitimate academic discipline, with online and offline centres of study, regular conferences, established academic journals, degree granting educational institutions and a canon of thinkers and theory builders[30] (Silver, 2000). The term *cyberspace* was coined by William Gibson in 1984 in his sci-fi novel *Neuromancer* and refers to 'a consensual hallucination experienced daily by billions of legitimate operators.... A graphic representation of data abstracted from the banks of every computer in the human system. Unthinkable complexity'.[31] The term caught on quickly and soon academic work began to evolve around cyberculture or the culture of cyberspace, especially from the early 1990s onwards, as the Internet began to make its presence more and more felt and online space began to be equated with cyberspace.[32] One can very broadly outline three stages of Internet studies[33] or critical cyberculture studies.[34]

The first stage was about euphoric utopian versus dystopian visions about the new technology and its effect on society at large;[35] about magazines like *Wired* (1993–date) and *Mondo 2000* (1989–1998) and Al Gore's evangelizing; about the optimism of John Perry Barlow and the Electronic Frontier Foundation ('the most transforming technological event since the capture of fire')[36]... tempered by the negativity of Hightower ('all this razzle-dazzle... disconnects us from each other');[37] about ambitiously titled books like *The Road Ahead, Being Digital* and *City of Bits: Space, Place, and the Infobahn* (by Internet prophets like Bill Gates, Nicholas Negroponte and William Mitchell respectively), sitting along shelves with titles like *Flame Wars, Data Trash* and *Cyberspace Divide*.[38]

The second stage was about online *versus* offline identities and communities, between the 'virtual' *versus* the 'real', 'the net' *versus* 'the self' (Castells, 1996).[39] Classics from this time, include cyber guru Howard Rheingold's *The Virtual Community: Homesteading on the Electronic Frontier* (1994), Sherry Turkle's *Life on the Screen: Identity in the Age of the Internet* (1995) and Julian Dibbell's account of *A Rape in Cyberspace* (1993).[40] Most of these early works are set in MUDs or MOOs[41]—and deal with the Internet, as it existed more than a decade ago.[42] This stage witnessed the publication of a slew of cyberculture related anthologies, by authors like Steve Jones (*Virtual Culture*, 1997; *Cybersociety 2.0*, 1998), Mark Smith and Peter Kollock (*Communities in Cyberspace*, 1998), David Bell (*The Cybercultures Reader*, 2000 [with Barbara Kennedy]; *Introduction to Cyberculture*, 2001) and David Trend (*Reading Digital Culture*, 2001). Most of these included pieces by the writers of the aforementioned classics, as well as other staples like Allucquère Rosanne (Sandy) Stone[43] and Lisa Nakamura.[44] This was also the age of large-scale Internet user surveys like the Pew Internet and American Life Project[45] and the World Internet Project[46] that 'counted the number of Internet users, compared demographic differences and learned what basic things people have been doing on the Internet' (Wellman, 2004).[47]

The third stage, or what Silver (2000) calls *critical* cyberculture studies [emphasis mine], is all about the intertwining between the online *and* the offline; context and interaction; social networks, and cultural specificity; where 'cyberculture is best comprehended as a series of negotiations that take place both online and offline'.[48] A good example of a work from this stage is *The Internet: An Ethnographic Approach* (2000) where the authors study the Internet and its impact on Trinidad via a combination of online and offline methods. Their ethnographic methodology includes interviews, participant observation and website research; they conduct house-to-house surveys and visits cybercafés; they explore the meaning of Trini identity not just among individuals located in Trinidad but also among the international diaspora and they contextualize all of this with a study of the political economy of the Internet in Trinidad and an examination of how business is done there. Within an Asian context, *Asia.com: Asia Encounters the Internet* (2003) is an anthology that attempts a similar grand sweep.

In my case, although I am working with relatively antiquated mailing lists and websites in this book, I believe that my work is extremely contemporary due to its scope and methodology employed, as well as the online-offline audience it studies and positions itself within this third stage.

I must stress that these three stages are meant to be understood as loose categories, which overlap and co-exist with each other. Thus we find that utopian (Katz and Aspden, 1997)[49] and dystopian visions of the technology (Kraut et al., 1998)[50] continue to persist; MUDs and MOOs are still being studied (Schaap, 2002); as early as 1997, there is a diversity of methodological approaches adopted by academics writing in this space, such as 'content analysis, Foucauldian discourse…communication history…online interviews…' (Silver, 2004)[51] and even in 1999, writers like Wellman and Gulia are already placing the Internet into a larger framework of 'transportation and communication connectivity, such as the telegraph, railroad, telephone, automobile and airplane' and examining how 'intertwined offline relationships were with online relationships'.[52] New spaces like weblogs continue to emerge out of earlier Internet and non-Internet spaces like magazines, Internet forums and letters.[53]

Researchers like Christine Hine (2000) have coined the term *virtual ethnography* for ethnographic research carried out in cyberspace. I hesitate to use the term to describe my work—first, because I carry out my research both in cyberspace as well as in the physical world and second, because like Campbell (2004), I am uncomfortable with the qualifier 'virtual'—it seems to suggest that online interviews are less real (and less important) than those conducted in the physical world.[54] My position is endorsed by Wilson and Peterson when they write that 'the distinction of real and imagined or virtual community is not a useful one',[55] and further, that an anthropological approach (such as mine) is well-suited to 'investigate the continuum of communities, identities and networks that exist—from the most cohesive to the most diffused—regardless of the way in which community members interact'.[56] I prefer to use the less judgmental sobriquets *online* and *offline* or *physical* instead to mark the distinction between the different environments I work in.

In general, I am skeptical of extreme positions. With the spurt in scholarship on online ethnography, there are diverse opinions as to what constitutes *real* research online and what does not. I do not agree with those that state that one can only conduct authentic research if it is conducted both online and offline (Turkle, 1995; Miller and Slater, 2000; Hakken, 1999)—I think it is perfectly valid if research is carried out online by itself (Markham, 1998; Dibbel, 1998; Schaap, 2002; Campbell, 2004) if the phenomena that are being studied exist only online. I am in agreement with Des Chene that 'to continue to valorize the face-to-face encounter will impoverish [ethnographic] accounts' and that 'it will be far more useful to attend to the relation between our research questions and the possible sources that will illuminate them, and to follow these wherever they may lead us and in whatever medium they may turn out to exist' (Des Chene, 1997).[57] The reason why my book consists of 'variously routed fieldworks' (Clifford, 1997)[58] situated online and offline, is that the community I am studying exists both online and offline—to do otherwise would be, in my opinion, doing my research injustice.

Gay and Lesbian Studies

Though there has been some questioning,[59] the still predominant belief in (Western) academia today is that 'prior to the late 19th century European sexologists' and psychologists' invention of labelled identity categories such as *invert, homosexual, lesbian* and *heterosexual*, inchoate sexualities and sexual behaviours existed but were not perceived or named as defining individuals, groups, or relationships'[60] (Vanita, 2002). Even the terms *homosexual* and *heterosexual* are quite modern (the Swiss doctor Karoly Maria Benkert [Kertbeny] coined *homosexual* in 1869 and *heterosexual* a few years after). Before the 19th century, *sodomy* (referring to a wide range of practices involving non-procreational, or *unnatural* sex, including anal intercourse) was considered sinful in the Western world but it was something that *anyone* could commit. Punishment for deviance was severe—in Britain, for example, until the 1880s, the punishment for 'The Abominable Vice of Buggery' was death (Sullivan, 2003).[61] From the 19th century onward, homosexuality was medicalized and brought under legal purview and a whole new discourse was created to describe sexual behaviours, which evolved new concepts of sexual identities. As Michael Foucault (1976) famously framed it—

> The nineteenth century homosexual became a personage, a past, a case history, and a childhood, in addition to being a type of life, a life form, and a morphology. Nothing that went into his total composition was unaffected by his sexuality.... It was consubstantial with him, less as a habitual sin than as a singular nature.... The sodomite had been a temporary aberration; the homosexual was now a species.[62]

Western society continued to persecute this *species* well into the 20th century; only the angle had changed—from a sin committer and a pervert who had to be imprisoned, the homosexual became a patient suffering from a medical condition that had to be cured. For gay and lesbian individuals living during that time, 'a kind of social contract emerged in the West. It had four elements. There was legal and social condemnation of homosexuality. Condemnation was offset by the closet trilogy of blindness...taboo...and secrecy'[63] (Sanders, 2004). There *were* social networks of gays and lesbians in existence in the US in the 1950s such as the Mattachine Society and the Daughters of Bilitis, but they were well below the radar. From the late 19th to the mid 20th century, there were several shifts in the medical and legal discourse surrounding homosexuality. The newly emergent fields of psychiatry and sexology played a significant role in its social construction, especially the work of Karl Heinrich Ulrichs, Richard von Krafft-Ebing, Havellock Ellis, Magnus Hirschfield, Edward Carpenter, Sigmund Freud and Alfred Kinsey.

There was a rupture in the late 1960s, which is when the modern gay and lesbian movement exploded (with 'the May 1968 events in Paris, the Binnehof protest in Holland and the Stonewall rebellion in New York')[64] as a component of the larger *liberation* movements—"New Left, anti-Vietnam War, counterculture, black and feminist'"[65]—of the time. Stonewall was especially significant. The fight by lesbian and gay street people and drag queens against the police at the Stonewall Tavern in New York City in 1969 became the catalyst of the gay liberation movement in the West and its most iconographic moment. The event marked 'the demand for a new social contract'[66]—and visible changes began occurring rapidly after that as part of an overall attempt to create 'a clear *social* identity organized around sexuality'[67]—symbolized by rainbow flags, pink triangles and parades. Around the same time, gay and lesbian studies began to develop within the academy (predominantly in Europe, North America, and Australia) as a field of theoretical discourse.

One can trace the origins of gay and lesbian studies to the work by British anthropologist Mary McIntosh on 'the homosexual role' in the 1960s[68]—the first wave of writing in the field included works like Jonathan Ned Katz's *Gay American History* (1975), Jeffrey Weeks' *Coming Out: Homosexual Politics in Great Britain* (1977) and John D'Emilio's *Sexual Politics, Sexual Communities* (1983).[69] Most of these early works 'narrated the formation of a collective lesbian and gay identity with its attendant processes of culture making, institution building and political activism and argued that this identity was crucial to the struggle of gays and lesbians to gain political legitimacy' (Corber and Valocchi, 2003).[70]

By this time, the gay community was experiencing a wide scale devastation due to the HIV and AIDS epidemic in the 1980s, which was pointedly ignored, especially by the governments of the US and the UK and accompanied by very strong societal homophobia. As a response to these multiple layers of discrimination, the movement began to cluster around two broad agendas, as outlined by Sanders (2004). The first was the *equality agenda*, focusing on equality-based human rights.

> Western activists use minority rights arguments in what is often called identity politics. The stigmatized identity is used to rally individuals in a movement for change. If the idea of a gay *identity* simplifies reality, it

is a simplification that large numbers of individuals happily accept. The homosexual identity now gives emotional support and forms the basis for collective action. (Sanders, 2004)[71]

Gay and lesbian studies was the academic complement to this agenda. Radical gay activism was tempered in favour of a programme more focussed on health issues, engagement with government and other authorities and to some extent, the invisibilizing of certain elements of the movement that straight society might be perceived to be uncomfortable with, such as drag queens and effeminate men; also, practices like sadomasochism and fetishism and race and class differences within the community were smoothened over.[72]

The late 1980s and 1990s were the age of continued mainstreaming— of straight acting people *coming out* and rapid gains being made in all spheres of society, especially in the workplace. There was another shift of activism in the 1990s from being individual-centered to family-centered. In 1989, Denmark allowed same sex couples the right to have registered partnerships and most legal rights as that of marriage. That shifted the focus of activism to fighting for marriage equality in the Western world. The field of gay and lesbian studies followed this historical process with felicity through its sociological, anthropological, historical and psychological works.

At the same time as all this was happening, there was also another agenda being pursued, though not as successfully and on a much smaller scale. This was the Liberation Agenda, academically articulated under the rubric of Queer theory, which attempted to become inclusive of a wide umbrella of sexual minorities (especially those that were feeling left out by the mainstreaming process described above) and was associated with social constructionism and post-modernism and inspired by French poststructuralist theory. Queer theory, with champions like Judith Butler, Eve Kosofsky Sedgwick, David Halperin and Michael Warner, is about playfulness, power, indeterminacy and performance. Gender and sexuality are seen as social constructs to be performed, reinforced through repetition and possibly subverted. These scholars were influenced by the works of Louis Althusser, Jacques Derrida, Michel Foucault and Jacques Lacan—they 'rejected the Renaissance notion of the subject [being] fixed, unifying and self determining... [and] argued that this notion... was an ideological fiction that worked to conceal, and thereby perpetuate, modern relations of power' (Corber and Valocchi, 2003).[73]

> The central tenet of Queer theory is a resistance to the normativity, which demands the binary proposition, hetero or homo.... If we can speak of the difference as one of emphasis, strictly gay and lesbian discourse more typically stresses the essentialist nature of sexuality over the socially constructionist nature embodied in Queer theory. (Hawley, 2001)[74]

However, while Queer theory has gained a fashionable legitimacy in universities, the Liberation Agenda has had a limited impact on the identity-based equality rights activism of the gay and lesbian organizations. Queer theory is essentially about opposing the heterosexual hegemony—but the reality is that the hegemony is really not being threatened. What *is* being imagined is 'a pluralist, multicultural mutual tolerance and over the past few decades, gay people in the West have built networks, organizations and media and colonized social spaces on that basis' (McIntosh, 2000).[75]

Now for some Indian history. As I have noted in the introduction to this section, most 'Western writings do not hold out a lost past that accepted sexual and gender diversity'.[76] But perhaps Foucault and his acolytes were simply ignorant. There is ample evidence that even in Western societies, terms like *Ganymede, sapphist, tribade* and *lesbian* were being used hundreds of years earlier (Vanita, 2002)[77] and that there were similar categories existing in other societies as well such as the *mahu* and *aikane* in Polynesia, *berdache* in Native America, *sekhet* in prehistoric Egypt, *eunochos* in ancient Greece and Rome, *saris* in ancient Israel and *mu'omin* in Syria (Wilhelm, 2004).[78] In ancient China, 'homosexuality acted as an integral part of society, complete with same sex marriages for both men and women' (Hinsch, 1990).[79] In Indian mythologies and ancient texts, one finds the mention of terms like *napumsaka* (gay men), *sandha* (transgender), *kliba* (asexuals), *kami* (bisexual) and *adhorata* (anal intercourse), (Wilhelm, 2004)[80] and in the recent past—*dogana* (lesbian or lesbian activity) and *chapti* (lesbian or lesbian activity)[81] (Vanita, 2001).

Ancient Indian texts from the Vedic period[82] and the *Kama Sutra* (a treatise on pleasure, penned by the Sage Vatsayana about 2000 years ago) all indicate that ancient 'Hinduism acknowledged a *third sex* or people who were by nature a combination of male and female and such people were considered special in many ways...'.

> People of the third sex were described as homosexual, transgender and intersexed people, they were such by birth and consequently were allowed to live their lives according to their own nature.... Even gay marriage... was acknowledged in the *Kama Shastra*[83] many thousands of years ago. (Wilhelm, 2004)[84]

In ancient texts like the *Artha Shastra*,[85] 'while homosexual sex is un-sanctioned, it is treated as a minor offence' and similarly in the *Manu Smriti* (Laws of Manu, another ancient text)—the penances for a man who has sex with another man are minor. In one case, 'the same penance [is] prescribed for stealing articles of little value' such as 'eating the five products of a cow and keeping a one night fast'[86] (Vanita and Kidwai, 2001).

Vanita and Kidwai have claimed on the basis on extensive research that pre-colonial India was generally tolerant.[87] In general, India, love between women and between men, 'even when disapproved of, was not actively persecuted'[88] and there are no records to prove that anyone was ever executed for homosexual behaviour in India. As opposed to this, 'for centuries in many parts of Europe, men found engaging in homo-sexual acts were vilified, tortured or legally executed'.[89] They argue that all evidence points to the 19th century being a 'crucial period of transition when a minor strand of pre-colonial homophobia becomes the dominant voice in colonial and postcolonial mainstream discourse'.[90] They indicate the 'homosexualization of the *ghazal*,[91] the suppression of *Rekhti*[92] and the introduction of the anti-sodomy law as three markers of this transition'.[93]

> British educators and missionaries often denounced Indian marital, familial and sexual arrangements as primitive.... Hindu gods were seen as licentious and Indian monarchs, both Hindu and Muslim, as decadent hedonists, equally given to heterosexual and homosexual behavior.... Educated Indians defending Indian culture, did not altogether reject

Victorian values but rather insisted that Indian culture was originally very similar to Victorian culture and had been corrupted during the medieval period. (Vanita and Kidwai, 2001)[94]

The British also collected, translated, rearranged and sometimes re-wrote Indian history as part of their *orientalist* agenda during the two decades of their rule and part of their rearrangement included eliminating or marginalizing all traces of positive same-sex references and correspondingly, showcasing texts or instances that glorified heterosexual masculinity[95] (Baccheta, 1999). Finally, in 1861, the British legal system was imposed on to India as the Indian Penal Code and Section 377 of this code was an offshoot of the British 1860 anti-sodomy law.

However, one must not blame colonialism for everything (although it is a rather convenient sitting duck). As Narrain (2004) pertinently points out, the continued perpetration of the stigma against homosexuality in India 'owes as much to nationalism as it did to colonialism'.[96] I shall discuss Section 377 and the Indian social stigma against homosexuality in later chapters.

Now, there is an ongoing debate within academia about whether one can use Western constructs like *gay* and lesbian when one studies the sexuality of people from non-Western locations. As Leap and Lewis (2002) write, the usage of these terms outside the North Atlantic domains might be considered problematic—

> Lesbian and gay are not context free categories, but express subjective understandings of gender, sexuality and social location closely linked to the historical emergence of North Atlantic capitalism and to the politics of cultural pluralism during the late modernity period.[97]

Within the Indian context, there in a vociferous constituency that protests the use of terms like *gay* for India's male homosexual population instead preferring the more functional *men who have sex with men* (MSM)[98]—

> In South Asia the socio-cultural frameworks are supremely gendered and often sexual relationships are framed by gender roles, power relationships, poverty, class, caste, tradition and custom, hierarchies of one sort of another. Here for many men or males we have gender identities, not

sexual identities. The phrase 'males who have sex with males', or 'men who have sex with men' is not about identities and desires, it is about recognizing that there are many frameworks within which men or males have sex with men or males, many different self-identities, many different contexts of behavior....

Hijras, transvestites, transgendered, gay-identified men, *kothis* or *dangas, panthis* or *giriyas*, double-deckers or *do-parathas* or *dubli* [referring to versatile sexual practices—that is, enjoying being penetrated as well as penetrating one's partner], men or males who have sex with other men or males, in all its variety of terminologies, behavioral choices, desires and constructions. Are we truly saying that we should reduce this diversity into the singular construction of a gay identity, a term that does not readily translate into the multiplicity of languages and dialects that reflect the diversity of South Asia itself? (Khan, 2000)[99]

Ruth Vanita (2002) is skeptical of this approach and wonders if organizations like the Naz Foundation, with their preference for *kothi* and MSM terminology over global terms like *gay* and *homosexual* are not merely branding themselves trendily *anti-colonial* in the grants bazaar.[100] She critically notes that 'it is usually those who have already obtained most of their basic civil rights and liberties in first world environments who object to the use of these terms in third world contexts'. The words *gay* and *lesbian* have gained significant currency over the past decade in the media—they are known, in HIV related work, 'the political visibility of a term like *gay* is likely to be much greater than a term like *men who have sex with men*'; and importantly, 'anti-gay groups have no compunctions in using familiar terms'. Thus, 'while intellectuals squabble about politically or historically correct language, Evangelical missionaries from the US are actively campaigning against *gay* and *homosexual* people in India'.[101] In any case, as Dennis Altman (1996) rightfully points out, terms like MSM too are hardly innocent—they are constructs, which have been created 'in a very Foucauldian way' along with other categories like *commercial sex workers* and *people with HIV/AIDS* primarily 'in the interest of preventing the spread of HIV'.[102]

In relation to this book, while I do see the relevance of terms like MSM for health and intervention programmes, I find identity-based categories to be more significant culturally, socially and vernacularly. I am working in a space widely considered *gay*—the name itself says it all: Gay Bombay.

Not Queer Bombay, not LBGT Bombay, not *Kothi* Bombay, but *Gay* Bombay. And yes, there are a lot of people in India who identify as *kothi*, *hijra*, or even perhaps MSM, but there are also many people who identify as *gay* and this book is about them. I have come to realize that to these folks, *gay* does not mean what it does in America, or the West at large. They have creatively played with it, modified it, made it their own, so that a married man is gay, an androgyne is gay; everyone in this universe is gay, in their own way. For my interviewees, 'what gay does label is the possibility of resisting local gender or sex norms. It gives a name to the idea that things might be different, that people marginalized within dominant gender or sex regimes can talk back and carve out spaces by strategic acts of subversion. It is in the imaginings of how things can be different at the local level that we find the source of the infectious excitement that surrounds the gay label'[103] (Jackson, 2000) in India. In short, I do not find the term gay limiting, if used specifically and appropriately.

It is my intention that my work in this book be considered as something that falls under the rubric of both gay and lesbian studies as well as Queer Studies. It looks at multiplicities at every level and plays with certainty and fixity, Indianness, globalization, belonging and imagination, as well as a reflexive writing style and could certainly be considered to *queer* established ways of seeing things. But even though my discussions often question identity politics, they are ultimately firmly rooted in them, as are the people whose lives this book professes to describe; thus gay and lesbian studies. In my interviews and during my research in Gay Bombay for three years, I did come across a few individuals that used the term *queer* to identify themselves,[104] but the only time I heard it being used in common parlance was at a sexualities conference I attended in Bangalore in June 2004.[105] [This has changed over the years, and as I re-read this book in the context of this special edition, I am struck by how much more common both the word as well as the identification with the word queer is in India today. This is why the title of my next book is *Queeristan*.] Most of my subjects accepted the homo-hetero binary (even if they played with this transgressively sometimes) and for them, identity and community (discovery, affirmation and negotiation) were extremely important. Moreover, they were not so much concerned with the *gay* versus *queer* binary as with questions of *gay* versus India's traditional sexuality constructs, or *gay* versus *straight* worlds.

My strategy within this book is to adopt a poly-vocal naming tactic—where naming is important but at the same time becomes irrelevant and intentionally confusing, reflecting the ground realities witnessed by me. Here, I am inspired by the persona in Suniti Namjoshi's novel *Conversations with Cow*, who 'gets frightened of her own changing self as well as those of others' selves' and 'is unable to name any of these selves until she adopts the strategy deployed by Hindu texts and practice...to call the gods and goddesses by thousands of different and often apparently mutually contradictory names' (Vanita, 2002).[106]

> This strategy serves to enable rather than paralyze. It also recognizes that all names, terms, signs and concepts...are constantly in flux and are only approximations necessitated by and necessary to human communication. (Vanita, 2002)

Thus, when I speak about my interview subjects or myself, I use *gay* as it is what most of us chose to be identified as. I make exceptions for those subjects who have chosen non-gay identifiers. I refer to other sexual minorities as need be—so when I talk about *Fire*, which was clearly projected as a lesbian film, I call it a lesbian film, likewise, when I discuss *hijras* and *kothis*, I address them by these specific terms. But when I talk of the larger context, I use *queer* as an inclusive, all encompassing umbrella term, following Narrain's (2004) lead, because first, as he notes, it is simply easier to use than the current alternative—LBGTKH[107] and 'has the potential of stopping this endless process of adding alphabets to the acronym';[108] and second, because I too believe that despite their differences, all the sexual minorities essentially 'question the heteronormative ideal that the only way in which two human beings can relate romantically, sexually and emotionally is within a heterosexual context'.[109]

Globalization Studies

Anthony Giddens points out that even as recent as the 1980s, the term 'globalization was hardly used, either in academic literature or in everyday language. It has come from nowhere to almost everywhere' (2002)[110] to capture the public imagination and might arguably be considered as 'the defining feature of human society at the start of the 21st century"[111] (Benyon and Dunkerley, 2000). Consequently, globalization or global studies has emerged as a new interdisciplinary field of study in several universities all over the world (and taken on an increased urgency in the volatile post 9/11 world scenario). The term globalization itself remains a contested concept, used on varying occasions 'to describe a process, a condition, a system, a force and an age (Steger, 2003).[112] Moreover, scholars have not only disagreed on how to define this term, but also on its scale, causation, chronology, impact, trajectories and policy outcomes'.[113]

Different theorists have established different endpoints for their speculation on when globalization began. Steger (2003) divides globalization into five periods—pre-historic (10000 BC–3500 BC), pre-modern (3500 BC–1500 AD), early modern (1500–1750), modern (1750–1970) and contemporary (1970–today).[114] For Robertston (1992), the categories are—phase one (1400–1750 or germinal), phase two (1750–1875 or internationalism), phase three (1875–1925 or take off), phase four (1925–1969 or struggle for dominance) and phase five (1969–today);[115] while Held *et al.* (1999) present the chronology as pre-modern (before 1500), early modern (1500–1850), modern (1850–1945) and contemporary (post 1945).[116] Friedman (2000) takes a more recent view; to him, globalization as we know it, spans only two eras (mid-1800s–late 1920s and 1989–today, separated by a *time out* period between the start of World War I and the end of the Cold War).[117] Although I recognize the importance of the earlier waves of globalization (expansion of religions, ancient and modern empires built through conquest, extensive international trade, the spread of science, and so on) I shall focus primary on this later period of post-1989 contemporary globalization for the purpose of this book.

The contemporary era of globalization has many different dimensions—economic (increased financial flows around the world, spread of free market capitalism, internationalization of trade, growth of multinational and transnational corporations, trading blocs, worldwide regulatory bodies like the International Monetary Fund and World Bank, international accords like the erstwhile GATT and current WTO),[118] political (collapse of communism, the increase in global terrorism and its countermeasures, advance and retreat of civil rights in different countries, international cooperation, political interventions by international organizations like the UN), cultural (global circulation of media and entertainment, fashions and lifestyles, tastes and habits, the predominance of English as the global language), technological (the personal computer revolution, emergence and spread of the Internet, miniaturization of technology), ideological (neoliberalism, protectionism, anti-globalization) and so on. All of these are inexorably intertwined.

Economic and technological globalization is now considered irreversible (and also faces the most flak from anti-globalization writers like Naomi Klein[119] and Arundhati Roy;[120] thousands of protesters in places like Seattle [anti-WTO, 1999] the Narmada valley [anti-dam, ongoing]; and at every iteration of the World Social Forum).

The end of the Cold War brought forward two significant and contrasting theses on political globalization—Francis Fukuyama (1992) proclaimed grandiosely that this was surely 'the end of history', while Samuel Huntington debunked this thesis (1996), proposing equally grandiosely that it was merely the beginning to an even bigger battle—the 'clash of civilizations'.[121] Neither of these rings completely true today and instead we find—

> both clashes of civilizations as well as the homogenization of civilizations, both environmental disasters and amazing environmental rescues, both the triumph of liberal free market capitalism and a backlash against it, both the durability of nation states and the rise of enormously powerful non-state actors. (Friedman, 2000)[122]

For this book, I am more interested in the area of cultural globalization, which might be defined as 'a social process in which the constraints of geography on social and cultural arrangements recede and in which people become increasingly aware that they are receding' (Waters, 1995).[123] Arjun Appadurai (1996) presents two perspectives from which we can view cultural globalization—homogenization and heterogenization.

From a homogenizing perspective, globalization might be seen as a force that erases difference. It is commonly perceived (using a centre-periphery scheme of understanding) as Westernization or Americanization. Other names for this force include 'coco-colonization' (Hannerz, 1990) and 'McWorld' (Barber, 1995)—where the global might of (mainly American) consumer goods and pop culture overpowers local habits and soon everyone is eating at McDonalds, sipping Coke, listening to Britney Spears and playing basketball while wearing Nike.

The heterogenizing view is more complex than the mere reverse of privileging local over global. Here globalization is understood to set up a 'dialectic between the local and global, out of which are…born increased cultural options' (Benyon and Dunkerley, 2002).[124] It challenges the assumption that globalization is primarily a Western phenomenon. It talks about multiple rather than one-way flows. It says that flows occur from the peripheries to centre as well as within the peripheries themselves. It also states that global products and processes are re-imagined, re-appropriated and reconstructed in their interaction with the local. It is characterized by paradoxes—such as 'the rise of multi-culturism and the celebration of ethnicity rather than its extinction' (Bhagwati, 2004).[125] Rosaldo and Xavier (2002) call this 'customization',[126] while Robertson (1995) deems it 'glocalization' (after a Japanese marketing term)—'the creation and incorporation of locality, processes which themselves largely shape, in turn, the compression of the world as a whole'.[127]

From this viewpoint, McDonaldization does not equate to Americanization or uniformity—thus the vegetarian McAloo Tikki Burger™ (spicy potato patty burger) I eat in my Bombay McDonalds is uniquely local, while the *sambhar* (lentil soup) and rice that I get with my Kentucky Fried Chicken in Bangalore will not even accompany the dish if I have it in Delhi (and if I am in a Paris McDonalds, I can order espresso and a *brioche* (a light textured French roll or bun) from the standard menu, which might be served to me inside a ski chalet themed restaurant interior).[128]

Some other examples of cultural heterogenization—The rise of China and India's soft power in America[129] parallel to the flow of capital and cultural commodities from America to these countries. The growth of *Hinglish* in post liberalized India, popularized by the fast talking MTV or Channel V video jockeys and captured so well by the umpteen number of tag lines for brands like Pepsi (*Yeh Dil Maange More*, 'This heart wants more') and Domino's (*Hungry, kya?* 'Are you hungry?');[130] and the simultaneous introduction of Hindi words (like *chai* [tea], *masala* [spices], *yaar* [friend], *chuddies* [underpants] and Bollywood)[131] into the global English speaking lexicon. Washing machines being used to churn *lassi* or buttermilk by restaurant owners in Punjab.[132] Bollywood films providing Nigerian viewers with a *parallel modernity*, closer to their own culture and a counter point to Hollywood cinema.[133] *Dallas* conjuring up different meanings when seen in Israel or Japan....[134]

Essentially, the heterogenizing vision of globalization re-imagines society as a *flow*—'of people, information, goods and...signs or cultural symbols' (Lash and Urry, 1994).[135] Some theorists have tried to create an opposition between 'the space of flows versus the space of places', (Castells, 1997)[136] but like Gille and O Riain, (2002) I do not find this notion very appealing as it makes 'places disappear entirely' and also ignores the 'agency of actors and their sense-making activities as forces in shaping the flows themselves'.[137] Instead, I prefer Sassen's pragmatic middle ground approach that sees 'globalization as a repatterning of fluidities and mobilities on the one hand and stoppages and fixities on the other' (2000).[138] As I wrote earlier, I feel that Appadurai's construct of intersecting *scapes* resonates most with the nature of my study; and in this book, I have tried to read Gay Bombay as a 'site for the examination of how locality emerges in a globalizing world...how history and genealogy inflect one another and of how global facts take local form' (Appadurai, 1996).[139]

The initial approaches to studying global homosexual cultures were of two types. Either the cultures being studied were exoticized by the anthropologists studying them—as something radically different, or, going in the exact opposite direction, Western style gayness was considered to be something universal (Berry, Martin and Yue, 2003).[140] The global queering debates in the academia (which started off between Dennis Altman and his peers in the *Australian Humanities Review* in 1996 and have been resonating ever since) spurred the creation of work that was not so essentialist in its approach. Altman set the terms of the debate by provocatively writing—

> There is a clear connection between the expansion of consumer society and the growth of overt lesbian or gay world; the expansion of the free market has also opened up possibilities for a rapid spread of the idea that (homo) sexuality is the basis for a social, political and commercial identity...change in America influences the world in dramatic way... American books, films, magazines and fashions continue to define contemporary gay and lesbian meanings for most of the world....[141]

Although he went on to concede that these non-Western gay movements might 'develop identities and lifestyles different to those from which they originally drew their inspiration', Altman's view came under immediate attack by his peers, for ignoring the *hybridity* of global-local interactions. For example—

> One of the things such as an account of the circulation of 'Western gay or lesbian identities' inside global space misses is the notion of hybridity— not as something that happens when transparently 'Western' identities impact on transparently 'other' cultures, but rather as the basic condition of cultures on both sides of the 'East or West' divide (wherever that might fall...) at this moment in the concurrent processes of decolonization and the globalization of economies. Altman's article assumes that the incursion of literature or imagery produced in the US, Australia and Europe into 'other' parts of the world means that 'a very Western notion of how to be homosexual' is swallowed whole and easily digested by women and men in those other cultures who then begin to exhibit the symptoms of the 'global gay or lesbian'—you see an American-produced poster in a women's bookshop in downtown Taipei, rush out and buy yourself a stick of Pillarbox Red at Watson's and BAM, you're a 'global lipstick lesbian'. This account assumes that it is always only the 'American' side of the exchange that holds the power; that the 'other side' will never return to seriously disrupt 'our' assumptions and forms (might this be one of the attractions of such an account...?) (Fran Martin, 1996)[142]

I am uncomfortable that Altman's hypothesis only lightly brushes by the rich diversity of specifically local sexualities (such as *kothi* culture). However, I am pleased to note that his 'global queering' does not only refer to fashion and entertainment but also to the positive effects of the global battle against the spread of HIV and AIDS—

> The imperatives of AIDS education have pushed embryonic gay communities in a number of non-Western countries to create organizations, usually along Western lines, to help prevent HIV transmission among homosexual men. In many parts of the world, you can now find 'gay' organizations, which use Australian, American, German literature and posters as part of AIDS education campaigns, and in doing so spread a very Western notion of how to be homosexual. (Altman, 1996)[143]

On my visits to the Humsafar centre in Bombay,[144] I have often observed some of these posters and it does feel a little strange seeing images of say, two white guys embracing each other advocating safe sex to Bombayites, so I turn back to Appadurai's heterogenization model as a way to break through this restrictive 'either global McGay or pristine local tradition' (Berry and Martin, 2003)[145] logjam, understanding that the poster means something else when viewed in Bombay. I also keep in mind that both the global queering and the local particularities line of reasoning have often been used by harsh governments to clamp down on their own citizens, even in India.[146]

Manfred Stegar notes that, 'Globalization is not merely an objective process, but also a plethora of stories that define, describe and analyze that process' (2003).[147] I hope that the evocative stories contained within this book will help create an understanding of some aspect of globalization as a lived experience *in* Gay Bombay (as well as the context *of* Gay Bombay), from a close to the ground perspective.

Net Gains

For someone who has covered the commercial arrival of the Internet in India extensively within the Indian press, organized one of the first mass surfing spectacles in Bombay through my newspaper youth club and been a part of every industry networking association in the city, gay chat is a pretty late discovery. I buy my first personal computer in 1996 at the age of 20, but it is not until 1998 that I get my first Internet connection—my primary use of the Net in the interim consists of checking my Hotmail account weekly at a friend's place. Having my own Internet account opens up the portal to the wonderful world of gay porn, informational websites and real-time messaging, which is where I first learn about IRC (Internet Relay Chat) and then the India-Countrywide room on Gay.com.

This is a place that is even harder to get into than the toniest South Bombay nightclub on a Saturday night. With entry limited to 50, it takes me 20 minutes of precious dial up time on my first attempt. The main room is full of bitchy regulars, flamers scrolling ANYONE 4 SEX 2NITE, MSG ME NOW and newbies like myself tentatively finding their way around. I learn the chatiquette fast enough and discover my personal predilections. This is the pre-photo profile era, so text is all one has. I look for chat bios with style—something spunky and original, not the run-of-the-mill 'Sexhunk

Bby...26...31w cs smth fair 7 uncut and hot lkng for some1 smlr' (read as: Nickname Sexhunk, located in Bombay, age 26, possessing a 31 inch waist, clean shaven, smooth bodied, fair, possessing a 7-inch-long uncircumcised penis and hot, looking for someone similar) types. So while A/S/L (age, sex and location) at the beginning of a conversation is standard fare—if someone asks me for my cock size within the first 5 minutes, I'm turned off. I want wit, intellect and pizzazz.

I am a king in this room because I have something that every horny gay man in India would give an arm and a leg for—a place. Thus, I can more or less pick and choose. Despite this, it's a fruitless endeavour on most nights. On the rare occasions that I find someone vaguely intelligent, the bloke gets disqualified because he lives in the suburbs, doesn't want to come to where I am even if he is in town, or doesn't break first in giving me his number. There's a well-defined ritual to follow if I manage to have a conversation half decent enough to warranty my interest in wanting to meet. First, we dither about who gives whom their number first. I'm firm on not giving mine out—it just depends on how easily the other person breaks. Second, there's the 'real name' exchange. Everyone in this room calls himself either 'Rahul' or 'Raj' (Actor Shah Rukh Khan's most common screen avatars). I fluctuate between the two, depending on my mood. My preferred meeting place is outside a coffee shop, down the street from where I live. It is public, crowded and it would not seem uncommon for me to be waiting there at midnight, for perhaps a friend, if my neighbours or local acquaintances see me.

If I'm especially horny or lonely, I lower my standards and settle for what's available on offer. Not all the encounters lead to sex. Sometimes, it is just coffee and/or a drive. Often, if the person is not how I imagined him to be physically, I lie that I have an emergency to attend and hence will not be able to continue the rendezvous. I hate it when I'm rejected by similar methods.

If sex eventually happens, I really don't like it all that much. I find it hard to get naked with someone who was a pixellated nickname a few hours earlier. I find the whole 'what do you like?' and 'what do you do?' pre-foreplay question-and-answer session too businesslike. I find it hard to look at people with their eyes closed when I am pleasuring them and wonder who or what they are thinking of. I find it demeaning to demand reciprocity after I've finished—isn't it simply the decent thing to do, to return the favour?

The two decent ones I manage to meet become regulars—to be met with one week's notice or less, for sex and nothing more, absolutely no strings attached. A is a psychology student studying for his Masters. Tall, dark, lean and broodingly beautiful, he takes three months to tell me his real name and that his entire life story that he had had me believe was a fabrication. He is extremely confused about his sexuality and tries hard to convince himself that sex with me is an experimental phase—what he really wants to do is have a girlfriend and live a normal life. On the other hand, C, a curly haired, boyish looking, mustached mid-level employee with a reputed public limited company, is completely comfortable with his sexuality. He is married, with two kids and fails to see why he should consider that to be an issue. I get it one way at home, another way with you—what's the big deal, he asks, insisting that it is a win-win situation. He is shocked when I wonder if he would be comfortable with his wife wanting the same deal and is certain that such an idea would never even occur to her.

My closeted friend Unni begs me to let him watch one of my Internet hook-ups and I am surprised at how easily I agree. (Am I an exhibitionist?) The guy we pick up is open to the idea of a threesome but he can't imagine why someone would just sit on the side and watch instead of performing. He's not aware of the concept of voyeurism and I don't feel like I want to broaden the vocabulary of someone whose real name I will never know.

* * *

There are two other terms that feature prominently in this book—identity and community—and I want to introduce these briefly at this point.

IDENTITY

(a) *The quality or condition of being the same as something else.*

(b) *The distinct personality of an individual regarded as a persisting entity; individuality.*

Both these dictionary definitions of identity[148] sit right next to each other, playfully demonstrating the challenge in pinpointing this concept down. In the West, the essentialist notion of identity (arising from the Cartesian concept of the subject being fixed and having an essential core that is stable) has been progressively eroded over the years, start-ing with the Enlightenment and Romanticism, when the human psyche began to be thought of as 'divided and... not whole or "one"' (Gripsrud, 2002)[149]—through Freud's differentiation between conscious and un-conscious identities, until the present day's social constructionist view, which 'stresses the temporal and spatial locatedness of identity, as well as identity as a process' (Bell, 2001). There have been many different terms used to describe this modern conception of identity, like 'protean' (Lifton, 1999), 'flirtatious' (Philips, 1994) and 'improvisational' (Barrett, 1998; Eisenberg, 1990; Hatch, 1999).[150]

> Identity can be seen as the interface between subjective positions and so-cial and cultural situations. Identity gives us an idea of who we are and how we relate to others and the world in which we live. Identity marks the ways in which we are the same as others who share the position and the ways in which we are different from those who do not.... Identities in the contemporary world derive from a multiplicity of sources, from nationality, ethnicity, social class, community, gender, sexuality—sources which may conflict in the constructions of identity positions and lead to contradictory, fragmented identities.... However, identity gives us a location in the world and presents a link between us and the society in which we live; this has made the concept the subject of increased academic interest as a conceptual tool with which to understand and make sense of social, cultural, economic and political changes. (Woodward, 1997)[151]

Identities are the names we give to the different ways we are positioned by, and position ourselves within, the narratives of the past[152] (Hall, 1990).

Jeffrey Weeks (1995) describes identities as necessary fictions people need to create, especially in the gay world,[153] implying like Foucault, that identities are essentially constructs. Eisenberg contends that socially created identities are a celebration of the 'multiplicity of selves' that individual perform continuously (2001),[154] echoing Butler's 'identity as a performance' (1990) and Giddens' 'identity as a project' (1991) para-digms. Weeks (1995) reminds us that if 'identities are made in history and in relations of power, they can also be remade. Identities then can be seen as sites of contention'.[155]

> Each of us lives with a variety of potentially contradictory identities.... Behind the quest for identity are different and often conflicting values. By saying who we are, we are also trying to express what we are, what we

believe and what we desire. The problem is that these desires are often patently in conflict, not only between communities but within individuals themselves. (Weeks, 1990)[156]

In the gay and lesbian world especially, as we have discussed before, there has been a conflict between those advocating identity politics (using fixed notions of gay identity as a rallying point for seeking legal and political inclusion into the mainstream) and those abhorring it as something that is restrictive and discriminatory.

We might distinguish between notions of identity constructed in Western (individualistic) and Eastern cultures (collective) (Eisenberg, 2001).[157] We might also distinguish between social or collective identity ('the identity we get from other people's perceptions of us and the collective contexts we are a part of'); Gripsud, 2002[158] and personal identity (that answers the question 'who am I?'; ibid.).[159] Closely related to one's social and personal identities is what Bourdieu denotes as *habitus* or the internalized social conditions that guide one's thoughts, actions and choices.[160] One's habitus is influenced by one's family background, upbringing and educational, workplace and other experiences—it is in a constant state of reshaping.

COMMUNITY

There is no consensually accepted definition of the meaning of community. In 1971, Bell and Newby analyzed 94 different definitions of the word, which had 'little in common other than their reference to people' (Kelemen, Mihaela and Smith, 2001).[161] Raymond Williams (1985), tracing the etymology of this word notes that it is 'the warmly persuasive word to describe an existing set of relationships; or the warmly persuasive word to describe an alternative set of relationships' that 'seems never to be used unfavourably and never to be given any positive opposing or distinguishing term'.[162]

Academically, the concept of community harks back to Ferdinand Tonnies, who in 1887 distinguished between community or *Gemeinschalft* (typified by home and village, family, friends and neighbours, where everyone knows everyone and there are strong and multiple bonds between people, with largely face to face interactions) and society or association or *Gesellschaft* (where social relations are brought about by urbanization).

One's *Gesellschaft* network is bigger than one's *Gemeinschalft*, but its bonds are shallow and weak, as everyone is busy and the city is too big. The multiple ways of defining community over the years either reinforced this divide between community and society (and within this reinforcement, privileged *Gemeinschalft* nostalgically) or questioned it Kelemen and Smith, 2001).[163]

Ahmed and Fortier (2003) list some of the different contexts in which the word community has been used in contemporary times.

> For some, community might be a word that embodies the promise of a universal togetherness that resists either liberal individualism or defensive nationalism—as a 'we' that remains open to others who are not of my kind (Agamben, 1993; Nussbaum, 1996) or 'who have nothing in common with me' (Lingis, 1994). For others, community might remain premised on ideas of commonality—either expressed in the language of kinship and blood relations or in a shared allegiance to systems of belief (Anderson, 1991; Parekh, 2000; Rorty, 1994), or community might be the promise of living together without 'being as one', as a community, in which 'otherness' or 'difference' can be a bond rather than a division (Blanchot, 1988; Diprose, 2002; Nancy, 1991). And for others still, community might represent a failed promise, insofar as the appeal to community assumes a way of relating to others that violates, rather than supports the ethical principle of alterity (Bauman, 2000; Young, 1990); that is, others matter only if they are either 'with me' or 'like me'. Community enters into the debate about how to live with others and seems to be as crucial as a name for what we already do (or do not do), what we must do (or not do), or what we must retain (or give up).[164]

'The present global context of flows and fluidity disturbs the temporal, spatial and emotive certainties of communities....' (Ahmed and Fortier, 2003). With the emergence of the Internet in this context, there have been reams and reams of writing on the virtual community and the differences between *real life* and the *virtual* world—whether real community can be sustained without a face to face interaction, the respective advantages and drawbacks of either, and so on. As I have already noted earlier, I do not find this *virtual versus real* debate useful or productive. People do not build silos around their online and offline experiences—these seep into each other seamlessly.

I am more inclined to agree with Anderson's (1983) contention that 'all communities larger than primordial villages of face-to-face contact (and perhaps even these) are imagined'.[165] Anderson concurs that communities only exist because people believe in them. Citing the example of the nation, he posits that the media and ceremonial symbols (like the national flag, national anthem, and so on) create a sense of time and space into which the national happenings and citizens can be positioned as occurring together and with a set purpose in mind. I find this construct of imagined communities to be a useful way of thinking about Gay Bombay. I am also intrigued by Maffesoli's (1996) conception of 'neo-tribe'[166] as a way of understanding the 'complex, heterogeneous and contested nature of community'[167] and by Oldenburg's 1991 contrivance of the term 'third space' ('a place separate from the home and the workplace').[168]

DANCING QUEENS

2003. The sky is pouring outside as I make my way to the Humsafar Centre. I have known Ashok Row Kavi and company socially—we have had many common friends—but I have always hesitated when invited to the Centre and backed off citing some excuse or the other. This time, two months before I leave for the US, there's a big group of people I know going for a special Sunday High meeting, so I decide to finally take the plunge. From the outside, the building looks old and unimpressive—but inside, the atmosphere is pure magic.

As I enter, two fabulous drag queens in saris sprinkle rose water on me, fold their hands in a dramatic 'namaste' *and hand me a* gajra *(bracelet) made of small jasmine flowers strung together that I wear on my wrist in total filmi style. The smell of incense is in the air. There are beautiful diyas (oil lamps) placed all round and soft pink curtains that cascade down the walls. There are white mattresses placed alongside the walls with rose petals scattered all over them. It is Indian style seating, arranged specially for the mujra (courtesan dance) performance that is to be the highlight of the evening. I sprawl on some cushions and exhale. Why was I so scared to come here for all these years?*

Needless to say, the dances are spectacular—they're all my favourite mujra songs—'Chalte Chalte' from Pakeezah, 'Maar Daala' from Devdas and 'Hothon Pe Aisi Baat' from Guide.... The crowd is going crazy, hooting and whistling with every swirl of hips, every lowered glance, every lip twitch.

I recognize the movements and mannerisms. Last year, I took some business clients from out of town to the famous Topaz dance bar in central Bombay and witnessed a dreaded gangster type nonchalantly shower a basketful of 500 rupee notes over the heads of the gorgeous fully clothed girls on the floor, who were winking and coyly making and breaking eye contact the same way as the drag queens at Humsafar are doing; except today, there's no money showering going on, only warmth and appreciation.

It is mesmerizing—the vocabulary of the erotic dance. I feel that I have always known it—and I have, in a way, having grown up on Bollywood. I suddenly realize that this is my first real contact with Indian drag queens— I have seen quite a few in the US while on vacation, but here, the connection is much more immediate. These are my songs, my music, my people and I watch the entire show with a foolish grin on my face. Maybe some day, I might be able to perform like them.

A few months later and I am at another show with similarly dressed dancing queens in Boston at a nightclub called Machine where the annual South Asian queer festival is being organized by the local Massachusetts Area South Asian Lambda Association (or MASALA). I've never been to a party like this before. A Pakistani boy called Yakub is busy crooning old Sridevi numbers on the nightclub stage and he is followed by a choli-clad Raees from Bangladesh dancing lustily to 'Choli Ke Peeche'. The Indian food ordered specially for the event has run out, so I munch on a loaf of sourdough bread and nurse my Diet Coke. I still don't have the balls to get on stage. Maybe next time?

* * *

A NOTE

[The identity of an object] is the retroactive act of naming itself; it is the name itself, the signifier, which supports the identity of an object (Zizek, 1989).[169]

Bombay was renamed Mumbai in November 1995 by the BJP-Shiv Sena coalition government in power. Gay Bombay was established three years later. However, the founders of Gay Bombay still chose to call themselves 'Gay Bombay'—not 'Gay Mumbai', aligning themselves with the notion of the city that was 'dynamic, intensely commercial, heterogeneous, chaotic, and yet spontaneously tolerant and open-minded...the Bombay of ethnic and religious mixing, of opportunities, of-rags-to-riches success stories, of class solidarity, of artistic modernism and hybridized energies....' (Hansen, 2001).[170] This mixing and matching and appropriating a variety of foreign influences to make them one's own is still the imagined inherent nature of *Bombay* and as I have observed during my study, of Gay Bombay as well. I have addressed the city as Bombay throughout this book to honour this vision of the city, even though I realize that it is and in fact, always was, quite frayed at its edges.

Notes

1. U2 'Walk On' *All That You Can't Leave Behind* (Santa Monica, USA: Interscope Records, 2000).
2. See—
    (a) Between the Lines—festival website: http://mit.edu/cms/betweenthelines/
    (b) Chavi Dublish, 'South Asian Gays Find US Voice', *BBC News*, 13 April 2004. http://news.bbc.co.uk/2/hi/south_asia/3620417.stm
    (c) Susannah Mandel, 'Between the Lines', explores South Asian LGBT identity', *Tech Talk*, 31 March 2004.
    (d) http://web.mit.edu/newsoffice/2004/arts-lines-0331.html
3. For reportage about *Freshlimesoda* and its online or offline activities, see—
    (a) Lindsay Perreira, 'Lime Lagao', *Rediff.com*, 22 September 2001. http://www.rediff.com/search/2001/sep/22fresh.htm
    (b) Georgina Maddox, 'Fresh and Tangy', *Indian Express*, 26 August 2001.
    (c) Varsha Shenoy, 'Budding Poets Squeeze Life Between the Lines', *Express Newsline: Indian Express*, 4 August 2000.
    (d) Tara Patel, 'At Chauraha, They Have a Good thing Going', *The Afternoon Despatch and Courier*, 7 August 2000.
4. John Edward Campbell, *Getting It on Online: Cyberspace, Gay Male Sexuality, and Embodied Identity* (New York: Harrington Park Press, 2004) p. 83.
5. David Silver, 'Communication, Community, Consumption: An Ethnographic Exploration of an Online City', in Beth Kolko (Ed.), *Virtual Publics: Policy and Community in an Electronic Age* (New York: Columbia University Press, 2003), p. 347.
6. Thomas Blom Hansen (*Wages of Violence: Naming and Identity in Postcolonial Bombay*, [Princeton, NJ: Princeton University Press, 2001, p. 235; footnote three to 'Introduction: The Proper Name' notes that while there have been some recent studied of urban India (Kumar, 1992; Breckenridge, 1996), the study of contemporary urban life in India 'is nowhere near the sophistication one finds in the study or urban practices in Latin America, for example, nor does it compare to the density of studies on rural India'.

7. *Time* magazine reported in March 2001 that in just five years, the Internet had done to Asia's gay and lesbian communities what Stonewall had enabled in the West over the past 25 years. See 'Boy's Night Out: We're Here. We're Queer. Get Used to It. Can Singapore Accept its Gay Community?', in *Time International* (Asia), 19 March 2001, as referred to in Chris Berry, Fran Martin and Audrey Yue (Eds), *Mobile Cultures: New Media in Queer Asia* (Durham: Duke University Press, 2003), p. 2.

8. For example—
   (a) Jose Quiroga, *Tropics of Desire: Interventions from Queer Latin America* (New York: NYU Press, 2000).
   (b) Neil Miller, *Out in the World: Gay and Lesbian Life from Buenos Aires to Bangkok* (New York: Random House, 1992).
   (c) Cindy Patton and Benigno Sanchez-Eppler (Eds), *Queer Diasporas* (Durham: Duke University Press, 2000).
   (d) Martin Manalansan IV, *Global Divas: Filipino Gay Men in the Diaspora* (Durham: Duke University Press, 2003).
   (e) Ruth Vanita (Ed.), *Queering India: Same-sex Love and Eroticism in Indian Culture and Society.* (New York: Routledge, 2002).
   (f) Wah-Shan Chou, *Tongzhi: Politics of Same-Sex Eroticism in Chinese Societies* (New York: Haworth Press, 2000).
   (g) Mark McLelland, *Male Homosexuality in Modern Japan: Cultural Myths and Social Realities.* (Richmond; Surrey, UK: Curzon Press, 2000).
   (h) Jeremy Seabrook, *Love in a Different Climate: Men Who Have Sex With Men in India* (New York/London: Verso, 1999).
   (i) Peter A. Jackson and Gerard Sullivan (Eds), *Gay and Lesbian Asia: Culture, Identity, Community* (New York: Harrington Park Press, 2000).

9. Peter Jackson, 'Pre-Gay, Post-queer: Thai Perspectives on Proliferating Gender/Sex Diversity in Asia, in Peter A. Jackson and Gerard Sullivan (Eds), *Gay and Lesbian Asia: Culture, Identity, Community* (New York: Harrington Park Press, 2000), pp. 1–2.

10. Jyoti Puri, *Woman Body Desire: Narratives on Gender and Sexuality in Post-colonial India* (New York: Routledge, 1999).

11. Brinda Bose (Ed.), *Translating Desire: The Politics of Gender and Culture in India* (New Delhi: Katha, 2005).
    Brinda Bose and Subhabrata Bhattacharyya (Eds), *Phobic and the Erotic: The Politics of Sexualities in Contemporary India* (London: Seagull Books, 2006).

12. See—
    (a) Zia Jaffrey, *The Invisibles: A Tale of the Eunuchs of India* (New York: Pantheon, 1996).
    (b) Gayatri Reddy, *With Respect to Sex: Negotiating Hijra Identity in South India* (Chicago: University of Chicago Press, 2005).
    (c) Gautam Bhan and Arvind Narrain, *Because I Have a Voice: Queer Polics in India* (New Delhi: Yoda Press, 2006).
    (d) Geetanjali Misra, Creating Resources for Empowerment in Action (CREA) and Radhika Chandiramani, Talking About Reproductive and Sexual Health Issues (TARSHI), *Sexuality, Gender and Rights: Exploring Theory and Practice in South and Southeast Asia* (New Delhi: Sage Publications, 2005).

13. Serena Nanda, *Neither Man Nor Woman: The Hijras of India* (Belmont, CA: Wadsworth, 1990).

14. The term *hijra* refers to 'a socially constructed role for a group of men with religious and cultural significance, whose primary belief is around the religious sacrifice of their genitalia and who act as women in exaggerated styles' (Shivananda Khan, 'Cultural

constructions of male sexualities in India', *Naz Foundation International*, June 1995). It includes 'men who go in for hormonal treatment, those who undergo sex change operations and those who are born hermaphrodite' (Arvind Narrain, *Queer: Despised Sexuality, Law and Legal Change.* Bangalore: Books For Change, 2004, p. 2). *Hijra* is 'not just a third gender' but 'also a third sex', with a 'well defined social identity... To be *hijra* the crucial step is to take the vow of *Hijra*hood and became part of the *Hijra* clan, which functions almost as a caste, with its own specific inner workings, rules, rituals, and hierarchy.... In the past kings and noblemen were their patrons... today... as they beg, sing, dance, bless and curse for a living, the public treats them with a mixture of awe, dread and disdain' (Devdutt Pattanaik, *The Man Who Was a Woman and Other Queer Tales from Hindu Lore.* New York: Harrington Park Press, 2002, pp. 11–12).

'*Kothi* is a feminized male identity which is adopted by some people in the Indian subcontinent and is marked by gender non-conformity. A *kothi* though biologically male, adopts feminine modes of dressing, speech and behavior and would look for a male partner who has masculine modes of behavior' (Arvind Narrain, 2004, op. cit., pp. 2–3).

15. See—
    (a) Jigna Desai's, *Beyond Bollywood: The Cultural Politics of South Asian Diasporic Film* (New York: Routledge, 2004). Deals with the gender and sexual politics of South Asian diasporas.
    (b) Gayatri Gopinath, *Impossible Desires: Queer Diasporas and South Asian Public Cultures* (Durham, Duke University Press, 2005).
    (c) Rajinder Dudrah, 'Enter the Queer Female Diasporic Subject', GLQ: *A Journal of Lesbian and Gay Studies*, Volume 12, Number 4. (Duke University Press, 2006), pp. 655–656.
    (d) Jasbir Puar, 'The Remaking of a Model Minority: Perverse Projectiles under the Specter of (Counter), Terrorism', *Social Text*—80 (Volume 22, Number 3), Duke University Press, Fall 2004, pp. 75–104.

16. In articles like 'Under the Rainbow Flag: Webbing Global Gay Identities' (from the *International Journal of Sexuality and Gender Studies*, July 2002 issue; Vol. 7(2–3), pp. 107–124), the authors compare and contrast the analyses of heavily trafficked US gay websites with gay, lesbian, bisexual and transgender sites originating in Mainland China, Japan and Germany. John Campbell's *Getting It On Online: Cyberspace, Gay Male Sexuality, and Embodied Identity* (New York: Harrington Park Press, 2004) deals with the construction of the gay male body in cyberspace. David Shaw has a chapter in the Steve Jones edited *Virtual Culture* (London; Thousand Oaks, CA: Sage Publications, 1997) titled 'Gay men and computer communication: A discourse of sex and identity in cyberspace' and Randal Woodland examines gay or lesbian identity and the construction of cyberspace in *The Cybercultures Reader* (London; New York: Routledge, 2000). From an Asian perspective, *Mobile Cultures* (Durham: Duke University Press, 2003) provides relevant and empirically grounded studies of the connections between new media technologies, globalization and the rise of queer Asia. There are also a few essays available, describing the Indian gay online experience, such as—
    (a) Chandra S. Balachandran, 'Desi Pride on the Internet—South Asian Queers in Cyberspace', *Trikone* (January 1996), pp. 18–19.
    (b) Vikram, 'Cybergay', *Bombay Dost*, Vol. 7(1), 1999, pp. 8–13.
    (c) Shrinand Deshpande, 'Point and Click Communities? South Asian Queers out on the Internet', *Trikone* (October 2000), pp. 6–7.

(d) Scott Kugle, 'Internet Activism, Internet Passivism', *Trikone* (October 2000), pp. 10–11.

(e) Sandip Roy, 'GayBombay', *Salon.com* 2 December 2002, http://archive.salon.com/tech/feature/2002/12/02/gay_india

17. Daniel Miller and Don Slater, *The Internet: An Ethnographic Approach* (Oxford/New York: Berg, 2000), p. 5, as cited in Samuel Wilson and Leighton Peterson, 'The Anthropology of Online Communities', *Annual Review of Anthropology* (Palo Alto, CA: Annual Reviews, 2002), Vol. 31, p. 453.

18. Dennis Altman, 'Rupture or Continuity? The Internationalization of Gay Identities', *Social Text* (Durham: Duke University Press, 1996), No. 48, p. 91.

19. Homi Bhabha, *Location of Culture* (London; New York: Routledge, 1994), pp. 1–2.

20. Outlined in Arjun Appadurai, *Modernity at Large: Cultural Dimensions of Globalization* (Minneapolis: University of Minnesota Press, 1996), pp. 27–47.

21. Ibid, pp. 32–33.

22. Ibid, p. 33.

23. Ibid, p. 37.

24. Arjun Appadurai, 'Grassroots Globalization and the Research Imagination', in *Public Culture* (Durham: Duke University Press, 2000), Vol. 12(1), p. 6.

25. Arjun Appadurai (1996), op. cit., p. 55.

26. Ibid, p. 3.

27. Arjun Appadurai (2000), op. cit., pp. 5–6.

28. Nancy Fraser introduces the notion of 'counter-publics' (or sub-groups within the mainstream that are critical of mainstream ideologies and practices) in her essay 'Rethinking the Public Sphere: A Contribution to the Critique of Actually Existing Democracy'. From *Habermas and the Public Sphere* (Ed. Craig Calhoun) (Cambridge, MA: MIT Press, 1991), pp. 109–142.

29. David Silver, 'Internet/Cyberculture/Digital Culture/New Media/Fill-in-the-Blank Studies', *New Media and Society* (London; Thousand Oaks, CA; New Delhi, India: Sage Publications, 2004), Vol. 6(1), p. 55.

30. See David Silver, 'Looking Backwards, Looking Forward, Cyberculture Studies 1990–2000', in David Gauntlett, *Web.Studies: Rewiring Media Studies for the Digital Age* London: Arnold, 2000), pp. 19–30.

31. William Gibson, *Neuromacer* (New York: Ace Books, 1984), p. 51, cited in David Silver (2000), op. cit., p. 21.

32. In this context, Allucquere Rosanne Stone's definition of cyberspace (from 'Will the Real Body Please Stand Up?: Boundary Stories About Virtual Cultures', in Michael Benedikt, [Ed.] *Cyberspace: First Steps* [Cambridge, MA: MIT Press, 1991], p. 85) would be more apt: '…incontrovertibly social spaces in which people still meet face to face, but under new definitions of both "meet" and "face"'. Reproduced in David Silver, (2000), op. cit., p. 21.

33. See Barry Wellman, 'The Three Ages of Internet Studies: Ten, Five and Zero Years Ago', *New Media and Society* (London; Thousand Oaks, CA; New Delhi, India: Sage Publications, 2004), Vol. 6(1), pp. 123–129.

34. See David Silver (2000). op. cit., pp. 18–30.

35. These utopian or dystopian visions are not unique to the Internet, but have accompanied every major new communication invention. See, for example—

(a) Daniel R. Headrick, *When Information Came of Age: Technologies of Knowledge in the Age of Reason and Revolution, 1700–1850.* (New York: Oxford University Press, 2000).

(b) Tom Standage, *The Victorian Internet: The Remarkable Story of the Telegraph and the Nineteenth Century's Online Pioneers* (New York: Berkley Books, 1998).

(c) David E. Nye, *Electrifying America: Social Meanings of a New Technology 1880–1940.* (Cambridge, MA: MIT Press, 1992).

(d) Elizabeth Eisenstein, *The Printing Press as an Agent of Change* (New York: Cambridge University Press, 1979).

36. John Perry Barlow, 'Is there a There in Cyberspace', *Utne* Reader 68 (Minneapolis, 1995) cited in Barry Wellman (2004), op. cit., p. 124.

37. Texas broadcaster Jim Hightower, quoted in Fox R, 'Newstrack' Communications of the ACM 38(8), 1995, pp. 11–12, cited in Barry Wellman (2004), op. cit., p. 124.

38. David Trend (Ed.), *Reading Digital Culture* (Malden, MA/Oxford, UK: Blackwell, 2001), p. 2.

39. Manuel Castells, *The Rise of the Network Society* (Oxford; Malden, MA: Blackwell Publishers, 1996), cited in Nina Wakeford, 'Pushing the Boundary of New Media Studies', *New Media and Society* (London; Thousand Oaks, CA; New Delhi, India: Sage Publications, 2004), Vol. 6(1), p. 132.

49. 'A Rape in Cyberspace; Or How an Evil Clown, a Haitian Trickster Spirit, Two Wizards, and a Cast of Dozens Turned a Database into a Society', *My Tiny Life: Crime and Passion in a Virtual World* (New York: Owl Books, 1999). This article first appeared in the New York based newspaper *Village Voice* in 1993 and has since been included in several cyberspace anthologies.

41. A MUD (multi-user dungeon/domain) is a multi-player Internet-based computer role-playing game, where players adopt *avatars* or roles of certain characters, see textual descriptions of rooms, objects, and other *avatars* within the game and interact with other players by using text commands. MOO stands for *MUD* Object Oriented and is a kind of MUD text-based virtual reality system that is programmable by utilizing the MOO programming language.

42. Frank Schaap, op. cit., p. 15.

43. Stone's oft quoted book is *The War of Desire and Technology at the Close of the Mechanical Age* (Cambridge, MA: MIT Press, 1996).

44. See Lisa Nakamura, *Cybertypes: Race, Ethnicity, and Identity on the Internet* (New York: Routledge, 2002) for an understanding of her key arguments.

45. See http://www.pewinternet.org/index.asp

46. See http://www.worldinternetproject.net/

47. Barry Wellman (2004), op. cit., p. 126.

48. David Silver (2000), op. cit., p. 30.

49. James Katz and Philip Aspden, 'Motivations for and Barriers to Internet Usage: Results of a National Public Opinion Survey' in *Internet Research: Electronic Networking Applications and Policy*, (Bradford, UK: Emerald Group Publishing, 1997), Vol. 7(3), pp. 170–188, as cited in Robert Burnett and P. David Marshall, *Web Theory: An Introduction* (New York: Routletdge, 2002), p. 65.

50. R. Kraut, V. Lundmark, M. Patterson, S. Kiesler, T. Mukopadhyay, and W. Scherlis, 'A Social Technology that Reduces Social Involvement and Psychological Well-Being?', in *American Psychologist,* (Washington, DC: The American Psychologist Association, 1998), Vol. 53(9), pp. 1017–1031, as cited in Burnett and Marshall, op. cit., p. 65.

51. David Silver (2004, op. cit., p. 57), makes this observation in his review of the Steve Jones edited *Virtual Culture*.

52. Barry Wellman and M. Gulia, 'Net Surfers Don't Ride Alone: Virtual Communities as Communities', in Barry Wellman (Ed.), *Networks in the Global Village* (Boulder CO: Westview, 1999), pp. 331–366; cited in Barry Wellman (2004), op. cit., p. 125.

53. Kris R. Cohen, 'A Welcome for Blogs', in *Continuum: Journal of Media & Culture Studies*, *Vol.* 20(2), June 2006, pp. 161–173.
54. John Edward Campbell, op. cit., p. 52.
55. Wilson and Peterson, op. cit., pp. 456–457.
56. Ibid.
57. Mary Des Chene, 'Locating the Past' in Gupta and Ferguson, op. cit., p. 78.
58. James Clifford, 'Spatial Practices: Fieldwork, Travel, and the Disciplining of Anthropology' in Gupta and Ferguson, op. cit., p. 218.
59. Most notably by John Boswell, who did not agree that homosexuality was a recent Western development. In his first book, *Christianity, Social Tolerance and Homosexuality*, (Chicago: University of Chicago Press, 1980) he argued that Christianity only became intolerant to homosexuals after the 13th century. In *Same-Sex Unions in Pre-Modern Europe*, (New York: Villard, 1994), he posited that the Christian church accommodated same sex unions and had rituals for the same.
60. Ruth Vanita (Ed.), *Queering India: Same-sex Love and Eroticism in Indian Culture and Society* (London; New York: Routledge, 2002), p. 1; as cited in Douglas Sanders, 'Flying the Rainbow Flag in Asia' Conference Paper—Second International Conference on Sexualities, Masculinities and Cultures in South Asia Bangalore, India, 9–12 June (2004), footnote 13, pp. 4–5. Though, as Sanders notes, 'some writings now suggest much more self-conscious homosexual groupings in the West in earlier periods'—like 'Graham Robb, *Strangers: Homosexual Love in the 19th Century* (New York: WV Norton, 2003) Louis Crompton, *Homosexuality and Civilization*, (Cambridge, MA: Harvard University Press, 2003)'.
61. Nikki Sullivan, *A Critical Introduction to Queer Theory* (New York: New York University Press, 2003), p. 3.
62. Michel Foucault, (Trans. Robert Hurley) *A History of Sexuality Vol. 1: An Introduction*. (New York: Pantheon Books, 1981 [1976]), p. 43. I disagree with him on this point, but Foucault is seminal reading for anyone interested in sexuality studies and his decision in *A History of Sexuality* to treat sexuality not as a biological or psychological drive but as an effect of discourse, as the product of modern systems of knowledge and power, represented a crucial political breakthrough for lesbians and gay men in the West.
63. Douglas Sanders, op. cit., p. 6.
64. Peter Drucker, *Different Rainbows* (London: Gay Men's Press 2000), p. 9 as quoted in Douglas Sanders, op. cit., p. 10.
65. Gary Kinsman, *The Regulation of Desire: Sexuality in Canada* (Toronto: University of Toronto Press, 1987), p. 179.
66. Douglas Sanders, op. cit., p. 10.
67. Jeffrey Weeks *Sexuality* (2nd Edition) (London/New York: Routledge, 2003 [Ellis Horwood and Tavistock Publications, 1986]), p. 80.
68. The now classic paper, Mary McIntosh's 'The Homosexual Role' (*Social Problems* Vol. 16(2), 1968 pp. 182–92) kick started the field, as well as the 'essentialist-constructionist' debate over homosexuality (that Foucault continued a few years later), which is still very much alive and kicking today.
69. Robert J. Corber and Stephen Valocchi, *Queer Studies: An Interdisciplinary Reader* (Malden, MA: Blackwell Publishers, 2003), p. 2.
70. Ibid.

71. Douglas Sanders, op. cit., p. 13.
72. Sanders (op. cit., p. 11) finds a parallel between the gay rights movement and the women's movement—'Just as gay men, striving for acceptance, disavowed drag queens and effeminate men for a period, the women's movement rejected lesbians. Feminism made striking gains, changing dramatically the expectations of young women about how they could live their lives. Western feminist organizations began to openly support lesbian rights'.
73. Corber and Valocchi, op. cit., p. 3.
74. John Hawley (Ed.), *Post-colonial, Queer: Theoretical Intersections* (Albany: State University of New York Press, 2001), p. 3.
75. Mary McIntosh, 'Foreword' in Theo Sandfort, Judith Schuyf, Jan Whem Duyvendak and Jeffery Weeks (Eds), *Lesbian and Gay Studies: An Introductory, Interdisciplinary Approach* (London; Thousand Oaks, CA: Sage Publications, 2000), p. xi.
76. Douglas Sanders, op. cit., pp. 8–9.
77. Ruth Vanita (Ed.), *Queering India: Same-sex Love and Eroticism in Indian Culture and Society* (London; New York: Routledge, 2002), p. 1.
78. Amara Das Wilhelm, *Tritiya-Prakriti: People of the Third Sex* (Xlibris Corporation, 2004), p. 32.
79. Brett Hinsch, *Passions of the Cut Sleeve: The Male Homosexual Tradition in China* (Berkeley and Los Angeles: University of California Press, 1990), p. 2; quoted in Douglas Sanders op. cit., pp. 19–20.
80. Amara Das Wilhelm op. cit., p. 32.
81. Ruth Vanita, and Saleem Kidwai (Eds), *Same-sex Love in India: Readings from Literature and History* (New York: Palgrave, 2001), pp. 220–221.
82. 'Vedic refers to ancient Hindusim, or the indigeneous religion and culture of India prior to any foreign inflience, based on traditional "veda" or "knowledge"... According to the scriptures... the Vedic age ended just over 5,000 years ago or about 3,150 BC, with the dawn of the *Kali Yug* era. Most modern historians place this date much later, at about 1,500 BC'. Amara Das Wilhelm op. cit., pp. xix–xx.
83. *Kama Shashtra*—'Vedic scriptures concerned with sense, pleasure and sexuality, set aside by Nandi at the beginning of creation'. Amara Das Wilhelm, op. cit., p. 192.
84. Ibid, pp. xvii.
85. *Artha Shastra*—'Vedic scriptures concerned with politics, economy and prosperity, set aside by Brhaspati at the beginning of creation'. Amara Das Wilhelm, op. cit., p. 184.
86. Vanita and Kidwai (2001), op. cit., p. 25.
87. Their book *Same-Sex Love in India: Readings from Literature and History* is divided into three parts. 'Ancient Indian Materials' covers the epics like the Sanskrit *Ramayana* and *Mahabharata*, the *Vedas* and *Puranas*, as well as early Budhist and Tamil texts between the period 1500 BC–8 AD. 'Medieval Materials' mainly deals with Persian and Urdu literary texts, poetry, Sufi writings and *ghazals* from the Muslim Mughal kingdoms from the 8 AD to the late 18th century. 'Modern Indian Materials' covers 19th and 20th century India, discussing material as diverse as *Rekhti* poetry, travelogues, homophobic fiction and positive and the negative media coverage of homosexuality.
88. Vanita and Kidwai (2001), op. cit., p. xviii.
89. Ibid, pp. 194–195.
90. Ruth Vanita (2002), op. cit., p. 3.
91. A *ghazal* is a 'Persian or Urdu love poem'. Vanita and Kidwai (2001), op. cit., p. 358.

92. *Rekhti* stands for 'poetry written by male poets in the female voice and using female idiom in Lucknow in the late 18th and 19th centuries'. Vanita and Kidwai (2001), op. cit., p. 220,

93. Ruth Vanita (2002), op. cit., p. 4.

94. Vanita and Kidwai (2001), op. cit., p 196.

95. Paola Bacchetta, 'When the [Hindu] Nation Exiles its Queers' in *Social Text* (Durham: Duke University Press, 1999), No. 61, pp. 146–147.

96. See Arvind Narrain (2004), op. cit., pp. 44–45.

97. Lewin and Leap, op. cit., p. 8.

98. This includes people like Anjali Gopalan and Shivananda Khan of the London-based Naz Foundation (a HIV/AIDS and sexual health technical support agency working in South Asia), British author Jeremy Seabrook and others like Indian activist Ashok Row Kavi (to some extent).

99. Shivananda Khan, '*Kothis*, Gays and (other) MSM' (Naz Foundation International, October 2000).

100. Ruth Vanita (2002), op. cit., p. 7.

101. Ibid, p. 5.

102. Dennis 'Altman (1996), op. cit.

103. Peter Jackson op. cit., pp. 21–22.

104. Over two-thirds of my respondents self-identified as *gay*; of the remaining, two called themselves *bisexual*; one preferred *same sex attracted person*; one chose *kothi*;one chose *hijra* and only two chose the sobriquet *queer*. In terms of gender, all except two respondents chose to categorize themselves as masculine. Nihar classified himself as *androgynous* ('I am he, I am she, I am a wo/man'); the *kothi*-identified Queen Rekha preferred the term *intergendered* and Savitri reiterated that she was *hijra*.

105. The 2nd International Conference on Sexualities, Masculinities and Cultures in South Asia. 9–12 June 2004. Bangalore. Conference website—http://www.dharanitrust.org/conf2004/index.html

106. Suniti Namjoshi *Conversations of Cow* (London: The Women's Press, 1985), as discussed in Ruth Vanita (2002), p. 6.

107. Lesbian + Bisexual + Gay + Transgender + Kothi + Hijra + Queer.

108. Arvind Narrain, op. cit., p. 11.

109. Ibid, p. 1.

110. Anthony Giddens, (revised edition) *Runaway World: How Globalization is Reshaping Our Lives* (New York: Routledge, 2002 [2000]), p. 7.

111. John Beynon and David Dunkerley, *Globalization: The Reader* (New York: Routledge, 2000), p. 3.

112. Manfred Steger, *Globalization: A Very Short Introduction* (Oxford: Oxford University Press, 2003), p. 7.

113. Ibid, p. 13.

114. Ibid, pp. 17–36.

115. Roland Robertson, *Globalization: Social Theory and Global Culture*, (London: Sage Publications, 1992), as referenced in Beynon and Dunkerley op. cit., p. 9.

116. Ibid, p. 10.

117. Thomas Friedman, *The Lexus and the Olive Tree* (Revised Edition) (New York: Farrar, Strauss and Giroux 2000 [1999]), pp. xvi–xvii.

118. IMF stands for the International Monetary Fund, established in 1947 to oversee the global financial system after the end of World War II. GATT stands for the General Agreement on Tariffs and Trade, the international global trade accord, which was in place between 1948–1994, when the WTO or the World Trade Organization replaced it.

119. See—
    (a) *No Logo: No Space, No Choice, No Jobs* (New York: Picador, 2000).
    (b) *Fences and Windows: Dispatches from the Front Lines of the Globalization Debate* (New York: Picador, 2002).

120. See *The Cost of Living* (New York: Modern Library, 1999).

121. See Samuel Huntington, *The Clash of Civilizations and the Remaking of World Order* (New York: Simon and Schuster, 1996) and Francis Fukuyama, *The End of History and the Last Man* (New York: Free Press, 1992).

122. Thomas Friedman, op.cit., pp. xx–xxi.

123. Malcolm Waters, *Globalization* (London: Routledge, 1995), p. 3.

124. Beynon and Dunkerley, op. cit., p. 27.

125. Jagdish Bhagwati, *In Defense of Globalization* (New York: Oxford University Press, 2004), p. 110.

126. Renato Rosaldo and Jonathan Xavier Inda (Eds), *The Anthropology of Globalization: A Reader* (Malden, MA: Blackwell Publishers, 2002), p. 30.

127. Roland Robertson, 'Glocalization: Time-Space and Homogeneity-Heterogeneity', from Roland Robertson, M. Featherstone and S. Lash, *Global Modernities* (London: Sage Publications, 1995), p. 40, as cited in Beynon and Dunkerley op. cit., pp. 20–21.

128. Shirley Leung, 'Armchairs, TV and Espressos—Is it McDonalds?', *Wall Street Journal* 13 August 2002, cited in Jagdish Bhagwati op. cit., (2004), pp. 110–111.

129. Soft power is a term made popular by Harvard professor Joseph Nye, which refers to the power of a country's culture as an influencing force, as opposed to its hard power or military and economic might. See the issue titled 'The Rising Soft Power of China and India', *New Perspectives Quarterly* (Oxford; Malden, MA: Blackwell Publishers, 2003), Vol. 20(1).

130. Scott Baldauf, 'A Hindi-English Jumble Spoken by 350 Million', *Christian Science Monitor Online*, 23 November 2004. http://www.csmonitor.com/2004/1123/p01s03-wosc.html

131. See Anushka Asthana, 'Kiss My Chuddies (Welcome to the Queen's Hinglish)', *Observer* 25 April 2005. http://observer.guardian.co.uk/uk_news/story/0,6903,1202721,00.html

132. See Sampa Chakrabarty Lahiri, 'A Peek Into the Rural Market', *ET Strategic Marketing* June–July 2002, for more examples of creative appropriations of consumer products by rural India. http://www.etstrategicmarketing.com/smJune-July2/art6_1.htm

133. See Brian Larkin, 'Indian Films and Nigerian Lovers: Media and the Creation of Parallel Modernities', in Inda and Rosaldo, op. cit., pp. 350–378.

134. See Elihu Katz and Tamar Liebes, *The Export of Meaning: Cross-Cultural Readings of 'Dallas'*, (New York: Oxford University Press, 1990).

135. S. Lash and J. Urry, *Economies of Sign and Space* (London: Sage Publications, 1994), paraphrased in Zsuzsa Gille and Sean O Riain, 'Global Ethnography', *Annual Review of Sociology* (Palo Alto, CA: Annual Reviews, 2002), No. 28, p. 274.

136. Manuel Castells, *The Information Age* (3 volumes) (Oxford; Malden, MA: Blackwell Publishers, 1996–1998), paraphrased in Gille and O Riain, op. cit., p. 274.

137. Gille and O Riain, op. cit., p. 275.
138. Saskia Sassen, 'Spatialities and Temporalities of the Global: Elements for a Theorization', *Public Culture* (Durham: Duke University Press, 2000), Vol. 12(1), pp. 215–232 paraphrased in Gille and O Riain, op. cit., p. 275.
139. Arjun Appadurai (1996), op. cit., p. 18.
140. Berry, Martin, and Yue, op. cit., pp. 5–6.
141. Dennis Altman (1996), op. cit.
142. 'Fran Martin responds to Dennis Altman', *Australian Humanities Review* (1996). http://www.lib.latrobe.edu.au/AHR/emuse/Globalqueering/martin.html#2
143. Dennis Altman (1996), op. cit.
144. The Humsafar Trust is an NGO formed in Bombay in 1991 by the famous LBGT rights activist Ashok Row Kavi with the mandate of working in the field of HIV/AIDS awareness or prevention in Bombay.
145. Chris Berry and Fran Martin, 'Syncretism and Synchronicity: Queer 'n' Asian Cyberspace in 1990s—Taiwan and Korea' in Berry, Martin, and Yue op. cit., p. 89.
146. In Peter Jackson (op. cit., pp. 8–9), he alerts us to the need to avoid 'over hasty generalizations in specifying what unites and what distinguishes different national or regional forms of g/l/t identity and culture'. The 'globally uniform view of gay identity' can also be negative—countries can use this to victimize their own people… The political complexities of taking either a 'global' or 'western influences' or local history explanatory line should be thought out.
147. Manfred Steger, op. cit., 'Preface'.
148. The American Heritage Dictionary of the English Language, Fourth Edition (Boston: Houghton Mifflin Company, 2000). Accessible on the world wide web through Dictionary.com http://dictionary.reference.com/
149. Jostein Gripsrud, *Understanding Media Culture* (London: Arnold Publishers, 2002), p. 7.
150. Eric Eisenberg, 'Building a Mystery: Toward a New Theory of Communication and Identity', *Journal of Communication* (Oxford, UK: Oxford University Press, 2001), No. 51, p. 537.
151. Kathryn Woodward, op. cit., pp. 1–2.
152. Stuart Hall (1990), op. cit., p. 225, as cited in Nayan Shah, 'Sexuality, Identity and the Uses of History', *A Lotus of Another Color* (Ed. Rakesh Ratti), (Boston: Alyson Publications, 1993), p. 121.
153. Jeffrey Weeks, *Invented Moralities* (Cambridge: Polity Press, 1995), p. 98.
154. Eric Eisenberg, op. cit., p. 537.
155. Jeffrey Weeks (1995), op. cit., pp. 98–99.
156. Jeffery Weeks (1990), op. cit., p. 115.
157. Eric Eisenberg, op. cit., p. 535.
158. Jostein Gripsrud, op. cit., p. 6.
159. Ibid, p. 6.
160. Bourdieu introduced this term in *Outline of a Theory of Practice* (Cambridge, UK: Cambridge University Press, 1977) and returned to it in other works such as *Distinction: A Social Critique of the Judgment of Taste* (Cambridge, MA: Harvard University Press, 1984).
161. Mihaela Kelemen and Warren Smith, 'Community and its Virtual Promises: A Critique of Cyberlibertarian Rhetoric', *Information, Community and Society* (Taylor and Francis [Routledge], 2001), Vol. 4(3), p. 373.

162. Raymond Williams, *Keywords: A Vocabulary of Culture and Society* (New York: Oxford University Press, 1985), p. 76, as cited in Maria Bakardjieva 'Virtual Togetherness: An Everyday-life Perspective' from *Media, Culture & Society* (Sage Publications, 2003), Vol. 25(3), p. 292.

163. Kelemen and Smith, op. cit., p. 373.

164. Sara Ahmed and Anne-Marie Fortier, 'Re-imagining Communities', *International Journal of Cultural Studies* (Sage Publications, 2003), Vol. 6(3), pp. 251–252.

165. Benedict Anderson, *Imagined Communities: Reflections on the Origin and Spread of Nationalism* (London: Verso, 1983), p. 18.

166. Neo-tribes are transient communities that we choose to become members of, just because we feel like it. Michel Maffesoli (*The Time of the Tribes: The Decline of Individualism in Mass Societies*, [London: Sage Publications, 1996], p. 6) calls them 'microgroups' which are inherently 'unstable, since the persons of which these tribes are constituted are free to move from one to another.

167. Kelemen and Smith, op. cit., p. 374.

168. Ray Oldernburg, *The Great Good Place: Cafes, Coffee Shops, Community Centers, Beauty Parlors, General Stores, Bars, Hangouts and How They Get You Through the Day* (New York: Paragon House, 1991), paraphrased in Kelemen and Smith, op. cit., p. 376.

169. Slavo Zizek, *The Sublime Object of Ideology* (London: Verso, 1989), p. 95, as quoted in Thomas Blom Hansen, *Wages of Violence: Naming and Identity in Postcolonial Bombay* (Princeton, NJ: Princeton University Press, 2001), p. 2.

170. Thomas Blom Hansen, op. cit., p. 4.

4

From This Perspective...

Scapes of Understanding

In this chapter, I shall elaborate on six of the seven scapes that I outlined in the introductory chapter, as a part of my larger attempt at conducting information arbitrage (Friedman, 1999)[1] throughout this book. A quick recap: Appadurai has outlined five dimensions of global cultural flows as *scapes* (mediascape, financescape, ideoscape, ethnoscape and technoscape)—these are perspectival constructs, the building blocks of what he calls *imagined worlds*. I am using Appadurai's grid of scapes as the theoretical framework of this book (and adding to them my own constructs of politiscape and memoryscape) so as to understand the *imagined world* of Gay Bombay. With their frictions, overlaps and disjunctures, these scapes will help us to contextualize the myriad online and offline circumstances that have made something like Gay Bombay possible and sustainable.

According to Appadurai, 'the various flows we see—of objects, persons, images, and discourses—are not coeval, convergent, isomorphic, or spatially consistent'—but in relations of 'disjuncture'.

By this I mean that the paths or vectors taken by these kinds of things have different speeds, axes, points of origin and termination and varied relationships to institutional structures in different regions, nations, or societies. Further, these disjunctures themselves precipitate various kinds of problems and frictions in different local situations. Indeed, it is the disjunctures between the various vectors characterizing this world-in-motion that produce fundamental problems of livelihood, equity, suffering, justice and governance.

Examples of such disjunctures are phenomena such as the following— Media flows across national boundaries that produce images of well-being that cannot be satisfied by national standards of living and consumer capabilities; flows of discourses of human rights that generate demands from workforces that are repressed by state violence which is itself backed by global arms flows; ideas about gender and modernity that circulate to create large female workforces at the same time that cross-national ideologies of *culture, authenticity* and national honour put increasing pressure on various communities to morally discipline just these working women who are vital to emerging markets and manufacturing sites. (Appadurai, 2000)[2]

These disjunctures produce problems and at the same time can be spaces within which these problems might be creatively tackled with, via the reconstitution of imagination 'as a popular, social, collective fact'.[3]

Appadurai builds his argument for the importance of imagination in today's world in three steps. First he notes that in the 'post electronic world', the imagination has 'broken out of the special expressive space of art, myth and ritual and has now become a part of the quotidian mental work of ordinary people…in…their everyday lives'.[4] Second, he notes that this imagination does not necessitate the diminishing of traditional values and religion and furthermore imagination is different from fantasy or escapism. 'Fantasy can dissipate…but the imagination, especially when collective, can become the fuel for action…and not only for escape'.[5] Third, Appadurai distinguishes between individual and collective imagination. Collective experiences of the mass media create communities of sentiment—or groups that 'begin to imagine and feel things together'. These sodalities are 'communities in themselves and potentially communities for themselves' and they criss-cross with one another, thus creating the possibilities of convergences…that would otherwise be hard to imagine.[6]

Let us attach this imagination lens on to six out of the seven scapes which constitute the different dimensions of our world of inquiry and explore what it means to be gay in Bombay, *in* Gay Bombay and *of* Gay Bombay, at this particular time in history. (I am excluding a detailed description of memoryscape from the mix here; it has been sufficiently defined in the introduction and in any case, is omnipresent throughout this work).

THE NOT SO GOOD DOCTOR AND OTHER STORIES

There's a masseur hiding under my bed, an irate grandmother in my living room and a phone call from work, asking me to come in as soon as possible. Good morning world—welcome to another fine day in the life of Parmesh Shahani, drama queen.

The masseur, Vijay, is easy to explain. Ramanmal Gangwani, an old friend (married with children of my age), who has tried to hit on me several times without success (and whose advice to me on leaving for America is to never come out but have my fun on the 'down low'), sends him over one morning, because I complain of a nagging backache. I soon discover that Vijay's repertoire consists of an extremely competent full body oil massage, plus a hand job for only a slight premium over regular rates; or what my friend Nil calls a 'happy ending'. Married men in their 50s are his regular clientele but of late, this has widened to include younger customers like me. We have weekly sessions—our arrangement consists of him phoning me regularly from a payphone to fix the time for the next week's appointment at my apartment.

This week, however, my grandmother decides to pay a surprise visit (she has a key to my flat) and I have swiftly managed to get clothed, push Vijay under my bed and emerge from my bedroom, looking like I've just woken up. Right then I get the summons from my office. My grandmother seems extremely suspicious; normally when she visits, I fuss over her and ask her to stay for tea. Today, I ask her to leave, as I have to get ready for work and don't want to be late. Her greatest fear now that I stay alone is that I will bring girls home and gain a bad reputation (that would be terrible for my marriage prospects, wouldn't it?) and since my grandparents function in loco parentis due to my parents being abroad, they obsess about my wellbeing, eating habits and chastity all day. I love it... except in situations like this.

Vijay is not pleased. He has had to stay under the bed for 45 minutes until I finally manage to sound the 'all clear'. I have to pay him double his rates and no massage in return. A few weeks later, post massage, he threatens to go out of my house and shout loudly about my homosexuality to the entire building, unless I pay him five thousand rupees at once. I wonder how many people he's extorted already, but resign myself to negotiating a fairer price, finally settling for two thousand. He never calls up again—I refuse to recognize him when our eyes lock in a crowded train some years later. The next time my back hurts, I try physiotherapy.

Joining my avert-eyes-from club is Dr Champak, who has his clinic at Fort. I go to him with a toe injury while in the first year of college. He asks me to lie down on his examining table and proceeds to tap my feet with a small rubber hammer. He then moves up to my knees, thighs and finally my crotch, asking me very considerately, to tell him if it hurts. Since I am too dumbstruck to respond, he assumed he has my consent to masturbate me.

I feel sorry for the doctor. He is smart, reasonably good looking and a charming conversationalist. I wonder why he would need to molest his male patients to get off. It is not difficult to find out information about him. I learn that he lives with his sister and mother in a flat nearby. Their father died recently and now, they are looking for a suitable boy for the girl. But how desperate can you be, if you are willing to risk your entire professional life, career and reputation by wanking off a patient on your examining table? On the other hand, is he really risking a lot? What man would file a complaint with the cops, alleging that his male doctor had fondled him? Besides being a direct affront to his masculinity, it would be a laughable matter for the cops and of course the doctor would completely deny it.

Dr Champak becomes a stalker. He manages to get hold of my number and calls me up at random hours. Follows me to college one day and begs me to come back to his clinic for a good time. Lands up at my house at midnight asking to be let in. I am not frightened, just utterly disgusted.

ETHNOSCAPE

My ethnoscape is the landscape of persons who constitute my world of inquiry—the online or offline inhabitants of Gay Bombay. They are physically *located* not just in Bombay, but in other cities in India and the rest of the world. They flow in and out of the different Gay Bombay spaces as per their needs and situation. I conducted formal interviews with 32 individuals from this ethnoscape over a period of two years, both online and in physical Bombay. (See the appendix for detailed interviewee demographics). Informally, I chatted with several other individuals over the course of three years that I spent on this project. Naturally, these informal interactions have influenced my analysis too.

This ethnoscape did not suddenly emerge out of nowhere; Gay Bombay was simply the latest addition to an already thriving existing gay scene in Bombay. From my discussions with some of my older interviewees and archival research, I have constructed a brief history of this scene from the 1970s to the 1990s, which I present below, followed by the origins and history of Gay Bombay from the late 1990s till the present date.

I am providing this origin story for two reasons. First, I want to resist the trap of researchers who willingly grant local affiliations like *kothis* and *hijras* histories and identities but do not do the same for those who profess a gay identity in non-Western locations 'and talk instead of "globalizing influences" and the "borrowing" of Western models' (Jackson, 2000)[7] for such people; as if to say that they have simply emerged suddenly and without any local back story. Second and on a related note, I want to avoid a simplified and linear relationship between the economic liberalization that I discuss shortly and the emergence of gayness. My argument is that the 1990s were important because they enabled gayness to be articulated above the ground—but this would not have happened unless there was already a foundation to build upon and Gay Bombay has built upon this foundation in a local and situationally specific way. So the group *does* have a back-story and it is *both* global and local.

* * *

Ashok Row Kavi (1999) writes,

> Bombay in the 1970s and 1980s was ripe for a gay sub-culture. A distinct class of salaried professionals had a firm grip on the city's cultural life. A corporate work ethic had finally evolved....[8]

Indeed, there was a rollicking time to be had for those in the know; popular cruising spots included the Chowpatty beach, the Gateway of India promenade, certain public gardens and train stations and of course, train compartments. There were female impersonators who danced regularly in elite restaurants like Talk of the Town. Bombay's first gay hangout was a tiny bar called *Gokul* located in a bylane behind the 5-star Taj Mahal Hotel in South Bombay. The availability of alcohol at affordable rates and the bar's convenient location resulted in it attracting a wide range of patrons, from advertising executives who worked in the office district nearby to Navy officers, stationed at South Bombay's Navy base a stone's throw away. Saturday evenings at *Gokul*'s become a regular event on the gay social calendar of Bombay in the 1980s.

From the beginning of the 1990s, private dance parties began to catch on. These were either hosted at the homes of rich volunteers, in rented bungalows on the beaches of faraway Madh Island or even in school premises over weekends. The private party phase coincided with the decline in the popularity of *Gokul* and the rise of Bombay's second gay hangout—Voodoo, a dance club, once again located in South Bombay's touristy Colaba area. Unlike *Gokul*'s casual and conversation oriented atmosphere, Saturday nights at Voodoo were loud, brash, noisy and for all practical purposes, standing only—an appropriate metaphor for the post-liberalization spell that urban middle class India was undergoing at that time.

The large private parties came to a halt, largely due to what is now known as the White Party fiasco of 1999. The White Party was billed as the biggest gay party ever to be organized in Bombay. The organizer—an heir to one of the country's large business empires—had cut no corners to ensure that his outdoor event was ultra luxurious, with firework displays, exotic flower arrangements, ice sculptures, floating water bodies, hundreds of scented candles and a male strip tease performance as the grand finale. Unfortunately, the police raided the party in large numbers just as the strip tease was in full swing, after having received a mysterious tip-off. The organizer was arrested and while his family pulled enough strings to ensure that the media reportage of the police raid made no mention of the fact that it was a gay party, the fear and humiliation experienced by all those present at the venue ensured that nothing on that scale was ever organized again in the city.

Parallel to the social scene, in the late 1980s and early 1990s, the city witnessed the growth of political and sexual health oriented activism, largely symbolized by the Ashok Row Kavi led *Bombay Dost*[9] magazine, established in 1990 and the Humsafar Trust[10] (1991). These grew in tandem with and often, in close interaction with diasporic south Asian groups like *Trikone* in the US and *Shakti* in England. Humsafar's gravitation towards an activist and health focussed agenda did not find favour among a certain section of Bombay's gay identified homosexuals—their sense of alienation and quest for a purely *social* interaction space, together with the fortuitous arrival of the Internet led to the birth of Gay Bombay.

When the Internet began in India in 1995, several gay men in India began to subscribe to an email list called *Khush*-list. Founded in 1992, this list (which continues to exist today) was then the oldest and most established online discussion space for LBGT identified South Asians. However, due to the location of most of its participants, the list predominantly discussed issues that were related to the lives of diasporic Indians from India and the UK, something that its subscribers located in India could not relate to. A few enthusiastic Bombay-based members of this list decided to create a separate list, modeled on *Khush*-list, that would discuss India-centric issues and thus Gay Bombay was launched on 31 December 1998.

The founders of the list had not planned for the group members to interact offline. However, most of the list's initial members were from Bombay and some of them decided to meet weekly on a trial basis. Many of these members had previously attended events organized by the Humsafar Trust and had either found them threatening or too stringent in their tone. They saw in their Internet-organized weekly meetings, a possibility of creating a social space that was non-threatening and also non-HIV focussed, as they felt that Humsafar Trust was beginning to become. Initially, these meetings were conducted over tea at the homes of some of these regular list members, but it was soon decided to open them up to the other list members as well. They followed a system of first assembling at a restaurant[11] and then moving on to the official meet venue. As the meetings continued, one of the group's expatriate American members, who was soon to leave India because of the completion of his posting, offered his spacious house to the group as a party venue. The experience was so good that the group members demanded an encore.

Due to the networking and organizational skills of one of their new members (a food and beverages industry professional), the group managed to host another large party at a centrally located abandoned warehouse in the city. It was decided that the party would be free, with a voluntary contribution to be accepted at the door, and subsidized by some of the group members, who chipped in with a thousand rupees each.[12] The huge success of this party too, along with a cash surplus from door collections, led the group to realize that they had a good thing going. The next step was to have an event at a more public space; a small bar located in the central Bombay locality of Dadar agreed to let its premises be used. The Group and other bars and nightclubs started following suit soon, once their owners realized how successful these events were becoming. Today, the Gay Bombay parties are a regular fixture on the city's social scene, taking place every fortnight at well-established trendy nightclubs.[13]

The different facets of Gay Bombay have grown in different ways over the years. The list, described to me as 'the pillar of the community' by its moderator has over 5,000 members (January 2007) and gets a healthy average of 450 postings per month. People who have newly joined the list first have their messages moderated. They gain direct posting privileges once the moderator deems it fit, usually, a few weeks after they join. The list has strict rules that the moderator follows diligently. For instance, no pornography and no classifieds. Some of the most common threads of discussion according to the moderator are those that deal with the topics of safe sex, relationships, married gay men, jokes, parties and cinema. Many times non-gay issues get discussed also. [A decade later, the list is not relevant any more, and main community forum for the discussions is the Facebook group.]

The Gay Bombay website is India's main website relating to information on gay issues. Depending on their popularity or necessity, various sections have been added (like Gay Bashing and Coming Out Stories) or dropped (like *Ghar*, aimed at people who were looking for gay flat mates) over the years. The most popular sections are the Calendar and Events sections.

The film festivals started off slowly—the venue for the first event was a hall in the distant western suburb of Kandivili and about 50 people showed up. However, when the venue was shifted to more accessible halls and college-based auditoriums the attendance more than doubled and currently, all screenings here are houseful. The films screened are mostly Western films, full and short length features and documentaries, without explicit frontal nudity and sex.

Special GB Sunday meeting events with themes related to marriage or the family, useful events like those relating to financial planning, or the much-awaited parents' meets garner a good attendance of between 40 to 80 individuals or so. The regular weekly events usually manage to have about 20 individuals attending them. The group also sporadically organizes different outings, like hikes to historical caves, kite flying events, food expeditions, etc. and so forth. Attendees at the GB events include a cross section of gay men living and working in Bombay city as well as out of town visitors. At the cost of seeming repetitious, I will say once again that what I constitute as my ethnoscape—that is English-speaking, upper middle class, largely gay-identified men—represents just a fraction of the larger queer population in Bombay city. There are several other queer communities, like *hijras, kothis* and lesbians, each with its own rich past and complex present.

As it stands today, Gay Bombay is not a formally registered entity.[14] While participation is encouraged from all, direct administration of the group's activities are carried out by a small number of members that currently call themselves GBAG (Gay Bombay Advisory Group) or the Core Group, whose genesis lay in the original bunch of people who had contributed for the first dance party. Over the time, some of these original contributors dropped out and currently, membership comprises 15 individuals all of who reside in Bombay. This residency is a prerequisite to be considered for admission into this inner circle. Other requirements include a deep interest in the work of Gay Bombay and an ability to get along with all the other members. The members have spread out the various tasks among themselves based on their personal preferences.

FINANCESCAPE AND POLITISCAPE

My financescape refers to the economic liberalization of India in 1991 that changed the fabric of the middle classes—the gay scene I talk about would not have been possible without these financial changes. Closely connected to this is the politiscape or the political landscape of the time. I will discuss these together.

1991 can be considered as the defining year for modern India. Internationally, this was the year that witnessed events like the collapse of the Soviet Union and the first Persian Gulf War. Within India, it was the year that the socialist leaning country undertook wide ranging economic reforms spurred by a massive balance of payments crisis—with spectacular results. The liberal-minded Rajiv Gandhi-led Congress Party government in the mid-1980s had attempted some reforms of India's severely protected socialist-leaning economy—but these faltered due to the controversies that the government got mired into and Gandhi was booted out of power at the 1989 polls. After two shaky hotchpotch coalition governments collapsed, another election was called in 1991. Tragically, Gandhi was assassinated by a suicide bomber during a campaign rally and in the sympathy wave that swept the nation, the Congress was voted back into power. The new government, headed by the demure intellectually-bent septuagenarian PV Narasimha Rao, took charge of a country in dire fiscal straits.[15]

The situation was so bad that there were only two weeks of foreign reserves in the government kitty to pay for imports—a bill that had risen dramatically due to the rise of oil prices during the Gulf War. The country was forced to ask the International Monetary Fund (IMF) for a US$ 2.2 billion bailout package, which necessitated the dispatch of a part of the country's gold reserves to London to serve as collateral. Rao's Finance Minister Dr Manmohan Singh, the Oxbridge-educated former Reserve Bank of India governor (who once again became India's Prime Minister in 2004), was the chief architect of the IMF mandated reforms implemented subsequently, which changed the structure of the Indian economy significantly. These included the devaluation of the Indian rupee by 20 per cent, the liberalization of the national trade policy, the abolishment of the licence-permit regime for industry, a severe cut in various subsidies and sops, tax reforms and a reign-in of governmental expenditure.

The Congress party initiated reforms were continued by the United Front and National Democratic Alliance coalition governments that followed and the country has grown rapidly ever since, which is evinced by even a cursory look at some economic indicators: If we use GDP (Gross Domestic Product)—the global standard indicator of economic progress—we see that India's GDP growth rate rose from 0.9 per cent between 1990–91 to 7.5 per cent between 1996–97.[16] For 2000–01, the GDP growth was 5.8 per cent[17] and it again sharply rose over the next few years to a 9.6 per cent growth rate for 2006–2007.[18] India's foreign exchange reserves rose from a paltry US$ 1 billion in July 1991 to US$ 159 billion at the end of August 2006.[19] From being shunned by investors due to the severe governmental constraints, India has morphed into a desirable global market—AT Kearney's 2005 Foreign Direct Investment Index ranked it as the second most attractive country in the world to invest in (it places after China, with the US coming in 3rd)[20] and at the 2006 World Economic Forum summit at Davos, India's business leaders, politicians and Bollywood stars combined efforts to brand *India Everywhere*, a blitzkrieg that had among others, summit chair Klaus Schwab dancing in a turban and shawl and extolling India's virtues.[21] Another indicator of India's reversal of fortunes is that it actually loaned US$ 300 million to the IMF as well as provided economic aid to 10 poorer countries in 2003.[22]

Noted economists like Delong (2003), Williamson and Zagha (2002) and Rodrick and Subramanian (2004) have disputed this popular narrative that ascribes India's current economic robustness to the 1991 reforms and argued that the growth upshift actually occurred in the 1980s itself. I acknowledge the veracity of their arguments, but still insist on treating 1991 as a watershed year for a variety of reasons.

First, as Rodrick and Subramanian themselves concede, the 1980 changes were pro-business (replacing government hostility towards large business houses with guarded support) rather than pro-market (structural reforms and trade liberalization)[23] and so their impact on the general population was rather limited. The impact of the 1991 changes, in contrast, was palpable; it resulted in the rapid emergence of a 'pan Indian domestic class of consumers'[24] (Khilnani, 2001), or what is now popularly known as the Great Indian Middle Class, the members of which constitute my ethnoscape. And for this class, as Pawan Varma writes, 1991 'removed the stigma attached with the pursuit of wealth. It buried the need for hypocrisy about the aspirations to become rich. Most import-antly, it made politics congruent with the temperament of the people.... Material wants were now suddenly severed from any notion of guilt'.[25] Consumption was cool. Fashion, lifestyle, beauty, celebrity, entertain-ment, dining out, travel, credit cards and malls were the new buzzwords and 'consumerism [became] an Indian value' (Fernandes, 2000).[26]

Second, along with a fast changing financescape, 1991 also wit-nessed sweeping changes in my mediascape and technoscape—changes without which the gayness I talk about would have been difficult to articulate. The mediascape is especially relevant; post 1991, the plethora of media outlets enabled the visuals of the new commodities and lifestyles available in the country as opposed to only being accessed *abroad* earlier, thus allowing the notion among the middle classes that finally, 'abroad [was] now in India'[27] to circulate widely. The flow was not a just one way—as India began to become an international buzzword, Indian IT engineers, skilled managers, models, and others began to flow out of India (and back) rapidly.

Third, as Das notes (2002), besides economic liberalization, there were many other liberations that the country went through during the period—political liberation (the passage of the 73rd Amendment by the Indian parliament in 1992 requiring every village and muni-cipality to have its own elected officials, one third of which should be women), social liberation (the rise of the backward castes post the implementation of the affirmative action Mandal Commission report in 1989; the rise in literacy from 52 per cent in 1990 to 65 per cent in 2000;[28] the fall in the poverty ratio from 39.4 per cent to 26.8 per cent in rural areas and 39.15 per cent to 24.1 per cent in the cities between 1987–2000;[29] a declining population growth rate of 1.9 per cent in the 1990s as compared to the 2.2 per cent of the three previous decades),[30] technological liberation (the spread of the Internet and telecommunications) and mental liberation (a positive new mindset among [certain] people).

Was it a coincidence that the Indian economic boom and liberaliza-tion of the 90s coincided with the rising Hindu nationalistic wave in the country throughout the late 1980s? The destruction of the Babri mosque in Ayodhya in 1992 was a cataclysm; it was followed by several waves of communal riots across different flash points in the country which culminated with a (Bharatiya Janata Party or BJP led) nationalist[31] government being established at the centre in 1998, as well as in several key Indian states from the mid-1990s onward, including Maharashtra (of which Bombay is the capital) in 1995. (Here, the BJP won power as part of a coalition with the nationalist Shiv Sena). Rajagopal (2001) argues that this was not coincidental at all and that economic reforms and Hindu fundamentalism were opportunistic bedfellows which fed off each other in the public imagination.

> Both militated against a *dirigiste* status quo and promised radical change if hidden social forces were emancipated, whether of the profit motive or of a long suppressed Hindu religion. Both drew on market forces energized in the process of liberalization, on the support of middle classes asserting their newly legitimated right to consume and of business groups seeking a successor to a developmentist regime in eclipse.... [Both] shared their technologies of transmission for expanding markets and audiences respectively....[32]

Now, these national and Maharashtra state governments *did* have extremely rigid notions of Indianness, tradition and purity. However, these were conveniently tweaked when necessary. So the West was evil, but only sometimes. Western culture was bad, but Michael Jackson was welcomed into Bombay as 'a part of our culture'[33]; capitalism was horrible and the corrupt American corporation Enron was first rebuffed, only to be heavily seduced shortly after; short skirts were frowned upon and bars were closed early, except when they were owned by the politicians in power... Kissing and Valentine's Day-style consumerism were supposedly degenerating Indian youth, but Bollywood films with frantic pelvic thrusts were presumably alright.[34]

This schizophrenia was manifested at the national level in the public debates around the BJP's platform of *swadeshi* (meaning 'from the home country', an appropriation of Gandhi's philosophy of self reliance that he advocated during and after the freedom struggle) policies, before and after its ascent to power at the centre in the mid-1990s. (In contrast, the 1991 reforms were passed without much debate and with much euphoria, because of their necessity and the dire situation the country was in then and also the inability of their opposers to get parliamentary consensus to vote against them). Before the BJP rose to power, it positioned itself as anti-globalization and pro-*swadeshi*—however, once it won the election, it did an about turn and redefined *swadeshi* as a pro-globalization philosophy. The incumbent finance minister conveniently called it 'pro-Indian without being anti-foreign'.[35]

I do not want to make it seem like the economic reforms of 1991 and the subsequent pro-globalization policy changes of the successive state and national governments in power have been accepted as an inevitable certainty within India—they were debated (and continue to be debated) across all strata of society and also through the ballot. (The verdict of the 2004 elections which booted the BJP-led government out of power, was widely perceived to be a silent revolt by India's poor voters that the economic benefits heralded by the government's much hyped 'India Shining' campaign has passed them by completely).[36] But while middle class India, whose lives the reforms have benefited immensely, worried about the loss of its cultural and social values, (or as Seabrook presents it: Liberalization—liberation or westernization?)[37] for poor India, the issues were much more serious—the loss of jobs, homes and often, even lives.[38]

MEDIASCAPE

My mediascape refers to the changing Indian urban media matrix, which has witnessed a significant growth over the past 15 years. There now exists in India an exciting array of media choices with a lot of envelope pushing as far as content is concerned and as a result of this changed media-scape, as we shall see in Chapter 6, gay images are flowing through Indian newspapers, magazines, films and on television to an extent un-imaginable even a decade ago.

Print Media

I identify two major trends that have changed the texture of how gayness has been covered in the English language print media since the 1990s[39]—the tabloidification of news and the boom in lifestyle-based publications. Tabloidification of news refers to the packaging of news into bite-sized capsules with a focus on light news and entertainment stories and a move away from weighty analysis of any kind. This approach, made popular by *USA Today* in the American market and followed in varying degrees worldwide through the 1990s has been accompanied by an eager willingness to bend the rules with regard to editorial content in India, especially by the *Times of India* group. This has led to some soul searching and hand wringing by media commentators but not much else; the *Times* juggernaut marches ahead at full steam[40] as does India's print media—it is expected to grow at a healthy annual rate of 12 per cent until the end of 2010.[41] As a key element of its strategy, the *Times* group launched *Bombay Times* in 1995 as a twice-a-week (extended eventually to a daily) eight-page colour supplement accompanying its flagship brand, the *Times of India*'s Bombay edition. Full of gossip, celebrities, fashion and film trivia and lavish photo spreads of the lifestyles of the country's rich, famous and beautiful people, the supplement heralded what is now popularly known as *Page 3 culture* in the county.[42] Other newspapers followed—most notably the *Indian Express* with *Express Newsline* and *Hindustan Times* with *HT City*—but *Bombay Times* (along with its other city avatars like *Delhi Times*, *Bangalore Times*, *Pune Times*, and so on) has consistently led the pack.

Page 3 culture means that the cult of celebrity has been yanked out of its hitherto confined space as an indulgence or a pastime (say, the monthly *Stardust* Bollywood magazine one bought, to flip through at leisure) and propelled on to the centre stage—as something that *has* to be consumed on a daily basis. This has necessitated the creation of Page 3 events by the media houses (the *Times* Group for instance, organizes the annual *Filmfare* Awards, the *Femina* Miss India Contest and the *Bombay Times* Party, to name just three) as raw material, to then be circulated around their various channels, as well as the building up of certain celebrities within the Page 3 circuit (only to bring them down viciously a little later, of course, all part of the game). All this is not new of course—but I find it interesting for this book because, within this Page 3 circuit, out gay celebrities like late filmmaker Riyad Wadia, hairstylist Sylvie, actor Bobby Darling, designer Krsna Mehta, and so on began to thrive and their gayness began to be consumed by mass media vehicles on a regular basis.

There have also been a great number of new national and international lifestyle magazines launched catering to different market segments like news (*Outlook*, 1995), women (*Cosmopolitan*, 1995; *Good Housekeeping*, 2004; *Marie Claire*, 2005), men (*Man's World*, 2001), youth (*JAM*, 1995; *Seventeen*, 2003), fashion (*Verve*, 1995; *Elle*, 1996; *L'Officiel*, 2002; *Vogue*, 2007), motoring (*Autocar India*, 1999), investing (*Intelligent Investor*, 1998), travel (*India Today Travel Plus*, 1997; *Outlook Traveler*, 2001) and food (*Upper Crust*, 2000). In the face of the challenge mounted by these new entrants, older and more established magazines have revamped into glossier avatars (like *Femina*, *Society*, *Savvy* and *Stardust*), changed their periodicity (the fortnightly *India Today* shifted to a weekly edition in the face of the competition from *Outlook*), or shut down (like the venerable *Illustrated Weekly of India*, 1880–1993).

Here, I must point out that though the urban English language press has certainly made important strides through the 1990s and beyond, 50 per cent out of a total print readership base of 222 million (as per the 2006 National Readership Survey) is rural and even within the urban press, the English language press is really not that large in terms of the overall number of readers. For example—vernacular dailies have 204 million readers while English dailies only have 21 million. Thus, though the *Times of India* is the most widely read English newspaper in the country with 7.4 million readers, it is well behind the national leader *Dainik Jagran's* 21.2 million readers.[43] However, the English press is considered most influential. It is called the *national* press (as distinguished from its *regional* or *vernacular* counterparts)[44] and receives a significant price premium in terms of advertising rates and hence a subsequently higher share of the advertising pie, because of the quality of its readers that it delivers to advertisers. As upper middle class English speakers in a country still struggling with high levels of basic illiteracy, they are the aspirational target groups and highly coveted.

Television

The Indian television scenario changed dramatically in 1991. Until then, there was only one terrestrial state-controlled network (called Doordarshan or DD),[45] along with a small homegrown cable industry in the cities,[46] which screened pirated Bollywood and English films, music and game shows.[47] The telecast of the Gulf War live on CNN in 1991 and the launch of Star TV[48] spurred the cable operators to buy satellite dishes and offer these new channels to their customers. Star's initial bouquet available in India included four English channels.[49] The tipping point occurred when Star TV entered into a joint venture with the Hindi channel Zee in October 1992.[50] Zee's programming mix of soaps, game shows and musical variety programmes[51] introduced viewers to an *Indian* consumerist lifestyle well suited for the roaring 1990s. In this environment 'money and good looks [were] the hallmarks of success'[52] and entertainment and fun were all that mattered. Films and film-based programming[53] became a key ingredient of the channel's programming mix. With Zee's success, a horde of other international, national and regional satellite channels began operations. Some of these have since shut shop (Home TV, BiTV, ATN, Jain TV) while others have been successful. (MTV, Sony, Sun, Discovery, HBO, Cartoon Network, AXN, Eenadu, SAB TV, Sahara). DD has responded by launching a slew of different channels (an upmarket Metro network, various regional language channels, sports channels, and so on) leveraging its vast terrestrial reach to attract viewers. MTV and Star's Channel V have become significant barometers of the tastes of Indian youth—their *Hinglish* speaking VJ's, sexy couture, racy videos and yet extremely Indian positioning has ensured their immense popularity among their target audience. Star's fortunes have soared since 2000—its flagship Star Plus (now completely Hindi) is the country's leading channel.[54] On a macro level, there are now 20 satellites beaming into South Asian homes with more than 300 accessible channels.[55] (About a 100 more channels are expected to be launched by 2008–09.)[56] The number of Indian television homes increased from 34.9 million in 1992 to 112 million in 2006—these include 68 million cable and satellite homes.[57] As we shall see in Chapter 6, gay issues have frequently come up as television news topics, as well as on popular soaps like *Jassi Jaisi Koi Nahin* (There's No One Like Jassi).

Radio

Like television, Indian radio was state controlled until 1993,[58] when the government opened up All India Radio's (AIR) FM channel and allowed private companies in different cities to buy time on it, brand their allocated time slots and resell commercial space on these slots. This move proved to be a big hit with urban India as there was no pre-censorship of the content that was aired—it could be Western music, talk shows, call-in requests, anything and soon, people were listening to FM radio in their homes and cars. In 2000, the government held an open auction for 108 radio licences;[59] once a company obtained a licence for a city—it could run its own complete station. Currently, there are several of these new stations operating in a very tightly competitive market, including Big FM, Radio Mirchi and Radio City. In 2005, the government opened up the sector to foreign direct investment and gave out 338 licences for 91 Indian towns and cities.[60] Radio is set to grow at a rate of 32 per cent per annum until 2010.[61] This explosion has resulted in several radio talk shows over the past few years discussing homosexuality—for example, on 3 May 2004, a phone-in show on Radio Mirchi at 10 a.m. raised the topic and had Bollywood stars Shah Rukh Khan and Isha Koppikar, as well as a psychiatrist from the city's Nanavati Hospital asserting that there was nothing wrong with being gay.[62] The real time and interactive nature of radio has been exploited by gay activists effectively. So, on Valentine's Day in 2006, a Get Your Gay Valentines Out Campaign was organized in Bombay where the organizers decided to bombard the different radio stations with same-sex Valentine dedications to their partners via call-ins and text messages—quite a few of these dedications landed up actually being read out on air.[63]

Internet

The Internet was officially launched in India on 15 August 1995 as a government-run monopoly service.[64] Its initial growth was slow and there were only 7,00,000 users within the country by March 1998.[65] After the government allowed private ISPs entry into the market in November 1998, the number of users increased to 3.7 million in 2000[66] and 18.5 million in 2004[67] and stood at 45 million in mid-2006.[68] On a related note, the Indian personal computers penetration too grew from 3,50,000 PCs in 1991 to 12 million in March 2004[69] and is expected to cross 80 million by 2010.[70]

These are still pretty low numbers. However, they are increasing sharply and the reach of the Internet at least within the demographic segment that I am concerned with, is pretty wide. Email usage is widespread. Popular gay-related websites among the men I interviewed included Gaybombay.org, Advocate.com, Guys4men.com and the chat rooms on Indiatimes.com and Gay.com—and as we shall see in Chapter 7, many of them look upon the Internet as a major factor in helping them acknowledge and gather more information about their sexuality. More recently, with the increased popularity of blogging worldwide, there has been a surfeit of gay blogs emerging from India as well.[71] [A decade later, this explosion continues. Newer forms of social media such as TikTok are now exciting spaces to view the articulation of queerness in India, especially in smaller towns and cities.]

TECHNOSCAPE

My technoscape refers to the emergence of the Internet and the tele-communications and technology booms of the 1990s and how both these were enablers of gayness. We have already discussed the emergence of the Internet above. Let us now turn to the telecommunication and IT (Information Technology) revolutions.

Telecommunications

Prior to 1992, the Government of India had a monopoly over telecom-munications in the country and there were only about five million fixed line telephones in India in 1990.[72] As part of the economic reforms process, the telecommunications sector was liberalized in 1992 and private sector participation was encouraged, especially in the cellular mobile services sector.[73] The number of cellphone subscribers in the country rose from about 8,00,000 in 1997–98 to 5.5 million users by the end of 2001—and then sharply rose again to reach 50.8 million in February 2005[74] and over 120 million by August 2006, by which time, India had become the fastest growing cellular market in the world.[75] The figure is expected to cross 500 million by 2010.[76] This cellphone boom has benefited India's gay population in general—the increasing ubiquity and constantly decreasing costs of handsets and phone rates has enabled even modest-income individuals to own their own phones and enjoy the benefits of private communication—this is something that used to be a luxury in India until a few years back. Gay Bombay makes an effective use of the thriving cellphone culture in the city to connect to its constituency virally—organizers regularly sent party announcements via SMS (short messaging service, or text messaging) to their phone lists—and these are forwarded all over the city, in a chain like manner, thus, having an effective blend of good old word-of-mouth and modern connectivity. More importantly, as Asim, one of my interviewees noted, with a cellphone number you can remain anonymous. You can give it out to other people without fear; something that you could not do earlier with a fixed line number because there was always a chance that your family would answer that phone sometimes.

IT

India's IT revolution of the past decade has been truly spectacular. From negligible revenues in the late 1980s, the Indian IT and ITES IT Enabled Services including Business Process Outsourcing and Call Center industry[77] has grown at an astonishing rate from the 1990s till the present day, exceeding US$ 36 billion in annual revenue in FY 2005–06. It made up about 5 per cent of the country's GDP in 2006 and employed 1.2 million workers.[78] The industry is expected to reach a size of US$ 100 billion by 2010.[79] This is not the space to go into why and how this technology and call centre boom happened;[80] I am interested in it because it of the empowerment it generated among the urban gay community involved within this industry.

As Carol Upadhya (2004) has noted, the bulk of Indian-owned software and ITES companies (including those located outside India, in Silicon Valley, which are not really Indian, but still appropriated by Indian media and included within the larger narrative of the Indian IT success story) have been founded by middle class engineers and entrepreneurs. These individuals (like Infosys' Narayana Murthy) became heroes for the Indian middle classes when their companies started doing well and symbols of the possibilities available in the Indian of the new millennium. For those working within this sector, like some of my interviewees, their employment had enabled them to achieve financial independence and articulate desires that would have been unthinkable for their parents' generation. In some instances, this had led them to gather up the courage to come out to their families. But even when this did not happen, the financial independence coupled with the high self-esteem and positive buzz around their professions had certainly inspired confidence. This confidence fuelled their desire to access the different gay outlets that were simultaneously becoming available and I could see that they were striving to imagine and then to live out a gay lifestyle of their choice.

AFTER READING GALATEA 2.2...

Picture a bus heading north. The red double-decker winds its way through Bombay's crowded streets. It coughs out smoke and jerks and jolts it way through the seething mass of humanity, miraculously managing to avoid direct contact with any one of the individuals that cross its path. On the bus are two young men with shiny happy faces who are oblivious to the mayhem that surrounds them. They sit close, their thighs fused together as one, just like their breath and their fingers gently caressing each other, just like their smiles, for they know that the journey is short and the night will be long.

Dear Z,

'It was like so, but it wasn't'. As I put the phone down after speaking to you for what I hope will be the last time in our lives, block you on MSN Messenger and tear up your photograph that has switched bedside tables via a 30-hour plane ride (but not your Valentine cards and scribbled pencil drawings of the two of us; I can't bring myself to tear those), the irony of Richard Powers' words does not escape me. All our dreams, our hopes, our destinies, were, yet plainly weren't. Langston Hughes once wrote about a dream deferred drying up like a raisin in the sun. But what about a dream shattered, Z, without the comfort of a slow burn? I need a metaphor for the way I feel.

When our love first blossomed, I was so full of it that I felt I would burst. I remember how I shouted out loud from my nani's building terrace at the passers-by walking below and wrote lovesick editorials on my web magazine till the readers pleaded with me to stop. How the crowds parted as we moved to the centre of the dance floor at our first (and only) Gay Bombay party together and looked on approvingly as our bodies swayed to our own private rhythm. How you would spend hours curled up against me in bed, happy to just trace the contours of my neck, my elbows and my heart. The superstitious before-exam walk on exactly the same route that we took every day, the redness of the sherbet your mother made for us when we returned home, the roughness of your braces as you carefully tried not to hurt me every time our lips met, your smell...our smell. The tenderness of your perfectly formed love-bites that I would wear as a badge to college for my classmates to raise their eyebrows in amusement. The radiant love, our exuberant foolish confidence in eternity. This relationship was supposed to work, damnit! We had everything on our side—love, togetherness, the approval of our families...it was the perfect Bollywood love story, a guaranteed blockbuster! How the hell did it flop so badly?

Now that it's over, I want to curl up into nothingness and am finding it difficult to type as my hands are shaking and my heart is empty. I have come to understand that to be 'as small as love' is still a very big thing and sometimes, your love doesn't want to fit in response. I don't want to buy the premise that 'a love fostered on caretaking cripples the loved one'. I want to believe that in some way, however small and however silly, you grew with me, as I with you. That despite all your bitterness, your tirade against me, your family, the people who love you the most, you will surely one day find the ability to uncoil, unburden, understand. Remember the magic we shared. And not break someone else's heart. I know that I hurt you. I am sorry that I was not more patient. How I wish things were different. But they are not and I am tired and don't want to play any more, Z. I wish you a good game, though. Best of luck and see the world...for yourself.

IDEOSCAPE

To understand contemporary Indian gay identity—we need to know its history and background, the forces that it is fighting against to assert itself and the global influences it is co-opting along the way.

The brief history and context of Indian gayness that I have narrated earlier constitutes one part of my ideoscape of gayness. I have narrated this history not just to provide a temporal background, but also because I believe that it is imperative that this history is known and constantly reiterated. First, this 'destabilizes opponents who argue that homosexuality is purely a Western import'[81] (Sanders, 2004). Of course, playing the blame game on homosexuality is nothing new. As Vanita and Kidwai (2001) point out—'Arabs argue that Persians introduced the vice and Persians blame Christian monks...many believe that the idea and practice of same sex love were imported into India by "foreigners"—Muslim invaders, European conquerors or American capitalists'.[82]

Also, 'the simple fact that there is history behind sexual variation is validating for contemporary gays and lesbians. They are not alone in history'[83] (Sanders, 2004). Indian historians especially, as Narrain writes, including highly esteemed figures like Romila Thapar and DD Kosambi, have either been completely silent on the issue—they have either dismissed it as something irrelevant, or have purposefully heterosexualized queer traditions[84] (Narrain, 2004). Reclaiming the right heritage of India's homosexual past and constantly emphasizing it, will provide hope and sustenance, more so for those who are living very difficult lives in very difficult circumstances.

Coming to Section 377 of the Indian Penal Code, which was introduced by the British in colonial India in 1861 and still stands in the country's books. [Of course, at the time of this revised edition in 2020, section 377 has been read down by India's Supreme Court after going through a see saw journey over the years. Still, as I have written in my short note at the beginning of the book, significant legal challenges remain for the LGBTQ community in India, and I would want you to read the next few pages in the context of these challenges.] The law, with the heading *Unnatural Offences* states—

> Whoever voluntarily has carnal intercourse against the order of nature with any man, woman or animal, shall be punished with imprisonment for life, or with imprisonment of either description for a term which may extend to ten years and shall also be liable to fine. Explanation— Penetration is sufficient to constitute the carnal intercourse necessary to the offence described in this section.

The statute does not clarify exactly what these unnatural acts are but 'the courts have interpreted the same to include anal sex, oral sex, intra femural sex [thigh sex] and mutual masturbation. In effect all the possible forms of sexual expressions between males have been criminalized' (Bondyopadhyay, undated).[85] Although a look at the history of the use of this section reveals that there have been very few charges under Section 377 in the courts for acts of consensual adult male sexual acts (it has mostly been used to prosecute cases of child sexual abuse),[86] the law has been used in public spaces by the police to abuse and blackmail gay people and harass outreach workers doing HIV/AIDS intervention work. The existence of this section also means that homosexual domestic partnerships and *hijra* kinship are not recognized by the law.

> Queers and *hijras* have had no rights to inheritance, adoption, custody, hospital visits, or to the bodies of their deceased partners or kin. It has been perfectly legal for employers to refuse to hire or once hired to fire someone simply because he or she is queer. Doctors have been able to refuse to treat queers with impunity. And the list of queer deprivation of basic citizenship rights goes on. (Bacchetta, 1999)[87]

Narrain and Bhan pertinently refer to Foucault's concept of the panoptic (2000) in the context of 377, or 'the idea that the law is internally manifested within its subjects and not just externally imposed upon them' and state that 'the very existence of Section 377 shapes people's beliefs about queer sexuality as they internalize the prohibition that the law puts forth.'[88]

There have been various debates in English newspapers about the pros and cons of abolishing Section 377 over the past few years; the topic remains contentious.[89] Legally, the section was first challenged in 1994, when the human rights activist group AIDS *Bhedbav Virodhi Andolan* (ABVA; Campaign Against AIDS Discrimination) filed a public interest petition in the Delhi High Court regarding its constitutional validity. However, the group became defunct soon afterwards and the petition was never heard.

In 2001, the legal process was revived, when the Naz Foundation (an India and UK-based AIDS prevention organization), represented by the Lawyer's Collective HIV/AIDS action unit, approached the Delhi High Court with a request to abolish Section 377 as it was violative of the Right to Equality (Article 14), Right to Freedom (Article 19) and Right to Life and Liberty (Article 21) guaranteed by the Indian constitution. This action was duly reported by the country's media.[90] The court wanted the

Central government's view on the subject before it issued its response and repeatedly sent requests to the Attorney General of India, asking for a clarification on the subject.[91] On 8 September 2003, after dilly-dallying for two years, the Indian Central Government finally informed the Delhi High Court that homosexuality could not be legalized in India as in their view, Indian society was intolerant to it. This decision and the protests by gay activists in its aftermath were widely broadcast in the media[92] as was the further dismissal of Naz's review petition in 2004 that asked the court to reconsider its stance.

This dismissal brought to the foreground the extremely homophobic nature of both the government and the court. The government passionately defended the section and argued that the petitioners had no *locus standi*, that there was no proof how HIV/AIDS interventions were affected by Section 377 and that it was a useful deterrent in punishing child sexual abuse. Three of the statements were particularly shocking—

Indian society disapproves homosexuality and this is strong enough to justify it being treated as a criminal offence.

Deletion of the said section can well open floodgates of delinquent behaviour and be construed as providing unbridled license for the same.

The right to privacy (in the case of homosexuals) cannot be extended to defeat public morality, which must prevail over the exercise of any private right.[93]

Arvind Narrain wondered in the *Hindustan Times*—

Why does [the government], in support of its contention on the need for Section 377, cite the fact that repressive intolerant regimes such as those ruling Burma, Zimbabwe, Egypt and Saudi Arabia, all have such laws? Why does it not instead cite countries which have contributed to an emerging human rights jurisprudence such as South Africa, Canada, Brazil and South Korea and argue for a repeal? What accounts for this deep-seated fear which refuses to acknowledge that sexual 'non conformity' is both a part of Indian history as well as part of contemporary culture?[94]

The petitioners then approached the Supreme Court and on 1 April 2005, the court directed the government to file its response.[95] The apex court ruled on 3 February 2006 to set aside the petition dismissal and referred the petition back to the High Court for reconsideration.[96] The case continues and developments since then have provided activists with some hope. The first has been the government's own lawyer, additional solicitor-general Gopal Subramaniam agreeing in court that the law needed to be reviewed.[97] The second has been the tremendous publicity generated by the letter writing campaign led by Nobel laureate Amartya Sen and author Vikram Seth (some of the other 100 signatories included leading Indian citizens from all walks of life such as Soli Sorabjee, Nitin Desai, Swami Agnivesh, Saleem Kidwai and Shubha Mudgal) as a direct appeal to the government and society to end discrimination against Section 377. This campaign is significant because for the first time, the country's leading gay and straight luminaries from all walks of life, have openly and jointly appealed to the government to reconsider their stand on the inhuman law and it has received a huge amount of press coverage both nationally and internationally.[98] The third has been the government's very own NACO (National AIDS Control Organization) throwing its hat in the ring—and offering official support to the abolishment of the section.[99]

Overall, the queer activist movement in India is broad and diverse, pursuing several legal and health agendas. Support groups include organizations like Gay Bombay, Lesbian and Bisexual Women in Action (LABIA), Stree Sangam, Anchal Trust and Humsafar Trust (Bombay), Good As You and Sangama (Bangalore), Solidarity and Action Against The HIV Infection in India (SAATHI) and Sappho (Calcutta), Organised Lesbian Alliance for Visibility and Action (OLAVA) and Queer Studies Circle (Pune), PRISM and Voices Against 377 (Delhi) and so on. Besides these, there have also been what Bhan and Narrain have described as community 'cultural interventions' by 'media activists collectives' like the Nigah Media Collective in New Delhi, Sarani (Calcutta) and Larzish (Bombay) that use films and other media to generate discussions in colleges and among young Indians about issues of sexuality.[100] A number of such different gay, lesbian, *hijra*, *kothi* and other groups came together under the umbrella of the India Network for Sexual Minorities (INFOSEM) in October 2003, in order to collectively advocate for their rights.[101] There are also resource centres like the South and Southeast Asia Resource Centre on Sexuality (Delhi) and legal support groups like the Lawyer's Collective (Bombay).

The current situation in India might be considered to be both similar and different to that of Western societies pre-gay liberation. It is similar in a sense because, the struggle to repeal Section 377 has helped in galvanizing LBGT activism in the country ('In Foucauldian terms, power elicits its own resistance...').[102] It is different because in India as with other Asian developing countries, 'official condemnation of homosexuality exists but based on much different concerns than in the West. It is part of a broader discourse about Western influence' (Sanders, 2004).[103] The drivers for *political* activism (besides Section 377) in India include economic growth, international LBGT NGOs, international human rights NGOs and the overall discourse around human rights, travel to the West (however, with Internet this has changed—as Sanders writes, 'the journey to the West no longer requires travel'),[104] help from the diaspora, technological changes and HIV/AIDS. With regard to AIDS, its role in the West is well documented, in India too, we see that first, the disease is creating spaces to discuss issues about sexuality and second, the majority of the Indian LBGT activist group[s] receive funding for HIV/AIDS related work.[105]

To wrap up this section quickly, what all of the above—the history, the legal challenges and the medical interventions—have done, is enable an ideoscape of gayness to be formulated and to circulate within the Indian society. There is an awareness of certain issues, an acknowledgement that gayness is something that exists in India and an imagination of the different facets of this gayness.

NOTES

1. 'Information arbitrage is the synthesis of information from disparate perspectives, woven together to produce a picture of the world that you would never had if you had looked at it from only one perspective'. Thomas Friedman, *The Lexus and the Olive Tree* (Revised Ed.) (New York: Farrar, Strauss and Giroux 2000 [1999]), pp. 19–20.
2. Arjun Appadurai, 'Grassroots Globalization and the Research Imagination', *Public Culture* (Durham: Duke University Press, 2000), Vol. 12(1), pp. 5–6.
3. Ibid.

4. Arjun Appadurai, *Modernity at Large: Cultural Dimensions of Globalization* (Minneapolis: University of Minnesota Press, 1996), p. 5.
5. Ibid, p. 7.
6. Ibid, p. 8.
7. Peter Jackson, 'Pre-gay, Post-queer: Thai Perspectives on Proliferating Gender/Sex Diversity in Asia', in Gerard Sullivan and Peter A. Jackson (Eds.), *Gay and Lesbian Asia: Culture, Identity, Community* (New York: Harrington Park Press, 2000), p. 9.
8. Ashok Row Kavi, 'Contract of Silence', in Hoshang Merchant, *Yaarana: Gay Writing from India* (New Delhi: Penguin India, 1999), p. 18.
9. This was the country's first gay magazine. It continues to be published very sporadically now; after the emergence of the Internet, its periodicity and circulation have dwindled. But for a few years in the early 1990s, it was the only source of gay information, narratives and networking, available to gay men in India.
10. The Humsafar Trust began its operations in 1991, with the mandate of working in the field of HIV/AIDS awareness or prevention. Today, it has grown into a large multifaceted organization with a drop in centre, a sexually transmitted diseases clinic and counselling, advocacy and outreach services.
11. Initially a suburban McDonalds; the current regular venue is a more spacious suburban coffee shop.
12. Approximately US$ 22, at early 2007 exchange rates.
13. The parties are of two types. 'Bar Nights' are usually held at smaller bars and clubs. The entrance fee is less (approximately Rs 250–350 or US$ 6–8 at early 2007 exchange rates) and this usually includes coupons for drinks or snacks, but no dinner. 'GB Parties' are held at large nightclubs—they usually cost Rs 450 (or US$ 10) and sometimes include a buffet dinner besides coupons for drinks and snacks. In May 2005, the group also decided to expand into hosting occasional Sunday brunches, with food and games, including speed dating.
14. The group website (created in 1999) states, 'There is nothing "official" about the group. There never was, and there still is not a membership form, registration fee, annual general meetings, minutes of meetings and voting or veto. Everyone is free to participate'. http://gaybombay.org/misc/aboutGay Bombay.html
15. In *The Idea of India* (New York: Farrar, Straus and Giroux, 1997, p. 94) Sunil Khilnani explains that in the 1980s, most of the Indian government's revenues came from indirect taxes, which it imposed through its 'protectionist regime of control and regulations simply to sustain itself, not for development reasons'. Despite having a fiscal deficit of around 10 per cent of the national income, the government continued to spend freely through the 1980s by borrowing either domestically from the national banks it controlled or from abroad in the form of low interest loans and aid. However, the international climate changed rapidly in the late 1980s and Rao's government was faced with the grim reality of a country on the verge of financial bankruptcy.
16. Rajiv Desai, *Indian Business Culture* (New Delhi: Viva Books, 1999), p. 85.
17. Sources:

   Government of India, *Ministry of Finance Economic Survey 2003–2004*, p. 2. Accessible on the Ministry of Finance website: http://finmin.nic.in/the_ministry/dept_eco_affairs/economic_div/eco_survey/index.htm

   World Development Indicators, 2007. Accessible on the *India Country Overview 2007* page of the World Bank website: http://www.worldbank.org.in/WBSITE/EXTERNAL/

COUNTRIES/SOUTHASIAEXT/INDIAEXTN/0,,contentMDK:20195738~menuPK: 295589~pagePK:1497618~piPK:217854~the SitePK:295584,00.html

18. '2006–07 GDP growth revised upwards to 9.6%' *Hindu Business Line*, 1 February 2008, http://www.thehindubusinessline.com/2008/02/01/stories/2008020151751200.htm

19. Sources: *Ministry of Finance Economic Survey* op. cit., p. 2; *Ministry of Finance Monthly Economic Report* (Government of India, August 2006) Accessible on the Ministry of Finance website— http://finmin.nic.in/stats_data/monthly_economic_report/index. html

20. AT Kearney, *FDI Confidence Index 2005* (Global Business Policy Council, December 2005), Volume 8. Accessible on the world wide web— http://www.atkearney.com/ main.taf?p=5,3,1,140,1

21. Fareed Zakaria, 'India Rising', *Newsweek* (U.S. Edition) 6 March 2006. http://www. msnbc.msn.com/id/11571348/site/newsweek/

22. Arun Shourie, 'Before the Whining Drowns it Out, Listen to the New India', *Indian Express Online*, 15 August 2003. http://www.indianexpress.com/full_story.php?content_ id=29666

23. See Dani Rodrik and Arvind Subramanian, 'From 'Hindu Growth' to Productivity Surge: The Mystery of the Indian Growth Transition' (*CEPR Discussion Papers* 4371, 2004) Downloadable—http://www.nber.org/papers/w10376.pdf

24. Sunil Khilnani, 'Many Wrinkles in History', *Outlook,* 20 August 2001, as quoted in Pawan Varma, *Being Indian* (New Delhi: Penguin/Viking, 2004), p. 160. Accessible online—http://www.outlookindia.com/full.asp?fodname=20010820&fname=Sunil+ Kilnani+%28F%29&sid=1

25. Pawan Varma, op. cit., (2004), pp. 88–89.

26. Anonymous magazine editor, interviewed by Leela Fernandes on 17 September 1998, for Leela Fernandes, 'Nationalizing "the Global": Media Images, Cultural Politics and the Middle Class in India', *Media, Culture & Society* (Sage Publications, 2000) Vol. 22, p. 614.

27. Leela Fernandes op. cit., p. 615.

28. Indian Census 2000 data, cited in Gurcharan Das, *The Elephant Paradigm: India Wrestles with Change* (New Delhi: Penguin Books India, 2002), p. 171.

29. Jagdish Bhagwati and Arvind Panagariya, 'Great Expectations', *The Wall Street Journal*, 24 May 2004.

30. Gurcharan Das (2002), op. cit., p. 253.

31. Paola Bacchetta ('When the [Hindu] Nation Exiles its Queers', *Social Text* [Durham: Duke University Press, 1999] No. 61 p. 141) describes Hindu nationalism as a 'extremist religious micronationalism of elites, in which elites make strategic political uses of elements drawn from one religion to construct a exclusive, homogenized, Other-repressive, "cultural" nationalist ideology and practice to retain and increase elite power.... Hindu nationalists ultimately propose to eliminate all non-Hindus from the citizen-body....'

32. Arvind Rajagopal, *Politics After Television: Religious Nationalism and the Reshaping of the Indian Public* (Cambridge: Cambridge University Press, 2001), p. 3.

33. See Farhad Wadia, 'Don't Rock Our Boat, Navalkarji', *Indian Express*, 11 April 1998. http://www.expressindia.com/ie/daily/19980411/10150944.html

34. See Arjuna Ranawana, 'Bombay's Cultural Wars', *Asia Week*, 7 August 1998, for an overview of the Shiv Sena culture policing of the mid-1990s. http://www.asiaweek. com/asiaweek/98/0807/feat1.html

35. In a speech addressed to Indian American and American business leaders in New York, then Finance Minister Yashwant Sinha said—'Swadeshi is pro-global but it is pro-Indian without being anti-foreign. And that's the important message from India.... If every country were to follow this policy and most countries are following it, we can have a better world....' Speech quoted in Narayan Keshavan, 'Swadeshi goes Global' *Outlook*, 27 April 1998, cited in William Mazzarella, *Shoveling Smoke: Advertising and Globalization in Contemporary India* (Durham: Duke University Press, 2003), p. 11.

36. See—
    (a) 'BJP Admits India Shining Error', *BBC Online*, 28 May 2004. http://news.bbc.co.uk/2/hi/south_asia/3756387.stm
    (b) M.G. Devasahayam, 'On Whom Does India Shine', *Hindu Online*, 23 March 2004. http://www.hindu.com/op/2004/03/23/stories/2004032300110200.htm

37. Jeremy Seabrook, *Love in a Different Climate: Men Who Have Sex With Men in India* (New York/London: Verso, 1999), p. 140.

38. See—
    (a) P. Sainath's series on rising farmer suicides in India on *Indiatogether.org*. http://www.indiatogether.org/opinions/psainath/suiseries.htm
    (b) Arundhati Roy's critique of big dams and nuclear bombs, 'The Greater Common Good', available online on *Narmada.org* http://www.narmada.org/gcg/gcg.html
    (c) Jean Dreze's overview of some successful pro-poor policies in different Indian states: 'Don't Forget India's Poor', in *Time Asia*, 6 December 2004. http://www.time.com/time/asia/covers/501041206/two_indias_vpt_dreze.html

39. I am focussing on the English language press because it is what is predominantly read by the middle class, both the subject and the context of this book.

40. Due to an astute strategy of price cutting, price differentiation and product diversification carried out by a team of marketing whizkids under the guidance of owner Sameer Jain, the *Times* group's revenues rose from rupees 4.79 billion in the year ended July 1994 to rupees 15 billion in July 2003, making it India's largest media company. Source: Vanita Kohli op. cit., p. 26.

41. 'The Indian Entertainment and Media Industry: Unraveling the Potential'—FICCI Frames 2006 Report (Bombay: Price Waterhouse and Coopers, 2006), p. 12.

42. For a closer look at Page 3 culture and the 2005 Bollywood film made on the subject, see—
    (a) Zubair Ahmed, Bollywood Director Eyes 'Tabloid Culture', *BBC Online*, 30 July 2004. http://news.bbc.co.uk/1/hi/world/south_asia/3929687.stm
    (b) Sukanya Varma, 'Madhur Bhandarkar Proves Himself Yet Again', *Rediff.com*. 21 January 2005. http://www.rediff.com/movies/2005/jan/21page.htm
    (c) Namrata Joshi and Lata Khubchandani, 'Page One and a Half', *Outlook India*, 7 February 2005. http://www.outlookindia.com/full.asp?fname=Film%20(F)&fodname=20050207&sid=1

43. 'Highlights from NRS 2006', *Hindu Business Line*, 30 August 2006. http://www.hinduonnet.com/businessline/blnus/14301801.htm

44. Rajiv Desai, op. cit., p. 66.

45. Television officially began in India in 1959, but it was not until the beginning of colour transmission for the 1982 Asian Games (hosted by New Delhi) that the medium really took off. India's former Prime Minister Rajiv Gandhi was deputed in charge of the

event by his mother, the then Prime Minister Indira Gandhi. Rajiv oversaw the smooth functioning of the games, including their national colour transmission, a first in the country's history. Prior to the games, the government had encouraged Indian industry to manufacture colour televisions and their import into the country was permitted at a lower rate of duty than that for other electronic items. Both these factors led to a spurt in colour television ownership. Soaps like *Hum Log* and *Buniyaad*, mythologicals like *Ramayan* and *Mahabharata* and Hindi song compilation shows like *Chhayageet* and *Chitrahaar* were the hallmark of the 1980s along with the sycophantic evening news bulletins and the staple Sunday evening Bollywood film—all screened on Doordarshan.

46. This began in the late 70s with the boom in the VCR market.
47. See Kinjal Shah and Seema Raisinghani, 'India—Cable TV Special Report', *Fitch Ratings*, June 2003, p. 2.
48. The channel was initially launched on the new Asiasat-1 satellite by Hong Kong based billionaire Li Ka Shing, who sold his stake to Rupert Murdoch's News Corporation in 1993.
49. These were Star Plus (with never seen before programs like *The Bold and the Beautiful*, *Santa Barbara*, *Baywatch*, *Oprah* and *Donahue*), BBC News World Service (an international alternative to DD), MTV (sexy videos, trendy Video Jockeys) and Prime Sports (with games like basketball and entertainment like WWF Wrestling).
50. MTV and BBC left the Star bouquet to go solo in 1993. Prime Sports in its newer avatar Star Sports entered into a 50:50 Joint venture with ESPN in 1996 and Zee's promoters bought out Star's stake in 1999 to form their own formidable network.
51. Zee's initial programming mix included the daily soap *Tara*, with its scandalous smoking, drinking, swearing and adulterous single women and weekly game shows like *Tol Mol Ke Bol* (the Indian avatar of *The Price is Right*), *Antakshri* (the popular Indian song game, now televised for large studio audiences) and *Saanp Seedi* (Snakes and Ladders, played in a studio with the slimy host Mohan Kapur).
52. Dr Chandraprakash Dwivedi, Former Head of Programming Zee TV, Bombay, May 1998, as quoted in Vanita Kohli op. cit., p. 141.
53. For example, the Bollywood song countdown show—*Philips Top Ten*.
54. For a list of the top 100 programs in India as measured by AC NIELSEN'S TAM people-meter—India's sole television rating agency, visit http://indiantelevision.com/tvr/indextam.php4 and http://indiantelevision.com/tvr/telemeter/indexteltam.php4 The site maintains separate rankings for Cable and Satellite Programmes and Terrestrial programmes, as provided by AC Nielsen.
55. Waseem Mahmood, 'Policy Analysis of Electronic Media Practices in South Asia'—a report prepared by the Baltic Media Centre for UNDP's PARAGON regional governance program, 30 August 2001, p. 7.
56. Ronnie Ganguly, 'Indian Media Industry' (Bombay: JP Morgan Asia Pacific Research 12 May 2005), p. 6.
57. Source—Various industry estimates in Vanita Kohli op. cit., p. 60 and Ashwin Pinto, '68 million C&S homes in India: NRS 2006' *Indiantelevision.com*. 29 August 2006. http://www.indiantelevision.com/mam/headlines/y2k6/aug/augmam122.htm
58. National radio had begun in India in 1921 and though the state controlled All India Radio (AIR) that began in 1932 greatly increased its reach during the post-independence years, it was slow to respond to public tastes—preferring instead to

adopt a paternalistic 'we know what's best for you approach' towards its listeners. For example, it took several years and severe competition from the Sri Lanka based Radio Ceylon before AIR launched *Vividh Bharti* (its 'light' service airing film based songs) in 1957.

59. The government suddenly disallowed private FM in 1998—however, intense lobbying by the public and media companies ensured that the space was once again opened up in 2000.

60. FICCI Frames 2006 Report, op. cit., p. 13.

61. Ibid, p. 12.

62. Source—Email posting to the *Khush*-List Yahoo! Group 'Abt the Radio Mirchi Show' by Nitin Karani, dated 4 May 2004.

63. Source—Email posting to the *Khush*-List Yahoo! Group 'Get Your Gay Valentines Out!' by Vgd67, dated 14 February 2006.

64. Anindo Ghosh, 'Outlook White Paper: Private Internet Service Providers in India' 15 October 1997. Published on the world wide web—http://www.india50.com/isp.html#6

65. Source—NASSCOM (National Association of Software and Services Companies) Internet Survey 2000, as cited in Puneet Gupta, 'India's Internet: Ready for Explosive Growth', *ISP Planet Market Research*. Available on the World Wide Web—http://isp-planet.com/research/india_stats.html

66. Ibid.

67. Source—'Internet Indicators: Hosts, Users and Number of PCs by Country', *ITU (International Telecommunication Union)*, 16 September 2004. Available on the World Wide Web—http://www.itu.int/ITU-D/ict/statistics/

68. Source—Kauffman Bros. Equity Research Industry Report on 'Internet and Digital Media', 22 September 2006. Analyst Sameet Sinha, p. 1. Accessible from the NASSCOM website—http://www.nasscom.org/artdisplay.asp?cat_id=447Kauffman

69. AP, 'Gartner Report Finds India's Computer Market Robust', *Yahoo! Asia News*, 16 November 2004. http://asia.news.yahoo.com/041116/ap/d86d17602.html

70. '80 Million More PCs in India by 2010', *Rediff.com*. 15 December 2004. http://in.rediff.com/money/2004/dec/15pc.htm

71. Popular blogs include *Talking Closets* (http://talkingclosets.blogspot.com/), *Queer India* (http://queerindia.blogspot.com/), *I *heart* Bombay...* (http://sourapplemartini.blogspot.com/) and *The Reluctant Observer* (http://mike-higher.livejournal.com/).

72. Gurcharan Das (2000), op. cit., p. 9.

73. AFP, 'Mobile Phones the Talk of India as Landlines Lose Out' *Sify News*, 25 October 2004.

74. In October 2004, the number of mobile phones in the country surpassed the number of landline users (44 million) for the first time. See—

(a) Arindam Mukherjee, '98 Tra La La 1000', *Outlook*, 4 April 2005. http://www.outlookindia.com/full.asp?fodname=20050404&fname=VTelecom+%28F%29&sid=1

(b) Official Cellular Operators Association of India (COAI) statistics. See http://coai.com/

(c) Anand Parthasarthy, 'Mobile Phone Growth Signals India's Telecom Maturity', *The Hindu*, 16 October 2004. http://www.hindu.com/2004/10/16/stories/2004101603401300.htm

75. Saritha Rai, 'India Leads World in Cellphone Expansion', *The New York Times*, 15 September 2006. http://www.iht.com/articles/2006/09/15/business/cell.php

76. Indrajit Basu (UPI), 'India's New Telecom Callers', *The Washington Times*, 25 June 2004. http://washingtontimes.com/upi-breaking/20040624-010347-8465r.htm

77. India's NASSCOM has co-opted IT Enabled Services within its ambit and includes ITES figures in its reporting. Source—Carol Upadhyay, 'A New Transnational Class', *Economic and Political Weekly*, 27 November 2004, footnote 2. Article archived on http://www. epw.org.in (Membership required)

78. Source—NASSCOM website. Key highlights: http://www.nasscom.in/Nasscom/templates/NormalPage.aspx?id=28485. Facts and figures: http://www.nasscom.in/Nasscom/templates/NormalPage.aspx?id=28487

79. 'IT Exports to Account for 30% Forex Inflows by 08: Maran', *Economic Times*, 20 October 2004.

80. For an excellent overview of India's emergence as an IT superpower, read *The Horse that Flew: How India's Silicon Gurus Spread their Wings* by Chidanand Rajghatta (New Delhi: Harper Collins India, 2001). Also read Devesh Kapur's essay 'The Causes and Consequences of India's IT Boom' in *India Review* 1(2), April 2002, 91–110.

81. Douglas Sanders, op. cit., p. 21.

82. Vanita and Kidwai (2001), op. cit., p. xxiii.

83. Douglas Sanders, op. cit., p. 21.

84. Arvind Narrain, op. cit., pp. 33–34.

85. Aditya Bondyopadhyay, 'MSM and the Law in India', Position Paper (Naz Foundation International, undated). Received via email, on request from NFI London office, on 14 November 2003.

86. Alok Gupta, 'The History and Trends in the Application of the Anti-Sodomy Law in the Indian Courts', *The Lawyer's Collective* (Bombay, 2002) Vol. 16, No. 7, p. 9, as cited in Gautam Bhan and Arvind Narrain, *Because I Have a Voice: Queer Polics in India* (New Delhi: Yoda Press, 2006), p. 7.

87. Paola Bacchetta (1999), op. cit., p. 159.

88. Bhan and Narrain (2006), op. cit., on p. 8, the authors refer to this concept taken from Michael Foucault, *Ethics*, (Vol. 1), London: Penguin, 2000.

89. See for example—
    (a) Anju Singh, 'An Unnatural Opposition to Section 377', *Indian Express* (Bombay), 1 October 2002.
    (b) Anubha Sawhney, 'A Flaw in the Law? Officially', *Times of India* (Bombay), 23 August 2004.
    (c) Vivek Divan, 'We're Only a Part of You', *Pioneer*, 26 March 2006. http://www.dailypioneer.com/displayit1.asp?pathit=/archives2/mar2606/sundaypioneer/assignment/assign2.txt
    (d) Arvind Narrain and Vivek Divan, 'Revise Section 377', *Times of India*, 12 January 2007.

90. See *Combat Law: The Human Rights Magazine*, Volume 2, Issue 4, October-November 2003. The entire issue is dedicated to different aspects of LBGT activism in India, mostly relating to Section 377.

91. See 'HC Asks Center to Clarify Stand on Homosexuals', *Telegraph* (Calcutta), 16 January 2003. http://www.telegraphindia.com/1030116/asp/nation/story_1578382.asp

92. See—
   (a) PTI, 'Allowing Homosexuality Will Lead to Delinquent Behavior: Indian Govt.', *Rediff.com*. 8 September 2003. http://www.rediff.com/news/2003/sep/08sex.htm
   (b) Kavita Chowdhary, 'Center Says Being Gay Will Remain a Crime, It's Reason: Our Society Doesn't Tolerate It', *Indian Express*, 9 September 2003. http://www.indianexpress.com/full_story.php?content_id=31224
   (c) Siddharth Narrain, 'Sexuality and the Law', *Frontline*, Volume 20, Issue 26, 20 December 2003–2 January 2004. http://www.frontlineonnet.com/fl2026/stories/20040102002209500.htm
   (d) Shibu Thomas, 'Mumbai Gays Against Center's Stance', *Mid-day*, 15 September 2003. http://web.mid-day.com/news/city/2003/september/63897.htm
   (e) Arvind Narrain, 'What A Queer Administration?', *Hindustan Times*, 3 December 2005.
93. The full text of the government response has been uploaded as a Word document on the website of the Interdisciplinary Humanities Center at the University of California Santa Barbara—www.ihc.ucsb.edu/research/ subaltern/events/facworkshops/reply.doc
94. Arvind Narrain, op. cit., 2005.
95. 'SC Notice to Government on Homosexuality', *Times of India*, 1 April 2005. http://timesofindia.indiatimes.com/articleshow/1067013.cms
96. 'SC Wants Rethink on Homosexuality PIL: HC had Dismissed NGO's Plea, Saying Indian Society Not Ready Yet', *Indian Express*, 4 February 2006. http://www.indianexpress.com/full_story.php?content_id=87254
   'Homosexuality: Govt. Relents', *Times of India*, 3 February 2006. http://timesofindia.indiatimes.com/articleshow/1400286.cms
97. 'Ban on Gays Under Review—Delhi HC to Decide on Validity of Law Against Homosexuality', *The Telegraph*, 4 February 2006. http://www.telegraphindia.com/1060204/asp/frontpage/story_5804545.asp
98. See—
   'Backing Gay Rights', *Times of India*, 17 September 2006. http://timesofindia.indiatimes.com/articleshow/1998671.cms
   'Dump Anti Gay Law', *DNA*, 16 September 2006. http://www.dnaindia.com/report.asp?NewsID=1053440
   Namita Bhandare, 'Time Ripe for Gay Rights', *Hindustan Times*, 15 September 2006. http://www.hindustantimes.com/news/181_1798316,0008.htm
   Amelia Gentleman, 'India's Anti-gay Law Faces Challenge', *International Herald Tribune*, 15 September 2006. http://www.iht.com/articles/2006/09/15/news/india.php
   Mark Williams, 'Great and Good Call on India to Scrap Gay Law', *The Scotsman*, 17 September 2006. http://news.scotsman.com/international.cfm?id=1373492006
   'Indian Author Vikram Seth Leads Fight Against Anti-gay Law', *Khaleej Times*, 16 September 2006. http://www.khaleejtimes.com/DisplayArticleNew.asp?xfile=data/subcontinent/2006/September/subcontinent_September585.xml&section=subcontinent
99. 'Law Against Homosexuality May Go: Health, Home Ministry Aim to Scrap Section 377 of IPC', *The Hindu*, 27 September 2006. http://www.hindu.com/2006/09/27/stories/2006092721241700.htm

100. Bhan and Narrain, op. cit., pp. 12–13.
101. INFOSEM's initial agenda is outlined as follows—(Source—personal email exchange with Ashok Row Kavi, dated 6 November 2003).

    (a) 'Work to abolish parts of Section 377 of the IPC that deal with consensual sex between adults, independent of their sexual orientation.

    (b) Work on very clear formulations of all forms of sexual assault and child sex abuse to be addressed by the law.

    (c) Make representations to the Constitutional Review Committee (CRC) seeking inclusion of sexual orientation as a group for non-discrimination in Part III of the Constitution of India.

    (d) Work for the recognition of the transgendered as a third sex in the Constitution of India.

    (e) Advocate for health awareness and care on a priority basis to fight HIV/AIDS and other STIs among LGBT people.

    (f) Help grassroots and emerging groups by providing input and training in conducting research and health, social and legal needs assessment; help in building their skills and resources; provide access to funding for their respective health and associated programmes; and share research and baseline data.

    (g) Set up consultations for lesbian sexual health and recognize their sexual health needs.

    (h) To encourage, advocate and work for capacity building of sexual minorities in India'.

102. Arvind Narrain, op. cit., p. 66.
103. Douglas Sanders, op. cit., pp. 38–39.
104. Ibid, p. 37.
105. See Arvind Narrain, op. cit., p. 67. Also Peter Jackson, op. cit., p. 1.

5

Up Close and Personal

The Pleasures and Complications
of Ethnography at 'Home'

SUGARLESS

It is the smoothness of E's skin that absolutely fascinates me. I have never seen anything like it. It is cream in colour and almost transparent—I can see the blue vein throbbing lightly under one temple and the sharpness of the Adam's apple. I am enamoured by its colour and texture that is so different from the fairness of the other Parsi boys in class. They are all either milky white and pasty or brown and dusty, just like everyone else. But E is creamy gold with shining skin that always smells fresh of Mysore Sandal Soap. His hair is brown, straight and soft and never stays combed, but flays about his forehead in uncontrolled wisps. Every six weeks, it begins to grow over his collar at the nape of his neck and shortly after that, he comes back to school with a ghastly crew cut.

I have been staring at E surreptitiously during class since the beginning of 8th grade, ever since the class teacher changed our places and made us 'partners'. We were mere 'hi...bye' acquaintances in 7th grade; now the daily proximity has led to a mutual affinity that includes sharing tiffins in short breaks, water bottles in case one's gets over early and compass boxes during geometry periods. It is the first time during my school life that I look forward to Monday mornings; I rush out of the BEST bus that I take to school daily and run up to class so that I can be there before E. Soon he enters the class with his water bottle dangling around his neck, top button always open and his tie knot askew. He places his faded brown 'He Man and the Master of the Universe' bag next to mine and eases into his seat.

Then our eyes meet and I feel a giant surge of happiness. I want to jump up and down and reach out and kiss him and do a hundred cartwheels all over the school compound, but I avert his eyes and pretend to arrange my belongings all over 'my' part of the desk.

During the Hindi language class, as the teacher drones on and on and all the students have lowered their eyes to follow the chapter in their textbooks, my eyes avert to E's lap and the smooth thighs peering out from the shorts that were a part of his previous year's school uniform. His mother has not stitched him a new uniform set for the 8th yet, though this is the year that most boys switch to long pants. He has spurted in growth since last year and now, when he sits in class, his shorts pulled up tightly around his thighs, there is a tight outline around his crotch that I shamelessly sneak peek at, whenever I can.

In my 12-year-old mind, I cannot yet comprehend the feelings that I am developing for E. I have a crush on Suraiya. That I know. She is wonderful to be with and when she speaks to me, it makes me happy. I blush whenever we are teased together and it makes me feel respected and appreciated amongst my friends, even though it is supposedly clandestine. But what am I to do with my feelings about E? I never stare at Suraiya the same way as I stare at E—have never thought of her at night and replayed the day's instances with her constantly in my memory, never felt the same thrill with her that I feel every time my leg brushes past E's as we sit together in class. Not even when we held hands on top of the giant wheel that we rode together at the previous year's annual school fete. I had 'proposed' to her and though she had laughed it away, at least she'd agreed to hold hands, so it had been nice and all my friends had envied me for days. But with E, it is something else completely. I just do not know how to explain it.

I wish that I had never started 8th grade. I wish I were back in the 6th. In Muscat, going ice skating on Friday afternoons followed by arcade games at Sinbad, burgers at Dairy Queen and late night WWF with Hulk Hogan. I miss all my friends from Indian School—Adrian and Kshitij and Romil and Vasundhara who I loved defeating for first rank and sports day and fancy dress and no knowing about shagging or the meaning of fuck and E has caught me staring at him. When school ends, I ask him if he wants to come to my place the next day, after school. He says no because he would like me to come to his place instead. His mom works and only returns back home a few hours after E reaches home. All right, I shrug. We both look pretty nervous.

We never ever talk about what we do. The first time, at his place, neither of us actually knows what to do, or how, but we learn soon enough; our bodies guide the way. Soon, we can't seem to stop. We're doing it in the school bathroom, on the sofa in my house, in his parent's bedroom on the dresser, after school… Once during extra French tuition classes, which we both joined together, we arrive early, and as we wait at the table for the other students to arrive and for the tuition teacher to descend from her room on the floor above, we make out under the table. When we emerge, we realize that the house help has been watching us from the door. He has a big grin on his face. He always winks at us after that whenever he sees us. It embarrasses E no end though I think it's kind of kinky.

I am on the phone with E. Fourteen years have passed since 8th grade and I've remembered his birthday and have called up to wish him. We drifted apart after school—I went abroad and he, to the world of architecture. We managed to meet up once a few years later when I was back in Bombay and it seemed like just the good old times, laughing, cracking each other up. He asked me then if I was happy. 'I guess', 'I replied'. 'Are you'? 'I guess', he repeated. But we never met up again.

He sounds different when he answers the phone this time. Distant. Careful. Emotionless. I have heard that he is engaged to be married but don't bring it up, waiting to see if he will, instead. He doesn't. 'Please don't call me up again', he states at the end of the conversation. 'My life is different now'. I am not surprised. Marriage is a different cup of milk. Unlike E's immigrant Parsi ancestors from the 8th century, ex-lovers might find it difficult to dissolve effortlessly. Better instead, to drink it sugarless.

'All discourse is "placed" and the heart has its reasons'.
—**Stuart Hall**, 1990[1]

ARRIVAL SCENE ONE: DARK STORMY NIGHT

What is ethnography without an arrival scene or two? (Or three?)

Cambridge, Massachusetts. December 2003. It is a dark, stormy night. A chilly wind rattles my dorm windows as the snow swirls around in concentric circles like a dervish. I brew myself a steaming cup of *masala chai*, cuddle with my laptop and type *gaybombay.org* into my Internet browser. It is strange that I have never visited the site before. The computer screen loads a cluttered white, lavender and pink homepage and I cannot help feeling nostalgic. I love America but at this very moment, I want a delicate *khaara* biscuit to dunk into my *chai*, not an oversized American cookie; I want to see pigeons and taste the sea breeze instead of snowflakes when I go out for a walk, be amidst brown faces and hear the unique cacophony of Bombay languages on the street that Rushdie calls 'hug-me' (Hindi, Urdu, Gujarati, Marathi and English) in *The Ground Beneath Her Feet*.[2] I want to be home instead of on a homepage.

The website is dense and information-heavy. The homepage has the Gay Bombay logo on the left (the letters *g* and *b* in small case, joined together), with a permanent picture of one of the Gay Bombay kite-flying events and a constantly changing (upon refreshing the page) gay-themed art picture below it. The two images are separated by links with information about Bombay, the gay community at large and the history of the Gay Bombay community. [The website has been redesigned over the years, of course, but as I read this section, a decade later, it feels like I've gone back in a time machine to the early days of the internet in our country!]

The central part of the homepage has direct links to the five main channels into which the topics of the site are categorized (*Events, Issues, Support Channels, Interactive Channels* and the *Reading Room*), as well as links to each of the sub-categories of each channel. There are alerts about the forthcoming events being organized by the group and an invitation to subscribe to the Gay Bombay mailing list. There is a prominent sprinkling of signifiers like *gay* and *homosexual* and rainbow imagery on the homepage and throughout the site. There are also small banner ads that change regularly exhorting the site's visitors to 'make gaybombay.org a habit' and 'attend GB events regularly'.

The *Events* channel contains a calendar of past and forthcoming events, including Sunday meets, parties, special outings and parents' meetings. There are first person reports about each of these events—written by members of the group. The highlights of the *Interactive Channels* section are the Gay Bombay mailing list (discussed below), *GBTalk2Me* (the one-on-one instant messenger service that enables users to chat with a Gay Bombay representative online) and *Neighborhood Watch* (an opportunity for interested persons to directly contact a Gay Bombay representative living in their vicinity). The *Issues* section contains very useful information on sex including details about safe sex and condom usage, oral and anal sex, HIV prevention information and Sexually Transmitted Diseases. There are also true coming out stories by Gay Bombay members and sub-sections on relationships and emotional issues, religion and spirituality, gay bashing and blackmail threats and legal information concerning homosexuality in India. The *Support Channels* provide useful services for the website's gay visitors. *Ask Doc Uncle* is an anonymous service that promises to answer visitor's medical queries related to gay or lesbian lifestyle. *Parent's Corner* aims to answer some common questions posed by parents of gay and lesbian children and provides resources for them to come to terms with their children's sexuality. There is also useful in-formation on recommended HIV testing centres in Bombay city and lists of support groups in India and around the world for the Indian LGBT community. The *Reading Room* contains gay themed poetry, all kinds of reviews and art images. Highlights of this section are the recipes provided by the site's regular visitors with names like *Sopan's Sudden Tomato Pickle for When Friends Descend*, *Hardley's Mother's Mutton Dhansak* and *Vikram's Versatile Ratatouille and Stoved Potatoes*.

ETHNOGRAPHY IN FLUX

The discipline of anthropology[3] has Western colonial origins, with its theories and concepts 'formulated from the point of view of Western ideology, Western needs and a Western way of life' (Jones, 1970).[4] The early anthropologists, mostly British, stayed at home and relied on third person accounts from soldiers, missionaries and other travellers for their studies. Their research was 'uninterested in the patterns of everyday life and grounded almost entirely in what people said, not what they did' (Van Maanen, 1988).[5] Bronislaw Malinowski, Franz Boas and AR Radcliffe-Brown changed the course of the discipline with their practice of actually living among their research subjects and documenting their daily lives and subsequently, this became a professional requirement. Thus social an-thropology became redefined as '"the study of small-scale society—ahistorical, *ethno*-graphic and comparative", with extended participant observation as its distinctive method' (Vincent, 1991).[6]

The method that these anthropologists used to conduct their research was ethnography, or the study of the day-to-day lives of people.

> Carrying out such research involves two distinct activities. First, the ethnographer enters into a social setting and gets to know the people involved in it; usually the setting is not previously known in an intimate way. The ethnographer participates in the daily routines of this setting, develops ongoing relations with the people in it and observes all the while what is going on. Indeed, the term participant observation is often used to characterize this basic research approach. (Emerson, Fretz and Shaw, 1997)[7]

The work of the ethnographer tends to be published in a written account, also called ethnography. 'Ethnographic accounts are both... descriptive and interpretative...ethnography requires analytical rigour and process, as well as inductive analysis (reasoning from the particular cases to general theories)' (Plowman, 2003).[8]

While pioneers like Malinowski advocated a detached and objective approach to their subjects, later ethnographers like Clifford Geertz chose a more involved participative style. Geertz (1973) recommended total immersion in the culture being studied for the ethnographer and the writing up of experiences and interpretations through the technique of 'thick description' or a detailed understanding and rendering of the 'multiplicity of conceptual structures' that the ethnographer encounters, 'many of them superimposed or knotted into one another...strange, irregular, and inexplicit'.[9]

However, Geertz's approach too was critiqued in subsequent years on both counts—'ethno' as well as 'graphic' (Witel, 2000).[10] Within the *graphic* critique, key terms include 'othering, authorial control, crisis of objectification, dialogical or polyphonic texts'.[11] The critique of *ethno* was predominantly against a limiting 'idea of "a culture out there"'.[12] In recent times, anthropology and ethnography found themselves once again at a crossroad—

> As groups migrate, regroup in new locations, reconstruct their histories and reconfigure their ethnic 'projects', the 'ethno' in ethnography takes on a slippery, non-localized quality, to which the descriptive practices of

anthropology will have to respond. The landscapes of group identity—the ethnoscapes—around the world are no longer familiar anthropological objects, insofar as groups are no longer tightly territorialized, spatially bounded, historically self-conscious, or culturally homogeneous.... The task of ethnography now becomes the unraveling of a conundrum: what is the nature of locality, as a lived experience, in a globalized, deterritorialized world? (Appadurai, 1991)[13]

This unraveling has included a reexamination of the field (Gupta and Fergusson, 1997), the conduct of multi-sited ethnographies (Marcus, 1998) and the growth of insider or native or indigenous ethnography (Hurston, 1935; Srinivas, 1976; Altorki and El Solh, 1998). Some of the other major changes in ethnographic practice over the years are the University of Chicago's urban ethnography (pioneered by Robert Park and his colleagues like WI Thomas and Ernest Burgess just before the Great Depression),[14] anthropology of women (Golde 1970; Reiter 1975; Behar and Gordon 1995),[15] gay and lesbian anthropology (Lewin and Leap, 1996, 2000; Weston, 1991, 1998; Walzer, 2000; Manalanson, 2003) and the use of ethnography as a qualitative research tool by scholars working under the umbrella of disciplines like cultural studies (Willis, 1977; Hebdige, 1979; Radway, 1984; Jenkins, 1992)[16] and cyberculture studies (Rheingold, 1994; Turkle, 1995; Markham, 1998; Smith and Kollock, 1998; Dibbel, 1999; Jones, 1997, 1998, 1999; Cherny, 1999; Hine, 2000; Schaap, 2002; Campbell, 2004). Currently, ethnography is also to be found being used in corporate circles (example, Cheskin's 'cultural sense-making',[17] Look-look's 'coolhunting'[18]) and fields as diverse as 'political science, law...social welfare, advertising, public administration, marine studies, education...criminal justice, and policy studies'.[19] However, the core of what constitutes ethnography still has not changed. 'Almost without exception, ethnography still involves the study of a small group of people in their own environment in order to test the ethnographer's hypothesis' (Plowman, 2003).[20]

I want to briefly focus my attention upon two changes in ethnography that have a direct bearing on this book—the changing concept of the field and the collapse of the subject/object divide.

The field denotes the site where an ethnographer produces his ethnography through fieldwork.[21] The traditional notion of the field is a place that is geographically defined and spatially separated from the home country of the anthropologist's origin.

> This separation is manifested in two central anthropological contrasts. The first differentiates the site where data are collected from the place where analysis is conducted and the ethnography is 'written up'. The second place the sharp contrast between 'field' and home and is expressed in the standard anthropological tropes of entry and exit from 'the field'. Stories of entry and exit usually appear on the margins of texts, providing the narrative with uncertainly and expectation at the beginning and closure at the end. (Gupta and Fergusson, 1997) [22]

With the various changes in ethnography, the notion of what constitutes the *field* has changed too. Marcus (1998) has introduced the concept of a 'multi-sited ethnography', which consists of 'research self-consciously embedded in a world system, that moves out from the single sites and local situations…to examine the circulation of cultural meanings, objects and identities in diffuse time-space'.[23] Gupta and Fergusson (1997) have suggested a 'decentering' of the field. They muse that so far, 'location has often been elided with locality and a shift in location has been reduced to the idea of going "elsewhere" to look at "another society"'. Instead, they propose that fieldwork be considered as 'a form of motivated and stylized dislocation', in which 'location is not something that one ascriptively has…[but] something that one strategically works at'. They speculate that in today's interconnected world, 'perhaps we are never really "out of the field"'.[24] On the same lines, Mary Des Chene (1997) imagines the field as 'a period of time, or a series of events, the study of which will take the researcher to different places' and raises interesting questions such as—'If one's work concerns events that have taken place in many locales, what renders one of these the primary site for research? If one's focus is on historical processes, what makes a geographically bound residential unit the obvious object of study?'.[25] She warns that 'to continue to valorize the face-to-face encounter will impoverish [ethnographic] accounts' and suggests that 'it will be far more useful to attend to the relation between our research questions and the possible sources that will illuminate them and to follow these wherever they may lead us and in whatever medium they may turn out to exist'.[26] Clifford (1997) imagines contemporary ethnography as the conduct of 'variously routed fieldworks—a site where different contextual knowledges engage in critical dialogue and respectful polemic'.[27]

* * *

Of all the oppositions that artificially divide social science, the most fundamental and the most ruinous, is the one that is set up between subjectivism and objectivism. (Pierre Bourdieu, 1990)[28]

Traditionally, students of ethnography were taught that detachment from the object of one's study was something that they must aspire to. In his critique of this viewpoint, Rosaldo (1989) writes—

The detached observer epitomizes neutrality and impartiality. The detachment is said to produce objectivity because social reality comes into focus only if one stands at a certain distance. When one stands too close, the ethnographic lens supposedly blurs its human subjects. In this view, the researcher must remove observer bias by becoming the emotional, cognitive and moral equivalent of a blank slate.[29]

In Morsy's (1998) equally scathing attack of this position, such a supposedly detached ethnographer would 'behave as if he has no judgment, as if his experiences were inconsequential, as if the contradiction between his origins and his vocation did not exist.... Moreover, he will imagine that he has no politics and will consider that a virtue'.[30] Morsy chronicles the historical refutation of the detached observer position in anthropological practice—

Affected by anti-imperialist struggles and changing global relations, the evolution of critical anthropological thought has challenged traditional disciplinary claims of objectivity and ethical neutrality. As Third World and radical critiques of anthropology exposed the discipline as a Western-dominated 'child of imperialism', anthropologists began considering not only the history of the 'people without history', but the history of anthropology itself. (Asad, 1973; Copans, 1975; Huizer and Mannheim, 1979; Leacock, 1982; Wolf, 1982). Calls for 'reinventing anthropology' (Hymes, 1974) followed critical assessments of the assumption of 'objectivity in anthropology'. (Maquet, 1964)[31]

In contemporary ethnography, it is increasingly being understood that 'because locations are multiple, conjunctural and crosscutting, there can be no guarantee of shared perspective, experiences, or solidarity....'[32] (Clifford, 1997); and the ethnographer's subjectivity is expected to be highlighted in his writing.

> To acknowledge particular and personal locations is to admit the limit of one's purview from these positions. It is also to undermine the notion of objectivity because from particular locations; all understanding becomes subjectively based and formed through interactions within fields of power relations. Positioned knowledges and partial perspectives are part of the lingo that has risen to common usage in the 1980s (Clifford, 1986, 1988; Haraway, 1988; Kondo, 1986; Rosaldo, 1989). (Narayan, 1993)[33]

This approach calls for the substitution of *unabashed subjectivity* in place of objectivity. 'Knowledge, in this scheme, is not transcendental, but situated, negotiated and part of an ongoing process.... By situating ourselves as subjects simultaneously touched by life-experiences and swayed by professional concerns, we can acknowledge the hybrid and positioned nature of our identities'[34] (Narayan, 1993). It is wrong to assume that 'an epistemology of "otherness"' is 'the best route to "objectivity"... "objectivity" is not a function of "distance"...'[35] (Passaro, 1997). In any case, distance is far too overrated—it can be replaced by making the ethnographer's identity and location 'more explicit' and by giving informants 'a greater role in texts'[36] (Narayan, 1993). However, this does not mean doing away with distance completely—

> To question the discipline's canonical; modes of objective distance is not however, to forfeit subjective distance and pretend that all fieldwork is a celebration of *communitas*. Given the multiplex nature of identity, there will inevitably be certain facets of self that join us up with the people we study, other facets that emphasize our difference. In even the closest of relationships, disjunctures can swell into distance; ruptures in communication can occur that must be bridged. To acknowledge such shifts in relationships rather than present them as purely distant or purely close is to enrich the textures of our texts so that they more closely approximate the complexity of lived interaction. (Narayan, 1993)[37]

Instead of asking, 'what fundamentally unites us or separates us?', we should be more concerned with 'what can we do for each other in the present conjuncture?' (Clifford, 1997).

What from our similarities and differences can we bend together, hook up, articulate…. And when identification becomes too close, how can a disarticulation of agendas be managed in the context of alliance, without resorting to claims of objective distance and tactics of definitive departure?[38]

The ultimate aim should be—

To represent and understand the world around us more adequately, to see beyond the epistemologies of received categories of collective identity and the assumptions about anthropology and fieldwork that continue to reinscribe various 'Others' of internal and external colonialism and thus, participate in ethnographic practices of liberation. (Passaro, 1997)[39]

PRICKED BY A THORN

The author R. Raj Rao, is visiting Bombay from Pune where he lives and teaches and he asks me to meet up with him at the infamous Voodoo club. For six days a week, the place is a seedy pick-up place for the Arab tourists that congregate in the area to pick up cheap hookers. But every Saturday night, it undergoes a magical fabulous transformation as hordes of gay men descend upon it and make it their own! Though it is located just off the street where I live, I have only been there once, with Riyad, maybe five years ago.

I arrive late, a little before midnight, pay rupees 250 to the old Parsi owner sitting at the counter (wasn't it 150 the last time?) and swing open the door. It is a lot smaller than I remember. I walk straight on to a packed dance floor. There is a tiny DJ booth to the right, a basic bar to the left. The walls are scribbled with neon graffiti; there are strange coloured shapes spray painted on to the ceiling. Very 80s. There are a few tables arranged towards the back of the club and a metal staircase that leads to a mezzanine observation lounge, as well as passages that lead to a more private lounge in the back of the club and to the toilets adjacent to this lounge. This is the make out lounge with soft sinkable sofas, slightly tattered and even lower lighting than the rest of the club.

I climb up the metal staircase and position myself midway, leaning on the railing, arms folded, just like I'd seen Riyad do the last time. (Maybe, he's watching me and smiling indulgently from somewhere way up there). From my perch, I can scan the crowd, predator-like. I lean over and chat with Raj, who is dancing on the floor with someone he has just met. I make polite conversation with an older guy and discover to my surprise that he is the uncle of A, former fuck buddy, brief crush and now soul brother. He is a jet-setting global academic and this is his first time out to a gay place in Bombay. I wish him all the best and continue sightseeing.

Tonight, I am horny and angry. B has just told me online that he has slept with a girl back in Boston, I don't know whether he is lying or not—but I despise myself for being head over heels in love with a stupid 18 year-old Venezuelan boy who has only just begun exploring his sexuality. I seek revenge. Someone random, someone I will never meet again. I see a possible candidate. A cute white guy, standing by himself in a corner of the club. Hmm. Why not? He's skinny and geeky; exactly my type. American? Perhaps European or Israeli. I ponder about whether I should descend and make a move, but before I can make a call, Charu (who I discover later is Nihar's ex-boyfriend and a complete slut) bags him—and within five minutes, they're the centre of attraction on the dance floor, groping each other all over. Sheesh!

I look away disappointed. On the floor, there is an assortment of men of all ages, sizes and shapes, merrily dancing away. This is not Gay Bombay crowd—it's more mixed—though I do see some familiar faces from the GB parties. One of these is Kirit. He is about five and a half feet tall. Twentyish. Very thin with a smooth body exposed due to the fact that his T-shirt is raised to his nipples, as his hips gyrate feverishly. He is surrounded by a pack of hungry wolves, but his eyes are closed as he dances. It's such joy—to see such beauty, such grace, such unabashed pleasure with one's own self. He moves confidently, assuredly, slickly. I was such a dork at his age—pondering over my sexuality, wasting all those years being scared.

With his eyes closed, Kirit looks a little bit like B and that does it for me. I alight, cut through the crowd with practiced ease and whisper into his ear while nuzzling his neck that he's the sexiest person I've seen all week. It's a really lame line, but Kirit giggles and pulls me close to him. Ten minutes later, we're on the sofa, in the make out lounge, kissing fervently. I pull him to me, but he wants to go back and dance to Kaanta Lagaa (Pricked by a Thorn)—*the hot new remix that the DJ has just begun*

> *playing—understandably, a gay dance floor favourite. We can do it after this song, he winks as he zips up and prances back on to the floor. I sit for five minutes on the sofa by myself. What the fuck do I think I am doing? And stupid, stupid boy. What kind of an idiot is he, wanting to 'do it' with someone he's just met in a club. Does he do this often? I want to go back to the dance floor, slap him and educate him about safe sex and being careful. But I slink away home quietly and jerk myself off to sleep.*

WHEN FIELD = HOME

[There] are people who belong to more than one world, speak more than one language (literally and metaphorically), inhabit more than one identity, have more than one home; who have learned to negotiate and translate between cultures and who, because they are irrevocably the product of several interlocking histories and cultures, have learned to live with and indeed to speak from, difference. They speak from the 'in-between' of different cultures, always unsettling the assumptions of one culture from the perspective of another and thus finding ways of being both the same as and at the same time different from the others amongst whom they live. (Stuart Hall, 1995)[40]

Over the next few paragraphs, I mull over some of the broad concerns regarding the practice of ethnography in one's own society (however, one may choose to define this *own*). In subsequent parts of this chapter, I will address specific instances of the challenges that I encounter in my fieldwork and how I respond to them.

To begin with, is it right for a researcher to exploit his background as a valid point of entry in his field of study? Gupta and Fergusson (1997) certainly think so and they contend that growing up in a culture could and in fact, should be considered as a 'heterodox form of fieldwork... an extended participant observation'.[41] Being an insider certainly has advantages. Such a researcher 'knows the language, has grown up in the culture and has little difficulty in becoming involved with the people' (Jones, 1970).[42]

The indigenous field worker has the undisputable advantage of being able to attach meanings to patterns that he or she uncovers much faster than the non-indigenous researcher who is unfamiliar with the culture of

> the wider society. Being part of the same cognitive world implies that the subject and object share a similar body of knowledge.... Being indigenous also implies the advantage of being able to understand a social reality on the basis of minimal clues; that is, the meanings of cultural patterns are more readily understood.... Indigenous researchers...are believed to be able to avoid the problem of culture shock.... They are expected to be less likely to experience 'culture fatigue', namely the strain of being a stranger in an unfamiliar cultural setting and the demands this places on their role as researcher. (Altorki and El Solh, 1998)[43]

On the flip side, there are also disadvantages to being an insider. One of these is that 'information may be withheld when it relates to behaviour that must be concealed from public knowledge. If one is outside the system, one's awareness of goings-on may not be problematic. But as a participant, the researcher constitutes a threat of exposure and judgment'[44] (Altorki, 1998). Therefore, one should be cautious not to excessively privilege the inside position over that of an outside researcher.

> One vantage point cannot be said to be better than the other. There are logical dangers inherent in both approaches. The outsider may enter a social situation, armed with a battery of assumptions, which he does not question and which guide him to certain types of conclusions; and the insider may depend too much on his own background, his sentiments, his desires for what is good for his people. The insider, therefore, may distort the 'truth' as much as the outsider...
>
> It is undoubtedly true that an insider may have easier access to certain types of information as compared to an outsider. But it is consistent to assume, also, that the outsider may have certain advantages in certain situations.... The crucial point is that insiders and outsiders may be able to collect different data; they also have different points of view, which may lead to different interpretations of the same set of data. (Jones, 1970)[45]

Also, as Weston (1997) warns, there is the danger that a researcher who chooses to study his own society is 'likely to be seen as native first, ethnographer second'.[46] If such researchers choose to use ethnography as a means of activism to bring about change in their own societies, they often have to 'confront charges of unprofessionalism and various labels of personality aberration, not to mention accusations of extremism'[47] (Morsy, 1998). On the one hand, these researchers are often viewed 'with suspicion, as people who lack the distance necessary to conduct good fieldwork; on the other hand, well-intentioned colleagues thrust upon them the responsibility for speaking their identity, thus inadvertently forcing them into the prison-house of essentialism'[48] (Gupta and Fergusson, 1997). Weston (1997) characterizes the native ethnographer as a 'hybrid'—one that 'collapses the subject or object distinction' by the 'act of studying "people" defined as one's own'.[49] This hybridity creates a *double bind* for the native ethnographer when it comes to writing up one's work—one has to surrender 'the intricate operations of hybridity to the oversimplifications of nativity or objectivity' and 'treat the components of [one's] hybridity as merely additive ('native' plus 'ethnographer') or split ('native' or 'ethnographer') by writing from only one subject position at a time...'.[50]

It is naïve to posit the insider or outsider dichotomy as a clash between subjectivity and objectivity, as both the researcher and the research subject are 'social persons with a certain position vis-à-vis one another with a common social structure' and thus, instead of wondering whether the indigenous ethnographer can be objective or not, the concern should rather be about how his 'relative social position...affects the methodology of research'[51] (Shami, 1998). In any case—

> For those engaged in working with their 'own' communities, engaged in activist organizing or for supporting financially strapped extended families, exoticism has no inherent value. Leaving their commitments and responsibilities for the sake of untethered research interests... [would imply] a betrayal of those people whose lives and livelihoods are inextricably linked to their own. (Gupta and Fergusson, 1997)[52]

According to Narayan (1993), as ethnographers, we all exhibit what Rosaldo (1989) has termed as 'multiplex subjectivity' with many cross-cutting identifications.[53] 'What facet of our subjectivity we choose, or are forced to accept as a defining identity can change depending on the context and the vectors of power'.[54] Thus, 'dismantling objectivism creates a space for ethical concerns in a territory once regarded as value-free. It enables the social analyst to become a social critic[55] (Rosaldo, 1989).

> One invariably takes a stand; indeed, one must take a stand, not as the waving of certain flags, but as a reflection on where one's allegiances and emotions are, what sympathies and empathies drive one to interpret events in certain ways rather than others. (Hansen, 2001)[56]

Kamala Visweswaran's (1994) differentiation between 'homework' and 'fieldwork'[57] that Clifford cites in his 1997 essay *Spatial Practices* is a useful one; it hints at a model in which ethnography does not succumb to a home or field divide—

> [For Visweswaran] Homework is not defined as the opposite of exoticist fieldwork; it is not a matter of literally staying at home or studying one's own community. 'Home'… is a person's location in determining discourses and institutions…a locus of critical struggle that both empowers and limits the subject wherever she or he conducts formal research. By restructuring the home or field opposition, Visweswaran clears space for unorthodox routings and rootings of ethnographic work.[58]

Clifford builds on this argument to envision the inclusion of the ethnographer's 'autobiography…the shifting locations of his or her own life'[59] as a part of this homework. In the same vein, Narayan reflects that 'people born within a society can be simultaneously both insiders and outsiders, just as those born elsewhere can be outsiders and if they are lucky, insiders too'.[60]

> The loci along which we are aligned with or set apart from those whom we study are multiple and in flux. Factors such as education, gender, sexual orientation, class, race or sheer duration of contacts may at different times, outweigh the cultural identity we associate with insider or outsider status. Instead what we must focus our attention on is the quality of relations with the people we seek to represent in our texts—are they viewed as mere fodder for professionally self-serving statements about a generalized 'other', or are they accented as subjects with voices, views, and dilemmas—people to whom we are bonded through ties of reciprocity and who may even be critical of our professional enterprise. (Narayan, 1993)[61]

ARRIVAL SCENE TWO: POST-IT NOTES

The Gay Bombay newsgroup[62] began on 31 December 1998 via the free group email service—Egroups, which was subsequently renamed Yahoo! Groups after its acquisition by Yahoo! in June 2000. Yahoo! Groups is one of Yahoo!'s many free services offered to its users. Through Yahoo! Groups, one can not just send and receive group messages, but also upload and download files, engage in online chat, work with photos and albums, link to other web pages using bookmarks, conduct online polls, maintain an online calendar, create online databases as well as maintain lists of members. The groups are indexed according to several categories. Yahoo! has a team of category editors, known as *surfers*, who go through the groups' directory constantly. If they feel a particular group has been improperly categorized, they may move it to a more appropriate location.

The person who starts or maintains the group and has administrative powers over the group functions is called the group's *owner* or *moderator*. The moderator can decide whether to restrict membership to the group, permit email attachments and let members post directly to the group or through the moderator.

I am a subscriber to the Gay Bombay Yahoo! newsgroup since August 2003, but my presence on it is that of a lurker—a silent observer of the postings. I need to clarify my purpose and intentions of my research clearly to the group before I begin my work here. I go to the Yahoo! Groups homepage (http://groups.Yahoo.com/) and create a separate Yahoo! identity (ID) just for research purposes.

I proceed to the Gay Bombay group page. There are five main sections here—the horizontal top bar, the horizontal bottom bar and the centre of the screen divided into three sections—a wide centre section and two narrow sidebars. The horizontal top bar is used to navigate to other sections of the site, the vertical bar on the left is used for navigation within the specific site.

I click on the link *Join this group* which is located on the top of the screen, in the centre. I am then asked for my preferences about messages—whether I wish to access them off the site, receive them in my Yahoo! Mailbox individually or in *digest* format (in batches of 25) or at some other email address. On confirming these preferences, one clicks on another link to join the group.

In March 2004, I post my first message to the newsgroup,[63] introducing myself and my research intentions—

```
From:"parmesh_mit_researcher"<parmesh_mit_researcher@y...>
Date:    Tue Mar 2, 2004 12:50 am
Subject:    Hello—and an introduction

A short note to say hello and that its a pleasure
to be here. My name is Parmesh. I am currently
studying and conducting research at MIT, in
Cambridge, MA, USA and my primary theme of inquiry
is the negotiation of gay identity among urban
gay individuals. Being both gay and from Bombay—
for me, being a participant in this group is
like being home in more ways than one and I'm
excited by the idea to academically consider it
as one of the "locations" for my study. I'll be
clarifying my ideas online within this space over
the next few months as both an observer and
an active participant in this community—I have
already begun a dialogue with some of the members
here—would love to continue it with others who
may be interested.

Best regards,
Parmesh.
```

I follow this up with a notice about *Between the Lines*, the LBGT Film Festival I am organizing at MIT in April 2004.[64] I do this because I want my position as an out gay student and event organizer in Boston to be known within the group. I think this would be an effective way of immediately establishing my credibility within the group as well as the integrity of my research intentions. However, to my disappointment, I only receive four responses. I was ambitiously hoping that the moment I declared my research intentions and MIT credentials, I would be flooded by a deluge of emails from eager members, all wanting to share their experiences with me…but this is clearly not happening.

It is time for plan B. I scan through the posts on the newsgroup of the previous six months and note down the nicknames of the regular posters. I then send each of them a personal email, introducing myself, outlining the nature of my work and requesting an opportunity to interview them using an instant messaging (IM) client such as MSN Messenger or Yahoo! Messenger. I mail 22 people—trying to construct a balanced mix of newsgroup administrators, regular posters, flamers and dissenters, as well as some completely random posters.

The response to my effort is more favourable this time. I receive replies from 14 of the 22 I have emailed, stating that they would be happy to be interviewed. However, I face another problem. Most of the respondents say that they are not comfortable with an online interview—they would rather have me compose a questionnaire and send it to them, which they can answer at their leisure and mail back. With others, the time difference becomes a factor. I schedule several interviews with one particular person based in India, but each time, either one of us cannot make it online at the required time.

At first, I am irritated as I see my plans of Annette Markham style chat-oriented data collection[65] disappear in smoke. On reflection however, I realize that this is fine and in fact, my idea of on online chat was quite silly considering that the newsgroup is asynchronous in nature—that is, messages on it are posted through email by its members at their own convenience and not in simultaneous real time. By carrying out email interviews, I am merely collecting my data from the group using the same device they use in their regular interaction with the group. It is as it should be. I interview a total of 12 individuals electronically, conducting only two IM interviews—the others are conducted via email.

I use an open-ended questionnaire, which I think will work both for online research and my subsequent physical world research in Bombay city. I divide the questionnaire into four different sections—*General Information*, *Being Gay in India*, *Gay Bombay* and *Identity*. I structure the questions in each section to move from general to the specific, trying to replicate textually the interview style I will use later on with my face-to-face respondents.

In cases where I feel I need clarifications on the answers I receive, I mail the respondents and they reply my queries promptly. Some of them are curious to know more about my research and me and I establish an informal bond with them through back and forth email correspondence. Others realize that they know of me through their friendship networks and mail me commenting about how small the world really is!

At the end of May 2004, I send out another email to the group, informing them of my three-month visit to India and seeking further inputs for my research. This results in six new responses that eventually translate into two productive interviews. I also mail the Bombay respondents of my questionnaire and ask them if they would want to be interviewed in person during my trip—almost all of them agree.

ARRIVAL SCENE THREE: HOME, SWEAT HOME

30 May 2004. 'We have now begun our descent into Chattrapati Shivaji International Airport...'. After 24 hours of non-stop travel, I stretch my legs as much as my cramped economy class seat can allow and look out of the window.

> *If you look at Bombay from the air, if you see its location—spread your thumb and forefinger apart at a thirty-degree angle and you will see the shape of Bombay—you will find yourself acknowledging that it is a beautiful city—the sea on all sides, the palm trees along the shores, the light coming down from the sky and thrown back up by the sea. It has a harbour, several bays, creeks, rivers, hills. From the air, you get a sense of its possibilities. On the ground, it is different.* (Suketu Mehta, 2004)[66]

I have made this descent into Bombay airport so many times in the past, but this time when the plane taxies to a halt on the shantytown hugged runway, my emotions begin to swell and by the time I emerge from the airport, they burst in a giant tidal wave of tears. Bombay is a visceral feeling; psychological as well as physical. Little beads of sweat begin trickling down my forehead—by the time I have walked to a taxi, the beads have turned into rivulets that are flowing liberally down my back. This city is unbearably hot, ugly, stinky and filthy, but it is home. Home, sweat home.

Three days later, I attend my first Gay Bombay Sunday meet. I am still a little jetlagged. I have been away for just one year; I should not feel out of place. Still, it was only five days ago that I walked down the street to the Central Square Red Line T... now, halfway across the world, I have to reorient myself to making another BEST bus number 123[67] journey, just to get to the train station.

> *Bombay, also known as Mumbai, is a city of 16 million inhabitants, of whom six million ride the city's three main lines daily—more riders than all of New York City's subways, buses, trains and ferries combined. Trains designed to hold 1,700 passengers carry as many as 4,700 during peak hours in a bone-crushing 1.4 bodies per square foot of space.*[68]

I am lucky to be travelling on a Sunday. Moreover, since I live in Colaba, the southern most part of Bombay, I board the train at its origin—Churchgate station, an ugly square monstrosity of a building, only 40 years old, so ordinary and squat in its appearance compared to it splendid predecessor just across the street (now a Railways office complex)! There are 28 stations between Churchgate and the suburb of Virar (a distance of 60 kilometres) on the western line that I am taking—its route hugs the western coast of Bombay, from south to north. On weekends, the traffic generally moves from the suburbs (north) to *town* (south)—and I am going against the flow, so I will be assured of a place to sit and there will be no crowds to crush my body against; no fond hopes of being fondled, as on previous weekday journeys. Today, the station is quiet—there is an indolent air to the proceedings.

> *The only hub of activity is a bookstall run by the famed A.H. Wheeler. Here, newsboys busily sort out bundles of Sunday newspapers to cater to the metro's news-hungry multitudes. (Later in the day, they can be seen hawking The Statesman and The Hindu that have arrived by air from Calcutta and Madras). Trains, of course, keep zooming in and out. But there are no stampedes on the platform.* (R. Raj Rao, 2003)[69]

I pick up copies of the *Sunday Express* and *Mid-Day* to read during the ride and buy myself a return *Card ticket II class* to Andheri (16 rupees, price gone up from last year!) from the expressionless spectacled clerk behind a cool-marbled ticket window, barely avoiding stepping on the mangy grey dog taking its siesta underneath. When I reach for my wallet to put my change back, I feel a nudge at my elbow and turn towards two yellow eyes, popping out of the brown-covered skeleton of a child not more than five, hand outstretched. It is perfect timing—I do not have much of a choice! I hand over a 10-rupee note, being careful not to make direct contact with the dirt-crusted hand.

I have nine minutes until the next slow train leaves and I decide to I pop in to see if anyone is cruising in the infamous loo. It has never been my scene, but I have accompanied friends there before and found it tremendously entertaining. Today, there is a middle-aged pot-bellied mustachioed man standing in a corner cubicle, playing with his dick. He looks inquiringly when I walk by, but I shake my head.

I go back to the cavernous railway platform covered with a metal gridlocked roof, opaque skylights running across its length. There are different benches nailed to the platform, some made of wooden slats, others from interlocking metal mesh and red trash cans attached to metal frames, again, efficiently nailed in. All kinds of things dangle from the roof—ineffectually rotating fans, tube lights, digital black train schedule display screens, giant clocks, huge backlit billboards with delicious smooth bodied men in skimpy VIP underwear who exhort me to *make a big impression,* funky looking *Dhoom* movie posters with leather-clad John, Abhishek and Uday straddling phallic red motorbikes....

I climb the maroon-yellow two-toned 12-coach Borivili-slow, snaked along platform number three, through its green always-open doors. The compartments are colour coded—yellow with red or green diagonal stripes means *first class*, dark yellow means *ladies only* and pale yellow is *gents regular*—where I belong. I am in a cage—the seats, sides, floors and roofs are all metal, painted in different hues of peeling yellow or green paint.

The train lurches forward; its noisy departure augmented by the rows of handles hanging over head, the loose broken In-Case-of-Emergency-Pull-Chain going clickety-clack and a blind middle-aged man led by two young children, one of them almost bent over under the weight of her harmonium. They are singing and playing *Pardesi Pardesi Jaana Nahin* ('O Stranger, Do Not Go Away') from the Bollywood film *Raja Hindustani* ('Indian King', 1996). I avoid making eye contact and stare instead at the *Kaya Kalp* International Sex Health and Clinic advertisement pasted above my seat; and then read the name of the stations on the route map, first in Hindi and then in English. Churchgate, Marine Lines, Charni Road, Grant Road, Mumbai Central, Mahalaxmi, Lower Parel, Elphinstone Road, Dadar, Matunga Road, Mahim, Bandra, Khar Road, Santacruz, Vile Parle, Andheri, Jogeshwari, Goregaon, Malad, Kandivali, Borivali, Dahisar, Mira Road, Bhayandar, Naigaon, Vasai Road, Nallasopara, Virar. The teenage boy next to me rolls some tobacco between his palms contentedly and leisurely inserts it between his lower lip and teeth.

Greater Bombay's population, currently 19 million, is bigger than that of 173 countries in the world. If it were a country by itself in 2004, it would rank at number 54...India is not an overpopulated country... it is the cities of India that are overpopulated. Singapore has a density of 2,535 people per square mile; Berlin, the most crowded European city has 1,130 per square mile. The island city of Bombay in 1990 had a density of 17,550 people per square mile. Some parts of central Bombay have a population density of 1 million people per square mile. This is the highest number of individuals massed together at any spot on the world. (Suketu Mehta, 2004)[70]

Andheri station, where I get down from the train, sure feels like this spot. I have been suffering from claustrophobia since the past six months in America, but that is a luxury I cannot afford to have in Bombay. I suffer a brief panic attack, but draw upon my crowd navigation skills, (luckily, like cycling and swimming, one never loses these) to emerge outside 10 minutes later.

The meeting venue is the McDonalds, in the bustling open-air market located right outside Andheri station. This is the norm—people collect at a restaurant and then are guided to the actual meeting (in someone's home) by volunteers. There are thousands of people milling about the market with noisy rickshaws, cars, bicycles, cows and goats, buses and the loud sales pitches of hundreds of street vendors all adding to the commotion. The restaurant is as densely packed as the streets outside; with families, groups of teenagers and swarms of children running around (or rather, squeezing their way around the crowds). The harried service people at the counter are trying their best to fulfill the incessant demands of Maharaja Macs, Vegetarian McCurries, spicy fries and cardamom tea. I am to look for a man wearing a black cap with *GB* written on it. I am a little nervous and wonder how I would be if I were not approaching this meet as an *out* researcher who has already appeared this year on the BBC and in the *Boston Globe* talking about my sexuality. Probably it would have been the same as last year, before I left. Sure about my sexuality, but not wanting to do anything publicly about it. Now, intoxicated with one year of reading *Out* and *The Advocate*, gay marriages in Massachusetts being a reality and the little bit of fame that my film festival generated, I cannot possibly go back to *what might people think* mode.

The group is easy to spot. I introduce myself to everyone around the table say eight or ten men, including a few first-timers who are shy and reserved. The veterans strike up a conversation right away. I am made to feel at ease. After half an hour, we rise and board a local bus. Joseph, who is in charge, buys tickets for everyone. 'Don't worry, we have a budget for this', he grins when I raise an inquiring eyebrow. We reach our destination, Pratham's home, singing film songs and laughing loudly, much to the consternation of the other bus passengers. I am happy as I walk with the group, making small talk and getting to know more about their lives.

Once inside, I introduce myself to the individuals already assembled there and tell them more about the kind of work I plan to do—these are people I will come to know intimately over the course of the next few months; and then years. Some of them recognize me from my emails on the mailing list, others are learning about me for the first time. I can see that they are intrigued by me—they wonder where I was all these years—if I was indeed living in Bombay and I wonder the same. They are taken aback by my shorts, blond-streaked hair and brazenly out attitude and I enjoy the attention I receive. My excitement is palpable and I know that the group members can sense it. It feels so good to be here…could Malinowski have felt the same rush as he pegged in his tent on an *alien* beach?

Two weeks later, I walk into the Bandra café *Just Around the Corner* with the practiced air of a Gay Bombay veteran. Enter. Find man with cap. Hug all around for those I know. Handshakes and smiles for the newbies. Small talk until we reach the actual meeting venue. Then ease into the meeting, observing, taking notes and interjecting as need be. In the interim, I have travelled to the southern city of Bangalore to attend the Second International Conference on Sexualities, Masculinities and Cultures in South Asia—which has been an eye opener for me in terms of making me aware of the momentum gathering around LBGT rights in the country.

Today's meet is in Karim's home. Karim is a journalist with one of the country's leading news magazines. He lives in an airy one-bedroom-hall-kitchen apartment. The décor is ethnic chic—cane furniture, hand woven rugs, low seating cotton cushions in pink, mustard, blue and lime green, wispy red curtains, potted plants and books. Paintings by the famous writer-artist Manjula Padmanabhan adorn the walls. Today, the room is cramped with 25 gay men—scientists, engineers, students, corporate executives; young twinks with coloured hair, in tight singlets, harem pants, jewellery and sunglasses; old butch men with paunches, glasses and salt and pepper beards. Bottles of Pepsi and Fanta are being passed around, as are fresh scones; courtesy Karim's excellent baking abilities.

The free wheeling discussion begins with the challenges and practical issues faced by gay men seeking long-term relationships in Bombay. Isaac suggests the organization of a match-making bureau for gay men, on the lines of the arranged marriage bureaus for straight people in India. Karim wonders if we are not fetishizing long-term gay relationships in India, just like the West. He informs the group that the gay guide *Spartacus* has asked them for an update on the India section and there is a debate on what locations to reveal in the guide. He also warns the group about Internet hustlers that have been operating in gay chat rooms, meeting people offline and then robbing or blackmailing them.

There are some tense moments at the meet. The first occurs when Isaac asks Homi, a shy newbie from Andhra Pradesh, to say something about himself. Daulat chides Isaac to stop treating the first-timer like 'an animal in a zoo'. Isaac angrily responds that he did not refer to the man as 'an animal'. Murgesh steps in to defuse the tension. Meanwhile, the object of this attention nervously observes the proceedings, silently. I find out that he is a Navy officer, recently posted to Bombay, but never see him at another meeting or dance party after this during the rest of my stay.

The second tense moment occurs during an argument about increasing the mandate of Gay Bombay to include more outspoken public activism. Senthil, Karim, Vidwan, Daulat and others are of the opinion that members of Gay Bombay should play a more proactive role in protests like the recent one organized by Humsafar against the obnoxious Bollywood film *Girlfriend*, be more visible on television and in the press and make financial contributions to other needy LBGT causes, such as the recent email appeal from a *hijra* group seeking funds for a new computer. Isaac, Pratham, Pulkit and others disagree and a heated argument follows. Murgesh proposes that a blanket decision not be made and each proposal be considered individually, based on its feasibility. Karim reminds the group that they had raised money for the Larzish Bombay gay and lesbian film festival through one of their bar nights last year and the same method could be adopted again, if everyone agreed upon it. Vidwan states that there is a difference between helping *hijras* and including them as part of the community; he feels that the Gay Bombay group is exclusionary to other sexual minorities, to which Pratham retorts—'Why should we be messiahs for the downtrodden? We are a social space for *gay* people, why be anything else?' Senthil counters this by reminding the group that even the existence of Gay Bombay as a social space might come under threat if right wing political organizations make gay people their next targets for victimization, or if their dance parties began to be raided by the police and in case such things happen, the only people who will publicly demonstrate are the *hijras*. I chip in with comments about us all having a conscience that we should be guided by, which receives indulgent smiles from the warring parties. It is evident that this issue is a deeply divisive one within the group; I am to encounter it at several times during my stay at several different levels. Over the next three months, on subsequent visits to India and after I relocate to Bombay in 2006, I attend many meetings like these.

I also attend a series of get-togethers organized by the Humsafar Trust every alternate Sunday called *Sunday High*. Some of these meetings discuss important issues faced by the community, like the threat faced by gay men from hustlers and blackmailers, while others are just occasions to unwind and watch films together. At these meeting I am exposed to a different kind of gay culture existing in the city; the issues faced by other sexual minorities like *hijras* and *kothis*.

Then there are the parties; not just regular Gay Bombay parties at night clubs but also private dinners in people's homes. I visit the Humsafar centre to see the HIV-prevention work they are doing and dig through their archives.

Throughout, I interview, interview and interview. I am lucky that each of my trips coincides with significant media action...2004 is a gay summer as the *Indian Express* calls it;[71] and I am there, bang in the middle of the action. Sexuality conference in Bangalore. Pride March in Calcutta. The Pushkin Chandra double murder case in Delhi. The *Girlfriend* controversy all over the country.... (See Chapter 6 for a discussion of the media coverage of all these events.) In 2005, I visit at the time of the release of the gay themed *My Brother Nikhil* and in 2006 I relocate to India bang in the middle of the letter writing campaign and court decision over Section 377. So much juicy material to dig into.

INTIMACY

I use the same questionnaire I designed for my online interviews as a guide for semi-structured personal interviews with individuals that I meet in the different Gay Bombay spaces as a participant observer. I use a snowball interviewing or friendship pyramiding technique format—I begin with a set of established contacts—including some of the Gay Bombay organizers and my online interviewees—and cull new informants based on their recommendations and also from my observations at Gay Bombay events. By using theoretic sampling, I try and maintain diversity among my respondents, with regard to factors like age, occupation and marital status as well as how they choose to access Gay Bombay (that is, via the net, meetings, parties or a combination of these). I also interview some leading gay and *hijra* activists from Bombay that have been critical of Gay Bombay in the past; even though their interaction with the Gay Bombay list or events is limited, I want to incorporate their viewpoints into my analysis.

Following my online questionnaire, I move from general questions to specific ones in my physical interviews—I work loosely within the framework of the questionnaire—but let the bulk of the agenda setting be directed by the respondents. I conduct some of my interviews with my participants individually and the others as dyads (interviewing two friends, partners or associates together).

The community welcomes me warmly. I think there are a number of reasons for this. First, my own homosexuality. Almost all my subjects first ask me if I am gay when I express an interest in interviewing them. My sexuality thus serves as my passport into the community. It helps me build rapport and gain the confidence of the community members. My forthrightness in revealing details about my own private life is also appreciated. Since, I am asking my respondents to be open and share details of their lives with me, I reciprocate by being honest about my life experiences and beliefs.

My interviewees are college students, working professionals and businessmen. They live either alone or with their partners, with their families as either out or closeted, or with their spouses and or extended families as married men. Those who can, invite me to their homes to conduct my interviews. Others ask me to come to their offices late, after office hours. I schedule interviews with those whose homes or offices I cannot visit, in different restaurants, at locations convenient to them and embark on a delightful gastronomical journey—*Vithal Bhelwala* near the Victoria Railway Terminus where I gorge on delicious *pani puris*, the best street food in the world; *Aswad* at Dadar with its Maharastrian *kothambir vadis* and *missal*; prawn *pulao* and *kheema parathas* at Jehangir art gallery's Samovar café; sizzlers at Yoko's in Santa Cruz—and when time is of the essence, the local Barista or Café Coffee Day.

I do not face any problems in explaining my research theme to my interview subjects—it is enough for them to know that it will be turned into my graduate thesis and a book later on. For some of them, anonymity is important; others insist that their real names and identities be used in my write up. (Ultimately, I decide to use pseudonyms for *all* respondents). They are conscious of their position as research subjects—and sometimes ask me, even after casual conversations, if I am going to use the conversations within my project.

A few of my respondents are skeptical—of both, my intentions and research methodology. They feel that I am exploiting my sexuality to gain currency in Western academia. Although they agree to be interviewed, they sometimes pepper their answers with cynical and often condescending judgements about me. Others strongly advise me that though my intentions are good, what is needed right now in India is hard activism on the ground and if I really cared as much about the gay community in India, perhaps I should come back and get involved in these grassroot efforts. Their comments strike a chord and I find myself getting very defensive whenever they are raised.

The majority, however, are appreciative that I have chosen to focus on issues dealing with contemporary gay life in Bombay. They respond to me personally and warmly—and go out of their way to help me in my efforts. Gopal offers to send me relevant magazine articles to Boston whenever required. Karim loans me his private collection of press clippings and makes sure that I am well-connected with a diverse range of people while I am in Bombay. Mohnish takes me to see a drag *lavni*—a traditional Indian folk dance being perfumed by male dancers in female clothing and make-up (it is a huge hit among the Marathi speaking audiences in Bombay)—and even arranges a private backstage inter-view with the performers and director. The Humsafar Trust opens up its premises and archives to me. Mike gives me his cellphone when mine stops working—and lets me keep it for the entire duration of my stay in Bombay. There are many other incidents, both big and small, but by far, the most important gifts that my interviewees give me are their valuable time and their fascinating stories.

I exploit my 'multiplex subjectivity'[72] to win the confidence of my po-tential interviewees in various ways. Sometimes, I utilize my privileged class background to gain access to people who might not have spoken to me otherwise. My relative youth and somewhat zany style-sense means that I can connect with a lot of people in their 20s and even younger, as a peer. When needed, I flaunt my academic punditry—and use my MIT research position as a door opener. In other cases, my prior life as a corporate citizen of Bombay comes in handy.

While I always try to be as much of *myself* as possible in my interactions with group members, I fine-tune certain aspects of my personality to suit the need of the hour. For example, if I feel that a particular interviewee might bond better with me if I act or sound a little campy, then I do so. Likewise, other decisions like meeting place and clothes to wear are all conditioned by my prior knowledge of the interviewee. If I feel that it is advantageous to bring up my American connection, I do so, but if I sense resentment, I quickly play up my innate Bombayness. My age is also a factor in the role that I play with my interviewees. Older respondents tend to treat me with indulgence. If we go out for a meal, they refuse to let me pay the bill and I feel pampered in their company, perhaps like a younger sibling. Correspondingly, with respondents who are younger than me, I tend to assume a big-brother kind of role, paying for our meals and advising them on their lives.

My respondents get irritated when I ask them for basic demographic information—they presume that I already know these details through my interaction with them. My strategy for asking open-ended questions is not always well received—some respondents interpret this as vague-ness. Sometimes, when I ask them basic questions that I should already know the answers to due to my *insider* position, they think that I am unprofessional and ill informed. Or they think that I am just joking or teasing them. Occasionally, they get angry and lash out that I should know *how it is*.

I want to tell them that I do know, but my situation is different. I have been very lucky actually—my parents have accepted my sexuality without a fuss (well, more or less). I am economically, educationally and socially privileged, I have always had a place of my own to bring guys to if I so desire, in Bombay. So, yes, I can speculate, but have no idea how it *really* is! Of course, I cannot say all this or I will lose my rapport. But I can certainly sense that I am a cause of resentment within some of my respondents (although they do not voice it directly) due to my upper-middle class South Bombay origins and my multiple-entry American visa that allows me to cross (at least certain) borders with ease.

I find it very hard to do research in the city in which I have spent most of my adult life. My non-researcher life is always trying to intervene. Because I am so involved with my field or homework, I do not return calls from friends, delay many personal appointments and even cancelled two out-of-town trips at the last moment. This causes a lot of irritation among my friends and family members. While doing research, I am constantly aware of the fact that my work is going to be judged by an audience for its professionalism and methodological and theoretical rigour. This is frustrating and quite nerve wrecking. On other occasions, like Joseph (1998), I find it 'difficult to think of my relationship with [my subjects] as a source of research data. They became active subjects, rather than objects of research' and I often forget to record important data while I am with them,[73] or as the following chat excerpt reveals, reverse roles with them—

Parmesh says:	Have you ever deceived or been deceived by someone online—and in specifically in settings like GB? If so, what was the experience like?
Ormus says:	Not applicable
Ormus says:	Never been deceived
Ormus says:	We could make this into a Drew Barrymore movie
Ormus says:	Have you?
Parmesh says:	Several times
Parmesh says:	In my youth
Ormus says:	Person turned out to be completely different from what he claimed to be, huh?

Parmesh says: You bet...
Ormus says: Are you happier now or were you happier then?
Parmesh says: Hehehe
Parmesh says: I'm always happy
Parmesh says: Or the reverse
Parmesh says: I'm never happy
Ormus says: How extremist...
Parmesh says: Is it me interviewing you? Or vice versa?

It is impossible to be emotionally detached. At one Gay Bombay meeting, I am carried away by the drift of my argument and maliciously attack Pratham, someone who I have just interviewed before the meeting, for not being *out* enough. For this, Karim publicly chastises me. I apologize to Pratham and he smiles and tells me to relax—it is no big deal.

There are many ways in which ethnographers may choose to disguise the identities of the individuals and community they research. These include 'creating composite characters out of individuals in the community, fictionalizing certain details and breaking identifiable individuals into multiple identities in the write-up'[74] (Cherny, 1999). In my case, because of the online or offline nature of my work, I decide to adopt Amy Bruckman's (2001) guidelines for treatment of names and online pseudonyms in published accounts.[75] She delineates a disguise 'continuum of possibilities' ranging from 'no disguise, light disguise, moderate disguise, to heavy disguise'. I choose *light disguise* as my strategy, which stipulates that—

(a) The group is named.
(b) Names, pseudonyms and some other identifying details (place names, organizational and institutional names, and so on) are changed.
(c) Verbatim quotes may be used, even if they could be used to identify an individual.
(d) Group members themselves may be able to guess who is being discussed.
(e) An outsider could probably figure out who is who, with a little investigation.
(f) Details that are harmful to individuals should be omitted.

I think that it would be difficult for an outsider to guess the identities of the individuals that are mentioned in my study. However, for those within the group—it may certainly be possible to guess which pseudonym stands for whom. In fact, as I mentioned earlier, a large number of my interviewees ask me to use their real names in my work; others ask me to use their online nicknames. I decide to change all names, instead of having a confusing mix of real character names and pseudonyms. I also change the names of some locations that are used by the community as meeting or party places. For the reflexive passages that deal with my own personal history, I use fictionalized initials for those who I have been in close sexual or emotional relationships with and fictionalize some but not all other names, thereby preserving a balance between authenticity and identity disguise. I acknowledge that my method may simply be 'a useless middle road between privacy protection and research rigour'[76] (Cherny, 1999)—but it is a road that I believe is a pragmatic one to take for a study of this nature.

Altorki and El Solh (1998) write that '[indigenous] fieldworkers are not only held accountable by those who constitute their academic frame of reference, but also may be expected to be conscious of their moral obligation to the subject of their study'.[77] I am acutely conscious of this unstated obligation; I am responsible to the Gay Bombay community for my actions and the way I write about them. I am also responsible to the greater Indian gay community at large.

> Describing and analyzing the culture of one's own community is also affected by the realities of one's group membership.... While all ethnographers have to deal with questions of confidentiality and exposure of data, for those who return to live with the people they study—even more for those who are participating members—these considerations have more drastic consequences. It is not whether a book will be read or not, assigned or banned from use. It is a question of potential and severe ostracism for the ethnographer. (Altorki, 1998)[78]

As a friend and community member, my respondents sometimes reveal very private information about their lives—although these revelations may be helpful, I do not include them in my write-up; I think that doing so would be both 'dishonest and disloyal' (Jones, 1970).[79]

Sexual involvement with one's research subjects has in general been taboo for ethnographers for a variety or reasons, including the power inequality that often exists between researchers and those researched. Recently, this taboo has begun to be questioned. Thus Clifford (1997) asks—'Why should sharing beds be a less appropriate source of knowledge than sharing food? There may of course be many practical reasons for sexual restraint in the field, just as certain places and certain activities may be off-limit to the tactful...but they are not off-limit in all places and at all times'.[80] Mark McLelland too argues against sexual prudishness in the field—in fact, he bases an entire study on sex that he has with participants encountered via the Internet.[81] Bell and Valentine (1995) declare—'Our research relationships and the way we report them cannot (and indeed must not) be kept impersonal and clinical. We must also be reflexive about how we feel about our respondents—owning up if we feel sexually attracted to them rather than struggling to maintain a false front of objectivity'.[82]

I acknowledge the existence of sexual tension between me and some of my respondents—both online and offline and adopt Campbell's methodological device of 'bracketing' as a means of addressing this tension; that is, being upfront with my respondents whether I am 'speaking to them as a researcher or as a friend and community member'.[83] Like Campbell, I avoid 'initiating any discussions I suspected would be construed as libidinous or even as deeply personal'[84] during formal interviews, leaving these for another occasion when I am not performing my researcher role. I am successful in this endeavour, however, like Campbell, I realize that my participants do not 'always observe such bracketing themselves'.[85] Sometimes, this makes for interesting scenarios—on one occasion, when I declared to an interviewee that I cannot respond to his sexual innuendo as we were in the midst of a formal interview, he volunteers to stop answering my questions so that I can start thinking of him as a sexual playmate instead of as a research subject! In another case, I am tremendously attracted to an interviewee and go out with him to a gay party where I try to hit on him, but am unsuccessful. One of my online interviewees happens to be someone at whose company I have interned many years ago as a fresh high school graduate. He is now married, with two kids and he reveals to me over email that he was very attracted to me during the time we worked together, but unable to declare his feelings.

One of the people I become close to is Ormus. He is the first person I contact off the Gay Bombay list, after reading a post by him describing his first experience at a Gay Bombay party. It is eloquently written and extremely expressive. I mail him immediately, telling him about my project and he agrees to be interviewed for it. Subsequent to that, we exchange emails, have several informal chats on MSN and speak to each other twice on the telephone, long distance. He tests the waters and flirts, not overtly, but using clever wordplay that could be read in multiple ways. I do the same.

We finally meet on MSN chat for a formal interview. As with our other conversations, we start off by catching up with our respective lives. Ormus knows about the film festival I have organized at MIT and wants to know how it went; he shares with me details about his recent out-of-town trip. He is training in the same professional school as my ex-boyfriend Z and so we have connections across several levels. Ormus has obviously read the questionnaire I sent to him in advance of our online meeting in detail—his answers are eloquent and well-framed. He is being honest and sharing intimate details of his life. I feel privileged to have this trust, but I also feel strangely exploitative. Is Ormus being so honest and open because he wants to make a good impression on me? Would he be so forthcoming even if we had not established our bond earlier? Am I attracted to him? I am enjoying the conversation immensely...we really have an excellent rapport and my previous conversations with him have meant that I have enough background information as well as a level of comfort established to ask him probing questions without wondering if I have gone too far. The formal interview goes off excellently.

Informally, we exchange pictures and decide to meet in Bombay for a date when I visit the city. During the course of this date, it is clear that there is a possibility of romance. Although this does not eventually materialize (we develop a platonic friendship instead), it results in my not conducting an offline interview with him and only retaining the online component as my data for research.

DEPARTURE SCENE: *KABHI ALVIDA NA KEHNA* (NEVER SAY GOODBYE)

I attend a Gay Bombay Sunday meet two days before I leave Bombay at the end of my summer break in 2004, to return to my graduate studies in Boston. It is the group's sixth anniversary—and it is being celebrated in style, with several events spread over a fortnight. The meeting I attend coincides with the festival of *Raksha Bandhan*—the Hindu festival commemorating brother-sister love. Appropriately, it is titled 'The Siblings Meet'. For old times sake, the meeting point is the Bandra McDonalds, just like it was at the first meet, six years ago. I climb upstairs to the second level of the restaurant and am met by Isaac, dressed in a splendid cream embroidered *churidar kurta* and the black GB cap identifier, greeting all the gay guests that arrive with a traditional hand folded *namaste*. As always, there are the old regulars and a bunch of (eight) newbies—a motivational trainer just relocated from Dubai, two guys from South Africa and Kenya, a group of shy college students, some software engineers…. There is also Upal, a brooding 20-something assistant film director from Delhi, who I am instantly attracted to—he looks like a young Matt Dillon, with his starving poet look, and blazing eyes. He had been introduced to me at the last dance party by my date for that evening; now I have the chance to chat him up as the group shifts to Sargam's aunt's place—again, a repeat of what took place six years ago.

The apartment is on the third floor of a building in a quiet by lane, off the crowded Pali Naka in Bandra. It has been recently renovated in the Palladian style common to upper middle class Bombay homes. Plaster of Paris false ceiling, lots of arches, sculpting, molding, cornices and scalloped curtains. Egyptian looking vases abound and there is abstract art on the walls. There are sofas arranged all around the apartment. By the time we arrive, it is already a full house with old timers who have come there directly. I make sure I squeeze myself right next to Upal. Sargam's two widowed aunts preside maternally over the proceedings—passing around sweets and drinks and urging everyone to speak up.

I hear several stories that evening. Robin talks about his brother's rejection upon learning about his sexuality, something that he did not expect at all, since his brother was a doctor who lived in America. Karim speaks about his sister's queasiness regarding his sexuality when it comes to telling her fiancé about it. He also feels strange that although she knows that he is in a long-term relationship, she avoids making any inquiries about his partner whenever they speak. Sargam feels that although his sister has accepted him for whom he is, she is still uncomfortable if he holds hands with his partner in her presence. He makes fun of her by threatening to attend her wedding in full bejeweled drag. Sankalp narrates his story of playing *doctor-doctor* with his cousin all through his childhood, which progressed into sexual action in their teens. Now, his cousin, married to a woman, constantly ignores him at family gatherings. Bhisham confides that he was blackmailed into having sex with his cousin and brother since the age of 12. There is a debate over the action of Isaac's brother—on coming out to him; he advised Isaac to leave the house and stay by himself, away from the family. Isaac chooses to interpret this as concern, the others feel it is selfishness and callousness on the part of the brother; instead of standing up for him, he is in fact shunning him, but Isaac is not convinced.

Shoeb, a software engineer who lives in California with his partner, has a happy tale. He came out to his family six years ago and now his parents and his partner's parents treat each other like in-laws. He advises that everyone should make their parents feel comfortable, answer their questions honestly and help them get over their fears. Likewise Senthil discloses that although his then 12-year old sister initially 'freaked out' when he came out to her at age 16, she was very supportive afterwards and even highlighted his sexuality in an admissions essay for a university in the US. (It worked, she was accepted!) He is not yet out to his parents though—he says that they are very conservative and might not be able to understand or accept. Joseph's story is unique—when he came out to his brother, his brother in turn revealed his own homosexuality to him—and now they are close confidantes.

The aunts interject with a list of concerns that parents might have on learning about their child's homosexuality. Who will look after him when he falls ill? What will happen when he grows old? They feel that gay men should be ready to answer these questions before coming out to their families. There is a general consensus that one should only come out after achieving financial independence. The meeting ends with a warm round of applause for the two aunts and their hospitality—and then its time for the great telephone number exchange to begin. The new guys mingle with the others, happy to be a part of this exciting community and old friends renew contacts. I am busy hugging everyone I know—saying goodbye!

Some of us decide to continue the evening by walking to the Bandra Bandstand Café Coffee Day. I am excited that Upal agrees to come along. He lights a cigarette the moment we are outside, which is a big turn off—but I am leaving in two days; it is not like anything is going to happen. I am happy to be among friends. Nihar, who I have grown exceedingly fond of; Bhuvan and Om, my first interviewees in Bombay; Murgesh, someone I have grown to admire; and beautiful, beautiful eye candy, Upal. The coffee shop is hunk paradise—it seems like all of Bandra's beautiful boys have decided to come out on this gorgeous Sunday evening. There is a cool breeze coming in from the sea and I look around at the chatter-filled café, at the smiling animated faces of my new friends and feel horribly, miserably, achingly sad to be leaving. Nihar sees my expression and envelopes me in a big bear hug. 'We will miss you Parmesh', he says simply. I nod back and continue sipping my coffee. When the waiter comes for the bill, I flirt with him shamelessly, much to the delight of my companions.

In Boston, a few months later, I come home from *Swades* (homeland); the latest Bollywood film playing at the Somerville theatre, with a song in my head that refuses to fade away.

Mitti ki jo khushboo, tu kaise bhoolaayega
Tu chaahe kahin jaaye, tu laut ke aayega
Nayi nayi raahon mein, dabi dabi aahon mein
Khoye khoye dilse tere, koyi ye kahega
Ye jo des hai tera, swades hai tera, tujhe hai pukaara
Ye woh bandhan hai jo kabhi toot nahin sakta

'How could you possibly forget the smell of the earth here?
It shall force you to return, however far you go.
While on newer routes, within your suppressed sighs,
Someone shall say to your lost, musing heart—
What calls out to you isn't just a country; it's your homeland.
Your bond with it is eternal and unbreakable'.

—**A.R. Rehman/Javed Akhtar** *Swades* (Homeland)[86]

I return to my dorm room and read and re-read my field notes spread out all over the floor. I am sleep deprived but when I close my eyes, I do not sleep.... Instead I see a small fishing boat bobbing solitarily on a tempestuous Arabian Sea from the windows of Kabir's gorgeously decorated Bandra apartment... Pulkit's kind mom insisting that I eat something before going back home after my interview... A casual conversation with Murgesh's school uniform-clad, video game-playing 16-year old nephew while Murgesh filters coffee in the kitchen... Yudhisthir's bedroom wall completely covered with Hulk Hogan posters... Red-eyed Nihar, drinking soup and pouring out his heart to me at a rooftop café in Colaba with the rain spattering on a blue plastic tarpaulin above our heads...Harbhajan's diamond encrusted gold watch, rings and chains clinking as he tells me about his wife....

Now I am panting heavily as I climb 12 floors to Isaac's friend's apartment in a new building near Bombay's Film City. (The construction symbolizes Bombay for me completely—brand new, surrounded by slums on a potholed and puddled road, with every amenity possible except a working elevator), to find an army of gay hotties sprawled around the living room, clad in only their boxers...an elevator that works—a rickety ride up to the Lawyer's Collective office in Fort where six diligent workers type away quietly at their computer screens, surrounded by stacks of papers and files and posters, badges and pamphlets that read 'Preventing HIV is very simple—just use your head'...giant puddles of water...flies, flies, flies...the hush in the dark, jam-packed National College auditorium before the start of the first film at the gay film festival; spicy hot *samosas* and juicy gossip in the interval.... Bhudev standing on a stool feeding the fish in his large office fish tank while talking about post-colonialism... a rainbow shining in a highway oil slick as my rickshaw speeds along with the driver humming *Jo Bhi Ho, Kal Phir Aayega* (whatever happens, tomorrow will come once again').

I smile as I think that perhaps Gay Bombay is a little like Hotel California—I can log off or fly out any time I like, but I can never leave. It is the culture that is so firmly stuck to my skin[87] that it cannot be washed away. As I wind up my formal research after three years, I find myself deeply entangled in the mesh of relationships that I have established. The project is as much a part of me, as I am of it. I am unable to let go.

I continue to read the posts on the newsgroup with delight every day and often visit the website to see if there is anything new. I continue to be in touch with most of my interviewees over email and on the phone from Boston and once I relocate to Bombay city, in person. With some of them I am a counsellor—Gul is miserable about his lack of success with men—and I soothe him that there is Mr. Right waiting for him, just around the corner. I follow up with Nihar about whether he is eating a big breakfast every day, sleeping well and cutting down on the partying; share his joy when he lands his dream job as a fashion stylist and send him my condolences when he loses his father. I am excited for Bhuvan when his television script gets accepted and he gets to quit his job and live out his dream of becoming a full time writer. Not all my correspondence is hunky-dory—when I mail a whole bunch of people, including my new Gay Bombay friends about my National Public Radio interview regarding gay life in India being broadcast in the US, I get a mail from Senthil wondering whether I am promoting the gay cause or my own self. I think about this for some time and then reply that I am doing both—at least in my world, they are deeply interlinked. There is sadness too; in mid-2007, one of my interviewees dies in hospital, after complications from a liposuction operation. I go back to my DV tapes and see him—happy, healthy, with a loud booming voice; so articulate and so full of life. [I must add here that my involvement continues even today, as a participant and also as a collaborator. We have often partnered with Gay Bombay through my Godrej India Culture Lab to organize events for Mumbai Pride over the years.]

WE ARE FAMILY

Nine p.m. outside VT station in September 2006 and a family of four walk out, after an exhausting but wonderful weekend picnic. They include D and E, two middle-aged men, myself a few years younger and A, a 20-year-old boy. We've just christened D and E the mama and the papa, A as the bachha *and myself as the* dadi-amma *of us all and while doing so, I have been reminded of Kath Weston's assertion that gays and lesbians create families of choice—in addition to, or sometimes, to compensate for the bonds experienced by their blood families.*

My observations at the Gay Bombay picnic throughout the day reinforced her claim. I met S and K—who have been happily married for the past four years. Tears welled up in my eyes as S and K described their relationship to me. Like many other gay couples in the city, they have managed to carve out their own piece of paradise and done so on their own terms. Coming from different religious backgrounds and with a significant age difference between them, I would have thought it might have been difficult, but on seeing the love and commitment that shone from their eyes as they recounted their marriage ceremony (yes, performed in India, in my very own Mumbai city, with garlands, an officiating Hindu priest and an audience of close friends and well-wishers), I realized that first, anything is possible and second, thank god for India, where such creative choices are within the realm of imagination.

There were so many other happy gay couples that I saw at the picnic. But it isn't just the couples that I choose to count as family units—it's the others too—the family-like units of close friends, who came together and hung around each other, caring for each other and laughing and joking with each other, in their own happy self-contained universe. The sexy sarong gang, the hot chaddi *company, the young twinkly twinks, the uncles and aunty brigade, the boys and their fag-hags groups, the international visitor and his posse…all these and more comprised the family-units that made up GB's picnic. Watching them mingle with each other on a rainy wind-swept Kihim beach off the coast of Bombay, was like watching the great Indian family drama play itself out in all its glory. While we were playing A's party games (pea in spoon race!), I really felt like I was an extra in the gay* Hum Aapke Hain Koun! *(There was even the obligatory dog, but unlike HAHK's* Tuffy, *this one didn't oblige by playing umpire and chose instead, to loll in a corner of the bungalow yard, disinterested. I suppose, you can't have everything!)*

Back to the scene outside VT station. My own picnic family of choice must drive itself back to four respective homes. Papa bear has work the next day; mama bear has to catch a flight to Bangalore. Baby bear reaches home and sleeps comfortably in his bed, wrapped securely in the love and support from a gay social network that his companions certainly didn't have at his age. (He's already agreed that he's one lucky bear, on that count!) And this particular bear continues to stare at another ceiling and wonder how his partner is doing, half way around the world.

Ye pal hai wahi, jis mein hai chhupi
Koyi ek sadi, saari zindagi
Tu na poochh raaste mein kaahe
Aaye hain is tarha do raahein
Tu hi toh hai raah jo sujhaaye
Tu hi toh hai ab jo ye bataaye
Chaahe toh kis disha mein jaaye wahi des
Ye jo des hai tera, swades hai tera, tujhe hai pukaara
Ye woh bandhan hai jo kabhi toot nahin sakta

'This moment right here, right now,
Encompasses an eternity,
Hidden within it is a lifetime.
Don't question your forked destiny,
Make sense of it. Choose wisely.
And then, whichever path you choose to walk on,
Know that it leads home.
What calls out to you isn't just a country; it's your homeland.
Your bond with it is eternal and unbreakable'.

—A.R. Rehman/Javed Akhtar *Swades* (Homeland)[88]

Just like the protagonist Mohan Bhargava in *Swades*, I too will eventually have to make sense of my forked destiny. I am back in India now—but do I want to stay and 'light a bulb'?[89] I am loving my job and feel like I kind of belong here. I have felt that in Bombay, since coming back, it has been comforting; but I also felt like I belonged to Boston for the last year of my stay there. At heart, I guess I am a gay Indian and a gay Bombayite most of all. There is a comfort and solidity to being in India that is hard to match anywhere else. But there are so many variables in play—material, emotional, the legal status of my sexual orientation in the two countries…my partner, who is still at MIT, finishing up his Ph.D. my own Ph.D. and academia aspirations, and my parents and old grandparents in India—bonds that have spurred my return to the homeland. I want to choose wisely. The Indian Prime Minister offered NRIs—Non Resident Indians living abroad, a PIO card in 2004 that enabled them to flow in and out of India with ease; perhaps I will go back to the US and choose to become one of them—another drop in the gigantic diaspora of *Non-Returning Indians* that visit the home country every few years, armed with bottles of imported mineral water and energy bars and complaining constantly of the heat and pollution. Or perhaps, I will choose to remain here in India and navigate our relationship via Skype and regular visits; figure out a way to be both here and there—to be multiple, be everywhere....

NOTES

1. Stuart Hall, 'Cultural Identity and Diaspora Identity', in Identity: *Community, Culture, Difference* (Ed. Jonathan Rutherford), (London: Lawrence & Wishart, 1990) p. 223; excerpted in Kathryn Woodward (Ed.) *Identity and Difference*, (London: Sage Publications, 1997), p. 51.
2. Salman Rushdie, *The Ground Beneath Her Feet* (New York: Henry Holt, 1999), p. 7.
3. Throughout, when I use the term 'anthropology', I refer to social or cultural anthropology and not the other anthropology subfields like medical anthropology and so on.
4. Delmos Jones, 'Towards a Native Anthropology', *Human Organization* (Winter 1970) Vol. 29(4), p. 256.
5. John Van Maanen, *Tales of the Field: On Writing Ethnography* (Chicago: University of Chicago Press, 1988), p. 16.
6. Joan Vincent, 'Engaging Historicism', in Richard Fox (Ed.), Recapturing Anthropology: Working in the Present, (Santa Fe: School of American Research Press, 1991), p. 55, as cited in Gupta and Ferguson, op. cit., p. 7.
7. Robert Emerson, Rachel Fretz and Linda Shaw, *Writing Ethnographic Fieldnotes* (Chicago: University of Chicago Press, 1995), p. 1.
8. Tim Plowman, 'Ethnography and Critical Practice' in Brenda Laurel (Ed.), *Design Research: Methods and Perspectives* (Cambridge, MA: MIT Press, 2003), p. 32.
9. Clifford Geertz, 'Thick Description: Toward an Interpretive Theory of Culture', in *The Interpretation of Cultures* (New York: Basic Books, 1973), p. 10.
10. Andreas Witel, 'Ethnography on the Move: From Field to Net to Internet', in *Forum Qualitative Sozialforschung/Forum: Qualitative Social Research.* (January, 2000) Available on the World Wide Web at—http://www.qualitative-research.net/fqs-texte/1-00/1-00wittel-e.htm
11. Ibid.
12. Ibid.
13. Arjun Appadurai, 'Global Ethnoscapes: Notes and Queries for a Transnational Anthropology', in R.G. Fox (Ed.), *Recapturing Anthropology* (Santa Fe: School of American Research Press, 1991) pp. 191–200; cited in Gupta and Ferguson, op. cit., p. 3.
14. John Van Maanen, op. cit., pp. 17–18.
15. Ellen Lewin and William L. Leap (Eds), *Out in Theory: The Emergence of Lesbian and Gay Anthropology* (Urbana: University of Illinois Press, 2002), pp. 2–4.
16. John Edward Campbell, *Getting It on Online: Cyberspace, Gay Male Sexuality, and Embodied Identity* (New York: Harrington Park Press, 2004), p. 7.
17. See http://www.cheskin.com/
18. See http://www.look-look.com/

19. John Van Maanen, op. cit., p. 24.
20. Tim Plowman, op. cit., p. 32.
21. Delmos Jones (op. cit., pp. 251–252) defines fieldwork as 'a process off finding answers to certain questions, or solutions to certain theoretical or practical problems. As such it involves a series of steps, from the definition of the problem to be studied through the collection of data to the analysis of data and the writing up of the results'.
22. Akhil Gupta and James Ferguson (Eds), *Anthropological Locations: Boundaries and Grounds of a Field Science* (Berkeley: University of California Press, 1997), p. 12.
23. George Marcus, *Ethnography through Thick and Think* (Princeton, NJ: Princeton University Press, 1998), p. 79; cited in Andreas Witel, op. cit.
24. Gupta and Ferguson, op. cit., pp. 35–37.
25. Mary Des Chene, 'Locating the Past', in Gupta and Ferguson (Eds), op. cit., p. 71.
26. Ibid, p. 78.
27. James Clifford, 'Spatial Practices', in Gupta and Ferguson (Eds), op. cit., p. 218.
28. Pierre Bourdieu and Richard Nice (Translator), *The Logic of Practice* (Stanford: Stanford University Press,1990 [1980]), p. 25.
29. Renato Rosaldo, *Culture and Truth: The Remaking of Social Analysis* (Boston: Beacon Press, 1989), p. 168.
30. Soheir Morsy, 'Fieldwork in my Egyptian Homeland: Towards the Demise of Anthropology's Distinctive-Other Hegemonic Tradition', in Soraya Altorki and Camilla Fawzia El-Solh (Eds), *Arab Women in the Field: Studying Your Own Society* (Syracuse, NY: Syracuse University Press, 1998), p. 72.
31. Ibid, p. 69.
32. James Clifford (1997), op. cit., p. 215.
33. Kirin Narayan, 'How Native is a "Native" Anthropologist?', *American Anthropologist* (Arlington, VA: American Anthropological Association, 1993), Vol. 95(3), p. 679.
34. Ibid, p. 682.
35. Joanne Passaro, 'You Can't Take the Subway to the Field', in Gupta and Ferguson (Eds), op. cit., pp. 152–153.
36. Kirin Narayan, op. cit., p. 680.
37. Ibid.
38. James Clifford (1997), op. cit., p. 215.
39. Joanne Passaro, op. cit., p. 161.
40. Stuart Hall, 'New Cultures for Old', in Doreen Massey and Pat Jess (Eds), *A Place in the World? Places, Cultures, and Globalization* (New York: Oxford University Press, 1995), p. 206.
41. Gupta and Ferguson, op. cit., pp. 31–32.
42. Delmos Jones, op. cit., p. 252.
43. Altorki and El-Solh, op. cit., p. 8.
44. Soraya Altorki, 'At Home in the Field', in Altorki and El-Solh (Eds), op. cit., p. 57.
45. Delmos Jones, op. cit., pp. 252–256.
46. Kath Weston, in Gupta and Ferguson (1997), op. cit., p. 167.
47. Soheir Morsy, op. cit., p. 73.
48. Gupta and Ferguson, op. cit., p. 17.
49. Kath Weston, in Gupta and Ferguson (1997), op. cit., p. 168.
50. Ibid, pp. 176–177.

51. Seteney Shami, 'Studying Your Own: The Complexities of a Shared Culture', in Altorki and El-Solh (Eds), op. cit., p. 115.

52. Gupta and Ferguson, op. cit., p. 18.

53. Renato Rosaldo (1989), op. cit., p. 168–195; cited in Kirin Narayan, op. cit., p. 676.

54. Kirin Narayan, op. cit., p. 676.

55. Renato Rosaldo (1989), op. cit., p. 181.

56. Thomas Blom Hansen, *Wages of Violence: Naming and Identity in Postcolonial Bombay* (Princeton, NJ: Princeton University Press, 2001), p. 17.

57. See Kamala Visweswaran, *Fictions of Feminist Ethnography* (Minnesota: University of Minnesota Press), 1994.

58. James Clifford, op. cit., p. 213.

59. Ibid, pp. 215–216.

60. Kirin Narayan, op. cit., p. 678.

61. Ibid, pp. 671–672.

62. A newsgroup (like its earlier avatar, the mailing list) is an asynchronous one-to-many online communication device—as opposed to asynchronous one-to-one online communication devices like email, or synchronous communication devices like chat and instant messenger. In common usage, the terms 'newsgroup' and 'mailing list' are used interchangeably and I shall be doing the same in this book.

63. Within this group, there is a provision to post messages to the entire group at large, or to individuals who have already posted on the list—by clicking on the (partially disguised) email link that appears besides their nickname, accompanying their posting.

64. See *Between the Lines: Negotiating South Asian LBGT Identity*, Official Festival Website— http://mit.edu/cms/betweenthelines/

65. In *Life Online: Researching Real Experience in Virtual Space* (Walnut Creek, CA: Altamira Press, 1998, pp. 62–67), Annette Markham conducts her research by carrying out what she calls 'User on the Net' interviews using various 'real time talk' software packages.

66. Suketu Mehta, *Maximum City: Bombay Lost and Found* (New York: Alfred A. Knopf, 2004), p. 14.

67. Brihanmumbai Electric Supply and Transport Undertaking or BEST is the public undertaking that operates Bombay's citywide bus services. Bus number 123 operates on a short route from RC Church in South Bombay to V. Naik Chowk in Tardeo. See official BEST website: http://www.bestundertaking.com/

68. Andrew Strickler, 'Officials in India Strive to Improve Rail Safety for Millions of Riders', *San Francisco Chronicle*, 12 November 2004. http://www.sfgate.com/cgi-bin/article. cgi?file=/chronicle/archive/2004/11/12/MNG2P9PCR11.DTL

69. R. Raj Rao, *The Boyfriend* (New Delhi: Penguin, 2003), p. 1.

70. Suketu Mehta, op. cit., p. 14.

71. Georgina Maddox, 'A Gay Summer', *Indian Express*, 18 July 2004. http://www. indianexpress.com/full_story.php?content_id=51228

72. Renato Rosaldo (1989), op. cit., p. 168–195; cited in Kirin Narayan, op. cit., p. 676.

73. Suad Joseph, 'Feminization, Familism, Self and Politics: Research as a Mughtaribi', in Altorki and El-Solh (Eds), op. cit., p. 35.

74. Lynn Cherny, *Conversation and Community: Discourse in a Social MUD* (Cambridge, UK: Cambridge University Press, 1999) p. 311.

75. Amy Bruckman, 'Studying the Amateur Artist: A Perspective on Disguising Data Collected in Human Subjects Research on the Internet'. Paper presented at the Computer Ethics: Philosophical Enquiries (CEPE) conference, held at Lancaster University, UK, 14–16 December 2001. Accessible on the World Wide Web—http://www.nyu.edu/projects/nissenbaum/ethics_bru_full.html

76. Lynn Cherny (op. cit., p. 312) writes that 'research rigour usually demands that the researcher provide a trail of supporting evidence for another researcher to duplicate her efforts and reach similar conclusions from the data.... privacy protection, on the other hand means thwarting just such a research duplication. However, the ethnographer must be pragmatic about how much effort anyone is likely to take to uncover identities and locations'.

77. Altorki and El-Solh, op. cit., p. 20.

78. Soraya Altorki, op. cit., p. 62.

79. Delmos Jones, op. cit., p. 255.

80. James Clifford (1997), op. cit., p. 202.

81. See Mark J. McLelland, 'Virtual Ethnography: Using the Internet to Study Gay Culture in Japan', *Sexualities* (Sage Publications: 2002) Vol. 5(4), pp. 387–406.

82. David Bell and Gill Valentine (Eds), *Mapping Desire: Geographies of Sexualities* (London: Routledge, 1995), p. 26; cited in John Edward Campbell, op. cit., p. 41.

83. John Edward Campbell, op. cit., p. 41.

84. Ibid, p. 42.

85. Ibid.

86. *Swades* (Homeland) title track (Bombay, India: Ashutosh Gowarikar Productions/T-Series Music, 2004). Music by A.R. Rehman, lyrics by Javed Akhtar.

87. I use the term affectionately, from the title of the opening note from Henry Jenkins, Tara McPherson and Jane Shattuc, 'The Culture that Sticks to the Skin: A Manifesto for a New Cultural Studies', *Hop on Pop: The Politics and Pleasures of Popular Culture* (Duke University Press, 2002), pp. 3–26.

88. *Swades* title track, op. cit.

89. The protagonist *in Swades* has to choose between returning to India to work on basic issues like electricity in his village, or remain at NASA in the US.

6

Media Matters

I begin this chapter by critically examining the coverage of gay-related stories by the Indian press between 1991 and 2007. My methodology consists of surveying over 300 press clippings sourced from the Quentin Buckle Library at the Humsafar Trust and several personal collections, as well as hundreds of web links. I focus on the English language press because it is what is predominantly read by the middle class, both the subject and the context of this book. I emphasize stories that are Bombay-centric although I also draw on all-India stories, whenever needed. This is not a comprehensive survey and since I am scrutinizing only the English language press, the viewpoints expressed are perhaps not exponentially applicable to the rest of India. However, in the face of the lack of alternatives, I am hoping that this work may serve as a precursor to an Indian gay news archive, which would include media coverage in Hindi and Indian regional languages besides English.[1]

Following my overview of the press coverage, I briefly touch upon the gay presence on Indian television in the past decade and Indian films with specifically gay themes. I end the chapter with a summary of select gay-themed books that have emerged from India over the past two decades, both fiction and non-fiction.[2]

My reasons for conducting this media overview are as follows—

(a) It provides a compelling framework of cultural artifacts with which to construct a timeline of the important events and issues in post-liberalized Indian gay history; useful markers of the changing attitudes and beliefs of upper and middle class Indian society during that time span. This attitudinal change along with the discourse around homosexuality in the media has helped catapult gayness into English speaking Indian mainstream consciousness—and as this chapter shows, it has been an interesting progression.

(b) I am in agreement with Appadurai's contention (1996) that since lives today are 'inextricably linked with representations', it is vital to incorporate the 'complexities of expressive representation' (such as the print articles, films, television shows and books I have documented in this chapter) into contemporary ethnographies—and 'not only as technical adjuncts but as primary material with which to construct and interrogate our own representations'.[3] The media and cultural background provided in this chapter segues into (and contextualizes) my respondents' comments quoted throughout this book. We notice that specific themes raised within this chapter regarding issues about family, coming out, neglect of HIV and so on constantly repeat themselves—both within my interviewee responses and my own memoryscape of experiences—and through these repetitions, a composite, fractal shape emerges of what it is like to be gay in contemporary urban Bombay.

LETTING GO

Q puts his hand over my hand in the car and together, we shift the gear stick into reverse. We are happy to have found a parking space near the Homi Bhabha Auditorium, located at the southern-most tip of Bombay in Navy Nagar. The hall inside is packed to its capacity crowd of 1,036 individuals. I often come to this part of the city to visit my friends living at the neighbouring Tata Institute of Fundamental Research housing colony and to take a walk at the complex's private corniche. Today, it is a date—the culmination of a long courtship that involved phone calls, online chat and occasional meetings spread over the past one-and-a-half years. The event is a dance performance by a visiting French troupe—modern ballet set to traditional Bengali Rabindra Sangeet. We are surrounded by Bombay's glitterati; people I know vaguely, having interviewed many of them for Bombay Times.

Soon we will drive back to his empty home (parents out of town for the weekend) and he will make me a candlelight dinner (fresh candles, microwaved dinner), followed by a night of intense lovemaking, where I will use a condom for a blowjob for the first time ever, after looking at Q's medical books about the consequences of not doing so. (The side effect of dating a doctor in training; it tastes ridiculous).

I will wake up at six the next morning, next to a lover for the first time in my life. We will cuddle and have a round of sleepy early morning sex, following which I will quickly grab my clothes and run out of his house to join my building friends—who have rented a bus for the day to take us all to the amusement park Essel World. There I will giggle foolishly in the giant wave pool and on prodding, pronounce mysteriously that the previous night had been the best night of my life.

I will bump into Q outside another auditorium five years later, where he will offer to introduce me to his current boyfriend. I will politely decline and tell him to fuck off, but we will start emailing each other once again. I will stay with him when I visit Boston two years after that, when he will try to feel me up while we share a common bed. I will push his arm away gently and he will mumble sorry and slink away to sleep on the couch. We will not talk about the experience until two years later in my MIT dorm room and then we will talk about everything and I will wish that things could be different. I will finally meet his boyfriend when I return to Bombay for my summer break and find him to be a wonderful, charming and utterly decent sort of chap. I will finally let go of Q.

PRESS COVERAGE OF GAY-RELATED ISSUES PRIOR TO 1991

There was a huge media hullabaloo around the 1927 release of Ugra's *Chocolate*—a compilation of eight short stories in Hindi, dealing with homosexuality. Vanita (2001) writes that this was probably the first public debate in the local Indian press on the topic.[4] Then in 1944, the famous Urdu writer Ismat Chugtai was accused of obscenity (and subsequently acquitted in court) for her short story *Lihaaf* (The Quilt). Published in the journal *Adab-I-Latif* in 1942, the tale 'depicts sex between a neglected wife and her maidservant, witnessed by a horrified girl child. The married woman's husband is only interested in boys'.[5]

Besides the odd scandal here and there, media coverage of gay-related issues in general was extremely rare in India prior to 1991 and limited to the occasional *letter to the editor* of newspapers like *Times of India* by Ashok Row Kavi in 1981 (about the country's first conference of homosexuals held in the city of Hyderabad that year).[6] An interview with *SK*, described as the president of the now-defunct organization, the *Lavndebaaz-i-Hind* (Homosexuals of India) in the 15–31 August 1977 issue of the now-defunct *Onlooker* magazine,[7] is significant because as student-activist Mario D'Penha writes in his blog *Historiqueer*—

> ...It was perhaps the first time in post-colonial India that an open articulation for a more positive recognition of homosexuals by the law was being made. Although, *SK* was asking for legalization and not decriminalization, which seems to be the more legally sound term (and since the original interview was translated by the magazine from Hindustani to English, there is a chance that this may have been lost in translation), I believe it is very significant that the linkage between harassment, the law and law-enforcement was being made and was being publicly articulated in 1977.[8]

D'Penha writes that SK seems to completely stump the interviewer 'because he breaks every stereotype of what one assumes homosexuals to be.... Here is someone who is "very masculine" and has a "deep bass voice" and "looks anything but a homosexual", but is so articulately flamboyant anyway, that he leaves you in complete and utter awe'.[9]

Towards the end of the 1980s, special features on homosexuality began to start appearing in weekly and monthly magazines, like the *Sunday* magazine cover story on Indian homosexuals dated 6 August 1988. This sensitive eight page article is a comprehensive account of the gay environment prevalent in the country then—it comprises interviews with gay men, their families and psychiatrists, lists of gay hangouts in major Indian cities, problems encountered by gay men at home and the workplace, the intense pressure to marry, the AIDS crisis, homosexuality in Indian prisons, class differences, extortion, police harassment, gay prostitution and the lack of a social network for Indian gay men.[10] Earlier that year, *Debonair* (India's *Playboy* equivalent) ran another sensitively-worded special feature on two officers of the women's company of the 23rd Battalion of the police (India's first women's police company) who had created a scandal with their *marriage* to each other (interestingly, by a Hindu priest who on conferring the scriptures maintained that marriage existed between two souls, not two sexes) and their subsequent discharge from the police force.[11] Articles like these played an important role in preparing both readers and journalists for the media deluge that was to follow in the 1990s.

PRESS COVERAGE OF GAY-RELATED ISSUES BETWEEN 1991 AND 2007

The coverage of gay-related issues in the Indian English language press has commingled around five distinct themes.

Being Gay in India

Since 1991, newspaper and magazine articles dealing with the existence of homosexuality in India began to appear on a regular basis. All my interviewees considered this to be a positive marker of change. Those who were in their thirties and older, spoke about their isolation while growing up and the paucity of reference material available for them to access, as well as role models to interact with or emulate. They mined college reference libraries and international magazines like *Time* and *Newsweek* for narratives that they could contextualize their sexuality in. They encountered very few gay people in their day-to-day lives and when they did, it was usually with a feeling of alienation.

In contrast, for my respondents in their twenties, access to information about homosexuality was not that much of an issue—as there was a plethora of press coverage about homosexuality in city tabloids like *Bombay Times* and *Mid-day*, national newspapers and a wide spectrum of magazines.

Some of these articles were positive and almost evangelical in their tone. Consider *Gentleman* magazine's 'Gay: Everything You Wanted to Know about Homosexuality but Were Afraid to Find Out,' published in

August 1991. Its writer, after tracing homosexuality down the ages from Greek mythology to the *Kamasutra* and its existence in India, covers a gamut of issues ranging from theories on what makes people homosexual, the Kinsey report, the difference between homosexuality and being gay, and how one cannot really recognize a gay person. He concludes by fervently declaring that '...nothing matters, not even the object of one's affections, whether it is man, woman, stone, tree, animal, music, ashtrays, penguins...nothing. Pure love—love for love's sake itself...".[12]

On the other hand, *Mid-day*'s 'I Want My Sex' (1993)[13] and *Sunday Mail Magazine*'s cover story 'Homosexuality: A Thorny Issue' (1991)[14] are uninformed, replete with negative stereotypes about homosexuality and gay men; and downright silly! The *Mid-day* piece talks about two different gay men—Shreyas and Rafiq. While the writer paints Shreyas as gay because of 'his childhood fetish for wearing his sister's clothes', Rafiq has been abused as a child 'at the hands of his homosexual uncle, which has led to his ultimate disorientation'. The *Sunday Mail Magazine* article is no better—it laments that since India's 'close-knit family structure' is so 'different from the West, such inclinations in one's progeny [are] very traumatic for the parents' and suggests among others, psychoanalysis and behaviour modification theory as two possible treatments for the 'habit'. It goes on to warn that 'the "gay" is more vulnerable' to AIDS because 'most of them do not stick to a single partner'.

From the end of the 1990s, we begin to see an articulation of a wider range of issues concerning gay life in India. There are many opinion pieces that argue for the acceptance of homosexuality as a part of Indian society.[15] 1998's *Sex Lies, Agony, Matrimony* reflects the changing norm of counsellors advising their gay clients to 'stay single and assert their identity' instead of being forced into an unwilling heterosexual marriage. It also estimates the number of gay people in India to be 13 million and claims that 10.4 million of these are married.[16] The writer of *Bi Bi Love* declares that 'eschewing labels like "straight", "gay" and "bi"' might 'be a move towards simply being a sexual being'.[17] *Men on Call* takes its readers into the world of Bombay's call-boys or male hustlers, 'anywhere between 15 to 25 years' old, who service both male and female clients and use the Internet and local classifieds to conduct their trade.[18] *I Want to Break Free* interviews parents of gay children and articulates their reactions, fears and concerns about their children's homosexuality. ('Love means acceptance. The bottom line is that I want my child to be happy. Unfortunately, the social reality makes this difficult').[19] Other interesting articles relate to depression in the gay community,[20] extortion of gay people via the Internet by blackmailing con artists[21] and the police,[22] efforts by gay support groups to explain that 'love's not only straight' at Bombay colleges on Valentine's Day 2003,[23] coverage of the Indian Roman Catholic church's position on the possibility of homosexuality among its priests;[24] and the debate over issuing condoms to male prisoners within jails as an HIV and STD prevention measure.[25]

Unlike earlier stories, with their 'names have been changed' disclaimers and shadowy illustrations, many 'coming out' stories after 2000 have featured gay men and women confidently being quoted with their full names and accompanied by their real pictures.[26] The excellently researched *Gay Spirit*[27] (2004) captures the confident tone of the emergent pan-Indian gay movement 'revolutionizing minds' across the country.

During our conversations, most of my respondents told me that the increased media coverage had enabled them to feel more confident about their homosexuality—they considered it a validation of their existence, a visibilizing of what was hitherto invisible.

Of course, not all the coverage was affirmative or balanced. Sensational news stories and scandals involving homosexuality tended to be reported (and often misreported) by the press with relish. *Gay couple stabs each other* describes the tragic suicide pact carried out to its conclusion by two men in 1992, 'following the non-recognition of their marriage by society'.[28] In a similar vein, *Lesbians' death wish* reports that 24 women, 'mostly from marginalized communities, especially Dalits, *Adivasis* and Muslims' committed suicide in the south Indian state of Kerala between the years of 1998–2004.[29] In 2005, a property feud among members of one of India's oldest business families received quite a bit of salacious coverage as it involved a sex change operation of one of the warring siblings.[30]

In 2001, the offices of the Lucknow-based HIV prevention NGOs—Naz Foundation International and *Bharosa*—were raided by the police and nine outreach workers from the two organizations were arrested. It is shocking to note that every major Indian newspaper misreported this incident based on a PR feed provided by the Lucknow police. So the *Asian*

Age story was titled *Two NGO-run gay clubs busted in Lucknow*[31] while *Indian Express'* headline ran as *Police busts gay clubs in Lucknow*.[32] The *Asian Age* story falsely reports that the police 'seized pornographic literature and blue film cassettes' from the offices of the NGOs while the *Express* story claims that the workers were 'charged with abetment of sodomy and criminal conspiracy' and quotes the Lucknow police chief saying that the gay clubs had a 'membership of at least 500'. On a positive note, these allegations by the police coupled with the media's callous coverage of the incident led to the galvanizing of several voices of dissent from the country's LBGT activist community and thankfully, some of these found their way into mainstream media reportage.[33] (Some of my respondents declared that they were drawn to activism after reading about this particular incident).

Five years later, a similar situation arose, once again in Lucknow and once again, the police-guided media coverage was sensational with headlines like *Gay club running on net unearthed—four arrested* and *Cops bust gay racket*. This time, the activists were ready to galvanize against the police brutality, with rallies in Delhi and Bombay which were covered by television networks like Sahara Samay, Aaj Tak, Headlines Today, CNN-IBN and Doordarshan, as well as several newspapers.[34] The police and state response to the NGO outcry was simply to assert that 'Homosexuality [was] a crime as heinous as murder'.[35] Here, I want to note some comments by the senior police and government officials handling the case, as carried by the news media, that highlight the thought processes, beliefs and actions of the authorities and sharply bring into light the need for repealing the Section 377 at the soonest.

Alok Sinha, principal home secretary—'The law of the land is against homosexuality, so the action taken by our police was absolutely valid… The men were arrested under the provisions of Section 377 of the Indian Penal Code (IPC) that prohibits homosexuality; and as long as the law prevails, police were well within their right to book people indulging in gay acts'.

Ashutosh Pandey, senior superintendent of police—'The group had established online Internet links with gay groups outside the country too and strictly speaking, these groups too could be liable under the abetment laws in India…. If laws were made against homosexuality in

India, it must have been done keeping in view the Indian social ethos and moral values.... The law prohibits homosexuality even with consent; and if a 10-year imprisonment is laid out for the offence, it ought to be treated as a crime nearly as heinous as murder'.[36]

Another sensational story was the murder of USAID employee Pushkin Chandra in Delhi in August 2004, along with his close friend Vishal (sometimes reported as being named Kuldeep). The initial coverage only tended to highlight the police discovery of the naked bodies of the victims in Chandra's home, the recovery of 'at least 100 nude photographs' of Delhi-based men that were 'said to have taken part in several orgies with him' and the conjecture that Chandra was part of a 'homosexual syndicate which went out of its way to rope in fresh members' and 'force' these new recruits into photographed sex.[37] As Vikram Doctor wrote in a *Times of India* op-ed—'One wonders why the killers of Pushkin are still bothering to hide the Delhi Police working through their tame media contacts has given them their defence. They simply need to claim that they were lured into the gay sex networks that we are told trap young men like this and forced into doing what they did'.[38] He adds that the murders should be seen against the backdrop of an increase in criminal extortion and blackmail and it is this that the police should 'focus on, rather than taking the easy way out by blaming the victim and letting the villain off the hook'. The quality of the coverage improved in the days that followed, no doubt, due to the active efforts of LBGT activists across the country.[39] The Pushkin case has been the most publicized, but there are several less high-profile *gay murder* stories that the media has had a field day reporting. (For example, *Horror story of unnatural sex and murder*).[40]

Gay Activism

The launch of Ashok Row Kavi's *Bombay Dost* in May 1990 was widely reported in the English language press. *Sunday Mid-day* provided an account of the launch party of the magazine where 'the editorial board of *Bombay Dost* went public with their identities'.

At the bash was a prominent architect with his live-in lover, a senior chartered accountant. A lesbian couple. And assorted gays, of both sexes. And all spoke to the media with little traces of hesitation....[41]

Bombay magazine declared that the advent of *Bombay Dost* 'usher[ed] in the gay revolution' in the country and presented a humorous account of the magazine editors' decision to mail out copies of the inaugural issue to select 'industrialists, businessmen, advertising and print media men', all 'ostensible closet queens', who, 'because of their public stature may be reluctant to "be a part of the movement" but might at least, at some point in the future, send *Bombay Dost* a few cheques!'[42] The article goes on to describe a very clear future trajectory for the magazine and its cause—and the press clippings collected over the years at the Quentin Buckle library bear witness to the achievements of each of the goals outlined by the magazine's founders in 1990. A parallel development was the establishment of the public charity—The Humsafar Trust in 1991, (again spearheaded by Row Kavi) with the mandate of working in the field of HIV/AIDS awareness or prevention (see section on HIV/AIDS below). The various activities of both organizations over the years are well documented, such as *Bombay Dost*'s incorporation (1993),[43] the establishment of the Trust's permanent centre on 31 October 1995 (in collaboration with the Bombay Municipal Corporation, which allotted it five rooms at its Municipal Health Building in North-West Bombay),[44] the creation of the country's first voicemail service for Bombay's gay community[45] followed shortly by a sexuality helpline manned by trained counsellors;[46] and the flashy inauguration of the spanking new drop-in centre at the trust's premises.[47]

Coverage of gay conferences and seminars increased significantly over the years, as the events themselves became more high profile and public in their nature. However, some things remained the same. Thus if 'secrecy was the hallmark of'[48] the first gay activists' meet organized by Humsafar and the Naz Foundation in Bombay in 1995, (an event attended by 'over 60 delegates from various Indian cities as well as from London, New York and Colombo')[49] the venue of a two-day workshop on 'Strategies to advance lesbian, gay and bisexual rights' conducted in Bombay in 1997[50] was hush-hush too, as was the location of the first Asian regional conference of the Brussels-based world wide International Lesbian and Gay Association (ILGA) held in Bombay in 2002. ('The participants fear it will be disrupted…').[51]

The ILGA conference drew an unprecedented amount of media coverage—photographs and interviews with international delegates like ILGA Secretary-General Anna Leah Sarabia De Leon and her partner Maria Victoria Dizon,[52] Sri Lankan activist Rosana Flamer-Caldera[53] and Sandip Roy, the editor of the US-based diasporic gay magazine *Trikone*[54] were circulated widely. There were also several quotes in newspapers from UNIFEM's (The United Nation Development Fund for Women) Shelly Kaw,[55] Naz Foundation's Shaleen Rakesh,[56] Sangini's Betu Singh,[57] Aanchal's Geeta Kumana[58] and Nepal-based activist Sunil Pant.[59] The sponsors of the conference—UNAIDS (The Joint United Nations Program on HIV/AIDS), UNIFEM, UNDP (United Nations Development Program), IAVI (International AIDS Vaccine Initiative) and the MacArthur Foundation[60]—were afforded a significant amount of publicity as well; and while the ubiquitous Humsafar naturally hosted the event (assisted by city-based lesbian support group Aanchal), the broad-based nature of the publicity garnered was significant.

Three other national gay conferences also drew media attention. The first was a National Law School of India public seminar on gay rights in 1997, held within the premises of the prestigious Bangalore institute, with the permission of the school authorities.[61] The second was a three day conference in Bombay in 2000, entitled 'Looking into the Next Millennium,' attended by activists from the country's LBGT communities, which discussed 'the new emerging identities of people having same-sex relations and problems arising from re-allocation of genders, the human rights issues around sexuality, the sexual health issues which confront gay women and men and the looming epidemic of HIV/AIDS in India'.[62] Finally, the International Conference on Sexualities, Masculinities and Cultures in South Asia was attended by over 200 delegates from all over the world in 2004 in Bangalore.[63] The World Social Forum, organized in January 2004 in Bombay, was another venue for the different Indian LBGT groups to espouse their cause in the full glare of the international media present. From the drag show by a Malaysian transgender performance troupe that had some nuns storm out of the event in disgust,[64] to the perceived neglect by some city based gay and lesbian groups to their cause by the Forum organizers,[65] the global media representatives that converged in Bombay for the event covered it all.

India's first public gay demonstration was organized by the collective AIDS *Bhedbav Virodhi Andolan* (ABVA, 'Campaign Against AIDS Discrimination') in front of the police headquarters in New Delhi as a protest against raids by the Delhi police on gay patrons of the city's Central Park. Photographs of the event were circulated via the Press Trust of India (one of the country's major news agencies) to most leading Indian newspapers. They show a group of activists holding up handmade banners and posters with slogans such as 'Human Rights is the Issue, Not Sexuality', 'Gay Manifesto: Gays of the World, unite. You have nothing to Lose but your Chains' and 'Down with Section 377'.[66] We have already examined the media coverage about Section 377 in Chapter 4.

The first Indian gay *pride march* was held in Calcutta on 29 June 1999, to commemorate the 30th anniversary of the Stonewall riots in New York City. Although only 15 activists took part in the initial 'friendship walk',[67] it became a recurring annual feature[68]—the 'Walk on the Rainbow' marches held between 2004–2007—have all had about 300 activists marching proudly through the city, escorted by the police[69] and followed by print and television news reporters. There have been media reports of marches and demonstrations in smaller cities like Patna as well.[70] Bombay's first public demonstration was a public protest on 27 September 2001 against the arrest of the Naz Foundation or Bharosa HIV/AIDS outreach workers some months earlier and it comprised protesters belonging to several city-based gay, lesbian and human rights organizations (including Aanchal, Humsafar, Stree Sangam, Lawyers' Collective HIV/AIDS unit, Forum Against Oppression of Women and the Arawanis Social Welfare Society) gathering together at the city's historic Flora Fountain.[71] There have been sporadic marches and public protests in the city since, duly covered by the media, such as the candlelight walk to commemorate World AIDS Day 2003,[72] or the 2004 march to protest the crusade of the political party Shiv Sena against the controversial film *Girlfriend*,[73] or the Rainbow March at the World Social Forum 2004 held in Bombay, which comprised gays, lesbians, *hijras* and sex-workers marching side by side.[74]

One can estimate the extent of progress of gay activism in the country through the 1990s by comparing two press clipping—just six years apart from each other. 1994's *Bringing down stonewalls* notes that 'if one would look more closely, there is a quickening pulse towards a formation of a gay and lesbian community in the country, which could, given a mass structure with aims and activities, turn into a movement'.[75] The article makes several sharp observations about the potential roadblocks on the way to the formation of such a movement (an insular Indian gay community, class barriers, differences with the lesbian movement). Fast-forward to *Action Stations* (2000)—'The disorganized gay community joins forces, starting a series of support groups, helplines, websites and networking opportunities'.[76]

An *Indian Express* article dated 17 July 1991[77] quotes an official from the Indian Council of Medical Research responding to a question of how he planned to work with the gay community regarding AIDS awareness. 'There may only be about 60,000 of them in India...[and] if they die, not many tears will be shed'. The article quotes Ashok Row Kavi's counter-assertion that using the Kinsey average of 5 per cent homosexuals in any society, India would have '11 million permanent practicing homosexuals' and goes on to list the magnitude of the problem that confronts the country. The journalist telephones 11 city-based doctors to see if they know what AIDS stands for and it is shocking to note that not even one of these can provide a completely correct answer—many of them simply hang up on him or refuse to answer!

The apathy towards any gay involvement in the governmental efforts to battle HIV/AIDS continued in 1992—an international conference on AIDS in Asia and the Pacific held in the country's capital, New Delhi, ignored homosexual concerns completely. The parallel AIDS meet organized by the international gay activists at a public park in the city was widely reported by the press.[78] Earlier that year, the World Health Organization at its annual AIDS congress in Amsterdam had cautioned the Indian govern-ment of 'a possible outbreak of AIDS among the homosexual population of Bombay' with the congress director warning that 'the fact that only very few HIV infected cases have been found so far in the gay population should not dull government's surveillance efforts'.[79] Humsafar's 2004 study of 240 homosexual men in Bombay city, conducted with the help of the Indian Market Research Bureau reported that 20 per cent of those surveyed were HIV positive, something that the press picked up on.[80] But my overall observation remains that the press coverage of HIV, whether gay-related or not, has been extremely disappointing in India. Given that the country now has the second highest number of AIDS sufferers in the world—official figures put the 2003 number at 5.1 million; only marginally behind South Africa's 5.3 million[81] (but most aid agencies say it is much higher and will reach 25 million by 2010)[82]—one sincerely hopes that they will pull up their socks soon!

Out Public Figures

While the Indian media has often speculated about the sexuality of celebrities from the world of entertainment, business and even politics, very few of these have actually unambiguously declared their homosexual orientation. Several of these celebrities live in pretty visible relationships with their same-sex partners and are often seen burning up the dance floors of their city discotheques at gay parties and events. While they might not publicly deny their homosexuality, they do not acknowledge it either.[83] For instance, the homosexuality of Rohit Khosla, India's first *haute couturier* was only written about at his untimely death.[84]

One of the first out Indian celebrities was the artist Bhupen Khakhar whose paintings (starting with 1981's provocative *You Can't Please All* and including among several others, 1987's *Yayati* and 1995's *Old Man from Vasad Who Had Five Penises Suffered from Runny Nose*) have become 'as Hockney's did in the West, emblematic for a whole generation of homosexuals in India'.[85] Khakhar's musings about his homosexuality in the press ('I told lies. I did not have courage to say I was going to meet my boyfriend. Gandhi spoke truth but I was coward';[86] 'There is no escaping the fact that homosexuality is an integral part of human existence').[87] forced 'the vast terrain of half-urbanized modern India'[88] that his work drew from, to deal with the subject, albeit flinchingly. Fashion designer James Ferreira has been direct about his homosexuality. ('I am what I am and I have never been ashamed of myself. I have had very intense meaningful relationships with men…').[89] In 2006, Mumbai's high-society designer Krsna Mehta came out in a newspaper interview.[90]

Another fashion designer, Goa based Wendell Rodricks, caused a stir when he exchanged vows with his French partner Jerome Marrel at a celebrity-studded event on 26 December 2002.[91] A senior consular official from the French government conducted the ceremony, at which the couple signed an official French Civil Solidarity Pact (PACS). Wendell and Jerome navigate the social high life very openly as a gay couple. Indian fashion's enfant terrible, designer Rohit Bal, has also been very open about his homosexuality—'I think I am too damn sexy. I am attractive because I am so cool about my sexuality. It is a part of me'.[92]

In June 2006, Prince Manvendra Singh Gohil of the royal family of Rajpipla—a small principality in the western state of Gujarat, came out as a homosexual in the media. The story was picked up by various national and international newspapers in India and abroad as *the gay Indian prince* story. Initially, the royal family reacted negatively to the publicity— effigies of the prince were burnt in the *Holi*[93] fire in Rajpipla and adver- tisements were published in local newspapers disowning him from his title. Within three months however, the prince and his family had reconciled and the prince was even contemplating adopting a child as his legal heir![94]

Writers like Firdaus Kanga, R. Raj Rao and Vikram Seth have all alluded to their own sexuality in their work. Rao has been publicly outspoken regarding his homosexuality and activist identity for many years. ('The word "activism" is not a dirty word for me as it is for other writers... I can- not stay in my ivory tower and ignore calls of help from gay men who are on the verge of committing suicide or are being hounded by cops or harassed by blackmailers').[95] As a university professor, Rao has started the Queer Studies Circle at Pune University, where he teaches and conducted informal courses on Queer Literature.[96] Other publicly out academicians include Somenath Banerjee, the Calcutta based transsexual senior professor of Bengali, who 'walks into class dressed as a woman, complete with showy earrings, matching lipstick and eye make-up'[97] and Hyderabad based professor/poet/activist Hoshang Merchant ('As everyone knows by now, I am a homosexual. To write this sentence and to speak it publicly, which is a great liberation, is why I write').[98] Seth's sexual- ity was often gossiped upon, but his *official* outing was in his mother's Justice Leila Seth's autobiography—*On Balance* (New Delhi: Viking, 2003),[99] following which he has become increasingly visible and involved in the campaign against Article 377 in India. In 2006, he was the spearhead of a very public letter writing campaign to repeal the law and in the several print and television interviews that he gave in relation to this initiative, he was comfortable to mention his bisexuality.[100] There have also been a few articles over the past few years where celebrities have been asked their views on homosexuality—and these have largely been positive, at least in the English press.[101]

Makeup guru Cory Walia,[102] late filmmaker Riyad Wadia[103] and the flamboyant actor Bobby Darling[104] are some of the other celebrities that have created a stir with their confident public assertion of their homosexuality. This list would not be complete without Ashok Row Kavi—he has single-handedly carried the responsibility of being the 'country's most public gay man'[105] for more than two decades.

Changing Public Perception

For this, let me point to three different sex surveys that span the 15 years of my research interests.[106] The *Debonair* magazine sex survey in 1991 claimed to present 'the country's first study of the sexual habits of Indian males'.[107] Despite its relatively modest base size of 1,424 respondents, the survey throws up some startling results with respect to homosexuality. For example, out of the respondents who have had sexual intercourse (81 per cent), 36.8 per cent report to have done so with another male. (This includes 32 per cent of married men and 41.7 per cent of unmarried men). Other interesting statistics are that the wives of 31 per cent of married men are aware of their homosexual behaviour and 17 per cent of the respondents claim to engage in homosexual group sex! The widely publicized[108] Kama Sutra Sex Survey 2004[109] conducted in the top 10 cities in India (sponsored by Kama Sutra condoms), is more comprehensive—it includes both men and women and has a much larger sample (13,437 married and unmarried individuals aged 18 and above). 17 per cent of the respondents acknowledge being attracted to a person of the same sex and within this category, 51 per cent acknowledge having had sex with a person belonging to the same sex. While 43 per cent believe that homosexuality is taboo, only 8 per cent feel that it is normal to be attracted to a person of the same sex. Sandwiched between these two reports is the *Outlook* magazine survey, conducted among 1,665 married men and women in eight cities in India in 1996, where 15 per cent of the respondents admitted to having engaged in homosexual activities and 30 per cent believed that homosexuality was 'a normal practice'.[110]

All these surveys were conducted in English, with highly educated urban respondents. (For instance, 67 per cent of the *Debonair* respondents and 88 per cent of the Kama Sutra respondents were university graduates). Yet, as the editors of *Debonair* point out in the piece accompanying their survey, the results are extremely pertinent—they 'reflect the behavior of an extremely important segment of the Indian population—the urban, middle and upper, socio-economic upwardly-mobile section'. And within this segment, as these surveys (and the many others along the same lines) so clearly point out—(*a*) Homosexual sex is alive and kicking and (*b*) Views on it are in a constant flux. Indeed, the concept of masculinity itself is changing—a 2000 survey conducted by the *Week* magazine reports that 71 per cent of the men polled (sample size 1,300) wanted to be seen as macho—but the meaning of macho as constructed by the article accompanying the poll is quite surprising. 'Macho is about all the things that macho was never supposed to be about.... Modern macho is about being a better woman than a woman'![111]

The *vox populi* sections of newspapers and magazines reflect this changing spirit. In 1997, a *Mid-day* question—'Should the law take any action against gays'[112]—received an almost equally split response; a larger survey, conducted by the research firm C Fore among 415 individuals aged between 15–25 in Bombay and Delhi and published in the *Hindustan Times* newspaper, reported that 50 per cent of the people polled were in favour of scrapping Article 377.[113] Respondents to a *Delhi Times* survey in 2004[114] about whether young Indians felt less conservative and more open about sexuality were mostly in the affirmative and a *Bombay Times* survey[115] the same year, about how the respondents would react if they discovered that a friend was homosexual received completely gay-positive reactions from those questioned.

We can also find traces of the changing perception about homosexuality in the advice given out by newspaper and magazine columnists to their readers. Shobha Dé has mostly campaigned for the right of gay men in India to exist with freedom, in her capacity as society columnist (For example—lauding the launch of *Bombay Dost*[116] and the Wendell Rodricks commitment ceremony)[117] and agony aunt.[118] Malavika Sanghvi,[119] Pritish Nandy[120] and Amit Varma[121] have all championed the gay cause in their columns, as have Kiron Kher ('So what if he [one's child] is gay? He is still very normal!')[122], Dilip Raote ('Gay and lesbian activism will transform the 21st century on much the same scale that Einstein and particle physics changed the 20th')[123] and Mayank Shekhar ('They are different people. But what the hell? They exist. That the government lives in denial is no reason why all should').[124] Advice columnists like writer Khushwant Singh,[125] sexologists Prakash Kothari,[126] Mahendra Watsal[127] and psychologist Radhika Chandiramani[128] always answer anxious readers' queries by assuring them that homosexuality is as normal as heterosexuality. Here is a particularly delightful piece of advice, published in the June 2006 issue of *Man's World* magazine—

My boss is a gay man. Everyone in the office knows this and seems to be fine with it. I am too. But how do I respond when he gives me compliments and says things like, 'You are looking great today?'

Do you know what the word *homophobic* means? It means heterosexual men who are shit scared of any sexuality other than their own. And you are a homophobe, you are. No, you did not say, 'Some of my best friends are gay', but you came close. What do you do when he gives you compliments? You do not have to get down on your knees. You just say, 'Hey thanks' and get on with it. Sexual harassment it is not. But then again, gay radicals, say homophobes, are actually closet gay men who cannot come to terms with their own identities. Dr Know does not think so. He thinks some heterosexual men are close-minded morons. Like you are.[129]

On the flipside, Farzana Versey has permanently carried a torch for the homophobes. Her 1990 columns in *Mid-day* are full of virulent gay bashing. Sample these quotes—'Those who go about in queer clothes with uncalled for behavior have no right to talk of acceptance? How many of these guys would not laugh at a circus clown?';[130] 'Homosexuality more often than not, works on the concept of multiple partners';[131] 'Instead of dumping the onus of sexual politics on heteros, it would help if gays took a look at their own sexual paranoia';[132] '...If there has been any infection at all, it has been one by a little virus that says "we will fight back"'.[133] In another column in 1991, she directs her ire at crippled gay writer Firdaus Kanga, urging him to 'get over...his wheelchair, his homosexuality—for the purpose of his literary endeavours'.[134] The vitriol continues in her 2000 piece *The gay glut* (with epithets like 'cocky community' and the by now familiar diatribe about homosexuals being

'the only people whose identity depends on their sexuality' and initiating 'young boys, who probably do not know which way they swing'
into the 'gay cult'),[135] as well as her 2006 column for the *Deccan Chronicle*
'Does it pay to be gay' ('the gay movement is a hugely successful public
relations exercise').[136] Other columnists like Swapan Dasgupta (*Rediff* and
DNA)[137] and Kanchan Gupta for *Pioneer* share Versey's distaste for homosexuals and express it in equally reprehensive language. Section 377 of
the Indian Penal Code is cheered ('Serves the buggers right, too!')[138] and
gay relationships are mocked.

> Imagine having a gay couple as your neighbour in the claustrophobic
> confines of a high-rise housing complex. Their sweet little adopted child,
> back from a friend's birthday party and eager to show off a gift, shrieks—
> 'Pappa*ji*, where is Mummy*ji*?' Daddy gay, who has just had a romp in the
> bed, sings out—'He is in the loo, darling!'[139]

Globalization

In 1980, Vijay Tendulkar's lesbian themed play *Mitrachi Goshta* ('A Friend's
Story') stopped its Bombay run after just 25 shows, 'because people were
simply not interested'.[140] Eighteen years later, the situation was a lot
different when Mahesh Dattani's *On A Muggy Night in Mumbai* had its
premiere performance in Bombay on 15 November 1998. The *Fire* controversy was blazing across the country (see the section on queer films below)
and the *Sunday Times of India* contextualized this play and *Fire* by framing
their openly gay and lesbian themes within a debate on globalization.
In a double spread special titled *Liberalism: can we handle it?* the newspaper stated that it wanted to present 'both sides of an issue that must
be addressed—the pleas of gays for acceptance as normal human beings
with merely another kind of sexual orientation and the arguments of
those who see this an aberration which cannot be allowed to warp a
society already struggling with confusing influences'.[141]

The recent media interest in matters regarding Section 377 also has
globalization overtures. One point of view wonders if it is right for a
country that aspires to be 'a' part of 'the' global scene to victimize its
minorities. As Karan Thapar writes in the *Hindustan Times*, 'by continuing to do so we make a mockery of our commitment to human rights;

leave aside all the Geneva conventions we have signed up to. So, for the sake of our democracy, this must be repealed'.[142] The counter-view wants to protect a certain notion of Indianness from the threat posed by globalization and this includes the threat posed by liberal ideas that deem homosexuality to be normal and legal.

The definitive 'pink' paper—the respected financial daily *Economic Times*—chooses to frame globalization by looking at whether the Indian work place can meet international requirements with regard to issues of sexual orientation.[143] But this is rare—a more typical representation of globalization and gayness in the Indian press would be through the prism of the burgeoning gay party scene. Though veering towards the stereotypical views of gay people as effeminate bitchy drag queens, the early reportage often comes across as hilarious and harmless and even positive at times. ('I ask myself, so what is the big deal anyway? I live my life my way, why should not Sanjay, okay, Mallika if you will—do likewise?').[144] Over the years, the jibes stop and the coverage turns more pragmatic. The Gay Bombay parties are well received ('For those with closed minds—no, this is not sleazy. It is a party, that is all'.);[145] after 2000, the monetary clout of the country's upwardly mobile gay population becomes the subject of a series of *Pink Rupee* articles. ('The business pie has a creamy pink slice and everyone wants a piece of it…pink nights, pink clubs, pink lounge bars and of course pink lifestyle products are the rage…').[146]

Television Coverage

While the satellite television revolution enabled the broadcast of Western television channels into Indian homes from 1992, Indian gay-related issues remained largely invisible until 1995, when a huge controversy erupted around the Star TV talk show *Nikki Tonight*. Ashok Row Kavi, invited on the show as a guest, called Indian independence hero Mahatma Gandhi a 'bastard' on the episode of the show aired on 4 May 1995, a remark that Kavi states was edited completely out of context.[147] The Indian parliament reacted strongly to the programme and Gandhi's great grandson Tushar Gandhi filed a suit for damages. The channel responded by yanking the show off the air and issuing an apology to its viewers. In a related incident, Bollywood actor Saif Ali Khan stormed into Kavi's home and punched him repeatedly over his remarks made about Khan's mother, the former Bollywood actress Sharmila Tagore.[148]

Ashok Row Kavi has remained a permanent fixture on the few talk shows and special reports telecast dealing with gay and lesbian related themes over the years. (A symptom of both, the media's failure to tap into other activists in the community, as well as the disinclination of other activists to be spokespersons for their constituencies, at least on national television, though this is now beginning to change). Thus, he appears on a Star News special report (telecast date 9 September 2003) along with lesbian activist Geeta Kumana, giving his reaction to the government's non-favourable response to removal of Section 377 and the next day on a SAB TV talk show hosted by actress and right-wing politician Smriti Irani—*Kuch Dil Se* ('From the Heart')—discussing the issue of married gay men. He is present once again as part of a panel discussion on the film *Girlfriend* on Doordarshan Marathi (telecast date 25 June 2004) where he draws the ire of the *Shiv Sainiks*[149] in the live audience for calling the Sena's cultural policing of films like *Girlfriend* 'a Taliban-like act'[150] and again, on NDTV (with Geeta Kumana) on NDTV 24x7's *The Big Fight* aired on 21 August 2004.

There has been an increase in gay-related news stories on all the major television networks, especially around controversies like *Fire* and *Girlfriend* protests and the 2004 gay double murders in Delhi. The special reports on homosexuality and gay rights in India produced by the television networks have ranged from uninformed (Zee News—'Homosexuality in India'; telecast date 5 December 2003) and bizarre (India TV—'Homosexuality and Astrology'; telecast date 7 October 2006) to energetic and encouraging (CNBC India—'Tonight at Ten'; telecast date 25 August 2004; Zoom TV—'Just Pooja' episodes'; telecast dates 16 April 2005 and 31 December 2005). I want to note the content and tone of one particular show here—a special programme on Zee News titled *'Pyar Ka Vyapar'* ('The business of love') telecast on 3 July 2006 at 9.30 p.m. The show, in Hindi, made outrageous claims equating gayness to prostitution and the spread of AIDS because of their 'addiction to gay sex' and also alleged that gay networks were slowly 'spreading their web' all over north India. It interviewed a few men who the reporter claimed had slept with '25–30' persons daily, without a condom; and concluded by informing viewers that some of these gay men had since given up their 'vice' and resorted to jewellery making as a means of earning an honest living. There was an equally misleading, misinformed and wrongly named series on CNN-IBN aired for one week, starting 10 April 2006, called 'The Third Sex', which reported luridly, among others, stories of a gay man acquiring HIV virus so as to be 'together' with his married male partner.

Just as they have done in print, India's gay celebrities, with the exception of some like Vikram Seth, have shied of talking to television media about their sexuality. The media, by and large, has tacitly complied with the subterfuge. Thus, an episode of the Star World talk show *Rendezvous With Simi Garewal* (telecast date 20 September 2002), where the host interviews the high profile gay fashion designer couple Abu Jani and Sandeep Khosla about everything—meeting each other for the first time, partnering each other at work, living with each other, tiffs and quarrels—everything except their homosexuality! The couple also co-anchored a reality show together (*Lakme Fashion House*, which was telecast between January to April 2005) where again, their coupledom was obvious and the participants and invited guests all clearly treat them as a couple, but it was never explicitly stated.

In contrast, ordinary gay men are slowly being visible on Indian television screens, mainly in talk shows and panel discussions related to homosexuality or Article 377. For example, the panel discussion show on CNN IBN *Minus 30* (telecast on 23 September 2006) had several ordinary non-celebrity, non-activist, just regular guy-next-door type of people, like Praful, a PR professional; and an episode of *Life's Like That* on Times Now (telecast on 12 September 2006) titled 'What's Life Like for a Homosexual in Urban India?' had corporate trainer Ali Potia and web developer Rudra, both in their mid-20s, frankly discussing their day-to-day experiences.

In late 2003, the popular Sony soap opera *Jassi Jaisi Koi Nahin* ('There's No One Like Jassi') was in the news[151] because of one of its characters—Maddy, a gay fashion designer with over-the-top mannerisms and a penchant for bullying Jassi, the show's main lead. Episodes of the show telecast on 1 December 2003 and 2 December 2003, featured a gay club, a gay kiss and a bet between Maddy and his boss (who visits the gay club searching for Maddy), which the boss eventually loses. The penalty—the boss dresses up in a drag (in the episode telecast on 19 January 2004) and accompanies Maddy to a party as his 'baby doll'!

CONTEMPORARY INDIAN WRITING ON HOMOSEXUALITY

The publication of the literature and reportage mentioned in this chapter has provided a vast account of the history and contemporary struggles around queer Indian sexuality—making it increasingly difficult for the mainstream to claim that queerness is a Western import. More importantly, it has enabled queer Indians (or at least those with access to such material) to find for themselves, the *narratives in an Indian context* that they so desperately sought.

In July 1991, a tiny boxed advertisement appeared in the inside pages of the *Times of India*, which read—'Book on Gays: A Delhi journalist, Mr Arvind Kala, is writing a sympathetic book, *The World of Indian Gays*. He invites gays to talk to him in confidence about their feelings and emotions. Telephone: 230247'.[152] A year and 112 interviews later, Mr Kala had churned out his book. Now titled *Invisible Minority: The Unknown World of the Indian Homosexual*,[153] the far-from-sympathetic account was published to almost universal denouncement as a 'badly written'[154] piece of work, intended perhaps for 'the round eyed, half-price scandal seeker'[155] instead of a more serious audience. Jeremy Seabrook's *Love in a Different Climate* (1999) turned out to be an infinitely better book produced using a similar methodology. (The author spent some months in 1997 interviewing 75 'men who have sex with men'[156] in Delhi. Most of the interviews were conducted in one of the city's public parks—a popular cruising ground and the subjects formed a cross section of Delhi's homosexual population).

Seabrook's book is elegant, intelligent and reflexive—his sensitivity to the testimony of his subjects and perceptive analysis is striking compared to the gross crudeness of Kala's effort. (Seabrook's attempt appears nobler too—his inspiration for writing stems out of the HIV prevention work being carried out by the Naz Project in Delhi, while it seems apparent that all Kala wants to do is milk a sensational topic for some quick bucks). Unfortunately, *Love in a Different Climate* is not available in

India; I wish the same could be said for Kala's book. Three other books conspicuous by their absence from Indian bookshelves are *Sakhiyani: Lesbian Desire in Ancient and Modern India* (1996), *The Man Who Was a Woman and Other Queer Tales* (2002) and *Tritiya-Prakriti: People of the Third Sex* (2003). Vanita (2001) also mentions Leslie de Norhona's *Dew Drop Inn* (1994) and P. Parivaraj's *Shiva and Arun* (1998);[157] neither of which is available within the country.

There have been four significant anthologies of Indian gay and lesbian writing published so far. First off the block in 1993 was Rakesh Ratti's (Ed.) *A Lotus of Another Colour: An Unfolding of the South Asian Gay and Lesbian Experience*. The book is primarily concerned with issues concerning the South Asian LBGT diaspora living in Western countries and aims at increasing their visibility in 'both the South Asian and gay and lesbian communities'[158] they inhabit. It consists of essays, poems, autobiographical and fictional short stories and interviews without South Asian celebrities like activist Urvashi Vaid and filmmaker Pratibha Parmar.

The two Penguin India releases in 1999—*Yaarana: Gay Writing from India* and *Facing the Mirror: Lesbian Writing from India* follow more or less the same formula, but with contributors that reside mainly in India. *Because I Have a Voice: Queer Polics in India* (New Delhi: Yoda Press, 2006) is another India-focused collection, edited by Gautam Bhan and Arvind Narrain. Narrain is part of a small but growing tribe of recent National Law School of India (Bangalore) graduates, committed to applying their legal background to queer rights and legal advocacy, while Bhan is a queer rights activist based in Delhi and one of the founders of the city's Nigah Media Collective. Their book has 30 contributors who are trying to create a conceptual framework for understanding the varied sexuality related struggles taking place in the country, narrating tales from the battleground, as well as their own personal journeys.

For many years now, R. Raj Rao (poet, professor, activist) has been the public face of gay Indian literature. His searing collection of short stories *One Day I Locked My Flat in Soul City* (1995) contains several angst-ridden gay-themed pieces. An obsessive and masochistic lover pining for his former flame (now turned straight); a patient narrating his wild sexual fantasies in a psychoanalyst's chamber; a homosexual rape in a police station; a gay man who has a sex change to capture the heart of his beloved and upon failing, decides to turn lesbian; a murderous rioter who decides to suck off his victim instead of killing him…Rao's world is melancholic and gritty, inhibited with characters that are both sad and mad. In 1996, six of Rao's poems from his still-in-progress *BomGay* were filmed by documentary filmmaker Riyad Wadia as India's first gay film—*BOMgAY*. In 2003, Rao released his first novel, *The Boyfriend*, which was widely publicized as India's first gay novel in English. (Authors like Vikram Seth,[159] Vikram Chandra[160] and Firdaus Kanga[161] had all written about gay themes, but Rao's work was the first to be fully pivoted around homosexuality).

The Boyfriend is bleak, hard-hitting and darkly funny. Rao is uncompromising in his examination of Bombay's gay subcultures and the thorny issues of caste, class and religion that are stirred up when 40-something freelance journalist Yudi picks up Milind, a 19-year old Dalit (lower caste) boy at a railway station public toilet and embarks on a tempestuous love affair with him, despite the odds being heavily stacked against its success. The book is peppered with a band of distinctive characters like stubborn fag-hag Gauri, AK modelling agency's pumped up gigolos, dance club Testosterone's feisty queens, blackmailing cop Dyaneshwar…. It literally throbs of Bombay—one can feel the crush of the sweltering train journeys up and down the city's longitudinal rail corridors, taste the grime of the putrid slums, witness furtive sexual encounters in public spaces and hear the earthy vernacular slang used by its homosexual inhabitants.

Ruth Vanita's three books—*Same Sex Love in India* (2001, Co-authored with Saleem Kidwai), *Queering India* (2002) and *Love's Rite: Same-Sex Marriage in India and the West* (2005)—are worthy of canonical status among the body of Indian LBGT writing. Vanita's agenda for *Same Sex Love* is simple—to 'help assure homoerotically inclined Indians that large numbers of their ancestors throughout history and in all parts of the country shared their inclination and were honoured and successful members of society, who contributed in major ways to thought, literature and the general good'.[162] The book has a grand sweep, which extends across ancient, medieval (Sanskritic and Persian-Urdu) and modern Indian texts (some of them in English, but most of them translated from different Indian languages like Tamil, Rajasthani, Gujarati, Bengali, Marathi and Oriya). *Queering India* is completely contemporary—comprised of academic essays divided into three sections—'Colonial Transitions', 'The Visions of Fiction' and 'Performative Pleasures in Theatre, TV and Cinema'. *Love's Rite* was released in the midst of the whole gay marriage debate in the US and it covers impressive terrain, discussing gender, spirituality, the law and the state, parenting, reproduction and the changing concept of families; from pre-modern to contemporary times.

Maya Sharma's 2006 book—*Loving Women: Being Lesbian in Unprivileged India*[163] is an account of the lives of 10 working-class lesbian women in north India—it is an important work that breaks the myth that lesbians, or queer people in general, in India, are upper class English speaking and urban.

The excellent report—*Less than Gay: A Citizens' Report on the Status of Homosexuality in India* was prepared by the New Delhi-based AIDS Bhedbhav Virodhi Andolan (ABVA) in 1991. There was a 10-year gap until the next widely circulated LBGT community report—2002's *Humjinsi: A Resource Book on Lesbian, Gay and Bisexual Rights in India*, published from Bombay.[164] The rise in Bangalore-based LBGT activism in the past few years has resulted in three major publications. PUCL or The People's Union for Civil Liberties in Karnataka (the south Indian state of which Bangalore is the capital) has published two reports documenting various types of harassments against India's different sexual minorities. The 44-page 2001 report titled *Human Rights Violations Against Sexual Minorities in India*[165] is divided into four sections. Section One provides an overview of the status of sexual minorities in India. Section Two lists various discriminations faced by LBGT people by the state (legal, system, police, and so on). Section Three lists societal discriminations (family, workplace, public spaces, medical establishment and the popular media); while Section Four deals with the impact of discrimination on the individual self. The organization's 2003 publication titled *Human Rights Violations Against the Transgender Community*[166] is more specifically focused on *hijra* and *kothi* sex workers being victimized by the Bangalore police and other authorities. 2004 witnessed the publication of Arvind Narrain's much-needed monograph *Queer: Despised Sexuality, Law and Societal Change*. Important sections of his monograph include an overview of the legal discourse surrounding queer sexuality in ancient, medieval and colonial India, the contemporary context in which the legal opposition to discrimination against queer sexuality in India is being played out (constitutional challenge to Section 377, campaign for progressive law reform, building a database of human rights violations perpetrated by the state against queer subjects) and a valuable resource list of groups working on sexuality issues throughout the country.

Sexuality, Gender and Rights: *Exploring Theory and Practice in South and Southeast Asia* (New Delhi: Sage Publications, 2005) is another recent book that aims at looking at sexuality rights discourse through a larger Asian prism; its editors Geetanjali Misra (from CREA or Creating Resources for Empowerment in Action, New Delhi) and Radhika Chandiramani (from TARSHI or Talking About Reproductive and Sexual Health Issues, New Delhi), have collated 15 essays from eight different countries, including India, that make relevant links between theory and practice, scholars and activists, rights, advocacy and outreach.

I wish to briefly reflect on two major gay *Indian* texts written before 1991–1932's *Hindoo Holiday* and 1977's *The World of Homosexuals*. *Hindoo Holiday* was written by J.R. Ackerley, a 20-something homosexual, Cambridge-educated, war-returned dilettante who spent five months in India in 1923 as the secretary to the (also homosexual) *Maharaja* of Chhatarpur. On his return to England, Ackerley fashioned his Indian diaries into a pacy travelogue and the book—published first in 1932 (when it was considered too sexy to be read aloud on BBC radio!) and then republished subsequently in more explicit editions in 1952 and 1979—became an instant classic. I am considering this as an *Indian* book because of its widespread availability in Indian libraries—for Indian homosexuals rummaging through library bookshelves and looking for characters closer to home in the decades prior to liberalization, this was often a refreshing find.

Hindoo Holiday weaves desire, palace intrigue and Indian customs adroitly together—laced with the wry humour that Ackerley would later become famous for as the literary editor of *The Listener* magazine from 1935 to 1959. By renaming Chattarpur as Chokrapur (City of Boys), Ackerley is upfront about his intentions. He vividly describes the physical attractiveness of the various young men he encounters during his travels and comically recounts the *Maharajah*'s pining for the performing boy actors of his kingdom. We learn, among several other juicy tidbits, that one of the king's peccadilloes includes forcing his young queen to make love with one of his regular bisexual playmates in his presence!

Ackerley's prose, as Eliot Weinberger writes in the 2000 introduction of the book's reprint edition, is 'entirely without the psychodrama or the Hellenistic pretensions that were common among gay writers at the time'[167]—it is natural, guilt-free, evocative and makes for extremely pleasurable reading. Although it appears light on the surface, the book is extremely sensitive to the myriad complexities surrounding issues of power, race, caste, sexuality and gender inequality observed by Ackerley during his sojourn. Consider this description of a kiss between the author and 20-year-old Narayan, who he has been lusting after ever since his arrival in Chokrapur.

> ...Narayan came down the path to meet me. I thought how graceful he looked in his white muslin clothes, the sleeves of his loose vest widening out at the wrist, the long streamers of his turban floating behind him. The breeze puffed at his *dhoti* as he approached, moulding the soft stuff to the shape of his thigh; then as he turned a bend in the path, another gentle gust took the garment from behind and blew it aside, momentarily baring a slim brown leg. I took his hand and led him into my tent....
> 'I want to love you very much', he said.
> 'You mean you do love me very much'.
> 'I want to'.
> 'Then why not'?
> 'You will go away to England and I shall be sorry. But you will not be sorry. I am only a boy and I shall be sorry'.
> ...He suddenly laughed softly and drew me after him. And in the dark roadway, overshadowed by trees, he put up his face and kissed me on the cheek. I returned his kiss, but he at once drew back, crying out—
> 'Not the mouth. You eat meat! You eat meat!'
> 'Yes and I will eat you in a minute', I said and kissed him on the lips again and this time, he did not draw away.[168]

The World of Homosexuals is a concise, detailed and enlightened examination of a wide range of issues surrounding homosexuality in the Indian context. It is by an unlikely author—the celebrated mathematics genius Shakuntala Devi—who beat the then world's fastest computer (the Univac 1108) at a competition to find the 23rd root of a 201-digit

number in the same year of the book's publication (1977)! She subsequently entered the Guinness Book of World Records three years
later, for mentally multiplying two randomly chosen 13-digit numbers
and correctly giving the 26-digit answer in 28 seconds! In *The World of
Homosexuals*, she declares at the outset that she is 'neither a homosexual
nor a social scientist, psychologist or a psychiatrist' and that her only
qualification for writing the book is that she is 'a human being'; and
wishes to shed light on a section of her 'fellow human beings who have
been little understood and forced to live in "half-hiding" throughout
their lives by a society that is merciless towards everything that differs
from the statistical norm'.[169]

Devi's research is meticulous; her sources include 'books, pamphlets,
departmental reports, parliamentary debates and even blue books [porn]'
and interviews with 'psychologists, social scientists, social workers, politicians, priests, doctors, lawyers, professors and many homosexuals
in India as well as in Canada, West Germany, the UK and many other
countries'.[170] The book comprises of 16 chapters. There are three extended interviews with Indian and Canadian homosexuals and chapters
dealing with historical, legal, religious and psychiatric perspectives
on homosexuality, commercialized homosexuality, homosexuality in
prisons, homosexuality in literature and films and *gay lib*. Devi's tone
is compassionate and sanctifying—throughout the book, she attempts
to clarify misconceptions about homosexuals, ('The most common
myth propagated about the homosexual is that he is effeminate. This is
far from the truth')[171] and present sexual information matter-of-factly,
('Sometimes men may indulge in what is popularly known as *69* where
they lie in such a way that they can simultaneously engage in oral-genital
contact')[172] and advocate for the complete normalcy of homosexuality.
('What people do not realize is the ordinariness and commonplaceness
of homosexuality. Every time we walk down the street, travel in a bus or
train, we shall probably pass homosexuals without knowing it.... Most
people will have at least one relative who is a homosexual').[173]

It is remarkable to observe just how much of the book rings true even
today, whether it is in the predicament of Indian gay men who have to
marry to conform to social norms,[174] or Western gay men who have to constantly struggle to preserve their hard-fought rights.[175] In the chapter

on homosexuals and community, I find a historical background to some of the issues surrounding kinship that I am exploring in this book—

> In India, where such [open] advertisements, bars, clubs or social groups are unheard of, homosexuals, men and women join small cliques of friends of long standing, who visit one another's homes, patronize the same cafés and meet at one another's parties.
>
> In ordinary company, many homosexuals who succeed in putting up a front of normality feel themselves outsiders merely pretending to share the lives and interests of the majority. Among their own kind, they can drop the mask; enclosed by their own tight little circle, insulated from the outside world, they can be completely at ease and they can enjoy the morale boosting effect of being accepted for what they are.[176]

QUEER INDIAN FILMS

Commercial Bollywood cinema has a long tradition of having comic sequences or songs featuring cross-dressing male stars (think Amitabh Bachchan in a sari in 1981's *Laawaris*—'The Orphan'; Rishi Kapoor in a dress in 1975's *Rafoo Chakkar*—'The Runaways') or any number of songs featuring *hijras*. It is becoming quite trendy to read Bollywood films as 'gay' or 'queer'.[177] Hoshang Merchant mentions the *Andaz* ('A Matter of Style', 1949) and *Sangam* ('Confluence', 1964) love triangles where 'the real love plot is...*dosti* or *yaaarana* [friendship] between the two heroes.... The female lead is there only to lessen the homosexual sting';[178] Shohini Ghosh reads *Dosti* (1964)—dealing with 'the intense friendship between two poor and physically-disabled young men who struggle to survive in the city'—as an 'allegory of homosexual love expressed through the metaphor of physical disability'.[179] R. Raj Rao, Gayathri Gopinath and Ashok Row Kavi have all queered Bollywood in a similar vein,[180] as have other writers for other Indian cinemas beyond Bollywood.[181]

Why, there are even now, a handful of explicitly gay-themed Bollywood films, or films which have visible LBGT characters, problematic as these might be. 1991's *Mast Kalander* ('Intoxicated') is a landmark in this context. It features Bollywood's 'first'[182] out and out *gay* character Pinku. If

Hollywood's first gay characters were either comic or villainous, Pinku was both and the critics had a field day!

> Pinku [is] a new generation gangster. In his flaming yellow or pink suits, Pinku is both pansy and comic rolled into one. A gay little tune strikes up whenever he enters. And just to make really sure that you are left in no doubt about him, Pinku in his opening scene runs his fingers over his father's brawny body and asks *'Daddy, hamara body aapke jaise strong aur muscular kyoon nahin hai?'* ('Daddy, why is not my body as strong and muscular as yours?') When Pinku is not plotting fell murders and kidnappings, he pleads for a motorbike ('Daddy, I want to live dangerously'), or chases men... And when all the thugs are finally rounded up in the police lock up, Pinku exults at what he sees as a heaven-sent opportunity.[183]

The gay sidekick is a regular comic character in many Bollywood films from the 1990s onward, like *Hum Hain Rahi Pyaar Ke* ('Companions on the Road of Love', 1993), *Raja Hindustani* ('Indian King', 1996) and *Taal* ('Rhythm', 1999); he has been replaced in more recent films like *Page 3* (2004) and *Let's Enjoy* (2004) with the debauched, decadent gay designer, hitting on straight men with impunity for his own sexual gratification.

Very rarely, we manage to find somewhat complex gay characters in films like *Bombay Boys* (1998) and *Split Wide Open* (1999), or *sensitive hijra* portrayals in films like *Bombay* (1995), *Tamanna* ('Desire', 1997) and *Darmiyaan* ('In-between', 1997). There have also been villainous *hijras* in *Sadak* ('Street', 1991) and the reality-inspired *Shabnam Mausi* ('Aunt Shabnam', 2005; the biopic of a high profile Indian *hijra* who was elected as a member of the legislative assembly in the Indian state of Madhya Pradesh).[184] The controversy that the lesbian-themed films *Fire* (1998; two sisters-in-law neglected by their respective husbands find comfort in each others arms) and *Girlfriend* (2004; obsessive lesbian ready to do anything to win her *girlfriend* back from a man) generate on their release, is well documented.[185] And then, of course, there is 2003's *Kal Ho Na Ho* ('If Tomorrow Does Not Come') and its arguably funny gay subplot between the two lead actors,[186] along with a slew of releases in the same year with both disparagingly camp or comic (*Out of Control, Masti* [Mischief], *Mango Soufflé, Market*) and somewhat non-stereotypical (*Rules,*

Chameli, Hyderabad Blues 2) characterizations that began full fledged mainstream media chatter about gay Bollywood.[187]

In 2006, *Quest*, a tedious and quite problematic look at the aftermath of a woman's life after she catches her husband in bed with another man, managed to slip under the radar on to urban multiplex screens, do a fairly good amount of business and slip away quietly. By 2007, there seems to be gay reference in almost every second or third Bollywood release. *The Bong Connection, Honeymoon Travels Pvt. Ltd., Marigold, Metro....* So much so that the Gay Bombay mailing list has begun conducting an online Gay Reference Audit for Bollywood—or GRAB![188]

I was in India in March 2005, when *My Brother Nikhil*, a Bollywood film dealing with the trials and tribulations of a gay champion swimmer who is found to be HIV positive (based on the real life story of Dominic D'Souza) hit the screen. My curiosity was piqued by the clever television promos, featuring a host of celebrities asking—'I care for *My Brother Nikhil*, do you?' When I went to see the film, I was blown away completely. As the *Outlook* magazine film critic wrote, the debutant director Onir had managed to tackle 'homosexuality without treating it as an ugly joke, a dirty alliance or an aberration'; in itself a cause for celebration.

> The gay relationship here is not designed to shock the audience or make them feel queasy but is so 'normal' that the two lovers seem just like any other couple—intimate yet jealous and insecure, happy but quarrelling, sharing and facing up to an imminent loss. It is the love and faith that matters, whether it is man-woman, man-man or woman-woman.[189]

Most of the mainstream English press was similarly deferential in the way they treated the film's gay theme.[190] There were also no angry protests from the cultural police and no theatre vandalism.[191] But more than the press reactions and the absence of a voluble public outcry, what struck me most as I watched the film in a houseful multiplex in South Bombay, was the reaction of the audience. They really seemed to *get* it—there were no hoots, no uncomfortable coughing when the couple was together. I was accompanied by a bunch of straight friends for *My Brother Nikhil*— and while they had been uncomfortable discussing my homosexuality before, now they had a context to ask me all the questions that they had wanted to. As I walked out of the film screening, I could see and hear animated conversations being carried out among the other viewers about different aspects of the story and the homosexuality of the protagonist... it was an extraordinary feeling.

I am also heartened to observe *Rules* director Parvati Balagopalan assert—

The gay couple was part of our script from the beginning. The movie spoke about various aspects of love and homosexuality is one of them. The movie was a discourse on love and we wanted to treat all kinds of love equally. There was no criticism, because there was no sensationalism at all. It was treated the way any other normal relationship would be.[192]

Shifting to non-commercial cinema, Riyad Wadia's *BOMgAY* (1996) is acknowledged as India's first gay film while *Gulabi Aaina* ('The Pink Mirror', 2003) has the distinction of being India's first *kothi* film.[193] They have been followed by a succession of diverse works

1. Tirthankar Guha Thakurta's *Piku Bhalo Achhey* from Calcutta ('Piku is Fine', 2004; a partly-fictional Bengali self-acceptance narrative)
2. Ligy J. Pullappally's *Sancharam* from Kerala ('The Journey', 2004; a lesbian love story set in the south Indian state of Kerala)
3. T. Jayshree's *Many People, Many Desires* from Bangalore (2004; a documentary about the LBGT community in Bangalore)
4. Santosh Sivan's *Navrasa* (2004; a look at the South Indian transexual Araavani community)
5. Shohini *Ghosh's Tale of the Night Faries* (2005; a debate over de-criminalization of sex work, explored through the narratives of five sex workers from Calcutta)
6. Sridhar Rangayan's *Yours Emotionally!* (2005; a cross-cultural 'gay' love story this time)
7. Ashish Sawhney's *Happy Hookers* (2006; a documentary about male commercial same-sex workers in Bombay)
8. Sridhar Rangayan's *68 Pages* (2007; a HIV-themed drama, produced by the Humsafar Trust)[194]

However, these films have only been screened privately or at festivals (they were either denied a censor certificate or did not bother applying), thus limiting their audience reach, despite the favourable publicity they received.

NOTES

1. There have been recent attempts at beginning this archival process online, through blogs such as *Queer Media Watch* (http://qmediawatch.wordpress.com/about/)
2. In addition, for an examination of 'queered' Indian advertising, I recommend Ruth Vanita's excellent essay 'Homophobic Fiction/Homoerotic Advertising: The Pleasures and Perils of Twentieth Century Indianness' in *Queering India: Same-sex Love and Eroticism in Indian Culture and Society* (London; New York: Routledge, 2002), pp. 127–148.
3. Arjun Appadurai, *Modernity at Large: Cultural Dimensions of Globalization* (University of Minnesota Press, 1996), pp. 63–64.
4. Ruth Vanita, 'The New Homophobia: Ugra's *Chocolate*', in Vanita Ruth and Saleem Kidwai (Eds), *Same-Sex Love in India: Readings from Literature and History* (New York: Palgrave, 2001), p. 248.
5. Saleem Kidwai, 'Introduction to Ismat Chugtai: *Tehri Lakeer*', in Vanita and Kidwai (2001), op. cit., p. 289.
6. Ashok Row Kavi, 'Homosexuals Meet', *Times of India* (Bombay), 18 December 1981.
7. 'Legalize Homosexuality', *Onlooker*, 15–31 August 1977.
8. Mario D'Penha, Comments on 'Legalize Homosexuality', *Historiqueer*, 13 August 2004. http://historiqueer.blogspot.com/
9. Ibid.
10. Mukund Padmanabhan, 'The Love that Dare not Speak its Name: A Journey through the Secret World of the Indian Homosexual', *Sunday Magazine*, 13 July–6 August 1988.
11. Mira Savara, 'Who Needs Men?', *Debonair*, April 1988.
12. Shridhar Raghavan, 'Gay: Everything You Wanted to Know about Homosexuality but were Afraid to Find Out', *Gentleman*, August 1991.
13. Anusha Srinivasan, 'I Want My Sex', *Mid-day* (Bombay), 30 June 1993.
14. Madhumita Ghosh, 'Homosexuality: A Thorny Issue', *Sunday Mail Magazine*, 1 September 1991.
15. For example—
    (a) Soraya Khan, 'Homosexuals—Should They Be Damned?', *Deccan Chronicle* (Hyderabad), 14 August 1993.
    (b) R. Raj Rao, 'Where are the Homosexuals? You don't have to Look too Far', *Indian Express* (Bombay), 2 September 2002.
16. Vijay Jung Thapa and Sheela Raval, 'Sex, Lies, Agony, Matrimony', *India Today*, 11 May 1998.
17. Kiran Manral, 'Bi Bi Love', *Saturday Times* (Bombay), 6 March 1999.
18. Sheela Raval, 'Men on Call', *India Today*, 27 January 2001.
19. Piyush Roy and Mamta Sen, 'I Want to Break Free', *Society*, October 2002.
20. Georgina Maddox, 'Gay and Gloomy', *Indian Express: Mumbai Newsline*, 24 June 2003. http://cities.expressindia.com/fullstory.php?newsid=55715
21. Neil Pate, 'Blackmailers Give Gays, Lesbians a Hard Time', *Times of India* (Bombay), 16 July 2004.
22. Neil Pate, 'Police Target Gays to Extort Money', *Times of India* (Bombay), 24 August 2004.
23. Sweta Ramanujan, 'Love in the Time of Cynicism', *Indian Express: Mumbai Newsline*, 14 February 2003.
24. 'No Gay Priests, We're Indians', *Mid-day*, 6 August 2003. http://web.mid-day.com/news/city/2003/august/60407.htm

25. Leena Mishra, 'Prisoners Turning Gay in Packed Cells', *Times of India* (Bombay), 12 July 2004.
26. See Georgina Maddox, 'Coming Out', *Sunday Express*, 27 July 2003. http://www.indianexpress.com/full_story.php?content_id=28237
Shalini Nair, 'Coming Out', *Indian Express: Mumbai Newsline*, 13 July 2004. http://cities.expressindia.com/fullstory.php?newsid=91232
27. Shefalee Vasudev, 'The Gay Spirit', *India Today*, 2 August 2004.
28. 'Gay Couple Stabs Each Other', *News Today*, 27 May 1992.
29. Ramesh Babu, 'Lesbians' Death Wish', *Sunday Hindustan Times*, 27 June 2004.
30. The female Aparna Mafatlal turned into the male Ajay Mafatlal in 2003 after a sex-change surgery. For an overview of the family feud as reported in the newspapers, see— Swati Deshpande, 'Bitter Mafatlal Feud Reaches Court', *The Times of India*, 10 November 2005.
31. '2 NGO-run Gay Clubs Busted in Lucknow', *Asian Age* (Bombay), 9 July 2001.
32. Reuters, 'Police Busts Gay Clubs in Lucknow', *Indian Express* (Bombay), 9 July 2001.
33. See—
    (a) 'NGOs Worry Over Arrest of Outreach Workers', *Times of India* (Bombay), 16 July 2001.
    (b) 'City Stands Up for Lucknow Workers in Jail', *Indian Express* (Bombay), 19 August 2002.
34. See—
    (a) 'Gay Club Running on Net Unearthed'—4 Arrested', *Times of India* (Bombay), 5 January 2006.
    (b) 'Cops bust gay racket...', *Hindustan Times* (Bombay), 5 January 2006.
35. 'Homosexuality, a crime as heinous as murder', *New India Press*, 11 January 2006. http://www.newindpress.com/NewsItems.asp?ID=IE420060111045619&Page=4&Title=Features+-+People+%26+Lifestyle&Topic=0 (Registration required)
36. Ibid.
37. 'Delhi Gay Murders Tip of Sleazeberg', *Times of India* (Bombay), 18 August 2004. Also see Swapan Dasgupta, 'The Problem is not Homosexuality', *Rediff.com*, 23 August 2004. http://us.rediff.com/news/2004/aug/23swadas.htm
38. Vikram Doctor, 'Less Than Gay', *Times of India* (Bombay), 24 August 2002.
39. See—
    (a) Suveen K. Sinha, 'The Nowhere Men', *Outlook*, 30 August 2004. http://www.outlookindia.com/full.asp?fodname=20040830&fname=Sex+%28F%29&sid=1
    (b) Suveen K. Sinha and Shobita Dhar, 'The Perfect Crime', *Outlook*, 30 August 2004. http://www.outlookindia.com/full.asp?fodname=20040830&fname=Sex+%28F%29&sid=2
    (c) Dibyendu Ganguly, 'A Friend Remembers Pushkin Chandra', *Times of India* (Delhi), 21 August 2004. http://timesofindia.indiatimes.com/articleshow/822313.cms
40. 'Horror Story of Unnatural Sex and Murder', *Indian Express* (Bombay), 13 October 2004.
41. 'Pop Goes the Myth', *Sunday Mid-day* (Bombay), 28 July 1991.
42. Pinkie Virani, 'Happy to Be This Way', *Bombay*, July 1990.
43. 'Bombay Dost Gets Company', *Mid-day* (Bombay), 13 November 1993.
44. See—
    (a) 'A Center in Aid of Gays', *Mid-day* (Bombay), 28 April 1994.
    (b) Shabnam Minwalla, 'Center to Help Gays Tackle Health Problems', *Times of India* (Bombay), 17 March 1996.
    (c) Saira Menezes, 'Room With a View', *Outlook*, 17 April 1996.

45. Ketan Narottam Tanna, 'Elephantine Problems of the "Invisibles"', *Hindustan Times* (New Delhi), 22 March 1996.
46. Shilpa Shet, 'Helpline for Men', *Mid-day* (Bombay), 1 June 1998.
47. 'Minority Support', *Times of India* (Bombay), 28 April 2004.
48. Harish Nambiar, 'Out of the Smogscreen', *Mid-day* (Bombay), 15 January 1995.
49. Milind Palnitkar, 'Gays Want Sexual Laws Changed', *Mid-day* (Bombay), 13 January 1995.
50. 'Gays Say Redefine Family', *Indian Express* (Bombay), 12 November 1997.
51. Kaniza Garari, 'Society Must Accept Us for What We Are', *Bombay Times*, 11 October 2002.
52. Georgina Maddox, 'Sexual Minorities Retie Umbilical Cord', *Indian Express* (Bombay), 12 October 2002.
53. Kaniza Garari, 'Society Must Accept Us for What We Are', *Times of India: Bombay Times*, 11 October 2002.
54. Georgina Madddox, 'Gay Diaspora Tries to Build Bridges', *Indian Express* (Bombay), 16 October 2002.
55. Georgina Maddox, 'Sexual Minorities Retie Umbilical Cord', *Indian Express* (Bombay), 12 October 2002.
56. Shibu Thomas, 'We Demand Our Rights', *Asian Age: Mumbai Age*, 13 October 2002.
57. Georgina Maddox, 'Sexual Minorities Retie Umbilical Cord', *Indian Express* (Bombay), 12 October 2002.
58. 'A to Z of India's Sexuality', *Asian Age* (Bombay), 10 October 2002.
59. Shibu Thomas, 'We Demand Our Rights', *Asian Age: Mumbai Age*, 13 October 2002.
60. 'A Platform for Lesbian, Gay Rights', *Afternoon* (Bombay), 10 October 2002.
61. K.S. Dakshina Murthy, 'Bangalore Pushed Out of the Closet', *Hindustan Times* (New Delhi), 15 September 1997.
62. 'Over 100 Delegates will Attend Three Day Conference of Gays', *Times of India*, 28 April 2000. http://timesofindia.indiatimes.com/articleshow/381076312.cms
63. 'A Focus on Sexuality and Related Issues', *Bangalore Times*, 10 June 2004.
64. Meenakshi Shedde, 'Humour Warms Up WSF', *Times of India*, 21 January 2004. http://timesofindia.indiatimes.com/articleshow/435951.cms
65. Shweta Shertukde, 'Gays, Lesbians Feel Neglected', *Asian Age* (Bombay), 20 January 2004.
66. *Times of India* (Bombay), 13 August 1992.
67. '15 Friends Walk with Gay Abandon', *Asian Age* (Bombay), 3 July 1999.
68. See Swagato Ganguly, 'India's Sexual Minorities—Gay Parade in Calcutta a Mark of Changing Mindsets', *The Statesman*, 27 July 2003. http://www.thestatesman.net/page.news.php?clid=3&theme=&usrsess=1&id=18938
69. See 'Gays, Lesbians Walk for Rights', *Times of India*, 27 June 2004. http://timesofindia.indiatimes.com/articleshow/755453.cms
70. See 'Gay March in Patna', *PatnaDaily.com*, 11 April 2007. http://www.patnadaily.com/news2007/apr/041107/gay_march_in_patna.html
71. See Ranjani Ramaswamy and Georgina Maddox, 'Out of the Closet, Asserting their Space in Social Fabric', *Indian Express: Mumbai Newsline*, 29 September 2001.
72. 'City Homosexuals to March for their Rights', *Mid-day* (Bombay), 1 December 2003.
73. See Ritesh Uttamchandani, 'Crowd Interrupted', *Indian Express* (Bombay), 20 June 2004.

74. Arvind Narrain, 'Marching to a Different Drumbeat: Culture and Queer Sexuality', *Humanscape Magazine* (December 2004). http://www.humanscape.org/Humanscape/2004/Dec/marching.php 'Another Gay March—Hum Hon Gay Kaamyaab is their New Slogan', *Indian Express: Mumbai Newsline*, 17 August 2005. http://cities.expressindia.com/fullstory.php?newsid=144126

75. Leela Jacinto, 'Bringing Down Stonewalls', *Metropolis on Saturday* (Bombay), 25 June 1995.

76. Anna M.M. Vetticad, 'Action Stations', *India Today*, 17 April 2000.

77. C.Y. Gopinath, '11 Million Invisible Men in the Decade of AIDS', *Indian Express* (Bombay), 17 July 1991.

78. See—
    (a) Kalpana Jain, 'Gays Hold Parallel AIDS Meet', *Times of India* (Bombay), 10 November 1992.
    (b) 'AIDS Congress Concludes Amid Protest', *Times of India* (New Delhi), 13 November 1992.

79. 'Bombay Gays Potential AIDS Carriers, Warns WHO', *The Daily* (Bombay), 28 July 1992.

80. For example—'20 pc of Mumbai's gays are HIV positive', *Times of India*, 21 May 2004. http://timesofindia.indiatimes.com/articleshow/690543.cms

81. 'India Vows to Check HIV Spread', *Times of India* (Bombay), 14 July 2004.

82. See Maxine Frith, 'India's Hidden AIDS Epidemic: Virus to Infect 25m by 2010', *Independent* (UK) 19 November 2003. http://news.independent.co.uk/world/science_medical/story.jsp?story=465047

83. Siddharth Srinivasan, 'Gays in India: Keeping the Closet Door Closed', *International Herald Tribune*, 17 September 2003. http://www.iht.com/articles/110147.html

84. Pritish Nandy, 'RIP: Requiem for our Heroes', *Daily* (Bombay), 27 February 1994.

85. Sunil Mehra, 'An Accountant of Alternate Reality', *Outlook*, 13 December 1995. http://www.outlookindia.com/full.asp?fodname=19951213&fname=profile &sid=1

86. Ibid.

87. Meher Pestonjee, 'Figure These Out', *Daily* (Bombay), 4 March 1991.

88. Timothy Hyman, 'Obituary: Bhupen Khakhar', *Independent* (London, UK), 27 August 2003.

89. Mini Chandran Kurien, 'When Jimmy Came Marching Home', *Saturday Times*, 27 July 1991.

90. Anil Sadarangani, 'I'm Seeing Someone', *Times of India*, 11 May 2006. http://timesofindia.indiatimes.com/articleshow/1526280.cms

91. See Georgina Maddox, 'Gay Partners Tie Knot Amid Hostile Laws', *Indian Express* (Bombay), 27 December 2002.

92. Vajir Singh, 'I'm Way Too Sexy', *Hindustan Times: HT Café* (Bombay), 1 February 2007.

93. Holi is an annual spring festival of colour, music and celebration, celebrated all over India but most popular in north India.

94. Peter Foster, 'Gay Prince is Cut Off from Fortune 'for Dishonouring his Family', *The Telegraph* (UK), 28 June 2006. http://www.telegraph.co.uk/news/main.jhtml?xml=/news/2006/06/28/wprince28.xml&sSheet=/news/2006/06/28/ixnews.html 'Gay Prince is Back in Palace', *Times of India*, 14 September 2006. http://timesofindia.indiatimes.com/articleshow/1988816.cms 'Disowned by Family, Gay Prince Opts to Adopt', *Deccan Herald*, 27 August 2007. http://www.deccanherald.com/deccanherald/aug272006/national19192006826.asp

95. Shibu Thomas, 'The Boyfriend Throws Light on Gay Culture', *Asian Age* (Bombay), 21 May 2003.

96. Personal conversation with R. Raj Rao, Cambridge, MA, 3 April 2004.

97. Jhimli Mukherjee Pandey, 'Even My Parents Have Not Accepted My Transsexual Identity', *Sunday Review*, 10 August 2003.

98. Hoshang Merchant, 'Rhythm of the Blood', *The Week*, 4 April 1999.

99. She writes that it was difficult for her and her husband difficult to come to terms with their son's bisexuality.... 'But we loved him and accepted it without understanding it'. (p. 429) *On Balance* (New Delhi: Viking, 2003).

100. In an interview on the news channel CNN-IBN aired 21 January 2006, Seth called the law silly, cruel and harmful. In an interview with *Outlook* magazine, he confessed that although he was a private person, he felt compelled to speak out because the happiness of millions of queer Indians was at stake.
See—Sheila Reddy, 'It Took Me Long To Come To Terms With Myself. Those Were Painful Years', *Outlook*, 2 October 2006. http://www.outlookindia.com/full.asp?fodn ame=20061002&fname=Anterview+Vikram&sid=1

101. For example—'Gay Men Make Great Friends', *Hindustan Times: HT Tabloid* (New Delhi), 22 March 2006. http://www.hindustantimes.com/news/7242_1656154,00180007.htm

102. See Pradip Rodrigues, 'Why do Gays Hate Women', *Savvy*, March 1993.

103. 'See Fahad Samar Pays Tribute to Riyad Wadia', *Mid-day*, 1 December 2003. http://web. mid-day.com/news/city/2003/december/70114.htm

104. See Lata Khubchandani, 'Gaywatch', *Mid-day* (Bombay), 4 May 2001. Also see novelist and blogger Sonia Faleiro's excellent inteview with Bobby Darling archived on: http:// soniafaleiro.blogspot.com/2005/11/liberty-equality-fraternity.html

105. Nonita Kalra, 'The Real *Maha Maharani*', [Queen of Queens] *Man's World*, June 2000.

106. I am alluding to these three as just representative samples out of a large range of sex surveys that have been conducted during that period. Over the recent few years especially, it seems every English media publication wants to bring out their own sexy survey!

107. '*Debonair* Sex Survey', *Debonair*, October 1991.

108. See for instance—
    (a) Anand Soordas, 'Indians Break Taboos But Play Safe: Survey', *Telegraph* (Calcutta), 2 June 2004.
    (b) Anubha Sawhney, 'Do You Get It? Indians Say Frequently', *Times of India* (New Delhi), 2 June 2004.

109. The Kama Sutra Sex Survey, 2004, Research findings may be viewed on the company's website—http://www.ksontheweb.com/64/category.ift

110. 'Sex in the 90s: Uneasy Revolution', *Outlook*, 11 September 1996. http://www.outloo-kindia.com/full.asp?fodname=19960911&fname=cover%5Fstory&sid=8

111. Kamran Abbasi, 'The New Macho', *The Week* (New Delhi), 30 April 2000. Also see Sunil Mehra, 'Vanity Fair', *Outlook*, 9 July 1997. http://www.outlookindia.com/full.as p?fodname=19970709&fname=coverstory&sid=1

112. 'Voices: Should the Law Take Any Action Against Gays?', *Mid-day* (Bombay), 22 July 1997.

113. 'India's Young People Inclined to Scrap Gay Ban', *Yahoo! News*, 25 September 2006. http://news.yahoo.com/s/po/20060926/co_po/indiasyoungpeopleinclinedtoscrap ga-yban

114. 'Sexuality No Longer a Taboo Subject', *Delhi Times*, 31 May 2004.

115. 'Just One Question', *Times of India: Bombay Times*, 19 July 2004.
116. Shobha Dé, 'Dé Dreaming', *Daily* (Bombay), 7 February 1991.
117. Shobha Dé, 'Love is a Many Splendoured Thing', *Times of India: Bombay Times*, 19 December 2002.
118. For example 'Many Homosexuals Do Marry', in *Mid-day* (Bombay), 10 May 1991, where she firmly chides a confused letter writer that 'dating attractive girls is not the answer or the "cure"' for his homosexuality.
119. See 'Mixed Media: The Gay Patriarch', *Sunday Mid-day* (Bombay), 4 August 1991.
120. See—
    (a) 'Extraordinary People: Combating Gender Stereotypes', *Times of India: Bombay Times*, 18 June 2002.
    (b) 'Extraordinary People: A Queen Without an Empire', *Times of India: Bombay Times*, 27 August 2002.
121. Amit Varma, 'These Songs of Freedom', *LiveMint.com*, 10 August 2007. http://www.livemint.com/2007/08/10232928/These-songs-of-freedom.html
122. Kiron Kher, 'Straight from the Heart: Gay Abandon', *Mid-day* (Bombay), 14 June 2002.
123. Dilip Raote, 'Sex Forecast', *Mid-day* (Bombay), 11 October 2002.
124. Mayank Shekhar, 'Gay Watch', *Mid-day* (Bombay), 17 September 2003.
125. See 'Ask Khushwant', *Daily* (Bombay), 19 October 1991.
126. See Prakash Kothari, 'What's So Unusual', *Daily* (Bombay), 19 July 1992.
127. Watsal's Column 'Ask the Sexpert' has been published daily in the newspaper *Mumbai Mirror* from 2005 onwards.
128. See Radhika Chandiramani, 'Everything You Wanted to Know About Midlife Crisis', *Asian Age* (Bombay), 10 October 1999.
129. 'Dr. Know', *Man's World* magazine, June 2006.
130. Farzana Versey, 'Flipside: Gay Power', *Mid-day* (Bombay), 1 September 1990.
131. Ibid.
132. Farzana Versey, 'Flipside: Verbal Touting', *Mid-day* (Bombay), 15 September 1990.
133. Ibid.
134. Farzana Versey, 'Not Novel, These Guys', *Mid-day* (Bombay), 7 September 1991.
135. Farzana Versey, 'Cross Connections: The Gay Glut', *Afternoon* (Bombay), 4 May 2000.
136. Farzana Versey, 'Does it Pay to be Gay?', *Deccan Chronicle*, 18 September 2006.
137. See—Swapan Dasgupta, 'The Problem is not Homosexuality', *Rediff.com*, 23 August 2004. http://www.rediff.com/news/2004/aug/23swadas.htm
138. Kanchan Gupta, 'Papa, Where's Mom? He's in the Loo!', *Pioneer*, 6 November 2004. http://headlines.sify.com/news/fullstory.php?id=13605608&headline=Column:~Dad,~where
139. Ibid.
140. Personal conversation with Vijay Tendulkar, Cambridge, MA, 2 November 2004. See 'Another Play on Lesbianism Ran Unopposed 18 Years Ago', *Asian Age* (Bombay), 4 December 1998.
141. 'Liberalism: Can We Handle It?', *Sunday Times of India* (Bombay), 22 November 1998.
142. See Karan Thapar, 'Sunday Sentiments', in *Hindustan Times*, 28 August 2004.
143. Lopamudra Ghatak, 'Does It Pay to be Gay in the World of Techies?', *Economic Times*, 12 May 2005. http://economictimes.indiatimes.com/articleshow/1108096.cms
144. Shayne Gonsalves, 'Dressed to Thrill', *Mid-day* (Bombay), 27 June 1991. See also 'A Single Girl at a Gay Party', *Island*, February 1992.

145. Kushalrani Gulab, 'It's Raining Men', *Times of India: Bombay Times*, 23 July 2001.
146. Shobha Dé, 'The Power of Pink'. *The Week*, 26 September 2004. http://www.the-week.com/24sep26/columns_home.htm
    Also see—
    (a) Gaurav De, 'The Pink Rupee', *Indian Express* (Bombay), 12 November 2000 and
    (b) Vishwas Kulkarni, 'Gay and Abandoned', *Mid-day*, 31 August 2004. http://ww1.mid-day.com/entertainment/news/2004/august/91248.htm
147. Personal conversation with Ashok Row Kavi, Bombay, India, 24 August 2004.
148. 'Star-TV Suspends TV Show After Row', *TeleSatellite Magazine*, 14 May 1995. http://www.funet.fi/index/esi/TELE-Satellite/TS950514.html
149. Cadre members of the right wing political party, the Shiv Sena.
150. 'Sena Men, Gay Activists Spar on Live TV', *Times of India* (Bombay), 26 June 2004.
151. 'Jassi Forges Ahead with a Bold Step', *Hindustan Times* (New Delhi), 4 December 2003.
152. The advertisement appeared in the *Times of India* (Bombay), 20 July 1991.
153. Arvind Kala, *Invisible Minority: The Unknown World of the Indian Homosexual* (New Delhi: Dynamic Books, 1991).
154. Pedro Menezes, 'On Gay Street', *The Daily*, 5 July 1992.
155. Kajal Basu, 'A Closet View', *India Today*, 15 June 1992.
156. The author prefers to use this expression as he feels that in India, like with several other non-Western countries, concepts of 'gay' or 'bisexual' may not be applicable to men that have homosexual intercourse.
157. Ruth Vanita, 'Introduction: Modern Indian Materials', in Vanita and Kidwai (2001), op. cit., p. 212.
158. Ratti Rakesh (Ed.), *A Lotus of Another Color: An Unfolding of the South Asian Gay and Lesbian Experience* (Boston: Alyson Publications, 1993), p. 15.
159. See—
    (a) *The Golden Gate* (New York: Random House, 1986).
    (b) *A Suitable Boy* (New York: Harper Collins, 1993).
160. See the short story 'Artha' in *Love and Longing in Bombay* (Boston: Little Brown and Company, 1997).
161. See Firdaus Kanga, *Trying to Grow* (London: Bloomsbury, 1990).
162. Vanita and Kidwai (2001), op. cit., pp. xxiv.
163. Maya Sharma, *Loving Women: Being Lesbian in Unprivileged India* (New Delhi: Yoda Press, 2006).
164. Bina Fernandez (Ed.), *Humjinsi: A Resource Book on Lesbian, Gay and Bisexual Rights in India* (Bombay: India Center for Human Rights and Law, 2002).
165. *Human Rights Violations Against Sexual Minorities in India* (Bangalore, India: PUCl-K, 2001). Accessible on the World Wide Web—http://www.pucl.org/Topics/Gender/2003/sexual-minorities.htm
166. *Human Rights Violations Against the Transgender Community* (Bangalore, India: PUCl-K, 2003). Report summary accessible on the World Wide Web—http://www.pucl.org/Topics/Gender/2004/transgender.htm
167. Eliot Weinberger, 'Introduction' in J. R. Ackerley (2000 reprint) *Hindoo Holiday: An Indian Journal* (New York: New York Review Books [1932]), p. xii.
168. J.R. Ackerley, op. cit., pp. 239–240.
169. Shakuntala Devi, *The World of Homosexuals* (New Delhi: Vikas Publishing House, 1977), p. vi.

170. Ibid.
171. Ibid, p. 16.
172. Ibid, p. 20.
173. Ibid, p. 17.
174. Ibid, pp. 1–10.
175. Ibid, pp. 127–142.
176. Ibid, pp. 105–106.
177. The Queering Bollywood website (http://media.opencultures.net/queer/) is an excellent resource for articles, reviews, web resources, and list of Indian films with queer possibilities.
178. Hoshang Merchant (Ed.), *Yaarana: Gay Writing from India* (New Delhi: Penguin India, 1999), p. xxiii.
179. Shohini Ghosh, 'The Closet is Ajar', *Outlook*, 30 May 2005. http://www.outlookindia.com/full.asp?fodname=20050530&fname=GShohini+Ghosh+%2F%29&sid=1&pn=1
180. See—
    (a) Gayathri Gopinath, 'Queering Bollywood: Alternative Sexualities in Popular Indian Cinema', *Journal of Homosexuality* (New York: Haworth Press, 2000) Vol. 39 (3/4) pp. 283–97.
    (b) R. Raj Rao, 'Memories Pierce the Heart: Homoeroticism, Bollywood-Style', *Journal of Homosexuality* (New York: Haworth Press, 2000), Vol. 39(3/4), pp. 299–306.
    (c) Ashok Row Kavi, 'The Changing Image of the Hero in Hindi Films', *Journal of Homosexuality* (New York: Haworth Press, 2000), Vol. 39(3/4), pp. 307–12.
181. For example, T. Muraleedharan and his work on male bonding and desire in Malayalam cinema. See—
    'Disrupted Desires: Male Bonds in Mohanlal Films', *Deep Focus*, Vol. 9, No. 1, 2001, pp. 65–75.
    'Crisis in Desire: A Queer Reading of Cinema and Desire in Kerala', in Gautam Bhan and Arvind Narrain (Eds), *Because I Have a Voice: Queer Politics in India* (New Delhi: Yoda Press, 2005), pp. 70–88.
182. Categories like 'first' are often contested and ambiguous. I am aware that *Badnam Basti* ('The Infamous Neighbourhood', 1971) had a bisexual gay lead character and an ambiguous ending, which suggests that he might have had a 'happily ever after' with another man. Likewise, the 1983 Hindi film *Holi* touches upon the subject of homophobia in a boys college, where an effeminate boy is driven to suicide by the violent harassment by his dorm-mates. However, I consider *Mast Kalander* as the first film with an explicit gay character—and it opened the door, even if slightly, for others to follow.
183. Gayatri Sinha, 'Bollywood Goes Gay With Abandon', *Indian Express Magazine* (Bombay), 21 April 1991.
184. See Rashid Kidwai, 'Real Cheer Dims MLA Jeers', *The Telegraph*, 18 May 2005. http://www.telegraphindia.com/1050519/asp/nation/story_4758092.asp
    See 'Eunuch MP Takes Seat', *BBC News*, 6 March 2000. http://news.bbc.co.uk/1/hi/world/south_asia/668042.stm
185. On *Fire*—
    See Praveen Swami, 'Furore Over a Film', *Frontline*, 19 December 1998–1 January 1999. http://www.frontlineonnet.com/fl1526/15260430.htm
    'Sainiks Spew Venom Against Dilip Kumar for Backing Fire', *Indian Express*, 13 December 1998. http://www.indianexpress.com/ie/daily/19981213/34750024.html

'Firepariksha—Replace Radha with Shabana', *Indian Express*, 14 December 1998. http://www.indianexpress.com/ie/daily/19981214/34850474.html

Suhasini Haider, 'What's Wrong With My Film? Why are People Making Such a Fuss?', *Rediff.com* http://www.rediff.com/entertai/1998/dec/10fire.htm

Sonia Trikha, 'Since Cricket Issues Didn't Work, People Picked on Fire, says Deepa', *Indian Express*, 6 December 1998. http://www.expressindia.com/ie/daily/19981206/34050764.html

On *Girlfriend*, see—

'Sena Turns the Heat on Girlfriend', *Times of India* (Bombay), 15 June 2004.

Srinivas Prasad and Sujata Anandan, 'Gay Groups Join Chorus Against Girlfriend', *Hindustan Times* (New Delhi), 16 June 2004.

186. The characters in the film are not really gay, but only pretend to be so, much to the disapproval of Kantaben, the housekeeper. The actors playing these two characters camped it up as emcees of the annual Filmfare Awards in 2004—a show that was broadcast to millions of viewers over television. Gay viewers I have spoken to, as well as the Internet discussions surrounding the film and the awards function have been polarized—some people saw these as stereotype indulging and mildly mocking, others found them to be liberating.

187. See Ziya Us Salam, 'Bold But Clichéd', *Hindu*, 18 June 2004. http://www.hindu.com/thehindu/fr/2004/06/18/stories/2004061801190100.htm

Parul Gupta, 'Bollywood Rocks, Both Ways', *Times of India*, 15 September 2003. http://timesofindia.indiatimes.com/cms.dll/articleshow?msid=183143

188. Message posted to the Gay Bombay Yahoo! Group by Vgd67, 'Gay Reference Audit for Bollywood (GRAB)—Seeking Volunteers' on 22 May 2007.

189. '*My Brother Nikhil*', *Outlook*, 11 April 2005. http://outlookindia.com/showtime.asp?fodname=20050411

190. For example—Priyanka Haldipur, '*My Brother Nikhil*', *Deccan Herald*, 27 March 2005. http://www.deccanherald.com/deccanherald/mar272005/mr1.asp

Mayank Shekhar, 'Film Review—*My Brother Nikhil*', *Mid-day*, 25 March 2005. http://ww1.mid-day.com/hitlist/2005/march/106267.htm

191. There could be several reasons for this lack of moral panic this time around. The fact that this was a 'multiplex' film (released to a select urban audience), the fact that the gay relationship was completely avoided in the promos enabling it to slip under the cultural police radar, the conjecture that because the film was about the men and not women, it was less threatening to the morality brigade and finally it's promotion by a phalanx of celebrity cricketers and film personalities, as an AIDS-sensitive goody-goody type of film.

192. 'Gay Lord', *Asian Age* (Bombay), 10 January 2004.

193. See—Jerry Pinto, 'Cinema Comes Out of the Closet', *Times of India: Sunday Review* (Bombay), 26 January 1997.

Shibu Thomas, 'India Finally Enters Gay World', *Asian Age* (Bombay), 31 January 2003.

194. I am only covering films made in India here—there have been several films made by the Indian diaspora, mainly in the US and UK...for a list of some of these, see—http://web.mit.edu/cms/betweenthelines/summaries.html

7

Straight Expectations
Interviews, Interpretations, Interventions

In this chapter, I have clustered the responses of my interview subjects around key themes that pervade this book and which I will further address in the concluding chapter. I conducted 32 interviews, of which, seven were conducted exclusively online, five were conducted both online and offline and three were begun online but completed offline. The remaining 17 were both arranged and conducted completely offline.

Individuals interviewed for this book comprised professionals and students from different fields (law, academia, medicine, media, stock trading, engineering). The age groupings were as follows—13 were between 20 to 29 years of age, 11 were between 30 to 39, six were between 40 to 49 and one was in his fifties. Half of those interviewed had graduate degrees (either Masters, postgraduate diplomas or Ph.Ds), 25 per cent held undergraduate Bachelor degrees and the others were continuing college students at either the undergraduate or graduate level. Five of the respondents were located out of India (in the US, Canada and UK). The others were from within India. Of these, most (80 per cent) were located in Bombay and the others across other metropolitan cities like New Delhi, Bangalore and Ahmedabad. Six respondents were members of Gay Bombay's managing committee—the *core group*, while seven respondents were actively involved in activism or gay organizations other than Gay Bombay, which included the Humsafar Trust and *Bombay Dost* magazine, protest rallies, workshops, legal activism and documentation. The remaining respondents were not directly involved in organizing Gay Bombay community events or activism at large.

Two thirds of the respondents declared that they were single. Of the others, seven were in same-sex relationship while three were in heterosexual marriage relationships. Half of the respondents were *selectively out* (mostly to close friends, but not family and or at the workplace). Of the remaining, three were *closeted*; the others were completely *out* to their families as well as at their work places. Over half of the respondents classified themselves as Hindu. Among other religions represented were Islam (three respondents), Christianity (three respondents), Zoroastrianism (two respondents), Jainism (two respondents) and Buddhism (one respondent). Three respondents declared that they had no religious affiliation whatsoever, three considered themselves to be atheist and one person declared himself agnostic. I think that my ethnoscape is reasonably diverse on most counts; however, it may seem weak in terms of the number of married gay men interviewed (only three) and those who consider themselves completely closeted (three). I found it very hard to find willing interviewees in both these categories, either online or offline.

As I have mentioned earlier, I have used pseudonyms to disguise my interviewee names and or email or newsgroup identities or chat handles. I have also used gender appropriate pronouns while describing the respondents, based on their declared gender orientation. Wherever I have used online or offline conversation or interview excerpts, I have either cut and pasted them verbatim from my saved records, or reproduced them within quotation marks. I have not edited the excerpts for minor grammatical or spelling errors; I want their original flavour to be retained and reflected within this book. (For more detailed interviewee profiles, kindly refer to the Appendix).

BEING GAY IN INDIA

Becoming gay or, rather, becoming aware of being gay is an organic process. More men in India are seeing themselves and their lives reflected in this idea and the individual testimonies often give a hint of the evolution within people's lives of that consciousness. (Jeremy Seabrook, 1999)[1]

Many people whom I interviewed considered their homosexuality to be normal, natural and just another personal choice. It was something that was intrinsic, 'as much a way of life as brushing your teeth in the morning or breathing' (Bhuvan). Others were grappling with self-acceptance.

MOHNISH: I AM GAY THOUGH I WOULDN'T LIKE PEOPLE TO CALL ME GAY, HOMO, QUEER, ANYTHING; IT IS STILL CONSIDERED ABNORMAL. I DON'T WEAR THE LABEL WITH PRIDE.

ORMUS: TO SOME EXTENT, ASKING ME WHAT MY PERSONAL VIEWS ON HOMOSEXUALITY ARE IS EQUIVALENT TO ASKING A JEWISH MAN IN A 1940S GERMAN CONCENTRATION CAMP ABOUT HIS VIEWS ON JUDAISM. DESPITE THE COMPLETE ACCEPTANCE OF ONE'S OWN NORMALITY, THE MANY WHIPS OF THE NAZI COMMANDANT CANNOT BUT CARRY THEIR OWN STING. NEVERTHELESS, THE MOMENTS WHEN I WISH I WEREN'T GAY ARE GROWING FEWER AND FEWER. THE PATH THAT I MUST FOLLOW, THOUGH ONE THAT WILL VERY FORESEEABLY BE STRUNG WITH OBSTACLES, IS ONE WHOSE ABILITY TO INTIMIDATE ME GROWS LESSER EVERY DAY.

For some respondents, being gay denoted a political stance or signified a social identity. A few considered it to be just a desire, or equated it with the sexual act—'Just sex, over and out. I know what I want. Seven inches and above' (Harbhajan). For others, it extended beyond their sexual urge into what Adam (2000) describes as the 'potential for emotional involvement and relationships'.[2] Thus, Asim, Mike, Yudhisthir and Mohnish portrayed being gay as being comfortable with one's own self, a state of mind, a spirit of being, a way of life, something that was both emotional as well as physical, as opposed to *homosexuality*, which was something just physical. Some respondents did not see the point in differentiating between the terminology of *homosexual* and *gay* (Nihar— 'Gay, queer, homosexual, potato, *batata*; it is all the same'; Rahim—'It is just men doing other men'), but for others, *homosexual* was a significant boundary that had to be crossed on the way to being considered *gay*. Jasjit differentiated between sexuality as a practice and as a lifestyle when he defined homosexuality as 'an innate personal trait that may or may not be translated into a conscious lifestyle decision'.

Most respondents noted that being gay in India carried its own unique set of connotations and experiences, mainly because of the cultural, social and religious structures, and family pressures that insist on conformity to traditional patriarchal, heteronormative values. Still, almost all were confident that India was becoming more open to the idea of homosexuality, although they qualified that this change was confined largely to urban areas and came accompanied by many riders.

JASJIT: *OPEN* IS A DECEPTIVE WORD IN MY OPINION—THE
           PARADIGMS OF SOCIAL ACCEPTANCE IT CONNOTES ARE
           ESSENTIALLY ROOTED IN WESTERN THINKING AND BASED
           ON INDIVIDUALISM AND RATIONALITY. PEOPLE IN INDIA HAVE
           VIEWED IT DIFFERENTLY…
VIDWAN: TO A LARGE EXTENT, THE INDIAN WAY OF LOOKING AT QUEER-
           NESS IS VERY DIFFERENT FROM THE WAY THE WEST SEES IT.
           THERE SEEMS TO BE A LOT MORE ACCEPTANCE OR AT LEAST
           TOLERANCE OF QUEERNESS IN INDIA AS LONG AS IT DOES
           NOT COME IN THE WAY OF HETEROSEXUAL PROCREATIVE
           ACTIVITY. THE RECENT VISIBILITY GIVEN TO AN OVERTLY
           POLITICIZED SEXUAL IDENTITY IS WHAT IS EXTREMELY UN-
           NERVING FOR MANY WHO SEE THEIR PRESENT POSITIONS
           IN SOCIETY, COMPROMISED BY A QUESTIONING OF GENDER
           AND SEXUALITY. AND YET, THERE IS CHANGE, MUCH OF IT
           POSITIVE—A LOT OF IT, COMING FROM THE ENGLISH MEDIA.
           IN URBAN HIP CULTURES, HOMOSEXUALITY IS FINE AND SO IS
           HAVING GAY FRIENDS, BUT SOME OF THE OLDER ATTITUDES
           PERSIST, SOMETIMES UNKNOWINGLY.

Many respondents echoed Vidwan's assertion that gay men in India
could easily compromise with straight society by existing 'within the
confines of a heterosexual framework' (Pratham). However, for others,
this 'silent acceptance' (Rahim) was a mirage, 'an existence in invisibility',
(Senthil) that would be shattered with increased visibility, which in turn
would almost certainly lead to 'more pronounced homophobia' (Nihar).

JASJIT: BEING GAY AND INDIAN WOULD, IN A TRADITIONAL CULTURAL
           SENSE, MEAN HAVING SEX WITH A MEMBER OF SAME SEX
           MORE AS A *HOBBY* OR *PASSION* (*SHAUK* IN HINDI), RATHER THAN
           TO TURN IT AN IDENTITY ISSUE, WHICH IS A POST-MODERN
           VIEW OF HOMOSEXUALITY, SO FAR AS INDIA IS CONCERNED.
           THUS, MANY INDIAN GAYS WOULD HAPPILY GET MARRIED AND
           HAVE FAMILIES. FAMILIAL GENDER BIAS AND THE GENERAL
           LACK OF INDIVIDUALISTIC THOUGHT, ESPECIALLY WHEN IT
           COMES TO WOMEN, HELP SUPPORT SUCH A SITUATION. ALSO,
           THE GENERAL MASS OF GAY INDIANS ARE QUITE UNAWARE OF
           THE HISTORICITY OF THEIR SEXUAL PREDILECTION AND SO IS
           THE SOCIETY AT LARGE—SO THE MAIN HOMOPHOBIC AGENDA
           FOR INDIANS CAN BE THAT BEING GAY IS ESSENTIALLY A
           WESTERN (LESS CHAUVINIST) OR ISLAMIC (MORE CHAUVINIST)

PHENOMENON AND IT NEVER EXISTED IN INDIA! THERE MOST CERTAINLY IS A UNIQUE GAY CULTURE. INDIVIDUAL TRAITS, WHICH IN TURN ARE CONVERTED INTO SOCIAL TRAITS THAT FOSTER AND CHERISH IT, ARE NARCISSISM, CHAUVINISM, ESCAPISM AND INDIVIDUALISM. OF COURSE THERE CAN BE MANY MORE, OFTEN HAVING THEIR OWN DIALECTIC (THESIS-ANTITHESIS-SYNTHESIS), RHETORIC AND POLITIC DYNAMICS.

RAHIM: A LOT OF GAY MEN ARE FINDING COMFORT IN THAT SPACE, WHICH SAYS—DO EVERYTHING, BUT BE QUIET! IF YOU ARE GAY, REMAIN GAY. IT'S OKAY. JUST DON'T WALK ON THE ROAD WAVING A FLAG. I HAVE A FRIEND, A GAY COUPLE, WHO HAVE BEEN LIVING FOR TEN YEARS IN A BUILDING SOCIETY. EVERYONE IN THE SOCIETY AND THEIR WORKPLACE KNOWS THAT THEY ARE A COUPLE BUT IT IS NOT TALKED ABOUT. IT GIVES THEM A GREAT SENSE OF COMFORT THAT WE ARE NOT A HOMOPHOBIC SOCIETY. THESE GUYS HAVE FOUND COMFORT IN A SOCIETY THAT IS WILLING TO OVERLOOK THEIR RELATIONSHIP AS LONG AS IT IS NOT ACKNOWLEDGED. WE ARE NOT A HOMOPHOBIC SOCIETY AS LONG AS EVERYTHING IS QUIET. THE MOMENT I GET UP AND SAY I WANT AN ACKNOWLEDGEMENT THAT I AM GAY AND AT PAR AS ANYONE ELSE IN SOCIETY, IS WHEN THE PROBLEM COMES UP.

However, it would be a mistake to assume that this *contract of silence* (Ashok Row Kavi, 1999)[3] existing in India is similar to the situation that prevailed in the West in the early and mid 20th century, where typically the gay son would leave home as soon as he could, 'both to move to a larger city and to keep his secret from kin' (Sanders, 2004).[4] In India, leaving home is an option that is rarely exercised, but even if this happens (as with Bhuvan, Yudhisthir and some of my other interviewees), the shadow of family continues to loom large in influencing the lives and decisions of gay men.

JASJIT: A PERSON'S EXISTENTIAL NOTIONS ARE STILL ROOTED INTO THE FAMILY AS OPPOSED TO THE INDIVIDUAL. SO THE FAMILY'S ROLE, ESPECIALLY WHEN IT COMES TO IDENTITY-BASED ISSUES LIKE *COMING OUT* FOR EXAMPLE, CAN BE CRUCIAL.

RANDHIR: THE MANIFESTATION OF THIS IN THE LIVES OF SAME-SEX ATTRACTED PERSONS IS MOST PROFOUNDLY FELT IN THE AREA OF (HETEROSEXUAL) MARRIAGE, WHERE THE PERSON

OFTEN CANNOT RESIST THE FAMILY PRESSURE AND DOES
CONCEDE TO GETTING MARRIED, THUS LIVING A DUAL LIFE
AFTER THAT!

The mythologist Devdutt Pattanaik (2002) attributes the unique marriage pressure on Indian gay men to the overwhelming influence of the 'Hindu way of life' in India.[5]

> For the sake of social stability, scriptures demand unquestioning obedience to sacred duties (*Dharma*) that are determined by one's inherited caste (*Varna*) and one's stage in life (*Ashrama*). One's duty, or rather a biological obligation, common to all castes, is to produce children, so as to facilitate the rebirth of ancestors and keep the cycle of life rotating.... The Hindu way of life also acknowledges that the humans need to earn a living (*Artha*) and enjoy life (*Kama*). However, the right to worldly goods and worldly pleasures comes only *after* worldly duties are performed. Thus, marriage is transformed into a key to worldly life. Unless married, the Hindu man has no right to own property or to perform religious rituals. He has no right to indulge his senses. The unmarried man is given two choices—remain a chaste student (*Brahmachari*) or turn into a celibate hermit (*Sanyasi*)... All hell breaks loose in a Hindu household not so much when a son or daughter displays homosexual tendencies, but when those tendencies come in the way of heterosexual marriage... Non-heterosexuality is ignored or tolerated as long as it does not upset the heterosexual world order.[6]

Indications of this tremendous pressure to conform to social norms were made visible to me in the case of the three married men who were a part of my survey. They all stated that they had got married as they felt that there was no other alternative. From among the others, I was struck that although only 21 years old, Iravan was already feeling the burden of this pressure when he insisted during our conversation that he had no choice but to get married. 'I am an only child and I have to do the best for my parents. I know that I am going to get married. [But] I do not know if I will be able to overcome my sexual attraction to men'.

This pressure, as Vidvan pointed out, is even more intense when the gay person is effeminate and thus visibly marked different—

BECAUSE SEXUALITY IS NEVER VERY OVERT, BUT GENDER OFTEN TENDS
TO BE SO, EFFEMINATE MEN AND BUTCH WOMEN OFTEN FACE GREATER

HURDLES THAN OTHERS IN QUEER CIRCLES. ALSO, MANY ARE OFTEN WILLING TO COMPROMISE FOR THIS ACCEPTANCE, LIKE GETTING MARRIED OUT OF FAMILY PRESSURE, WHILE THE FAMILY REMAINS SILENT OVER MANY CONTINUING RELATIONSHIPS.

Rebellion against this pressure can sometimes mean banishment (Queen Rekha revealed that her decision to come out as *kothi* led to her estrangement from her family), but in most cases, the child is not thrown out, but pressurized to change his ways in order to maintain the family *izzat* (honour).

On the issue of coming out, my understanding is that although all respondents had shared information about their homosexuality with their friends to some extent or another, most equated *coming out* with coming out to their families. Here, the first obstacle as Ormus lamented, was that 'in India, there does not exist a respectable vocabulary for homosexuality. If I were to come out to my aunts and uncles, I have no idea what words I would ever use'. Students Gul, Nihar and Om shared with me their deep desire to come out, but only after they graduated and achieved financial independence from their families, as they were apprehensive about their reactions. For Ormus, Divakar, Taksa and Husain, fear of confrontation with their families led to their eliminating all traces of their homosexuality within the family presence. Even in situations like Mohnish's where he acknowledged that his family might be understanding ('they are broadminded, liberal, discuss homosexuality often'), there was still a fear that 'their condition would be quite miserable… if they found out that their own son was gay'.

On the other hand, for openly out respondents like Kabir, Cholan, Rahim, Karim, Harbhajan and Mike, the family helped serve as a vital source of support.

MIKE: I'VE BEEN RAISED IN A PSYCHIATRIST'S HOUSE. SO THERE HAVE NEVER REALLY BEEN ANY ISSUES OR TABOOS. SOME OF MY PARENTS' CLOSEST FRIENDS ARE GAY, SO IT WAS MUCH EASIER FOR ME TO ACCEPT MYSELF AND TO REALIZE THAT I'M NOT A GENETIC DEFECT OR SOMETHING.

CHOLAN: MY FATHER'S FIRST REACTION WAS, 'LETS CHALLENGE THE LAW.' HIS SECOND REACTION WAS, 'I WANT TO READ SOME BOOKS ON THIS TO UNDERSTAND IT BETTER.' HIS THIRD REACTION WAS, 'YOU KNOW I'VE BOUGHT A SMALL FLAT IN

BOMBAY, IT'S NOT READY BUT WHEN IT IS, I THINK YOU NEED YOUR OWN SPACE AND I THINK YOU SHOULD HAVE IT.' HIS FOURTH REACTION WAS, 'I WANT TO MEET OTHER PARENTS.' I DON'T KNOW ANY OF MY FRIENDS WHO'VE HAD SUCH A COOL EXPERIENCES WITH THEIR PARENTS. SIX YEARS AGO, THEY ASKED ME, 'CHOLAN YOU ARE OF MARRIAGEABLE AGE, IF OUR FRIENDS ASK US, WHAT DO YOU WANT US TO SAY?' I TOLD THEM TO SAY WHATEVER THEY THOUGHT WAS APPROPRIATE. THEY SAID, 'WE WANT TO TELL THEM THAT YOU'RE GAY.' I WAS LIKE, WELL THAT'S THE ULTIMATE EMPOWERMENT, IF YOU CAN BE SO MATTER OF FACT ABOUT IT.

Yudhisthir described his coming out as a *necessity* due to the extreme anxiety that he was experiencing while being in the closet, which was affecting his health and studies. 'I was a nervous wreck. After coming out, the headaches have gone and the anxiety levels are lower. I am not compulsive or neurotic any more'. Harbhajan, who was married and forced to come out due to blackmail threats he was receiving from one of the male prostitutes he frequented, received rock steady support from an unexpected source—his wife!

SHE WAS RELIEVED. OUR RELATIONSHIP FINALLY MADE SENSE TO HER, THAT THERE WAS NOTHING WRONG WITH HER. SHE SAID THAT SHE DIDN'T HAVE A PROBLEM BUT WE SHOULD KEEP IT WITHIN OURSELVES. THE FIRST TWO YEARS AFTER I CAME OUT TO HER WE DECIDED NOT TO HAVE A CHILD BUT THEN DECIDED THAT WE WANT TO BE TOGETHER AND WE WANT TO HAVE A CHILD TOGETHER. WE HAVE BEEN MARRIED FOR SEVEN YEARS NOW AND HAVE A DAUGHTER. I NOW TELL HER EXACTLY WHAT GOES ON IN GAY BOMBAY MEETINGS, FILM SCREENINGS, PARTIES, EVERYTHING. SHE EVEN MAINTAINS ACCOUNTS FOR THE [GAY BOMBAY] GROUP! I AM SUCH A LUCKY BASTARD. I DON'T KNOW WHY I HAVE GOT ALL THIS LUCK, I DON'T DESERVE IT.

Gopal's insistence on speaking to the press about his homosexuality was a contentious issue with his family. 'They say, ok, you are gay; why do you have to be in the press? Others can do it. My answer is that yes, there are others doing it too. And many more are required as well'. Other respondents like Husain and Pratham walked a tight rope while negotiating space for themselves and their homosexuality within their family systems—a *don't ask, don't tell* policy that ensured that everyone was happy. Pratham revealed, 'There has been silent support—by which I mean I have never been forced in marriage. They are aware that my partner lives with me. My sister and nieces in the US always bring or send gifts for him'. For Murgesh and Asim, tacit acceptance by the family had led to their making professional or personal sacrifices, that they said they were perfectly happy making.

ASIM: TO ME, NOT GETTING MARRIED WAS A FAR MORE IM-PORTANT ISSUE. I WAS VERY CLEAR THAT I WAS GOING TO FIGHT DESPERATELY FOR THAT. I WASN'T READY TO PICK ANOTHER FIGHT ABOUT WHERE I WAS GOING TO WORK. I GAVE IN ON THAT [AND JOINED THE FAMILY BUSINESS] BECAUSE I NEEDED TO PROTECT MY SEXUALITY BY NOT GETTING MARRIED.

MURGESH: IF YOU FEEL YOUR FAMILY IS SACRIFICING IN ACCEPTING YOU (PRIDE, SOCIAL STATUS AND SO ON)—YOU CAN ALSO SACRIFICE. MOST OF MY FAMILY KNOWS—ALTHOUGH WE DON'T DISCUSS IT. I AM WILLING TO MAKE THE SACRI-FICE OF NOT BEING OUT COMPLETELY FOR THEIR SAKE.

As it could be expected, the geographical location of the respondents influenced greatly their capacity to network and meet other gay people. For the respondents living outside India, coffee shops, bars, cafés, pubs, malls, gay video parlors and the Internet were all possible venues for inter-action. For those within India, parks, public toilets, trains and railway stations and other cruising areas, the Internet and Gay Bombay parties were some of the options listed. Taksa even provided a detailed stat-istical breakdown of the people he met in Bombay—'Internet—70 per cent; railway stations in Bombay—3 per cent; through other people—25 per cent; gay group meetings—2 per cent'.

GAY BOMBAY: ACCESS AND IMPACT

My respondents came to know about Gay Bombay by reading about it in city newspapers like the *Bombay Times,* searching for, or stumbling upon it on the Internet and through word-of-mouth publicity. Some accessed the group exclusively online (either because they were apprehensive, married, lived out of Bombay or simply did not have the time to attend any of its offline manifestations) and for these individuals, the website and newsgroup engendered a kind of 'immobile socialization'[7]—enabling them to feel connected to the Gay Bombay community at large. Those who lived in Bombay and were comfortable attending the local events, equated Gay Bombay primarily with the city based events and not with the list or website. Even here, there was a split between those who thought of it as primarily a party space and those who thought of it as a space for other kinds of community events.

For the newsgroup subscribers, the reasons for signing up were varied. For some it was just curiosity, for others, a way to know more about the emerging gay world in India. Vidvan said that he was 'fascinated at being able to interact with other gay people in Bombay, while being anonymous at the same time'. The respondents from out of India looked at the group as a connection to their home country. Thus, Husain had experienced a 'craving for my countrymen' and could 'relate better to men who think and act more in line with my culture and traditions'. For activists like Randhir and Gopal, the possibility of advocacy and working for the issue of LBGT rights was the lure. For Murgesh, it was the chance to share his poems and romantic musings with other gay people. 'It is a readymade market—I would post my work and receive all *oohs* and *aahs*—people would write back and say, its so lovely…it felt good. I felt euphoric'. Often, it was simply a search for empathic gay friends.

Respondents like Kabir and Asim, who had their fill of Madh Island parties and cruising and dancing at Voodoo through the 1980s and the 1990s, accessed the various Gay Bombay spaces out of a sense of 'wanting to do more for the community' (Kabir). 'You see younger people and you do not want those who are 15 to have the same experiences as you did and make the mistakes you made'. Asim found the sense of community he obtained through Gay Bombay as a progression from his promiscuous earlier days, in which 'being homosexual was just about partying and sex'.

Once the respondents had signed up for the online group, they continued to subscribe for a variety of reasons. For Karim, Pratham, Randhir and Queen Rekha, it had become a community that they were deeply involved in and knew the other members. 'It is a largely *non-cruisy*, moderately intelligent e-list', said Randhir. 'I continue to visit it mostly to update myself on what is happening and also to update others with information that I may be privy to. I also like to read up on the various articles that get posted there regularly'. It was also important to know 'who is bitching about whom…' (Vidvan). For Husain, Jasjit and Taksa who lived out of India, the chance to keep in touch with the happenings back home and participate in the discussions were the biggest draws, so that when they visited Bombay on their holidays, they could plug into the offline community easily. In contrast, Mike who lived in the US, declared that he had unsubscribed from the newsgroup and only occasionally visited the Gay Bombay site. His main interest in the group was the parties that he attended whenever he was in Bombay, but he was beginning to find even these to be boring.

Mike says:	Going every fortnight for the event gets very boring.
Parmesh says:	Why is that?
Mike says:	Same people, trashy place, waste of money and at Gay Bombay, there's a 90–10 trash-cuties ratio.
	I think Gay Bombay is more about shedding inhibitions, learning to love sleaze and having a good time.
Parmesh says:	In terms of activities?
Mike says:	Dancing.
Parmesh says:	You see it primarily as a party organization?
Mike says:	I know they have other events too.
Parmesh says:	Yes.
Mike says:	But I would get bored at those events.
Parmesh says:	Why?
Mike says:	Because they're more for people who are coming to terms with their sexuality.
Parmesh says:	Ah!
Mike says:	That is phase 1.
Parmesh says:	And you are in?
Mike says:	Probably phase 3.

For those respondents who accessed Gay Bombay offline, a pleasant first experience was the main motivating factor for them to keep on returning to the group's events. Gul utilized the *Neighbourhood Watch* service provided on the Gay Bombay website and mailed one of the volunteers who had contacted him and encouraged him to come for the meeting.

When Gul subsequently expressed his apprehension about going for the Gay Bombay party the week following the meeting, the volunteer kindly told Gul that he could attend the party along with him and his boyfriend. Before attending his first meeting, Harbhajan was nervous that his married status might be a problem for some of the other members. Their unequivocal acceptance of him into their fold was a huge relief. 'From then on, I attended each and every meet'. Bhuvan established at his very first meeting that this was a group he could 'relate to'.

> BHUVAN: THESE ARE THE KINDS OF PEOPLE I WANT TO BE WITH. ISSUES BEING DISCUSSED IN SUCH A NON-PERSONAL WAY. THERE WAS A STUDENT, WHO HAD JUST DIED, PEOPLE HERE WERE RE- MEMBERING HIM WITH ENOUGH SENSITIVITY, WITH DUE RESPECT TO HIS MOM. IN A WAY IT WAS COMFORTING THAT IF I CHOSE THIS PATH, AFTER I DIE PEOPLE ARE THERE... WHEN SOMEONE IS SO SENSITIVE ENOUGH TO SEE ISSUES CLEARLY WITHOUT GETTING FILTERED, THAT'S WHEN YOU KNOW THE PERSON IS SENSIBLE AND WHEN YOU HAVE ONE MORE SENSIBLE PERSON LIKE THAT IN A GROUP, GOOD; IF YOU LOOK UP TO THAT, YOU WANT TO BE LIKE THAT, THEN YOU WANT TO COME BACK AND GAIN THAT KIND OF KNOWLEDGE. AT [MY FIRST] PARTY I SAW THE PEOPLE BEHIND THE SCENES, SAW HOW SENSIBLE AND SENSITIVE THEY ARE WHAT KIND OF THOUGHT PROCESS GOES BEHIND THE SCENE. THESE ARE RESPONSIBLE PEOPLE.

My interviewees came up with a wide range of positives attributed to Gay Bombay's presence. For Taksa and Mike, the online world of Gay Bombay had not emphasized individual differences as much as diminished them, while Pratham thought that it had resulted in making people more 'individualistic and helped them live a gay lifestyle'. Karim felt that it had 'literally changed the life of so many people'—helped many people come out, given younger people confidence and enabled at least some people to withstand marriage pressure.

> ASIM: PEOPLE FROM MY PAST WILL TELL ME THAT I WAS DULL. PEOPLE TODAY SAY I AM ONE OF THE MOST TALKATIVE PEOPLE AROUND. PROBABLY THIS HAS BEEN DUE TO THE FACT THAT I HAVE BEEN ABLE TO FIND A COMMUNITY AND EXPRESS MYSELF FREELY. MAYBE MY PREVIOUS RESERVE WAS A SHELL IN WHICH I USED

TO KEEP MYSELF. YES, I HAVE NO QUESTIONS ABOUT THE FACT
THAT GAY BOMBAY HAS HELPED ME. I KNOW TODAY THAT MY
DEGREE OF OPENNESS COMES TO A LARGE EXTENT FROM MY
INTERACTIONS WITH GAY BOMBAY.

On the other hand, Queen Rekha and Gopal commented that the group
may have had a negative impact on the lives of homosexuals in India, either
because, they have 'made it easier to stay closeted' (Queen Rekha) or, as
Gopal wrote, 'often consciously, encouraged the evolution of a gutless,
closeted, urban gay male who is mainly a sexual creature. Through mutual
complicity, they have sanctioned and strengthened language, class and
gender barriers between emerging gay cultures'.

'The catch phrase for Gay Bombay is that "come to the meets, it is
people like us"', said Senthil. 'What do *people like us* mean? Middle
class, working, having jobs, English speaking not doing drag—"normal"
people. [Gay Bombay is] creating normativity in the gay scene by excluding others...people who are effeminate, from a working class
background...'

COMMUNITY

The interviewees reported experiencing community differently. For
some, it indicated the network of friendships they had been able to form
through Gay Bombay, both online and offline; for others, just being a
part of Gay Bombay itself gave them a feeling of community.

NACHIKET: GAY BOMBAY IS A COMMUNITY, BOTH ONLINE AND OFFLINE.
IT IS NOT A PICKUP SPACE, LIKE A LOT OF OTHER ORGAN-
IZATIONS IN OTHER CITIES. IT ACCOMMODATES A DIVERSE
RANGE OF VIEWS, FROM THE TRULY OBNOXIOUS AND
HOMOPHOBIC, TO THE MAINSTREAM, TO THE LIBERAL.

Woolvine (2000) contends that gay men in the West generally tend to
break down *Gemeinschalft* or *Gesellschaft* distinctions in their organizations[8] and membership within a gay organization—social or political—
tends to result in both primary and secondary groupings. The scenario in
India is clearly different; as per my observations, the primary affiliation

group for most respondents was their own blood family. Though many of them did form pretty 'intimate secondary relationships'[9] (Wireman, 1984) within the various Gay Bombay spaces, with 'informal, frequent and supportive community ties'[10] (Wellman and Gulia, 1998) binding these relationships, the group functioned more as a neo-tribe—with partial and shifting affiliations; it 'did not have a complete and total hold' over them (Charles and Davies, 1997).[11]

There were different reasons provided for attributing *community* to the Gay Bombay experience. For Vidvan, Om, Isaac, Asim and Bhuvan, the wide range of safe spaces engendered by Gay Bombay were the 'locus for "expressive" and "emotionally reciprocal" behavior' (Woolvine, 2000).[12] The group functioned as a 'third space' for its members, a place other than home or work (Oldenburg, 1991) that provided them the capacity to just be *themselves* without any fear of discrimination. I noticed that the constant interaction between members online and offline had produced a kind of community feeling and loyalty to the group. Individuals like Rustom and Husain who primarily accessed the group online, described this community feeling as an ability to recognize the names of regular posters; (Rustom—'They are becoming personalities or individuals in my mind'), while Kabir and Harbhajan pointed to the range of regular social events that Gay Bombay organized as well as the services provided like *Neighbourhood Watch* as an indication that Gay Bombay was a vibrant and thriving community.

KARIM: IT IS A COMMUNITY—BUT IT DOESN'T MEAN THAT EVERY GAY PERSON HAS TO BE FRIENDLY WITH EVERY OTHER GAY PERSON. IN MANY CASES WE DON'T EVEN GET RECOGNITION FROM GAY PEOPLE. BUT A LARGE NUMBER OF PEOPLE WHO COME FOR OUR PARTIES FEEL THAT THERE IS A CERTAIN KIND OF COMMUNITY THEY ARE BEING A PART OF AND THEY HAVE A CERTAIN LEVEL OF APPRECIATION FOR WHAT GAY BOMBAY DOES. IF SOME-THING AWFUL HAPPENS WOULD THEY COME TOGETHER IN SUPPORT? I DON'T KNOW, PERHAPS NOT. THAT'S SOMETHING THAT CAN ONLY BE TESTED. WE'VE REACHED OUT TO A WIDE RANGE OF PEOPLE—WITHIN THAT THERE WOULD BE SOME PEOPLE WHO ONLY THINK OF US AS PARTY ORGANIZERS, BUT THERE ARE STILL ENOUGH PEOPLE WHO WOULD THINK THAT IT IS A COMMUNITY…

Karim also drew on Granovetter's notion of strong and weak ties[13] (1973) to reason that the success of GB as a community lay in its online origins.

KARIM: WE ALWAYS THINK OF A COMMUNITY AS ONE WITH STRONG LINKS. STRONG LINKS HAVE PROBLEMS—LOT OF BONDING AND LOT OF FIGHTING ALSO. WEAK LINKS ARE USEFUL BECAUSE THEY PROVIDE A CERTAIN CONTINUITY BUT THEY PREVENT PEOPLE GETTING BORED OR BECOMING TOO MUCH OF A BURDEN. PURELY BY CHANCE, WITH THE INTERNET WE HAD A TECHNOLOGY THAT WAS GREAT AT PROVIDING WEAK LINKS— IT WASN'T OPPRESSIVE OR PUSHING ITS ATTENTION ON US ALL THE TIME. IT WAS THERE AND WE COULD FOCUS ATTENTION ON IT WHEN WE WANTED TO.

Both Vidvan and Karim touched upon the *imagined* nature of Gay Bombay, as a part of a larger imagined gay community in India. Vidvan empha-sized—'Even if there is no such thing as an Indian community right now, it is important to address yourself as a community; in the very process of calling yourself a community, the community gets formed'. Karim agreed and stated that from the point of view of the organizers—

WE'RE OUT TO CREATE A *GAY* COMMUNITY. GAY BOMBAY IS JUST INCIDENTAL. A FACILITATOR. WE WANT PEOPLE TO FIND THEIR OWN LEVEL OF COMFORT. THERE IS A REAL BENEFIT IN PROVIDING DIFFER-ENT SPACES FOR PEOPLE TO FIND THEIR OWN LEVEL OF COMFORT... HOPEFULLY WITHIN THESE SPACES THEY WILL MOVE ON TO LARGER EDUCATION WITHIN THE GAY COMMUNITY... AS IN, THINKING OF THEMSELVES AS A GAY PERSON—WE DON'T PARTICULARLY WANT PEOPLE TO THINK OF THEMSELVES AS 'A GAY BOMBAY PERSON'.

Woolvine (2000) has described the 'divided community' as the corollary to imagined community;[14] several of my respondents articulated this division and simultaneously emphatically denied community status to Gay Bombay.

BHUDEV: NO. I AM BECOMING VERY DISILLUSIONED. ACCORDING TO ME, THERE ARE NETWORKS FOR MEN FUCKING MEN. WAY ACROSS CLASS AND GENDER. I DON'T THINK THERE IS ANY TOGETHERNESS.

Randhir, Nihar and Cholan felt that community was too big a word to describe gay Bombay and called it 'a reasonably successful group', 'a driving force' and 'a loose collective' respectively. Mike contemptuously referred to it as 'scattered cliques who refuse to recognize each other in public'. For Pratham and Jasjit, it was a virtual community rather than a real world one, while Gopal indicated that it was more of a 'social network' since 'a dozen people do not make a community; there has to be a much larger number of people who relate to each other and have characteristics, needs, desires, goals and so on that coincide to a high degree'. Rustom and Yudhisthir concurred and referred to the *hijra* community as a case in point.

> YUDHISTHIR: I THINK A COMMUNITY NEEDS TO HAVE A DEEPER SENSE OF BONDING, WHICH GAY BOMBAY DOESN'T HAVE. THE *HIJRA* COMMUNITY HAS A TREMENDOUS SENSE OF BONDING. IF YOU TALK ABOUT PEOPLE WHO DO DRAG OR THE TRANSVESTITE POPULATION, THEY ARE A COMMUNITY. BUT GAY BOMBAY IS A GROUP, A BIG SOCIAL GROUP…CATERING TO PEOPLE WHO WANT TO DO THINGS OTHER THAN SEX.

GLOBALIZATION AND LOCALITY

All the respondents felt that globalization (which they largely perceived to be financial, technological and communication focussed in nature) had had some impact on their lives and on the larger gay scene at large within India. Many respondents praised the international media that were available in India post 1991, as the harbinger of a liberal worldview towards homosexuality.

Queen Rekha pointed out that globalization had provided her with employment in the call centre industry. For Nihar and Senthil, globalization presented an opportunity for the young Indian gay movement to learn from the legal, media and social battles already fought in the West. Nachiket theorized that 'globalization and the rising middle class' led to 'increased travel, increased opportunities…as more and more material desires get satisfied, your aspiration levels increase in terms of finding your identity and expressing it and being honest about it'. My other interviewee responses seemed to confirm his hypothesis.

Travel was a theme that came up again and again in many of my interviews with respondents located in India. Whether this referred to travel to Bombay from a smaller city in India (Om, Nihar, Senthil), or to travel out of India for study (Murgesh, Mike, Cholan, Rustom), leisure (Harbhajan, Asim, Karim, Gul) or work (Nachiket, Cholan, Bhudev)—all the respondents spoke about it as a positive experience in helping them learn more about themselves and their sexuality.

NIHAR: WHEN I CAME TO BOMBAY [FROM BHOPAL], IT WAS GAY EL DORADO... IF I HADN'T GOT IN TOUCH WITH THE GAY WORLD, I WOULDN'T HAVE BEEN SO LIBERAL. I WOULD HAVE BEEN A PRUDISH PERSON—SOMEONE WHO GETS SCANDALIZED EASILY... STRANGELY, IT WAS MY FATHER WHO WANTED ME TO COME HERE. HE SAW WHAT A SISSY I AM—HE WANTED ME TO BE IN THE BIG BAD WORLD AND LEARN THINGS OF MY OWN. I THINK IT WAS A GOOD DECISION!

Some of the older interviewees described themselves as *passport princesses*—privileged gay men who could travel abroad to experience a gay lifestyle there (which they equated with being out, gay parties and activism). Among this generation, Murgesh and Cholan spoke of leaving India in search of their gay identity, but returning in disappointment—their experiences in foreign lands were an affirmation of their separateness from Western gay culture instead of the utopia they had hoped to find.

MURGESH: I DECIDED THAT THERE IS NO WAY I CAN FIND AN IDENTITY IN INDIA. SO I SAID, OKAY, I CAN BE GAY IN AMERICA. THIS WAS 1978. I KNEW THERE WAS A MOVEMENT IN THE WEST— AND I WANTED TO BE PART OF IT. BUT WHEN I WAS THERE, MY CULTURAL IDENTITY, WHICH I THOUGHT WAS NOT SO IMPORTANT BEFORE GOING TO THE US, BECAME A BIG STRUGGLE. I COULDN'T ADJUST TO A WESTERN LIFESTYLE. IN THOSE DAYS, UNLESS YOU WERE IN A BIG CITY, YOU WERE INVISIBILIZED UNLESS YOU DID NOT ASSIMILATE. AND FOR ME, I DID NOT WANT TO. I WAS MISSING INDIAN FOOD, INDIAN FILMS AND MUSIC. MAYBE IF I HAD FOUND

SOMEONE IN THOSE VULNERABLE YEARS, I WOULD HAVE
SETTLED DOWN IN THE US. BUT SINCE IT WASN'T THE
PARADISE THAT I HAD THOUGHT IT WOULD BE AS FAR AS
BEING GAY WAS CONCERNED, I RETURNED.

CHOLAN: I WENT TO CHRISTOPHER STREET. I WENT TO THE CASTRO.
I KNEW I WANTED TO COME BACK AND TELL MY DAD AND
BE HONEST TO PEOPLE THAT MATTERED. WHETHER THERE
WOULD BE SPACES OR NO SPACES, IT DIDN'T MATTER. I WAS
LOOKING FOR SPACE WITHIN FAMILY. I WASN'T LOOKING
FOR SPACES LIKE CHRISTOPHER STREET.

In contrast, younger interviewees, already exposed to the international gay scene through television and the net, used their travels abroad to either access support and counselling services that were difficult to find in India (Rustom), or voraciously consume the gay pop culture that they were already vicariously previously clued in to (Gul)—and both these acts served as confidence building measures for living out a gay lifestyle *in* India on their return.

GUL: IN AMERICA, THE WORD 'GAY' IS SO OPEN ON AMERICAN
TV—I SAW *QUEER EYE, BOY MEETS BOY, THE REAL WORLD,
QUEER AS FOLK*. BEING GAY IS OK. I WENT TO SAN FRANCISCO;
SAW CASTRO, THE RAINBOW FLAGS AND ALL THAT. THEN
THERE WAS LAS VEGAS, SEX AND SLEAZE... WENT TO NEW
ORLEANS. I WENT TO ALL THESE BARS. I WENT AND SAW A
DRAG SHOW, A STRIP CLUB WHEN I CAME BACK, I WAS MUCH
MORE CONFIDENT. I WAS GOING FOR GAY BOMBAY EVENTS
REGULARLY. NOW IT IS A LIFESTYLE FOR ME.

Many respondents indicated that the Internet was extremely crucial in helping them formulate their own personal conception of an imagined gay world.

BHUVAN: IF THE NET WEREN'T THERE, MY LIFE WOULD HAVE BEEN
HELL. EVERY STEP OF MY DISCOVERY PROCESS—HAS
BEEN TOTALLY INTERNET DRIVEN. WHEN I WENT ONLINE I
STARTED KNOWING GAY PEOPLE AND REALIZED THAT THEY
ARE NORMAL PEOPLE, THEY HAD DECENT LIVES, THEY
WERE EDUCATED... BUT STILL THEY WERE GAY. I CAME TO
KNOW THAT I LIKED THIS. I CAN LOOK AT MEN AS SEXUAL

PARTNERS. I STARTED EXPLORING THE NET. EVEN IN
READING PORN STORIES, IF THEY ARE NOT ENCOUNTER
STORIES, THEY ARE RELATIONSHIP STORIES AND I GOT
THE IMPRESSION THAT TWO GUYS CAN LIVE TOGETHER,
BE HAPPY TOGETHER. THERE IS A POSSIBILITY FOR A
HAPPY LIFE APART FROM THE 'FAMILY, FAMILY' THAT
I'VE BEEN TOLD ABOUT. SO WHAT I WISH IS NOT A
PATH TO DOOM AS PEOPLE CLAIM. BUT RATHER IT CAN
BE SOMETHING ENRICHING, SOMETHING THAT I LOOK
FORWARD TO.

YUDHISTHIR: THROUGH THE NET, WE INTERACT WITH GAY PEOPLE IN SO
MANY DIFFERENT CITIES. WE COME TO KNOW THAT IT'S
NOT SUCH A BAD THING BEING GAY... I MYSELF AM NOT
A PARTICULARLY POSITIVE GAY GUY. I'M A MELANCHOLIC
GUY, KIND OF PESSIMISTIC. I HAVE DISCOVERED THAT YOU
DON'T HAVE TO BE GAY AND BE DEPRESSED; YOU CAN BE
GAY AND CHEERFUL.

PULKIT: IT HAS BROUGHT A FEELING OF SAFETY, WHICH WASN'T
THERE INITIALLY. BROUGHT ABOUT THE POSSIBILITY OF
PROTECTING YOURSELF WHILE TRYING TO CONNECT TO
OTHERS.

However, respondents like Gopal, Vidvan, Randhir, Queen Rekha and
Jasjit also implicated the Internet and globalization at large for further
dividing the rifts between those who identified as gay and those who
identified as *hijra* or *kothi* or MSM—largely on class lines.

VIDVAN: BECAUSE OF THE ANONYMITY IT OFFERS, [THE INTERNET]
IS PREFERRED AS A MEANS OF INTERACTION, BY THOSE
WHO CAN AFFORD IT OR UNDERSTAND HOW TO USE IT. UN-
FORTUNATELY, THIS USUALLY INCLUDES ONLY THOSE WITH
SOME DEGREE OF A WESTERN ENGLISH EDUCATION AND
THOSE FROM THE UPPER OR UPPER MIDDLE CLASSES. MANY
OTHER QUEER MEN HAVE TO CHOOSE THE TRADITIONAL
MEANS OF INTERACTION, ESPECIALLY SEEKING RECOURSE
TO CRUISING AREAS. THIS RESULTS IN A CLASS-BASED (AND
OFTEN CASTE-BASED) MEANS OF INTERACTION.

GOPAL: FUNNILY, I AM TOLD THAT IN THE PHILIPPINES, BECAUSE OF
THE INTERNET, IT HAS ENCOURAGED AN EXPLOSION OF OUT
GAY CULTURES, STORES, RESTAURANTS AND HANGOUTS. IN
PLACES LIKE INDIA, IT HAS JUST HELPED PEOPLE TO FIND

FUCKS, REMAIN IN THE CLOSET, GET MARRIED AND GET ON
WITH THEIR LIVES.

RANDHIR: 'GAY' PEOPLE NOW HAVE A BETTER AND MORE VARIED
CHOICE OF BARS, PUBS AND DISCOS, SO THEY CAN BE 'JUST
LIKE THEM' MORE EASILY. IT'S NEVER BEEN BETTER FOR
THEM SINCE GLOBALIZATION. NOW THEY CAN SAVE MUCH
MORE BY GOING ON FEWER FOREIGN TRIPS THAT THEY WERE
COMPELLED TO GO TO EARLIER 'JUST TO BE GAY'. FOR THE
NON-GAY IDENTIFIED, THINGS HAVE ALSO CHANGED. NOW
WORK IS HARDER TO FIND, THINGS ARE MORE EXPENSIVE
AND THERE ARE THAT MANY MORE GIZMOS ON THE SHELVES
TO ASPIRE FOR. SO MANY MORE ARE GETTING INTO SEX
WORK, GETTING INFECTED BY HIV AND SO ON.

Pratham was concerned that globalization had resulted in a change of
aesthetics for Indian gay men—'We all want our men to look like Western
role models. There was a time when all our men would have mustaches,
now nobody wants them. I wonder how people…can train their mind
to like only a certain kind of person?' Gul, who was very conscious of
his weight, echoed Pratham's views—'Look at me. Nobody wants to be
with a fat guy sexually. Even in parties, they see me dancing and move
away. I have thought you only needed to have a hot body to find people'.

The best term to summarize the relationship between globalization
and Gay Bombay would be 'glocal' (Robertson 1995).[15] Due to its usage
of the Internet as its major conduit, Gay Bombay is 'simultaneously
more global and local, as worldwide connectivity and domestic matters
intersect' (Welman and Gulia, 1998).[16] Karim contended—'To a large extend you could say that it is a global gay identity. We have in Gay Bombay
taken many images, stereotypes, inspirations, whatever, from the gay
movement worldwide…'. But at the same time, he noted, as did Vidvan
and Husain, that the group's tradition of respecting Indian culture and
family ethics gave it a strong Indian flavour. This included sometimes,
subversion as well. 'Gay Bombay has often taken uniquely Indian festivals
such as *Holi, Raksha Bandhan* and the *Iftaar*[17] and subverted them' (Vidvan).
For Pulkit, the Indianness of Gay Bombay was not a response to or a
subversion of 'Western notions of being gay'; rather it was more an appropriation of 'Indian notions of what it means to be straight', while
for Rustom, it was not as much an issue of subversion as of synthesis.

RUSTOM: WE ALL ARE IN THIS MICRO STRATA OF SOCIETY. WE'VE GROWN UP WATCHING AMERICAN TV SHOWS, AMERICAN MUSIC, AMERICAN MOVIES. BUT I WILL NEVER ACCEPT IF SOMEONE TELLS ME THAT BECAUSE ENGLISH IS YOUR FIRST LANGUAGE, YOU ARE NOT INDIAN. I THINK THAT IDEAS OF FAMILY, NOTIONS OF SACRIFICE, STORIES MOVIES BOOKS AND SO ON... ARE ALL THINGS THAT YOU SUBTLY IMBIBE AS YOU GROW UP. SO DOES GAY BOMBAY HAVE SOMETHING DISTINCTLY INDIAN ABOUT IT? YES OF COURSE, THERE IS SOMETHING DISTINCTLY INDIAN ABOUT THOSE WHO TAKE PART—BECAUSE THEY ARE INDIAN. THERE HAS TO BE. I DON'T THINK THEY DISSOCIATE THEIR GAY IDENTITY WITH NOT BEING INDIAN—I DON'T THINK THERE IS AN ASSOCIATION OF BEING GAY WITH BEING WESTERN. AS A PROUD HOMOSEXUAL AND ALSO A PROUD INDIAN, HOW CAN YOU DISSOCIATE THE TWO?

Many respondents agreed that Gay Bombay could be considered to be a part of a larger global gay community.

BHUVAN: I SEE THAT A PERSON SITTING IN ATLANTA WHO HAS NEVER BEEN TO BOMBAY IS STILL A PART OF THE COMMUNITY. A PERSON WHO... COMES TO BOMBAY AND WANTS TO SEE IF THERE IS A GAY SCENE HERE, GOES TO THE WEB AND DOES A SEARCH AND COMES TO KNOW.

PRATHAM: THE GAY BOMBAY LIST EXPOSES THE SUBSCRIBER TO A WIDER WORLD, INFORMS YOU OF THE FRESH DEVELOPMENTS IN THE LIBERATED PARTS OF THE WORLD AND AT THE SAME TIME ALLOWS EACH MEMBER TO GROW AND EVOLVE AT HIS OWN PACE.

For Nachiket, Gay Bombay was 'a part of the global movement in terms of a broad search for identity', but he asserted that the variables in India were different from the variables in other developed or even developing countries. 'At the broad macro level there are similar issues, but the specific issues are completely different'. Jasjit pointed out that 'most "gay communities" would see each other as a part of a "global" political agenda and Gay Bombay being bereft of any such, would not qualify on those terms', while Vidvan questioned the very notion of a 'global gay community'.

IDENTITY AND NEGOTIATION OF SELF

For some respondents (Kabir, Mike, Nihar and Yudhisthir), being gay was the most important marker of their identity. For, Yudhisthir it was a 'big stressor' that consumed a large part of his life. Kabir felt that it had 'affected and impacted every area' of decision-making.... 'My family, friends, lifestyle, work...my planning, financial sorting, insurance, the way I live my life, the way I spend my money, the lifestyle I have... I live alone, I know I will not have kids to save for their education....'. The majority of my respondents though described being gay as just one part of their overall identity—and not the major part at that. Thus, Murgesh described his identity as the intersection of his family positioning, caste and artistic affiliations. For Bhuvan it was a composite of his physical location and his sexual preference—'I associate with the city on a personal level. Wherever I will be, I will be a gay Bombayite'. Nachiket revealed an obsession with corporate success to be the most striking component of his identity. 'The focus of my life is my career. I like to lead. My aim in childhood was to be on the cover of a magazine'. Isaac expressed similar views. '"Gay" should be my second identity, an important part, but not the major part. I would be happy if I was identified more with being a business tycoon first and then gay'. Pulkit chose to define himself politically, as 'a left centrist' and Asim highlighted his membership within his religious community as something that he derived his identity from and also something that he felt he needed to keep separate from his gay identity—

I DO A WHOLE LOT OF WORK WITHIN THE COMMUNITY, WHICH HAS NO CONNECTIONS WITH THE FACT THAT I AM GAY, BUT WHICH WOULD PROBABLY CREATE PROBLEMS FOR ME WERE I TO COME OUT. I WORK WITH A WHOLE LOT OF KIDS. A LOT OF PARENTS MAY HAVE A PROBLEM WITH THE FACT THAT I AM GAY. BUT IT'S SOMETHING I WANT TO DO FOR THE COMMUNITY AND AS LONG AS I KNOW THAT I AM GOING TO BE FAITHFUL TO THE TRUST THEY HAVE PUT IN ME. I DON'T SEE WHY IT'S RELEVANT TO KNOW ABOUT MY SEXUALITY... I WANT TO DO MY BIT FOR THE COMMUNITY AND I AM.

Queen Rekha said the only construct that she was comfortable with identifying was her religion—

I USED TO IDENTIFY AS A QUEER BLACK CATHOLIC (OR A CATHOLIC *ZENANA KOTHI*). HOWEVER, SINCE I'VE BEGUN TO REJECT THE QUEER OR STRAIGHT AND BLACK OR WHITE DICHOTOMIES AS ARTIFICIAL CONSTRUCTS, I HAVE BEGUN TO FEEL EXTREMELY UNCOMFORTABLE DESCRIBING MYSELF AS ANYTHING MORE OR LESS THAN ROMAN CATHOLIC... I MEAN I INCREASINGLY SEE GENDER AND RACE AS INCIDENTAL, OVERLAPPING AND IRRELEVANT (SHADES OF A CONTINUUM)... AND I'LL BE DAMNED IF I CAN EXPLAIN THAT IN A LUCID OR COHERENT FASHION...

Many respondents reported the existence of gay friendships as an important component of their gay identity. Murgesh drew comfort from the fact that he had an increasing circle of gay friends as the years went by.

MOHNISH: MAYBE, PART OF MY GAY IDENTITY IS HAVING MORE GAY FRIENDS. BEFORE, I USED TO HANG OUT WITH STRAIGHT FRIEND MORE, NOW I HANG OUT WITH GAY FRIENDS MORE. SEX IS NO LONGER THE ONLY THING. WHEN I AM MEETING A GAY GUY FOR WHATEVER REASON, SEX IS NOT THE MAIN CRITERIA ALL THE TIME. EVEN ON CHAT, THESE DAYS I PREFER MEETING GUYS ALONG WITH MY FRIENDS. I SAY, OK, THERE ARE SOME OF US FRIENDS HERE, WOULD YOU LIKE TO JOIN US FOR COFFEE? BEFORE IT WAS A SEX ACT OR A CHAIN OF ACTS, NOW IT IS AN IDENTITY.

Cholan, who identified as queer, confessed feeling strangely disconnected from the 'gay world' as most of his friends were straight and most of his interests were not 'conventionally gay'. 'I am a big sports fan, I love cricket. I prefer rock and roll, Bruce Springsteen to Kylie Minogue'.

With regard to gay identity theory in particular, there have been two main schools of thought. The first comprising linear stage models, such as those provided by Cass (1979) and Sophie (1986) typically construct gay identity as something that is acquired at the end of several stages, starting with apprehension and questioning and ending with a full and complete acceptance and pride.[18] Within this model, the essence of an individual's identity would be, to borrow a phrase from Giddens, 'the capacity to keep a particular narrative going'.

The individual's biography, if she is to maintain regular interaction with others in the day-to-day world, cannot be wholly fictive. It must continually integrate events, which occur in the external world and sort them into the ongoing 'story' about the self. (Giddens, 1991)[19]

Several of my interviewees (Mike, Pratham, Karim, Rustom, Mohnish, Murgesh, Senthil, Yudhisthir) structured such a linear story of their selves and narrated a step-by-step discovery and acceptance tale of their gay identity to me.

The second school of thought is derived from Butler's conceptualization of identity as a performance that can be played with, within constraints.[20] I found the Gay Bombay newsgroup to be an excellent site to observe the performative aspects of my respondents' identities. Many of them used their own names while accessing the newsgroup. This would not be typical of the list per se, but has to be contextualized by the fact that my interviewees included the organizers, list moderator and other regular posters who were comfortable with their real names being known. But I was surprised to note that some individuals who considered themselves pretty closeted in the offline world, also posted using their real names! For example, Nachiket, who was married, with two kids, but identified as gay, posted using a combination of his first name and surname. ('I could have chosen any other name. But I have chosen this. It is simple; I am not cheating on anyone or hiding anything. What would happen?') When the respondents did chose nicknames, they did so primarily to 'preserve anonymity' (Harbhajan); however, as Donath points out, 'it is important to distinguish between pseudonymity and pure anonymity'.

> In the virtual world, many degrees of identification are possible. Full anonymity is one extreme of the continuum that runs from the totally anonymous to the thoroughly named. A pseudonym, though it may be untraceable to a real-world person, may have a well-established reputation in the virtual domain; a pseudonymous message may come with a wealth of contextual message about the sender.... (Donath, 1998)[21]

Donath further suggests that each part of the message (the account name, the voice, the language, the signature) provide a great deal of information about the sender's identity. I could verify this from observing the interviewees that I connected with, both online and in physical Bombay. Gopal ranted about the 'gay' centred-ness of the group and parties consistently, online as well as in his face-to-face interview to me. Randhir was as serious and queer activism focused in person, when

I met him in Bangalore, as he was over email—on the newsgroup too, he constantly posts about the various human rights organizations he is in daily contact with regarding abuses against homosexuals in different parts of the world. The Gay Bombay administrators Pratham and Karim were authoritative in their comments to me over email and in person, staunchly defending their vision of Gay Bombay. Ormus' newbie status within the group was obvious in his online interview as well as at the Gay Bombay meets I observed him at—his language was earnest and he tried hard to be proper—and his posts to the newsgroup did not have the casual familiarity that regulars like Queen Rekha, Karim or Randhir had managed to cultivate, even as they disagreed with each other on several points.

The choice of my respondents' online nicknames typically resonated with their own sense of self or certain affiliations they wanted to highlight. For Husain, and Murgesh their IDs were a combination of their religious and Indian identities; Queen Rekha chose her nickname as a tribute to an iconic lesbian filmmaker. Cholan's online ID was the title of his favourite Bruce Springsteen song and there were many nods in the direction of famous poets, fashion designers and characters from literature and cinema.

MURGESH: I DON'T USE MY REAL NAME... [FOR] MY ONLINE POSTS BECAUSE IT IS A MUSLIM NAME. MUSLIMS MAKE UP 16 PER CENT OF THE POPULATION IN BOMBAY—IF I HAD A COMMON NAME LIKE 'RAVI'—FROM 84 PER CENT THERE CAN BE SO MANY 'RAVIS'; BUT WITH A NAME LIKE MINE, IT IS DIFFICULT—I THOUGHT PEOPLE WOULD KNOW. I USED THE NAME OF A MUSICIAN. I CHOSE A MUSLIM PSEUDONYM HERE—I WAS CLEAR THAT PEOPLE SHOULD KNOW THAT THERE ARE MUSLIM GAYS AS WELL... I CONTINUED USING THE NAME DUE TO VANITY... AND IT STUCK FOR MANY YEARS.

Unlike Murgesh, who had affiliated himself to one online nickname and cultivated it over the years, respondents like Nihar and Mohnish shifted between using multiple nicknames while posting to the group.

NIHAR: I ENJOY HAVING MULTIPLE NICKS. THEY ARE JUST DIFFERENT NAMES. I LIKE PLAYING WITH WORDS. BUT I DON'T HAVE MULTIPLE PERSONALITY DISORDER.

Some respondents stated that their identities were the same online and offline. But the majority reported consciously activating a change in their online persona and performing it with pleasure. Gul and Nachiket used their online selves to be more bitchy and flirtatious, something that they could not imagine doing offline because of shyness (Gul) or being in the closet (Nachiket). Pulkit, the list moderator, presented himself as a 'champion of the smaller voices'. Asim said that he had actively cultivated a fixed online persona—

> I TEND TO BE VERY VIOLENT AND OPPRESSIVE IN MY WRITING THAT I AM NOT IN REAL LIFE. I TAKE STRONG POSITIONS ON THE LIST, WHICH I PROBABLY WOULDN'T BE RIGID ABOUT IN REAL LIFE. IT'S A REASONABLE FIXED ONLINE PERSONA—BASTARD. IT DEFINITELY COMES ON WHEN I AM ONLINE, WHEN I POST... I TAKE PLEASURE WITH MY ONLINE PERSONA. I ENJOY PERFORMING. PEOPLE EXPECT SOMETHING OF MY WRITING...

Judith Donath (1998) has observed with regard to newsgroup behaviour—

> There is no editorial board ensuring the standards of reliability; each posting comes directly from the writer. Thus the writer's identity—in particular, claims of real world expertise or history of accurate online contributions—plays an important role in judging the veracity of an article... Identity also plays a key role in motivating people to actively participate in newsgroup discussions...reputation is enhanced by contributing remarks of the type admired by the group.[22]

Within my interviewees, I noticed that Yudhisthir and Karim, both professional writers, were conscious of the popularity of their online identities—their popularity was reflected in the special treatment accorded to them by the rest of the group as 'high status participants'.[23]

> YUDHISTHIR: I LOVE WATCHING FILMS, SO I WRITE A LOT ABOUT FILMS. NOT JUST GAY FILMS BUT ALSO FILMS IN WHICH SOMEONE HAS PERFORMED WELL, OR LOOKS GOOD, OR IS SPECTACULAR THAT I THINK PEOPLE ON THE LIST MAY LIKE TO READ ABOUT. I AM A BIT OF A SOCIAL COMMENTATOR... I TRY AND DO ADVERTISING CONNECTS ALSO... PEOPLE KNOW ME BECAUSE OF MY POSTS, IF I WOULD GO TO A MEET AND SAY MY NAME, IT WOULD

	BE RECOGNIZED. IN A WAY MY PERSONA HAS BECOME BUILT…
KARIM:	AS A NEWSPAPER WRITER, YOU'RE TAUGHT TO WRITE SHORT CRISP SENTENCES AND THAT HELPS YOU TO POST ON EMAIL FORUMS. I WROTE SLIGHTLY BETTER THAN MOST PEOPLE, SO I FOUND LOTS OF PEOPLE READING MY POSTS AND THAT WOULD SPUR ME TO POST A LOT. IN CERTAIN WAYS, I WAS PROVOKING THE LIST, BRINGING UP ISSUES, CONSTANTLY WRITING ON THEM. THE EMAIL LIST WAS A SPACE WHERE I COULD USE MY WRITING SKILLS. IT MADE ME FEEL PRETTY GOOD.

I discovered that significantly, for several respondents, the real issue was about identity in gay versus straight settings, rather than online versus offline identities. Several of my interviewees spoke about having distinct gay identities that they revealed or *performed* in settings in which they were comfortable.

ISAAC:	WITH GAY PEOPLE, I BITCH WITH CLOSE FRIENDS, I TRY TO BRING OUT GAYNESS IN ME, MANNERISMS, TALKING; WITH STRAIGHT PEOPLE I AM NORMAL. WITH GAY PEOPLE I AM IN A GAY MOOD—TALK FOR FUN… WITH STRAIGHT PEOPLE I AM CONSCIOUS THAT I DON'T TALK TOO MUCH ABOUT GAY THINGS.
OM:	I DO CHANGE MY MANNERS IN DIFFERENT SETTINGS. [THIS IS] HYPOCRISY AS IT EXISTS IN INDIA AND I AM A PART OF IT.
BHUVAN:	I DON'T THINK OF IT AS HYPOCRISY. YOU EXPRESS YOUR-SELF NATURALLY, BUT SENSIBLY. YOU DON'T QUESTION ACCEPTABILITY. IT'S LIKE GOING OUT FOR A BLACK TIE DINNER, HOW DO YOU ACT? BEING WITH STRAIGHT PEOPLE IS SOMETHING LIKE THAT.
OM:	LIKE THIS INTERVIEW WITH YOU. IF IT WERE A STRAIGHT PERSON SITTING RIGHT THERE, I WOULD NOT BE AS VERBAL OR AS OPEN AS I AM WITH YOU RIGHT NOW.
BHUVAN:	ME TOO.
OM:	IT'S VERY OBVIOUS. EVERYBODY DOES IT.

Nihar expressed pleasure at being able to perform his identity play-fully within the Gay Bombay spaces. He identified as androgynous—'I feel an electricity of masculine and feminine energy in perfect harmony—it gives me such peace—I feel so fulfilled…'.

I DIDN'T CONSTRUCT THIS ANDROGYNOUS IDENTITY. IT WAS ALWAYS THERE. NOW I CHOOSE TO ENACT IT. WHEN I WORE HOT PANTS TO A PARTY RECENTLY, I HAD BLEACHED MY HAIR AND I WORE BOOTS AND A SLEEVELESS T-SHIRT. THE NEXT DAY I CALLED UP THIS FRIEND OF MINE AND HE TOLD ME THAT SOME PEOPLE THOUGHT I WAS A BRITISH DYKE. I LOVE IT. I LOVE CONFUSING PEOPLE… I LIKE DRAMA—I LIKE BEING FLAMBOYANT. I LIKE DANCING, WEARING SKIMPY CLOTHES, DESIGNING SEXY OUTFITS FOR EVERY PARTY, MAKING AN ENTRY, PUSHING LIMITS AS FAR AS I WANT TO. ALL MY LIFE I WAS ASEXUAL. NOW I AM REVELING IN MY SEXUALITY. IT GIVES ME ENERGY… BEING ANDROGYNOUS GIVES ME THE FREEDOM TO PLAY CRICKET AND DO EMBROIDERY AT THE SAME TIME. IN ANY CASE, WHAT IS MASCULINE OR FEMININE? A BABY DOESN'T CHOOSE TO BE WRAPPED UP IN A BLUE TOWEL—WE DO THAT! IT IS CONDITIONING. I ENJOY BREAKING THE BOUNDARY—PLAYING WITH BOTH THE BALLS IN MY HAND….

Kabir, Asim, Murgesh, Mike and Yudhisthir also stated that they tended to become more camp in the company of friends or in gay settings. Queen Rekha described consistency itself as 'the refuge of a fool' and further added—'I am a drag queen, honey! I perform *always*…'. In contrast, Ormus who had been an effeminate child while growing up, said that he tried hard to perform being non-effeminate. For him, both his on-line and offline identities were a reflection of this quest. '*I absolutely* wanted to change, I wanted to fit in and I do not think my current self is a put-on'.

Conflict

For a long time, Humsafar was the only gay-related organization in Bombay. Humsafar's open-to-all Friday meets were very well attended by the city's gay identified men. However, the organization's increasing foray into HIV and health related activism alienated these men. 'They were not willing to serve as volunteers', recounted Senthil, 'but *kothis* and *hijras* were'. Also as Pulkit recalled, there was a growing sense of discomfort among the gay identified men who attended Humsafar events about its overtly camp nature—'I noticed that if you go to Humsafar, you have to behave in a certain way. If you are not effeminate, if you do not have a limp hand, if you do not refer to each other as "she" instead of "he", you do not feel you belong, you are like an outcast'. These two factors resulted in the Humsafar space being used more and more by *kothis* and *hijras*—while the gay men started to access the nascent Gay Bombay spaces as alternative and more comfortable environments. Eventually, there was an almost complete absence of a gay presence from Humsafar events like the Friday meets, while Gay Bombay supported events and activities began to flourish.

During my initial interactions with my interviewees online and the observation of some of the newsgroup postings, I had already had a preview of some of the simmering tensions between members loyal to both organizations. On my visit to physical Bombay, I discovered that there was cordiality on the surface. But the moment I scratched just a little, the emotions poured out fast and hard. The contentious relationship between these two organizations was by far the most polarizing subject of discussion for my interviewees. It was more intriguing because a lot of the current Gay Bombay regulars had cut their teeth organizing Humsafar events or editing *Bombay Dost* in the early 1990s, or used the Humsafar space to come out and even among the younger lot, there were many who were affiliated to both organizations. Further, the higher-ups in both organizations often collaborated on events together, despite being vocal about their differences. In any case, there were six key flash points that emerged during my conversations and I want to discuss each of them briefly over here.

Straight Acting Men Versus Effeminate Men, Drag Queens and Hijras

Several individuals I spoke to had based their gay identity and some-times, their entire life, battling the notion that a gay person is 'a pansy effeminate guy' (Isaac). They prided themselves on the fact that they were 'just like everyone else' and were deeply vested with creating 'a culture where it is okay to be "straight acting" gays' (Asim). Indeed, as Pulkit stated, Gay Bombay was formed on the very premise of creating a space for 'middle class straight acting men. It was for the people who get embarrassed when they walk with a very effeminate man in public and who do not like it when they are referred to in the female pronouns, as *she* or as *mother* or *sister*'. For these men, Humsafar's in your face championing of camp behaviour ('Being gay and queeny with a mission', as Isaac put it) was a negation of everything they had tried so hard to not be and a threat to the *straight-acting* image that they had tried to cultivate and project of themselves and the gay community, either overtly or implicitly.

This discomfort with effeminate behaviour was translated into the strict no-drag policy framed by Gay Bombay for its parties. Revoked in 2005, the policy came in for some fierce criticism, both from within Gay Bombay and outside. In fact, matters came to a clash on New Year's Eve of 2004, when The Humsafar Trust decided to have a competing drag-friendly party in the suburbs in response to Gay Bombay's no-drag city-based party, offering tickets at a substantial discount to Gay Bombay's prices and including incentives such as special rates for college students. The spat even made it to the pages of some of the country's newspapers.[24]

Karim justified the reason for the policy's existence and subsequent withdrawal—

MOST OTHER GAY GROUPS HAVE PRIVATE SPACES—OFFICES AND FACIL-ITIES—WHERE THEY CAN RETREAT AND DO DRAG. WE ARE A CURIOUSLY PUBLIC GROUP—WE MEET IN PUBLIC SPACES, HAVE PARTIES IN PUBLIC SPACES, EVEN THE MEMBERS' HOUSES THAT WE HAVE OUR MEETS IN ARE APARTMENTS IN LARGE RESIDENTIAL COMPLEXES. THE FACT THAT WE ARE A PUBLIC GROUP HAS INFLUENCED OUR POLICIES. A LOT OF GUYS ARE VERY PHOBIC ABOUT DRAG—WE DID FEEL IT WAS BETTER TO DISCOURAGE DRAG FOR GUYS WHO WERE COMING FOR MEETINGS THE FIRST TIME... THIS COINCIDED WITH THE FACT THAT IT WAS DIFFICULT TO DO DRAG IN PEOPLES HOUSES—OR EVEN IN NIGHTCLUBS THAT ANYWAY WERE WARY OF HOSTING GAY NIGHTS FOR US—THEY WOULD SAY YES AS LONG AS YOU ALL ARE DECENTLY DRESSED, WHICH MEANT NO DRAG. SO FOR PRACTICAL REASONS WE PUT IN THE 'NO DRAG' RULE. IT WAS NOT SOMETHING THAT WE WERE COMFORTABLE WITH. WE'VE GOT A LOT OF FLAK FOR IT AND DESERVEDLY SO... WE'VE WITH-DRAWN IT NOW BECAUSE BY NOW, THE GROUP AND MOST PEOPLE WHO COME TO THE GROUP CAN DEAL WITH IT AND EVEN PRACTICALLY, NOW WE ARE WELL ESTABLISHED AND NIGHTCLUBS KNOW US AND WE HAVE

GOOD RELATIONSHIPS WITH THE MANAGEMENTS. BUT EVEN BEFORE WE DROPPED THE 'NO DRAG' RULE OUR POSITION WAS THAT IF SOMEONE HAS THE BALLS TO COME DRESSED UP IN DRAG, THERE IS NO WAY THAT WE WILL TURN THEM AWAY.

Gopal, Bhudev and Rahim considered this change to be progressive but they pointed out that Gay Bombay's acceptance of drag was only for Western style drag. Thus, a Malaysian drag group that came down for the WSF was invited to perform at a Gay Bombay party but Indian drag groups have been constantly ignored at such events. 'Indian drag, *lavni*, is down-market', jibed Rahim. 'Malaysian drag is upmarket because it is foreign'.

There was great divisiveness within the group when it came to the issues of *hijras*—like Isaac, a large number of individuals felt that 'eunuchs and gays are two different identities' and that Gay Bombay's mandate was only to cater to gay people. Karim explained that while they were 'supportive and friendly to everyone', the founders had 'consciously defined a narrow focus [for Gay Bombay]—gay men'. However, others like Senthil felt that it would be a smarter move to expand this vision to include non-gay identified sexual minorities, out of self-interest, if nothing else—

SENTHIL: THIS IS THE PROBLEM OF GROUPS LIKE GAY BOMBAY; THEY DON'T REALIZE THAT SOMEDAY THERE COULD BE BACK-LASHES… IF THERE IS A GAY BOMBAY PARTY TOMORROW THAT GETS RAIDED, THEY WILL NEED HELP FROM ALL THESE PEOPLE—THE ACTIVISTS, THE PEOPLE WHO MARCH—ITS NOT THE GAY MEN, HONEY, ITS THE *KOTHIS* AND *HIJRAS*….

Class Differences and Language Barriers

The responses of my interviewees provided an indication of the 'vast social gulfs across which people in India must face each other' (Seabrook, 1999).[25] There was more or less a consensus that Gay Bombay was an organization that catered to a narrow English speaking, upper middle class segment of the homosexual population, though Karim was insistent on emphasizing that this still constituted a considerable amount of 'diversity within a band—actually a fairly wide range of people'. This stratification was a source of comfort for many of my interviewees who were upfront in stating that their interactions with those beyond their class boundaries were limited. Pratham said—'Though I would not like to admit it, I prefer to hang out with people more or less from the same socio-economic background. I do not treat them differently but beyond "hi" and "hello", I am not too comfortable spending time with self identified *kothis*'. Jasjit was quick to clarify that his stance did not indicate that he was a 'class-chauvinist'—

IT JUST MEANS THAT EACH INDIVIDUAL REVOLVES AND INTERACTS WITHIN THE RIGID AREA OF HIS CLASS WITH A FEW GREY SHADES ABOVE AND BELOW THAT SOCIAL STRATUM AND IT TAKES A LOT OF EFFORT TO BREAK THESE BOUNDARIES, UNLESS THERE IS AN OVERWHELMING REASON TO TRANSCEND IT. I IDENTIFY MORE WITH URBAN, MIDDLE CLASS, INTELLECTUAL PEOPLE AND DO TEND TO GET MY OWN PHYSICAL AND PSYCHOLOGICAL STIMULI RESPONDED BY THEM, SO THERE ISN'T MUCH REASON FOR ME TO LOOK BEYOND THAT GROUP.

NIHAR: PEOPLE CRITICIZE GAY BOMBAY FOR BEING A SEGREGATED GROUP OF UPPER MIDDLE CLASS PEOPLE—THE BOURGEOISIE… BUT CLASS DOES SET IN—YOU CAN'T AVOID THAT. BIRDS OF A FEATHER FLOCK TOGETHER AND THAT'S WHERE THEY ARE COMFORTABLE… THE KIND OF PEOPLE THAT ARE MEMBERS OF GAY BOMBAY… THEY ARE ENGLISH SPEAKING UPPER MIDDLE CLASS…. I COULD HOLD A CONVERSATION WITH THEM AND WOULDN'T NEED SOMEONE TO INTERPRET THINGS… THEY COME FROM THE SAME LEVEL OF CULTURE… THAT'S WHAT MAKES A COMFORT ZONE FOR PEOPLE LIKE ME… REGULAR COLLEGE GOING BOY, SOMEONE WHO IS WORKING IN A CALL CENTRE… BY CULTURED I MEAN SOMEONE WHO IS WELL READ AND HAD AN ENGLISH EDUCATION AND CAN TALK ABOUT ART AND MUSIC AND SHIT LIKE THAT—SOMEONE WHO HAS HAD HINDI EDUCATION IS CULTURED TOO, BUT IN A DIFFERENT CONTEXT. IF SOMEONE CAN'T TALK IN ENGLISH, THEN THERE WOULD BE A COMMUNICATION GAP. I AM MUCH MORE COMFORTABLE IN ENGLISH. I'M NOT SAYING THAT THE NON ENGLISH-SPEAKING PEOPLE SHOULDN'T BE CATERED FOR—I'M JUST SAYING GAY BOMBAY SHOULDN'T CHANGE… IT'S A POLITICALLY INCORRECT THING, I KNOW.

ASIM: PERSONALLY I DON'T HAVE ANY APOLOGIES… WHEN YOU SAY
THAT YOU ARE ELITIST AND CATERING ONLY TO A CERTAIN SEG-
MENT, YOU ARE IMPLYING THAT THE SEGMENT DOESN'T NEED
SUPPORT. THIS IS BULLSHIT.

Viewpoints like the above came in for strong criticism from respondents
also affiliated with Humsafar.

BHUDEV: PEOPLE'S DISCOMFORT HAS A LOT TO DO WITH CLASS AND
OPENNESS OF TALKING. BECAUSE [HUMSAFAR] IS SO OPEN,
PEOPLE ARE AFRAID. ACCESS TO SOME OF [GAY BOMBAY'S]
PARTIES IS ACCESS WITH MONEY. THEY KNOW THAT THEY ARE
MIXING WITH THEIR OWN CLASS; HERE YOU DON'T KNOW
WITH WHOM YOU ARE MIXING. THAT SCARES THEM. AGAIN IT
IS CLASS POLITICS. WHEN THEY COME HERE AND HEAR THE
GUYS TALKING OPENLY ABOUT THE PEOPLE THEY HAVE FUCKED;
THEY HAVE NEVER HEARD THIS TALK. THE WHOLE DISCOURSE
OF OPEN SEXUALITY THAT IS REALLY PART OF THE INDIAN
STREET SCENE, IS NOT PART OF THE MIDDLE CLASSES.

Rahim pointed out the hypocritical nature of some of the prejudices expressed by the members of Gay Bombay—while there was resentment
among Gay Bombay people to interact socially with people from the
non-English speaking classes, many of them had no qualms in exoticizing
them in their sexual fantasies or even picking them up for random sexual
escapades, when they desired so!

Differing Views of Activism

Om, a 22-year old student and a regular Gay Bombay party presence,
shared his experience about volunteering at the Humsafar stall at the
World Social Forum (WSF) in Bombay in early 2004—

DURING WSF, HUMSAFAR HAS PUT UP A STALL ON GAY ICONS. THERE
WAS NO BIAS ABOUT THESE ICONS THAT THEY HAD CHOSEN, BUT GAY
BOMBAY CHOSE TO IGNORE IT. IF THE PEOPLE FROM GAY BOMBAY MET
PEOPLE FROM HUMSAFAR, THEY JUST SAID 'HI' AND WALKED BY. THERE
WERE TALK SESSIONS HAPPENING AND OTHERS, WHERE I DIDN'T SEE
PEOPLE FROM GAY BOMBAY AT ALL.

Similarly, Rahim, who worked full time at Humsafar, was very anguished by Gay Bombay's lack of active interest in anything political. He presented three accounts of his experiences and observations—

(a) [THE TWO NEW YEAR'S EVE PARTIES THE PREVIOUS YEAR, OR-GANIZED BY GAY BOMBAY AND THE HUMSAFAR TRUST, HAD COLLECTIVELY DRAWN AROUND A THOUSAND PEOPLE]. BUT THE FACT REMAINS, WE ARE ONLY ASSEMBLING PEOPLE FOR PARTIES. WHAT I AM SEEING IS THAT PARTIES ARE HAPPENING FOR SO MANY YEARS, BUT PEOPLE ARE NOT GOING BEYOND THAT.

(b) [HUMSAFAR HAD APPROACHED SOME OF ITS YOUNGER GAY IDEN-TIFIED VOLUNTEERS THAT ALSO ACCESSED THE GAY BOMBAY SPACES, TO FORM A SELF-HELP SUPPORT GROUP CATERING TO THEIR SPECIFIC NEEDS]. WE'VE BOUGHT A LCD PROJECTOR AND A SCREEN—THEY CAN HAVE SCREENINGS, DISCUSSIONS, PLANNING OF MEETINGS AND SO ON. WE CAN OFFER ALL THE SPACE HUMSAFAR HAS AND FACILITIES. NOW BEYOND THAT, I AM CONVINCED THAT AN 18-YEAR OLD SHOULD SHOW MORE ENERGY THAN A 40 OR 50-YEAR-OLD. WHERE IS THE ENERGY? I TOLD THEM THREE MONTHS AGO—BUT THEY STILL HAVEN'T COME BACK.

(c) [HUMSAFAR STARTED A PROGRAM CALLED *HUMSAFAR DOST*, WHERE THEY HAD ASKED INDIVIDUALS TO CONTRIBUTE A THOUSAND RUPEES PER ANNUM, OR US$ 23, AT EARLY-2007 CONVERSION RATES, AS A DONATION FOR VARIOUS HUMSAFAR HEALTH PROGRAMS]. THAT IS 80 RUPEES PER MONTH FOR SOMEONE LIKE YOU AND ME— OR THE COST OF A CIGARETTE PACK. TODAY, *HUMSAFAR DOST* HAS 38 MEMBERS AND OF THESE 38, 22 ARE LIVING IN THE US. HERE, WE HAVE APPROACHED AS MANY PEOPLE AS POSSIBLE, BUT THEY DON'T WANT TO GIVE EVEN A THOUSAND RUPEES PER YEAR. PEOPLE ARE SPENDING ON THEMSELVES, THOUSAND BUCKS PER NIGHT EASILY; BUT NOT TO CONTRIBUTE FOR THE WELFARE OF THE COMMUNITY.

Rahim and Bhudev were both skeptical of activism over the Internet. Rahim noted that there were 'thousands of mails being exchanged on the net' regarding Article 377, but when the case came up in the Delhi court, only a few well known activists were present. Bhudev insisted that the real activism was on the ground, 'not in cyberspace which... dominates Gay Bombay'. 'Gay Bombay is having rights without responsibilities', he continued. 'It is a dream factory. Their parties are like Bollywood'.

'So what?', countered Isaac. 'I feel that if I become successful in what I do and I am also out as gay, then it will give it more credibility than if I go and become a full time gay activist'. On a related, but different note, Nachiket, who was married and closeted, argued that he was as much an activist as Bhudev—albeit, in a different setting and armed with a different strategy. Despite being closeted, he attributed a large part of his confidence to 'being a member of an online community where I know that there are at least 2,000 people more like me'.

I HAVE GREAT RESPECT FOR THE OUT ACTIVISTS LIKE BHUDEV. ACTIVISTS DISCOUNT THE POSSIBILITY THAT THE PEOPLE WHO ARE MAKING CHANGES ARE NOT THE ONES ON THE STAGE. SO YOU WILL NEVER FIND ME AT A MARCH. BUT I AM MAKING CHANGES. IN THE SPACES I WORK IN. SO SOME DAYS BACK, THE PERSON WE OFFERED A JOB TO WAS A MAN WEARING EARRINGS. WE OFFERED HIM THE JOB AND THE PERSON WHO WOULD HAVE BEEN HIS BOSS AND THE PERSON WHO WOULD HAVE BEEN HIS BOSS'S BOSS WERE EXTREMELY COMFORTABLE WITH HIM. HE DIDN'T JOIN US ULTIMATELY, BECAUSE HE GOT A BETTER JOB, BUT I WOULD COUNT HIS SELECTION AS AN ACHIEVEMENT. SO PEOPLE LIKE ME ARE THE ONES MAKING THE CHANGES. THAT IS WHAT IT BOILS DOWN TO. IRONICALLY, IF I WERE OUT AT MY POSITION IN THE COMPANY AND IN MY PROFESSION, I WOULD BE AN OUTCAST. BECAUSE I AM IN, I AM GIVEN ADMISSION INTO INNER CIRCLES AND GIVEN OPPORTUNITIES TO INFLUENCE CHANGE. I BELIEVE I AM AN ACTIVIST IN MY OWN WAY. FUNDAMENTALLY, BUSINESS IS NOT GOING TO CHANGE IF YOU ATTACK IT FROM THE OUTSIDE. YOU HAVE TO EARN YOUR STRIPES AND BE IDENTIFIED AS A PART OF THE BUSINESS IF YOU WANT TO MAKE ANY CHANGES. OTHERWISE YOU ARE JUST ONE OF THE LOONIES GOING AROUND. I THINK THE OTHER TYPE OF ACTIVISM IS IMPORTANT TOO—BUT BY ITSELF, IT IS NOT ENOUGH. FRANKLY, THE AWARENESS DOESN'T COME WITHOUT PEOPLE LIKE HIM, BUT CHANGE DOESN'T COME WITHOUT PEOPLE LIKE US. IT CUTS BOTH WAYS.

For Nachiket, as for many of my interviewees, Gay Bombay's appeal lay in the fact that it was not an activist organization. Karim explained—'Our strength is not in gay activism and marching on the street, which is great and some of us do want to do that. But for the larger group, it is in creating safe spaces and helping gay people come into the community'.

Harbhajan pointed out that the parties that Gay Bombay organized at different venues all over the city were a kind of activism in their own way—'an eye opener for the hotel manager and staff'. Pratham opined that it was futile to just pick up political causes 'to feel better about what we do…'.

WHAT DOES ONE MEAN BY ACTIVISM? A GUY PROACTIVELY COMING TO A PARTY IS AN ACTIVIST TOO. EVERYONE IS AN ACTIVIST. PLACES LIKE HUMSAFAR ARE POLITICAL ACTIVISM. POLITICAL ACTIVISM IS NO LONGER THE CENTRE OF THE WHOLE HOMOSEXUAL IMAGE NOW. AT ONE POINT, FROM AN OUTSIDER'S POINT OF VIEW, POLITICAL ACTIVISM THAT HUMSAFAR DID OR THE WORK DONE WITH HOMOSEXUALS WAS WHAT WAS THE DEFINING VIEW. NOWADAYS, WHEN THE MEDIA WRITES ABOUT THE GAY COMMUNITY, IT IS NOT NECESSARILY ABOUT ACTIVISM; IT IS ABOUT PARTIES AND OTHER THINGS. SO I SUPPOSE THE PUBLIC PERCEPTION HAS BECOME BROADER.

But Senthil, while agreeing with Pratham and Harbhajan that being social was its own kind of activism, was perplexed as to how this could not translate into a political statement. According to him, this extreme aversion to political activism was a myopic position to adopt and emblematic of the intrinsic failure of the middle class that most of Gay Bombay's members counted themselves as members of—

THIS IS THE BIGGEST CRITICISM OF THE MIDDLE CLASSES THAT GAY BOMBAY IS A SYMBOL OF. IT IS SO AVERSE TO THE IDEA OF POLITICS. THERE'S A MORAL JUDGMENT AGAINST IT THAT IT'S WRONG. IT'S NOT FOR US. IT'S AGAINST EVERYTHING WE ARE ABOUT. IT'S WRONG IF YOU LIVE IN A SPACE AND WANT IT TO EXIST AND GROW, POLITICAL GROUPS HAVE TO HAVE A SAY IN IT…. LET'S NOT BE AVERSE TO IT. YOU CAN'T BE ANTI-POLITICS.

The Importance of Coming Out, Closeted Men and Married Gay Men

Most of the respondents were appreciative of Gay Bombay's non-judgmental policy with regard to their status as out or closeted. As Karim noted—'We cannot force guys to come out of the closet, lead an open gay lifestyle; we can just help guys help themselves. We can just create spaces for them'. However, critics like Gopal and Rahim argued that this policy, coupled with the social focus of the group was creating a feeling of complacency among people who accessed its spaces—and falsely leading them on to believe that they were out just because they had attended a gay event in a safe space, when in fact, it was nothing more than a 'High Tech Closet'.[26] The challenge, as Rahim noted, lay in being visible 'outside the safe spaces we have created for ourselves' and this was simply not happening with Gay Bombay. He was critical that several people from Gay Bombay had posted excitedly on the group about attending events like San Francisco Pride and New York Pride, but the same people, when called, refused to show up at a Humsafar-led silent walk in Bombay to commemorate World AIDS day. 'A gay man from Bombay, dancing on the streets of San Francisco or New York is going to make no difference to Bombay. I need a few faces to be seen at a certain place, where showing a few faces would make a difference. But I do not see this'.

Humsafar was also presumed to be too harsh towards married gay men. One of my married interviewees recounted his experience of going to one of Humsafar's events and then receiving a call from them the following day asking him not to come to any future events because of his married status. He contrasted this with Gay Bombay's acceptance of him into their fold. Karim explained Gay Bombay's approach to this issue—

ONE OF THE POSITIONS THAT THE GROUP DOES TAKE IS THAT IT IS WRONG TO BE MARRIED TO SOMEBODY [IF] THE WOMAN DOES NOT KNOW ABOUT YOUR SEXUALITY. IF SHE KNOWS AND IS OKAY WITH IT, THEN IT'S DIFFERENT. MOST OF US ARE QUITE WILLING TO BE SYMPATHETIC AND TO BE FRIENDS WITH SUCH GUYS, BUT THAT SYMPATHY SHOULD NOT BE TAKEN TO IMPLY THAT ONE APPROVES OF WHAT THE MARRIED GAY GUY HAS DONE AND TO SUGGEST THAT GAY GUYS MARRYING WOMEN WITHOUT COMING OUT TO THEM IS IN ANY WAY THE RIGHT COURSE OF ACTION TO TAKE. GUYS WHO DO THIS KNOW THAT WE DISAPPROVE, SO THEY DISTANCE THEMSELVES FROM THE MEETS. THEY MAY STILL COME FOR THE PARTIES—A LOT OF MARRIED GUYS COME FOR THE PARTIES. BUT THEY KNOW THAT THEY AREN'T 100 PER CENT WELCOME AT THE MEETS.

HIV

Several respondents, including Isaac and Asim, attributed Gay Bombay's tremendous success to its no-sex policy. Pulkit too indicated that this policy, though an indicator of the group's 'prudish values that come from the straight community', had served it well. However, for the respondents who were involved in voluntary HIV prevention work like Bhudev, this attitude was 'anti-sexual' and more devastatingly, 'HIV phobic'. 'They do not like to talk about sex. For them, gay is a lifestyle'. This squeamishness with anything sexual meant that health issues like risky behaviour and the huge HIV crisis that the community was facing, were being swept under the carpet. Rahim was very concerned—

THE DIFFERENCE THAT I SAW ON MY VISIT TO THE US AND IN INDIA IS THAT IN THE US, AN AVERAGE MIDDLE CLASS GAY MAN IS VERY AWARE OF HEALTH ISSUES AND HIS RISK BEHAVIOR. IN BOMBAY, I DON'T THINK IT MATTERS. FOR ME WHAT WAS MOST SHOCKING WAS THAT LAST YEAR, WE DID A HUGE STUDY—A 10-MONTH STUDY. THE FINDINGS OF THAT STUDY, INCLUDING THAT OF A LARGER SURVEY WE HAVE CONDUCTED FOR FOUR YEARS INDICATE THAT 17–20 PER CENT OF THE GAY MEN IN THE CITY ARE HIV POSITIVE! THIS IS A VERY HIGH FIGURE, BUT IT HAS BEEN STABLE FOR THE PAST FOUR YEARS. *MID-DAY* CARRIED A HUGE STORY SAYING 20 PER CENT OF BOMBAY'S GAY MEN ARE HIV POSITIVE. BUT THE FIRST REACTION FROM THE GAY COMMUNITY IN BOMBAY WAS ANGER. OUR WHOLE IDEA OF THE SURVEY AND FINDINGS WAS TO TAKE THIS ISSUE TO THE MAINSTREAM SOCIETY, NOT CREATE SENSATIONAL HEADLINES. BUT OK, ON SECOND THOUGHTS, MAYBE I SAID, PEOPLE WILL NOW GET UP AND REALIZE. BELIEVE ME, FOR THE TWO WEEKS FOLLOWING THE SURVEY, THROUGH INTERNET LISTS... I HAD 120 RE-QUESTS FOR THE COPY OF THE STUDY AND NOT ONE REQUEST FROM BOMBAY! I WAS SO DEMORALIZED. WHY AM I DOING WHAT I AM DOING WHEN PEOPLE DON'T GIVE A FUCK? WHEN NOBODY IS BOTHERED.

A LARGE AMOUNT OF WORK THAT HAPPENS AT HUMSAFAR, CENTRES AROUND THE LOWER INCOME GROUP—MSMS—BUT THE SURVEY AND STUDIES THAT WE HAVE CONDUCTED HAVE LOOKED AT DIFFERENT INCOME GROUPS. THE FEAR IS THAT IF YOU ARE A PART OF HIGHER IN-COME GROUPS IN BOMBAY, YOU MAY THINK THAT HIV IS SOMETHING THAT ONLY LOWER INCOME MSM PEOPLE IN BOMBAY HAVE; BUT IT IS NOT TRUE. I WAS TALKING TO AN 18-YEAR OLD WHO IS A GAY BOMBAY REGULAR AND I ASKED HIM HOW OFTEN HIV WAS DISCUSSED AMONG

HIS FRIENDS. HE SAID 'NEVER'. NOW IF FOR AN 18-YEAR OLD TODAY, IT IS NOT AN ISSUE AT ALL, THEN IT IS VERY DANGEROUS. ARE WE GROWING UP WITH A GENERATION THAT IS IMMUNE TO THE DANGERS POSED BY HIV OR ARE WE GROWING UP WITH A GENERATION THAT IS JUST NOT AWARE? BOTH ARE SCARY.

Registration

The people that I interviewed affiliated with Humsafar were disappointed that Gay Bombay had not got itself registered formally as a charitable organization. This, they felt would give them official stature in the eyes of the law and also enable them to be part of initiatives like INFOSEM (Indian Network for Sexual Minorities), an umbrella groups of organizations working all over India on issues of sexuality, health and human rights. However, the members of Gay Bombay's core group were reluctant to do so for a variety of reasons—first and foremost, the unpopularity of this measure among most of its members and second, even if the group wanted to be registered, it would have to do so under a health agenda, like Humsafar, as there was 'no standard in Indian law' (Harbhajan) that would recognize Gay Bombay's profile. Karim stated that the group had no pressing needs for registration of any kind—

WE ARE NOT AN AMBITIOUS GROUP. WE ARE ALSO SELF-SUSTAINABLE. PRESSURE OF LOTS OF EXTERNALLY FUNDED GROUPS IS THERE TO PERFORM; HAVE LONG-TERM PLANS AND SO ON; BY FUNDING AGENCIES NATURALLY. WE DON'T HAVE FUNDING AGENCIES. WE HAVE VERY FEW EXPENSES—A SMALL MARK UP ON SOME PARTIES GOES TO FUND OUR ACTIVITIES LIKE WEBSITE AND SO ON. NO LONG-TERM PLANS AND AMBITIONS.

* * *

While the points of disagreement were many, I also saw enough indications that bridges between the two organizations and the viewpoints they represent could and indeed, were being built. To start with, most of the interviewees, even while expressing critical views, were deeply appreciative of the work being carried out by both organizations. David Woolvine (2000) has called this 'tactical pragmatism'—or the 'ability to distance [oneself] from [certain] organizations and from some of the goals or tactics of the organizations while at the same time supporting the organizations'.[27]

GUL: I THINK HUMSAFAR IS GOOD—AT LEAST THERE ARE SOME PEOPLE FIGHTING FOR US. I DON'T THINK I COULD DO THE SAME. I DON'T HAVE THE BOLDNESS AND STRENGTH THEY HAVE.

OM: I WONT BE ANTI-HUMSAFAR OR ANTI-GAY BOMBAY— HUMSAFAR IS DOING GOOD WORK. HUMSAFAR HAS THE INFRASTRUCTURE AND THE GOVERNMENT SUPPORT THAT THE COMMUNITY NEEDS RIGHT NOW. GAY BOMBAY IS ALSO DOING GOOD WORK.

RAHIM: HUMSAFAR MAY BE DOING CERTAIN WORK. I AM NOT AT ALL DISCREDITING GAY BOMBAY, THEY ARE ALSO DOING THEIR OWN WORK... AS LONG AS WE ARE NOT OBSTRUCTING EACH OTHER'S WORK AND ALL CONTRIBUTING...

HARBHAJAN: ALL OF THEM ARE PLAYING A ROLE... IF I LAND UP AT GAY BOMBAY AND NOT KNOW WHAT THEY ARE TALKING ABOUT, I WILL FEEL ISOLATED. I MAY DISCOVER A BETTER PLACE IN ANOTHER GROUP. SIMILARLY FOR ME, I WAS DIS-ILLUSIONED AT HUMSAFAR, BUT I FOUND MY PLACE AT GAY BOMBAY. THESE COMMUNITIES WITHIN THE LARGER GROUP ALL HELP EACH OTHER. YOU FIND YOUR CLIQUE SOMEWHERE.

Second, I felt that it was too pat to simplify, as many of my interviewees seemed to do, that Humsafar is equal to *kothis*, *hijras*, HIV work and hatred of married gay men, while Gay Bombay is equal to dance parties, upper class people and Internet. I observed that Humsafar organized social events regularly, for example, a weekly open-to-all meeting at its premises called 'Sunday High', which took the form of discussions, film screenings and sometimes live performances. They also organized New Year's Eve parties, regular Friday town hall style gatherings and other smaller scale events. Likewise, despite criticisms of sex phobia and drag phobia, I gathered that Gay Bombay had organized a drag party privately, in one of the core group member's homes and also held well-attended community events like workshops on safe sex, including HIV. For example, a Gay Bombay Hepatitis B vaccination drive that included providing free vaccinations along with an information session on STDs, had 63 people in attendance on a Sunday afternoon.[28] Other interesting events have included meetings on financial planning (3 October 2004) and on knowing the law (25 September 2005). Moreover, its website is a useful provider of HIV-related information, including gay-friendly testing centres in and around Bombay. In 2007, the group started the GB Poz online forum as an offshoot of the main group, 'to discuss, provide support and share stories about what it means to be gay and positive and living in India.'[29] Again, despite the notion that Humsafar was anti-married gay men, I discerned that a lot of their services, including HIV-related and other type of counselling, were directed towards married gay men and their spouses, across all income categories.

As I have mentioned earlier, *Bombay Dost* magazine and the Humsafar Trust played an important part in the narratives of my interviewees. For several respondents who had previously only referenced Western material, discovering *Bombay Dost* was their first experience with 'narratives in an Indian context' (Karim). In fact, a lot of the older respondents and current Gay Bombay regulars like Pratham, Pulkit or Cholan, used to help publish or promote the magazine, conduct Humsafar's intervention programs or simply attend the regular Friday meets; and I also observed several college going students like Om and Senthil who continued to volunteer at Humsafar while simultaneously attending Gay Bombay events and parties in the present day. I sensed complex feelings and deep divisions within them about how they wanted Gay Bombay to be perceived as and the direction in which it should head. There were heated debates at several of the Gay Bombay weekend meetings that I attended; I have observed regular flare ups about the key issues noted above on the Gay Bombay mailing list over the past few years and I am aware that the core group has been meeting regularly to discuss this topic.

Several of my interviewees reasoned that there were disagreements in every community (Murgesh—'I do not think there is a united gay identity anywhere else in the world') and in fact, in India, the divisions within the queer community were not as deep as they were in some other countries. While some felt that the differences could not be resolved and were best left alone, others were of the opinion that a united front was possible and desirable (Om—'[It] is what any minority does') and the need of the hour was for the two organizations to work together.

GOPAL: DO WE HAVE TO BE LIKE THE REST OF SOCIETY? MAYBE NOT
UTOPIAN, BUT WE ARE THE ONES WHO ARE EXCLUDED ALL THE
TIME. MAYBE THE LEAST WE CAN DO IS NOT CREATE BARRIERS,
NOT BE EXCLUSIVE.

I found some indications of an emerging unity during my time in
Bombay when I understood that the Gay Bombay and Humsafar organizers had mutually decided to hold their events every alternate Sunday, so
that the Gay Bombay meets and Sunday Highs would not clash and cross
attendance would be possible. I attended one such Sunday High meeting
at the Humsafar Trust premises that dealt with the rising problem of
male hustlers in Bombay city and noticed the presence of several Gay
Bombay regulars there. Likewise, there have been Humsafar volunteers
present at the Gay Bombay picnics and film screenings and Humsafar
head Ashok Row Kavi often posts his praise for Gay Bombay's various
achievements on different online forums.[30] In fact Kavi presided over
GB's 8th anniversary party in 2006 as the chief guest and the two groups
collaborated for the subsequent movie screening of the gay themed
film *Quest*.

I also discerned that Gay Bombay members did attend political meetings in their individual capacities and Gay Bombay as a group, despite
the objection of some of its members, but staying within the ambit of the
social space that it was comfortable operating in, had already started
to take small steps towards becoming less insular.

'Without feeling that it will threaten its own system', (Murgesh) the group
had begun to structure some of its dance parties as fundraisers for projects organized by other LBGT groups such as the Larzish LBGT film
festival in 2003 and the Calcutta Pride walk of 2005.

KARIM: THERE ARE PEOPLE WITHIN THE CORE GROUP WHO ARE
CLOSE TO OTHER GROUPS. SOME OF US ARE FRIENDLY WITH
HUMSAFAR, OTHERS WITH THE *KOTHI* COMMUNITIES OR
LESBIAN COMMUNITIES. THROUGH THE DIFFUSE NATURE OF
THE GROUP, WE MANAGE TO COMPACT OTHER GROUPS. WE
HAVE REALIZED THAT WE DO NEED TO DO THIS IN A FORMAL
WAY, WHICH IS WHY WE HAVE THE CONCEPT OF FUNDRAISERS.
IF SOMEONE APPROACHES US WITH SPECIFIC PROJECTS THAT
WE THINK WORTHWHILE, WE DO ORGANIZE FUNDRAISERS. WE

RECOGNIZE THAT THROUGH OUR PARTIES AND FILM FESTIVALS, WE CAN ACCESS THIS LARGER QUEER COMMUNITY—SINCE WE HAVE THIS ABILITY TO REACH OUT, WE SHOULD USE IT. THE ONE THING THAT FRUSTRATES ME PERSONALLY ABOUT THE PARTIES IS THAT WE GET ALL THESE GAY GUYS TOGETHER AND ITS AMAZING, BUT MAYBE WE SHOULD DO A LITTLE BIT MORE THAT MAKES THEM THINK OF THEMSELVES AS A COMMUNITY AND ITS ARGUABLE THAT ITS NOT POSSIBLE TO DO THAT IN A PARTY; BUT MAYBE WE SHOULD STILL TRY.

WEEKEND REVIEW

My weekends in Cambridge are so different from the ones I enjoy in Bombay. In Bombay, the routine is set...wake up early, go to my regular New Paris Hairdresser for a head massage (alternating between Parachute coconut oil, Dabur Brahmi Amla Kesh Tel, *Dabur Vatika and the Navratna* Thanda Thanda Cool Cool *red oil every week), buy all the weekend newspapers from the regular newspaperwallah, go home for a snacky breakfast of poha, or tomato omlet...shampoo and bathe at 1 p. m., lunch at grandparents soon after. A play at the National Centre for the Performing Arts or some kind of outing in the evening with friends, dinner outside, maybe a drive and that's another Sunday well spent.*

In Cambridge, it's a little different. I spread my movie, theatre and other cultural outings over the week unless it's something spectacular like Shakespeare in the park or a 4th of July concert that happens to fall on the weekend. J and I usually catch up on our laundry and grocery shopping over the weekend. Occassionally, we do meet up with friends—and in the past few years, we've formed our own little network. Straight friends, gay friends, singles, couples, with kids and without.... Mostly though, we just laze about in bed. We try and do brunch at least once (Sunny's, on Mass. Ave. is our favourite—a little Italian diner, where the propreiter knows us well). We cook at home—this is the only day of the week that we're not totally exhausted and we try and cook up a nice meal. Today's was shrimp, garlic, spinach and scallion pasta, with tofu and snow pea miso soup with whole-wheat olive bread, layered with fig, almond and olive spread. Yummy!

I still catch up with all my Indian newspapers—but online and in between the weekend work pile, instead of leisurely, while J plays the piano or violin—mostly Bach but every now and then, he'll surprise me with an ener-getic Bollywood rendition—the Hum Tum *title tune is his current favourite. Then naturally, I have to put my laptop away and do a little dance on the bed, to accompany him.*

I want to be married to J. We've discussed this endlessly. I've pro-posed to him on multiple occasions and he's accepted each proposal, even though he thinks it's a bourgeois idea and is not at all convinced that it will add anything more special to the bond we already share. We've had our queer friends walk down to the Cambridge city hall and walk out with their marriage licences—its literally so easy. Maybe he would be happy with something that simple, but not me. No, no, no, no, no, no. Too much Bollywood in my blood, honey. I want cartloads of flowers. At least four or five different parties. Thousands of guests. A procession on an elephant. Turbans, palaces, dancing, scented candles and every damn cliché in the book. Followed by a walk down the aisle, wearing matching tuxedos, while our fam-ilies dab at tears (of happiness, naturally) on the sidelines. Or a Disneyland fairy tale wedding, with seven roller coaster circles around a giant fireball in the sky—the symbolic seven circles round the fire ritual from Hindu wed-dings, reinterpreted Parmesh style. Until we reach some kind of agreement, he's agreed to wear a silver quasi-engagement ring that I got for him from a trip back to India. Good enough, for now. I can develop my big fat Indian wedding plans at leisure.

The Imagined Future

How did the inhabitants of Gay Bombay imagine their own personal futures as well as the future of the group? Many respondents were confident that India would become more gay-friendly in the future.

NACHIKET: FRAGMENTATION OF THE FAMILY AS A UNIT; ECONOMIC INDEPENDENCE WILL INCREASE AND START COMING AT AN EARLIER AGE. THERE IS GOING TO BE A DISTINCTLY GREATER SENSE OF EXPOSURE TO EUROPEAN AND AMERICAN LIFESTYLES. ALL THESE WILL MAKE A DIFFERENCE.

Some were apprehensive that the divisions within the gay movement in the country 'on the basis of class, gender and politically too', (Vidvan) would hamper the cause. Murgesh and Cholan felt that although there was a lot of progress being made in terms of gay visibility, the real challenges lay ahead and the path would not be easy.

MURGESH: IT IS WONDERFUL THAT WE ARE A DEMOCRACY, BUT THERE ARE VERY FRIGHTENING FRINGE GROUPS. THERE ARE ALSO A LOT OF VERY INTELLIGENT, INTELLECTUAL PEOPLE WORKING FOR THE COMMUNITY—FROM THE MEDICAL COMMUNITY AND LEGAL COMMUNITY. THESE PEOPLE KNOW ABOUT HUMAN RIGHTS, THE RIGHTS OF MINORITIES... THEY HAVE BEEN HELPING US ON THEIR OWN, WORKING IN OUR FAVOUR. HELPING US TO FIGHT AGAINST 377, WILL HELP US FOR GAY MARRIAGES TOO... IT WILL TAKE VERY LONG... BUT I AM CONFIDENT THAT [PROGRESS] WILL COME ABOUT.

CHOLAN: WHAT WE HAVEN'T DONE IS TALK TO THE BIGOTS. WE HAVE BEEN CONFIDENCE BUILDING BETWEEN EACH OTHER AND SAYING WE ARE OKAY AND WE HAVE THESE SUPPORT STRUC-TURES. BUT LET US TAKE THIS TO THE BIGOTS NOW AND REASON WITH THEM AND SAY 'STOP ALL THIS BULLSHIT ABOUT GAY MEN IN INDIA SPREADING HIV'. I MEAN—COME ON—STRAIGHT MEN IN THIS COUNTRY ARE SPREADING HIV. LETS NOT HAVE ALL THIS TALK ABOUT WESTERN CULTURE, BECAUSE WE ARE THERE EVERYWHERE; LET'S BE MORE VISIBLE ABOUT IT. THERE HAVE BEEN FEW SMALL LINKS MADE WITH POLITICAL PARTIES. I THINK NOW WE CAN PROBABLY CALL THE BIGOTS AND SAY 'LETS HAVE A MATURE DISCUSSION AND A DEBATE', WHICH YOU COULDN'T FEW YEARS AGO'. NONE OF THIS COMES WITHOUT A COST, OF COURSE THERE WILL BE UPS AND DOWNS LIKE WITH ANY OTHER MOVEMENT AND THERE WILL BE A COST FOR SOME PEOPLE INVOLVED.

With regard to the future of Gay Bombay, many respondents were comfortable with it exactly as it existed. Some of the core group members wondered if it was not getting too 'jaded...mechanical and streamlined' (Murgesh). From the others, some pitched for an increased engagement with activism and inclusiveness of 'not only of lower-income groups, but also queer women' (Husain). Cholan and Asim suggested steps that Gay Bombay could take, even while staying true to its mandate of not being involved in political activism. Asim was keen that the group promote a vaccination drive for hepatitis B (something that was accomplished sub-sequently), while Cholan suggested using the group's different channels to route out important information within the community, such as 'health information, information about how to deal with hustlers, awareness on how to protect yourself, STIs [Sexually Transmitted Infections] and HIV, coming out…'.

> CHOLAN: IT SEEMS THAT THERE IS A YOUNGER GENERATION OF PEOPLE THAT COME INTO GAY BOMBAY AND THEN MOVE OUT AFTER HAVING FOUND THEMSELVES QUICKLY AND THEN JUST ATTENDING THE PARTIES. I THINK IT WOULD BE GOOD TO HAVE A SENSE IN THE YOUNGER COMMUNITY THAT THIS IS NOT JUST ABOUT ME; IT'S ALSO ABOUT A WHOLE LOT OF PEOPLE WHO DON'T HAVE ALL THE SUPPORT STRUCTURES… I THINK GAY BOMBAY DOES A GREAT SERVICE THROUGH PARENTS' MEETS—BUT IT'S DIFFICULT TO BROAD BASE THAT. I THINK IT WOULD BE NICE IF EVEN 30 PERCENT OF THE PARTY CROWD SITS AND THINKS ABOUT THEIR RESPONSIBILITY BEYOND THE PARTY SCENE TOWARDS THE LARGER COMMUNITY.

On a personal level, Mike wanted to become a 'role model for the community' and 'start scholarships and increase awareness'. Rustom, who was located in Ahmedabad, expressed a desire to start a gay support group in the city, on the lines of Gay Bombay. (I was happy to note that he achieved this goal a few months subsequent to our interview). Several respondents who were single, imagined a life with a boyfriend, a life partner or a husband.

> GUL: I THINK THE COOLEST THINGS WOULD BE TO HOLD HANDS AND WALK ON THE ROADS OF BOMBAY WITH MY LOVER. THAT IS MY DREAM. BEING WITH SOMEONE, CANDLE LIGHT DINNERS IF POSSIBLE, STAYING WITH THAT LOVER…
>
> NIHAR: I WANT A LOVER. IF NOT CHILDREN, AT LEAST A DOG OR A CAT. I WANT A HOME. I AM AFRAID OF ENDING UP ALONE. MY FRIENDS TELL ME THAT FOR 20, THAT'S STUPID THINKING. BUT I AM AFRAID.
>
> MOHNISH: MY DREAM LIFE WOULD BE TO LIVE WITH THAT PERSON IN INDIA AS A COUPLE… I WOULD LOVE IF HE STAYS WITH MY FAMILY AND ME, WITH MY MOM AND DAD. BUT THAT IS ALMOST IMPOSSIBLE.

ISAAC: I WILL HAVE A GAY MARRIAGE. MY FAMILY WILL COME AND DANCE. SING WEDDING SONGS. I JUST HAVE TO FIND A GUY.

Some who were already in relationships, imagined cementing their relationship and things like joint bank loans, common property and so on—once Section 377 was removed, or being able to finally declare the true nature of their relationship to neighbours and office colleagues. Others, like Yudhisthir were fearful of the future—

RIGHT NOW IT DOES LOOK A LITTLE DEPRESSING. I AM 30, I HAVEN'T HAD A RELATIONSHIP AND I DON'T KNOW IF I WILL EVER HAVE ONE. I AM LOOKING AHEAD TO 30 YEARS OF LIVING ALONE. IT LOOKS SCARY SO I TRY NOT TO THINK ABOUT IT. PARENTS—WHEN YOU COME OUT TO THEM, AFTER THEY HAVE GOTTEN OVER YOU BEING GAY AND THEM NOT HAVING GRANDCHILDREN AND STUFF… THE ONE THING THEY ARE CONCERNED ABOUT IS—HOW WILL YOU MANAGE WHEN YOU ARE ALONE? THAT'S A BRIDGE I WILL CROSS WHEN I COME TO IT. THAT IS TOO SCARY FOR ME. WHEN YOU READ ABOUT PEOPLE WHO LIVE ALONE AND ARE KILLED AND STUFF… I DON'T WANT TO GO THERE NOW.

NOTES

1. Jeremy Seabrook, *Love in a different climate: Men Who have Sex with Men in India* (New York/London: Verso, 1999), p. 50.
2. Barry Adam, 'Love and Sex in Constructing Identity Among Men Who have Sex with Men', *International Journal of Sexuality and Gender Studies* (Kluwer Academic Publishers, 2000), Vol. 5(4), p. 322.
3. This phrase is the title of Ashok Row Kavi's essay 'Contract of Silence in Hoshang Merchant's, *Yaarana: Gay Writing from India* (New Delhi: Penguin India, 1999).
4. Douglas Sanders, 'Flying the Rainbow Flag in Asia', Conference Paper—Second International Conference on Sexualities, Masculinities and Cultures in South Asia Bangalore, India, 9–12 June (2004), p. 7.
5. Hinduism is the predominant religion in India. According to the 2001 census, about 83 per cent of the population identified as 'Hindu'. The latest Indian census facts and figures may be viewed on the world wide web—http://www.censusindia.net/
6. Devdutt Pattanaik, *The Man Who was a Woman and Other Queer Tales from Hindu Lore* (New York: Harrington Park Press, 2002), pp. 5–8.
7. Maria Bakardjieva, 'Virtual Togetherness: An Everyday-life Perspective', from *Media, Culture & Society* (Sage Publications, 2003), Vol. 25(3), p. 291. Bakardjieva reverses Raymond Williams' 1974 concept of 'mobile privatization'; her term 'immobile socialization' denotes the 'socialization of private experience through the invention of new forms of intersubjectivity and social organization online'.

8. David Woolwine, 'Community in Gay Male Experience and Discourse', *Journal of Homosexuality* (New York: Haworth Press, 2000), Vol. 38(4), p. 21.

9. Peggy Wireman, *Urban Neighborhoods, Networks, and Families: New Forms for Old Values* (Lexington, MA: Lexington Books, 1984); cited in Barry Wellman and M. Gulia 'Net Surfers Don't Ride Alone: Virtual Communities as Communities', in Mark Smith and Peter Kollock (Eds), *Communities in Cyberspace* (London; New York: Routledge, 1998), p. 176.

10. Barry Wellman and M. Gulia, 'Net Surfers Don't Ride Alone: Virtual Communities as Communities', in Smith and Kollock (Eds), op. cit., p. 181.

11. N. Charles and A. Davies, 'Contested Communities: The Refuge Movement and Cultural Identities in Wales', *Sociological Review* (Blackwell Publishing, 1997), No. 45, pp. 416–436; as cited in Mihaela Kelemen and Warren Smith, 'Community and its Virtual Promises: A Critique of Cyberlibertarian Rhetoric', *Information, Community and Society* (Taylor and Francis [Routledge], 2001), Vol. 4(3), p. 374.

12. David Woolwine, op. cit., p. 21.

13. 'Weak ties are more apt than strong ties to link people with different social characteristics. Such weak ties are also a better means than strong ties of maintaining contact with other social circles'. M. Granovetter, 'The Strength of Weak Ties', *American Journal of Sociology* (University of Chicago, 1973), 78(6), pp. 1360–1380; referred to in Wellman and Gulia, op. cit., p. 176.

14. David Woolwine, op. cit., p. 30.

15. See Roland Robertson, 'Glocalization: Time-Space and Homogeneity-Heterogeneity,' in Mike Featherstone, Scott Lash and Roland Robertson (Eds), *Global Modernities* (London: Sage Publications, 1995), pp. 25–44.

16. Wellman and Gulia, in Smith and Kollock, op. cit., p. 187.

17. *Holi* and *Raksha Bandhan* are Hindu festivals and national holidays in India. *Iftaar* is the daily fast breaking meal performed during the holy month of Ramadan in the Islamic calendar.

18. See Sally Munt, Elizabeth H. Bassett and Kate O'Riordan, 'Virtually Belonging: Risk, Connectivity, and Coming Out On-Line', *International Journal of Sexuality and Gender Studies* (Kluwer Academic Publishers, 2002), Vol. 7 (2,3), p. 127, for an overview.

19. Anthony Giddens (1991), *Modernity and Self- Identity, Self and Society in the Late Modern Age,* Cambridge (Polity Press), p. 54 quoted in David Gauntlett, *Media, Gender and Identity: An Introduction* (London/New York: Routledge, 2002), p. 99.

20. See Munt, Bassett and O'Riordan, op. cit., p. 128, for an overview.

21. Judith Donath, 'Identity and Deception in the Virtual Community', in Smith and Kollock (Eds), op. cit., p. 53.

22. Ibid, pp. 30–31.

23. Ibid, p. 44.

24. See Ketan Tanna, 'Bombay Gays' Night Out—New Year's Eve Parties', *The Hindustan Times*, 31 December 2003. http://www.hindustantimes.com/news/919_514378, 001800010001.htm

25. Jeremy Seabrook, *Love in a Different Climate: Men Who have Sex with Men in India* (New York/London: Verso, 1999), p. 75.

26. Read 'GayBombay', *Salon.com* (2 December 2002), where the writer Sandip Roy speculates whether the Internet keeps 'gay men from really coming out' and instead,

puts them 'in a giant virtual closet'. http://www.salon.com/tech/feature/2002/12/02/gay_india/print.html

27. David Woolwine, op. cit., pp. 16–17.

28. Source—Email posting to the Gay Bombay Yahoo! Group 'Hep B inoculation meet so many pricks' dated 27 June 2006.

    In this post, Vikram describes how a medical type of event becomes into a party. 'Boyfriends would hold their partners hands as they got inoculated, much to the amusement or envy of everyone else there. Then people started forming circles and when the guy at the centre got his dose, everyone around him would scream—so that he didn't have to!'

29. Message to the Gay Bombay newsgroup 'Announcing the GB Poz Forum' posted by vgd67 on 29 July 2007.

30. For example, Kavi's post on 3 August 2006 on the Lbgt-India Yahoo! Group ('Re: 5th GayBombay Parents and Relatives Meet—A Report') where he states that 'what GB is doing is great and absolutely worthy of every support.'

8

Disco *Jalebi*

Observations, Concerns, Hopes

Often truth is neither this nor that. Or rather it is a bit of both—this and that. The truth can rest on the threshold, in the twilight, somewhere in the middle, between contradictions, slipping in as a possibility between two realities....[1] (Devdutt Pattnaik, 2002)

This chapter covers my analysis of how Gay Bombay came about, what being gay means to its members and how they negotiate locality and globalization, their sense of identity as well as a feeling of community within its online or offline world. My conclusion aims at a compromise between the need to make a fully knitted closure—weaving all my threads together in a giant sweep—and the realities of ambivalence and the futility of drawing any definite end results from such a poly-vocal endeavour. My compromise, just like the rest of the work, is a little bit of this and a little bit of that.

WHO AM I?

Friend cosmopolitan grandson top shopaholic son boss gay teacher brother versatile male Hindu Bombayite student entrepreneur advisor Indian TV junkie gossip shy homo ingénue researcher foodie catalyst Bollywood fan scholar corporate fashionista NRI...oh, fuck it! How do they expect me to compress my identity into a little Friendster box that says 'About Me'? I write—'I'm fun loving, trusting, sensitive, high-spirited, curious, zany and passionate. I love meeting new people with interests and passions different from mine. I enjoy hugs, languid afternoons in bookstores, picnics by the river, love stories with happy endings, orange sunsets, railway stations, Pringles Sour Cream and Onion, chicken a la Kiev, the colour red, Acqua Di Parma, masala tea, oxidized silver, sunshine... I believe in both eternity and transience' and stop. It seems so put on and incomplete. Is this really the way to meet Mr Right?

I am a time traveller slithering in and out of many skins, crossing time zones into different Bombay worlds every day. Shop, shop shop. This could be New York or Paris. Except that couture doesn't cost you an arm and a leg (Oh dah-ling...I just made a pair of fah-bu-lous gold raw silk pants from my tailor.... You'll never believe how good they look!) and you can have Pepsi and lassi next to each other. International cable and local mafia. Expensive Martinis and 40 different types of coffees. Tall buildings right next to slums. Fucking outstanding street chaat on hellish post apocalyptic streetscapes. Twisted metal forms melting into stinking garbage mounts amidst an ever-pervasive stench surrounding another gelato parlour franchise.

Ha! It all sounds so fucking clichéd, that it's laughable. (Like one of those desi writers who exoticize India and make fat sums of money writing for the West and then jealous journalists back home enjoy ripping them apart to shreds while secretly wishing that it would have been them, but their manuscript came back, rejected, so sad...what to do...we are like this only, par aakhir dil hai Hindustani, baba!) But these are also my clichés and I'm sorry that they're so pathetically lame but really, what to do, man... I am always reflexive in India. I mean, how can you not, na—when the entire world and their country cousins come to India for their Karma Cola® spirituality fix and dump their angsty shit on it—why the fuck shouldn't I, you know? I belong here after all. Yes? I belong here. Right?

I am Bombay. Pukka, 100 per cent (guaranteed, otherwise free exchange, boss—tension kaikoo leney ka?) I belong to Colaba and Churchgate and Bandra and Lokhandwala in a way I have never belonged to Cambridge or Manama or anywhere else I have lived. I am a kitsch Krishna poster on the street outside the Prince of Wales museum. I am the frenzy of Oval maidan cricket. I am soft Holi gulal smeared on a wet forehead. I am a crunchy papad in a Chinese restaurant. I am Irish coffee at Prithvi theatre. I am the first edition of Mid-day, read from back to front. I am a game of Antakshri played on a six hour bus ride back home from a picnic. I am the indignation and exuberance of Shilpa Shetty on

Big Brother. *I am a pink feather boa draped Hema Malini, slowly descending in a basket, from the sky singing* 'Mere Naseeb Mein'.

I am a bright orange disco jalebi, *hot and soft and syrupy, eaten after dancing for three hours non-stop at a Gay Bombay dance party, with random strangers who've suddenly become my new best friends. I climb back into the basket and rise high above the heat and noise in my circular* jalebi *pattern that makes me dizzy.... From far above, this seems to be any group of gay men dancing anywhere in the world. Same dance floor layout. Same crystal ball. Same strobe lights. Same DJ booth, same smoke, same everything, yaar. Except that I can hear the faint strains of* 'Hai Re Hai Tera Ghungta' *playing, and I have a sweet aftertaste in my mouth. And this feels like home in a way no other place in the world does. Another night, another place.* Sholay *party, New York. Same brown gay men. Same Bollywood music. Same heat. Inexplicably different.*

I am gay Bombay. I am straight acting gay Bombay. I am straight acting and hating it gay Bombay. I am straight acting and enjoying my straight acting life gay Bombay. I am I wish I could change but I can't gay Bombay. I am I change a little bit every day gay Bombay. Perhaps I am a coconut. Brown outside, white inside. (But not white white. Brown white. But brown is the new white, didn't you know... India shining, India poised and all that? Not the new black? So confusing. Not really. It's simple—repeat after me—same, only different. Same, only different!) I am a spice. ('Namaste!' Ka-ching. *Same only different). Exoticize! It's an order. No, subvert, subvert, you're a subaltern who speaks, no? Subsume. Subvert. Subjugate.* Subkuch. *Follow?* Yessir. *Sameonlydifferent.*

I float high above...now everything is a speck. I am a cloud, evaporating in Bombay's sweltering heat... I can feel the monsoon pouring out from within my skin...I am feeling alive and full and soon, I will burst open...but till then, I am pregnant with infinite possibilities... I want to float, float, float...float away. Happily ever after.

HOW DID GAY BOMBAY COME ABOUT?

A simplistic linear explanation would go something like this—Globalization and liberalization happened, media exposure to gay lifestyles happened, bars and social spaces opened up, gay activism began, and then

Gay Bombay came about. While this line of logic is not entirely wrong, it is un-nuanced. There were several forces at work that led to the unique set of circumstances in which Gay Bombay was engendered; the post 1991 changes in India were only the last piece within the larger jigsaw.

The initial piece would have to be the existence of a significant English speaking population in India, which can be attributed first of all, to the colonial exercise of 'creating a class of persons, Indian in blood and colour, but English in taste, in opinions, in morals, and in intellect'.[2] The British pursued this goal by spreading missionary style English education throughout the country and following that up by opening up certain jobs in the British Indian administration to Indians, who spoke and wrote English. After the British left India in 1947, India's southern states vehemently opposed the imposition of Hindi (the language of central and northern India) as the national language. Prime Minister Nehru's solution was a compromise which stated that 'while Hindi would remain the national language, it would not be imposed on non-Hindi speaking states. Instead, English would henceforth enjoy the status of the official language'[3] (Kapur, 2002). This compromise ensured the continuation of English's predominance over the years (in parliament, in the courts, in trade and commerce and especially in higher education) and proved to be beneficial for the creation of Gay Bombay in many ways. To list just two—

(a) When the Internet emerged, predominantly in English, there was already a ready constituency of English speaking, upper middle class gay men, ready to exploit its opportunities and utilize it for their benefit.

(b) The IT and IT-enabled services boom, when it happened, found a treasure trove of ready and able workers, including Gay Bombay's members, who could leverage their English speaking abilities as their passport to a better life.

Second, as Varma points out in his book *Being Indian* (2004), India after independence pursued a lop sided and 'socially callous' educational policy—tertiary education received more funds than primary education and basic literacy training; 'while the campaign against illiteracy languished...some of the finest technical institutions were set up as part of an enviable infrastructure of higher education'[4] and thus, today, 'a country with the largest number of people in the world who cannot read and write produces a veritable army of technically proficient graduates'.[5] Entrance to this army is highly competitive (for example, in 2003, over 2,00,000 students took the entrance examination for admission into the Indian Institute of Technology, but only 2,000 were admitted, a success rate of less than 1 per cent)[6]—but once you are in, the rewards in terms of salaries and the ability to lead a life of privilege are sumptuous. I do not want to comment on the social inequality of the system here, but for the purpose of this book, it is clear to see that the technology and job booms that followed the opening up of the Indian economy in 1991 (and their subsequent ripple effects on Indian gayness, as noted in previous chapters) would not have been possible, had there not been an already existing structure of higher education that shepherded young and ambitious Indian graduates on to the assembly line to a shining techie future.

Third, as we have also seen in Chapter 4, there was *already* a thriving social gay community existing in Bombay city during the 1970s and 1980s. In the 1990s, the pioneering efforts of *Bombay Dost* magazine and the Humsafar trust had laid the groundwork for the possibility of Gay Bombay with their constant outreach through the media. One should remember that even in the Western world—sexual politics and social formations only came to the forefront after the 1960s and took off in the 1970s and 1980s. Jackson has pointed out that there were gay cultures in countries like Philippines, Thailand, Australia and New Zealand even in the 1960s, just like in India. I am saying this because I want to emphasize that it would be wrong to consider the emergence of gayness in India (and in Bombay, specifically) entirely as an after effect of globalization or an emulation of Western standards, instead, as Jackson suggests, we could consider it as a 'parallel development'.

> The issue is not so much to consider how these cultures appeared after they did in the West, but rather how they emerged at much the same time as they did in many parts of the West. It may be necessary to revise current accounts which imagine the West, in particular the United States is the original site of contemporary gay and lesbian identities and instead see these identities emerging by a process of parallel development in diverse locales. (Jackson, 2000)[7]

The above three factors were vital in creating the context for the birth of GB and eventually, Gay Bombay came to be born in the late 1990s out of the friction, overlaps and disjunctures of the six scapes we have recounted in Chapter 4.

We saw in Chapter 5 that the changed mediascape played a significant influence in enabling news stories about gay rights and gay cultures and lifestyles from abroad to circulate freely within the Indian imagination. As my respondents noted, it was a big thing for them just to be able to see the existence of gay people in other countries; it validated their own existence and made them feel that they were not alone. More importantly, the changed mediascape allowed stories about *Indian* gay rights and gayness in an *Indian* context to circulate widely and the coverage, while not always positive, was often supportive, at least in the English language press. The issues covered were diverse (gay activism and conferences, the pink rupee, lesbian suicides, corporate HR policy and LBGT issues…); in some cases, the media reflected societal concerns (for example, in framing the emergence of homosexuality in the popular perception as a debate on globalization), in other cases, it played advocate (as in the articles advocating for the abolishment of Section 377). Page 3 culture and the press tabloidification of the 1990s contributed significantly to the discursive idea of gayness as a part and parcel of everyday urban life. The media also contextualized Indian gayness within the larger scheme of Indian sexuality as a whole, through its periodic sexual surveys.

Thus, the (English) media performed the important role of an ambassador of gayness in the minds of Indian middle and upper middle classes. It enabled gayness to be brought out of the closet, into the public sphere. It activated the imagination of a larger gay Indian community than what already existed. Every time there was a story that could be used as a hook (the *Fire* controversy of 1998, the Pushkin Chandra double murders of 2004, Vikram Seth's open letter in 2006 and so on), the media upped the ante by using the story to debate and discuss Indian homosexuality at large, thus constantly reinforcing the imagination and construction of Indian gayness with every iteration. Indian literature, films and English theatre as performed in the country, all added to the news media's deliberation of the gay cause. All this cemented the emerging gay ideoscape.

There were two other important factors without which the media's impact might have been lessened, and I am grateful to my respondent Karim for discussing these with me. One was HIV/AIDS which helped to mainstream gayness from a marginal issue by riding on the health agenda. The government is now entwined with gay organizations like Humsafar (through its agencies like NACO) because of this agenda and the basis of the motion for the repeal of Section 377 is HIV/AIDS. The second that at least there is a rudimentary human rights framework in place in India for groups like women, religious minorities and so on, that sexual minorities can appropriate, learn from and also appeal to, in contrast with countries like Egypt which in many other ways parallel India, but where the queer movement is nowhere as close.

The financescape of economic liberalization and the subsequent rapid economic growth within the service sector (especially retail, technology and BPO services) resulted in the rapid expansion and transformation of the great Indian middle class into a 'pan Indian domestic class of consumers' seeking a '[commodified] Indianness' (Khilnani, 2001).[8]

The pressures of the market, both global and local...[are] producing what one might call a commodification of Indianness. The workings of the market are creating a pan-Indian domestic class of consumers who wish to have diversity packaged and served up to them. The new taste for unfamiliar food from other parts of the country (think of the invention of 'regional cuisines'), fashion, domestic ornament, *vaastu*, astrology and now a search for new travel destinations, all are signs of this new hunger for consuming India. It is a strategy of internal exoticisation and domestication. (Khilnani, 2001)[9]

Side by side to this commodification and consumerization of Indianness was the creation of what Varma (2004) calls 'pan Indian culture'—

The new supranational Indian culture...has given common symbols and icons to Indians even in the remotest parts of the country. Riding on a media and communications revolution, it has spread faster than any cultural development before. It permeates every aspect of everyday life—dress, food, art, language, employment and entertainment. It has the arrogance of the upstart and the self-absorption of the new. Irreverent in expression, it is dismissive of critics and has no time for apologists. What it lacks in pedigree, it makes up for in confidence, for it can count on the support of the people. Its greatest strength is that—excluding perhaps the absolutely marginalized, it includes more people across India in a common language of communication in more areas of everyday life than ever before. The new culture is still evolving. It is difficult to define exactly, but impossible to ignore in the nationwide appeal of masala *dosa* and *tandoori* chicken, the rhythms of Daler Mehendi and A.R. Rahman, the evolution of 'Hinglish', the ubiquity of *salwar-kameez*, the popularity of Hindi films, the audience for cable television, the mania for cricket and the competition for IIT-JEE, to name just a few. What has facilitated the growth of this pan-Indian culture? Certain answers are obvious, such as the reach of Indian films and the exponential growth in the popularity of television. The revolution in communication has helped, as has the huge increase in mobility. Common aspirations and the solidarity imparted by similar constraints...the gradual but definite democratization of the social order...countrywide opportunities, standard institutions and curricula...the presence of the Indian state...the consequence is a far more homogenized India than Indians are aware of or willing to accept. (Varma, 2004)[10]

For many years, the semi socialist state had been thrusting its definition of what was modern and national down the throats of the citizens... But...'micro narratives of film, television, music and other expressive forms...allowed modernity to be rewritten...as a vernacular globalization... (Appadurai, 1996).[11]

This globalization was accepted as something very *Indian*—its framing as something that was vernacular, ensured its success. To inelegantly adapt some more Appadurian terminology, there was a case of cultural homo-Indianization and cultural hetero-Indianization occurring simultaneously with vernacular globalization. It is important to remember (and this is a salient feature of cultural heterogenization, as we have encountered in Chapter 3) that various Indian historical traditions continued to flourish along with the reformulated modernity. For example, the popularity of Indian pop music was accompanied by a revival of interest in Indian classical music (Varma, 2004).[12]

For our purpose, we can see that this timely emergence of pop cultural homogeneity, pan-Indianness and vernacular globalization enabled gay identified Indian individuals to *imagine* a distinctly *Indian* gay identity, in opposition to a Western gay identity. As we read in Chapter 7, my respondents were adamant that they were both *Indian* and *gay*; they had created this composite identity by drawing on and appropriating Western cultural elements in combination with the aforementioned homogenous Indian elements that were being articulated at the same time.

Appadurai points out that the work of imagination 'is neither purely emancipatory, nor entirely disciplined, but is a space of contestation....'.[13] I was witness to this contestation taking place as my respondents answered me about how they negotiated this imagined hybrid gayness, individually and collectively. (It is this combination of radically diverse elements that is perhaps, the defining factor of Indianness—never a case of eitherness, but always of bothness; both this *and* that. This can be frustrating, but also liberating, as we shall see later).

Anyway, in a scenario like the above, the advent of the Internet proved to be the tipping point, which served as a catalyst for the expansion of the gay community. It was the right technology that emerged at the right time and soon enough, Gay Bombay was born. Its anonymity (one needed an email address to access it—and one could easily get an email address with a nickname, without having to reveal one's real identity) and asynchronous nature (both the site and mailing list did not need to be accessed in real time; thus people did not need to have their own computers—they could go to cyber cafés whenever convenient, or access the service from their offices) made it an instant hit among the educated, English speaking men that it targeted.

In Chapter 4, I commented that all the recent changes in the Indian gay landscape occurred within the *Hindutva* (Hinduness) charged, schizo-phrenic political environment of the mid 1990s and wondered why the establishment did not jump upon these as yet another Western influence to be fought tooth and nail and squashed. My explanation for this official tolerance of gayness through the 1990s is as follows.

First, it must be understood that the changes we are talking about were really very tiny and only affected a small section of urban India. Homosexuality is in any case pretty much a non-issue for any Indian political party—national or regional; it is not even a blip on their pol-itical agenda radars and I certainly do not see that changing in the immediate future. This does not mean that the governments in power, at both the state and central level in the 1990s, were not aware of the existence and spread of Gay Bombay; they certainly were, but it is my contention that gayness in general was tolerated by subsuming it into the *imagination* of the ideal nation state.

The mid-1990s were a period of increased political chauvinism; the cultural *threats* supposedly posed by globalization and the opening up of the economy had resulted in a hybrid outward looking or inward looking behaviour amongst the mainstream middle classes. Being Indian took on a shrill jingoistic fervour after the nuclear bomb explosions of 1998 and the Kargil battle with Pakistan in 1999. The BJP-led government tried to forge an identity for India that stood for belligerence and nationalistic assertion. India was no longer to be imagined as an idealistic Gandhian state, a poor country cousin of the world's superpowers, but a proud international nuclear world power, that would deal with the world on its own terms.

It should be clear that both the BJP government at the centre and the BJP-Shiv Sena government in power in Bombay from the mid 1990 onwards were extremely homophobic; both explicitly and implicitly and practiced what Bachetta (1999) has called 'the dual operations of xenophobic queerphobia and queerphobic xenophobia'. Within xenophobic queerphobia, being gay or queer is positioned as being non-Indian—it is a marked as a Western import and something against Indian culture. Within queerphobic xenophobia—'queerdom is assigned (often metaphorically) to all designated others of the nation, regardless of their sexual identity'.[14] Within their kind of nationalistic imagination, there was, of course, no place for homosexuality or difference of any kind, but if by chance, any difference did manage to raise its head, it was not cut off, but immediately marked and made powerless, and thus non-threatening.

We can see this subsumption of difference in operation within the *Hindutva* inspired Bollywood films churned out during that period.

[They] created the apparently contradictory images of a marginalized, stereotyped and yet benign religious minority and of overwhelmingly harmonious relations between members of the dominant Hindu culture and the Muslim minority; a set of circumstances not unlike those found in the American cinema with regard to that culture's African-American minority. Hindus and Muslims do not normally contest for superiority, women, or other prizes in the Hindi cinema. (Booth, 2005)[15]

I want to specifically point to *Hum Aapke Hain Kaun* ('Who Am I of Yours?' 1994), the extended marriage video of a film, released in the aftermath of the terrible riots and bomb blasts of 1993, as an excellent example of this display of hegemony. In this film, the Muslim *threat* is addressed not by exclusion, but by othering. As Kazmi (1999) notes, the only Muslim presence in the film is the jovial doctor couple, who are *othered* by religion, speech (*adaabs* galore, lots of *shaayiri*) and dress (*achkans* and *ghararas*).[16] They function as support staff, offering sage words of advice only when asked, completely marginal to the main plot. Laloo, the main servant, is quite an important character. Of course, his servant stature is constantly emphasized throughout, whether through his own expressions of gratitude at the benevolence of his masters, or their continuous insistence that he is *like a* son or a brother to them. The loyalty of both—the servants and the Muslim friends—is made explicit; they exist within the periphery of the main Hindu family—that is their place and that is how they must live and as long as they understand that, it is good. I am reminded of Hardt and Negri's contention that 'Empire does not fortify its boundaries to push others away, but rather pulls them within its pacific order, like a powerful vortex'[17] (2000).

One can read the entire slew of Bollywood films that emerged in the 1990s with gay sidekicks keeping this operation in mind. The markedly effeminate, comic gay characters (almost always men) were ridiculed but also indulgently patronized by the protagonists and effectively neutralized. Thus, a Bobby Darling is teased and mocked in whatever film he is a part of, but his place in the youth gang is never in doubt. It is of course understood that he will never behave transgressively with the hero, coo over him or insinuate desire for him. He is accepted, despite being different, because his loyalty as a friend and overall integration into the master narrative overrule his effeminate behaviour and implied homosexuality. In *Hum Aapke Hain Kaun* itself, there is a song and dance sequence where the lead heroine performs a raunchy sex simulation act with another cross dressing woman, at the end of which, they are both joined by the film's hero, in full drag, but the transgressive element of all this is neutralized due to the comical presentation. Similarly, in the public eye, the outspoken Ashok Row Kavi is *othered* and then indulged as a firebrand activist, because ultimately, he is *one of us*—with his impeccable Hindu credentials and so on.

But let us not forget, whenever the situation gets non-comical, like with the *Fire* controversy, this indulgence stops and the response is vicious and often violent. *Fire* was deemed as an attack by 'ultra westernized elite' on 'the traditional set up' through 'explicit lesbianism and other perversities'[18] (Bhatia in *Organizer*, 1998).

> It proves that modern India wants to become as modern as ancient Greece. And for those who think that this is going backward, the answer is simple—West is best and nothing coming from the West, ancient or modern, can ever go out of fashion for us. (*Organizer*, 1999)[19]
>
> That way, one day all the pornographic flings of Mona (sic) Lewinsky-Clinton duo may become the role model, if the aim is to disintegrate the family a la western society. (Bhatia, 1998)[20]

We see countless other instances of clamping down on gayness whenever the discourse around it becomes too public, or too threatening. For example, Naz Foundation workers were arrested in 2001 for running a *gay sex club* when they were in fact, simply doing HIV prevention outreach (see Chapter 6), the government and the courts constantly decry homosexuality (see Chapter 4) and former Indian prime minister, Manmohan Singh, clearly flustered by a question about same sex marriages by a Canadian journalist, emphasized that 'these kinds of marriage are not appreciated here [in India]'.[21]

To summarize, Gay Bombay was formed as a result of the intersection of certain historical conjectures (including an already existing gay history) with the disjunctures caused via the flows of the radically shifting ethnoscape, financescape, politiscape, mediascape, technoscape and ideoscape of urban India the 1990s. It was allowed space to exist due to its upper class orientation and the relative insignificance of gayness in the larger socio-political scheme of things. Of course, my explanation for the above is 'radically context dependent'[22] (Appadurai himself has emphasized that his theories—my reference grid—are insufficiently developed to be even parsimonious models at this point, much less to be predictive theories');[23] however, I find it to be extremely relevant in dispelling the simplistic one sided linear theory (as evinced within the global queering debate, discussed in Chapter 3) that gayness is a Western thing and that its history and circulation in other countries will follow the same path that it has done in the West.

WHAT DOES BEING GAY MEAN IN GAY BOMBAY?

Large numbers of Asian men and women continue to live within the 'traditional' spaces for gender or sex difference and to understand themselves and their lives in 'pre-gay' terms that often relate more to the pre-industrial rural pasts of their societies than to the post modernizing urban present. However, there are also large numbers of men and women who are reacting against what they see as the historic constraint on homoeroticism in their respective societies and who are actively engaging in relocating homoeroticism from the shadows and the periphery, to the centre stage of their lives. (Jackson, 2000)[24]

I encountered two opposing conceptions of homosexuality among my interviewees. One version equated homosexuality with being *gay*; this camp wished to assimilate and appropriate the term within the Indian context, recognizing fully well the unique set of circumstances within which this would take place. For them, social interaction was the key to building a sense of gay community in Bombay, but they recognized that cutting across class and gender norms may be a problem within these kinds of interactions. The other version of homosexuality I encountered questioned terms like *gay* and deemed them Western imports and negative influences and preferred to use *gay* as just one term, alongside indigenous terminology such as *kothi* or functional terms like 'MSM'. They were interested in social interaction across class norms, an assimilation of the various LBGT identities that exist in India and were also concerned with issues such as HIV/AIDS. Proponents of both these views used the gay Bombay newsgroup as well as real world events like parties and meetings as a battleground for their respective ideologies. The archive facility of the Gay Bombay newsgroup provides a fascinating and rich look at their debates as they have played out through the volatile posts over the years.

However, this is not to suggest that these were the only two positions that my respondents adopted—as we have seen in Chapter 7, there existed a variety of other stances that were sandwiched between and around these two prominent takes on the nature of Indian homosexuality. Many of these included reconciliatory stances advocating a middle ground, which echoed Shivananda Khan's (2000) line of reasoning that 'to say gay is appropriate and right. But at the same time to denigrate or deny other frameworks of identities and choices is not…'.

> Let us stop seeing a debate that pits those who work for *gay* rights and those who work in preventing HIV/AIDS, among men who have sex with men, against each other. Let us work together, whatever our own frameworks and priorities and recognize that in a region of over one billion people there is space for everyone to work out their destinies. (Khan, 2000)[25]

Indeed I find it difficult to look at things in black or white after my experiences in the field. What people said often contradicted with what they did and people's views changed over the course of my research. Take the case of Harbhajan to whom being gay was 'just sex, over and out' and who was also married to a woman who was aware of his sexual orientation. I observed him at several GB events and he was an intrinsic part of the organizing committees for these. It was clear that he experienced his sexuality as something much more than 'just sex'. He felt a part of the community and there was camaraderie between him and others. Or Bhuvan, who clearly told me that he was not willing to shout out in public about his sexuality. Two years later, he was one of the lead panelists at a CNN talk show, openly discussing his life as a gay man on television!

For the gay identified respondents, being gay signified different things to each of them. For some *gay* just represented their sexual desires, for others it was a political statement or a social identity. Many respondents felt that it was a state of being or a way of life, while some spoke of it as an emotional commitment to other men. For all of them, the common element about being gay was the imagination of themselves as gay, in whatever way they wished to articulate this imagination. It was fascinating to meet someone like Nachiket, for example. He was married with kids, had never had sex with another man, but still described himself as gay, because he *imagined* himself so.

Many respondents felt that they were bound by the *contract of silence* and that being discreet about their sexuality was the pragmatic thing to do. Within this silent space, they found society to be pretty flexible and accommodating with regard to their sexuality. Some, citing responsibilities towards their parents, families and society, had either chosen to get married, or were contemplating doing so in the near future. As Vanita (2001) writes, this is typical in India—

> The parental family remains a major locus of social and emotional interaction for adults. There are few public places where people can comfortably interact, so friends are entertained at home and absorbed into the family or turned into fictive kin. The family is also the only form of social security and old age insurance available to most people. This means that heterosexual marriage and parenthood hold many attractions even for homosexually inclined people. Many deal with the dilemma by marrying and then leading a double life.[26]

For these married men, or soon to be married men, marriage did not indicate a change in their sexual identity. They were clear that their marriage was an obligation, but that their sexual gratification would continue to rest with men, even after marriage. There was very little sensitivity expressed towards the feelings or desires of women in these worldviews.

Other respondents were avoiding marriage and devising means to negotiate what was best for them. For some of these individuals, this meant coming out, for others it meant discreetly fighting for what they felt was important and making creative compromises to attain their goals. But for all respondents, there was a constant reflexivity— an acute consciousness of their thoughts and actions vis-à-vis their sexuality.

Overall, I think that to be gay in Gay Bombay signifies being *glocal*; gayness here stands for *Indianized* gayness. So, one might dance in a Western style disco anywhere else in the world, but one can only munch on a post-dance *jalebi*[27] in India. My respondents wanted to selectively draw on a buffet of Indian and western influences in conjuring their own *thali*[28] of gayness! Most of them, even those who had access to the El Dorado of *abroad*, still wanted to configure their gay experiences within an Indian matrix. As Cholan said, hanging out in the Castro was not important, but coming back home and being with his father was. Even for the younger Gul, travelling to America opened his eyes to *Queer as Folk* and gay strip bars, but he used the experience to be more confident *in* India.

Gay Bombay is certainly inspired by Western notions of what it means to be gay—its dance parties, PFLAG[29] style meets, website and so on, have all drawn from Western experiences; but they have been customized, glocalized and made uniquely Indian, uniquely Gay Bombay. Thus, as I noted in Chapter 3, even though I talk about flows throughout this book, I do not want to diminish the agency of my respondents or their locatedness in Bombay itself. For Gay Bombay, as I have realized, place does matter and this is true both offline and online, where even though it is a *virtual* world, it is still a manifestation of Bombay and Indianness at large.

How is Identity Negotiated in Gay Bombay?

The politics of identity generally is driven by the paradox that no identity, no sense of community and no imputed property of a place ever can be self evident or stable. There are always multiple meanings, many narratives and inherent instabilities within such entries. (Hansen, 2001)[30]

As we saw in Chapter 7, for most of my respondents, being gay was just one aspect of their identity and not the dominating aspect. Family and related obligations and duties were a much more important aspect. This is in line with other studies like that of Seabrook (1999) where he commented that the 'English speaking and educated to university level' men that he interviewed did not see 'being gay as the main constituent of their identity'. 'They did however, express relief at being able to name this aspect of themselves'.[31]

For my respondents, their gay identity was something that was both fixed and negotiated. Being gay was something that was often considered intrinsic—'I always knew that I was this way ever since I can remember' was a popular refrain—but alongside, it was also something that was constructed and played with performatively, in an acutely reflexive manner.

Online, my respondents used the Gay Bombay newsgroup as a 'tool, a place and as a way of being',[32] in order to better understand and makes sense of their sexual and other identities. For them, the Gay Bombay newsgroup (and this was similar to what Berry and Martin concluded from their 2000 study of queer people and the net in East Asia) was 'neither a substitute for nor an escape from real life. Nor [was] it simply an extension of existing offline communities and identities. Instead, it [was] a part of lived culture, informed and informing other parts of [their] lives,'[33] and often functioned as a 'testing ground for possible selves that can then inform offline identity'.[34] Like Campbell (2004), I too saw my respondents 'integrating their online and offline experiences into a broader understanding of the reality of everyday life'.[35]

In any case, for most of my interviewees, online versus offline distinctions were not as significant as the distinctions between their *gay* and *straight* identities. Several of them reported purposefully constructing a straight-acting offline identity that they performed for the outside world and in their day-to-day lives, while their gay side was only to be revealed in safe spaces like Gay Bombay and among close friends.

It was clear that the habitus of my respondents fixed their notion of social identity a great deal. As I have already iterated, being *Indian*, however the respondents chose to define it, was a common thread running through the responses. My interviewees were in a constant state of internal negotiation between their Indianness (and its related social and family expectations and obligations) and what were to them considered to be more Western ideals, such as the quest for personal space and self-centred happiness. Thus, though cultural globalization as defined by Apppadurai (flows and so on) did take place in Gay Bombay, factors like nationality and cultural origins mattered, perhaps more to my respondents, as did their educational and social background. I saw this happening again and again in my interviews. I perceived each individual's identity as the product of his own personal interaction between his habitus and the extent to which he was able to stretch that habitus to allow him to tap into the rapid changes occurring all around him.

At the same time, as Bourdieu himself noted, habitus is not something that is constant. It also involves choice and reasoning and while it continues to be affected by geography, family background, gender and so on, it can definitely change based on one's life experiences. According to Appadurai (1996), the *improvisational* quality of habitus is now being stressed.[36] Certainly, I witnessed a tremendous amount of creativity and improvisation being carried out by my respondents with regards to their habitus and the various Gay Bombay spaces served as both—the facilitator and the locus—of these changes.

Is Gay Bombay a Community?

Yes, I think so. My respondents had mixed feelings about this but to me, Gay Bombay is a 'community of sentiment'[37] (Appadurai, 1996), of 'affirmation and solidarity...[and] self-discovery' (Campbell, 2004)[38] and a gay *third space*, borne out of the collective imagination of its constituents, representing a variety of meanings for them. It is a fluid community—its name fixes its location geographically—but its membership is global. It is an imagined community (Anderson, 1983) and also a divided one (Woolvine, 2000). Its inhabitants, predominantly English speaking upper middle class urban gay men, connect to this *imagined world* via a tangle of wires, satellite signals and fragile human networks.

Unlike other gay communities in the West (or even some of the other non-gay identified sexual minority communities like the *hijras* in India), I feel that Gay Bombay serves as a secondary community for its members rather than their primary community. Insofar as one's primary community is concerned, the blood family still rules the roost here.

I rather like Phelan's notion of community as a process (1994), 'which... is always in a state of becoming and thus is open to and requires negotiation'.[39] This resonates with Ahmed and Fortier's suggestion of thinking about communities as 'never fully achieved, never fully arrived at, even when "we" already inhabit them';[40] sites of possibilities as well as reality. Drawing on these accounts, I view Gay Bombay as a site that is 'lived through the desire for community, rather than a site that fulfils and "resolves" that desire'.[41] It is more a common ground rather than a site for commonality—both a space and a place—where community is created as an effect of how the members of gay Bombay 'meet on this ground... a ground that is material, but also virtual, real and imaginary'.[42]

In Memoriam

1998. I am so glad to be at Elle. *For a while, I thought I was doomed to a corporate existence at my previous marketing job and it is good to be working creatively with words and images again. I am also beginning to think about my sexuality in concrete terms. I have blanked it out of my head for the past six years, but am not so uncomfortable with the thoughts these days. Why don't we do an article on the gay scene in Bombay, I suggest in all seriousness at an edit meet one week. Why, what's happening out there, the editor queries. I don't know, I reply defensively—how would I know, I mean—but it'd be cool to find out, right?*

The piece never gets written. At my first interview, I meet Riyad Wadia, future friend, mentor and guide. The scion of the legendary Wadia Movietone film production studios, Riyad is flamboyantly high after the success of his latest gay themed documentary, BOMgAY. He had given me his phone number when he showed his film to a roomful of gasps at my film study course last year. Darling, he drawls as he drags on a Marlboro light, at his elegant Worli sea face apartment one late afternoon. Let's drop this article crap, shall we? You're a faggot. Deal with it. I feel a huge weight lift off my shoulders.

I stay on at his house for a party he is hosting that evening. It is just like any other party, except that it is full of gay men. Diamond merchants, film-makers, artists, bankers, corporate executives, consulate staff. (Do they send all their gay employees to India?). Everyone's rich, successful and happy looking. I'm the youngest and the only one wearing shorts. I can feel eyes on me. They won't bite you, Riyad nudges, as he circulates, Martini glass in hand, even though you're looking very bitable. Go talk to someone.

I encounter an interesting group. Mostly older men, who are not really my scene, but this is my intro to gay life 101 and I still have a lot to learn. François, from the Alliance Française in Bombay, cooks me fabulous meals at his Malabar Hill apartment. Ben, from the Israeli consulate is great for going out with, because we always travel in a cavalcade of cars, with flashing lights and a jeep-load of stone-faced Mossad bodyguards to give us company. Ram, from Calcutta, is married and comes to Bombay on weekends where he puts up at the swanky Oberoi Hotel and enjoys the good things in life like sex accompanied with Absolut Citron shots. I laugh at them when they tell me they have fallen in love with me! I can afford to; I am 20 years old, tight-bodied and smooth skinned.

Riyad introduces me to his world of Voodoo's and the Walls and late night cruising and the concept of sex without love. We never sleep with each other, which is why I think that the relationship is so special. He feels protective about me. If we have sex, I doubt we would be as good friends. Not that he doesn't try. One night, early in our friendship, after a party from which he is dropping me home, I casually ask him up for coffee, not knowing its implications on the scene. Are you sure, he raises an eyebrow. He is amused when I emerge from the kitchen with two steaming cups but leaves after a pleasant conversation. A few weeks later, he instructs me never to invite a gay man up for coffee unless I want to sleep with him. I keep that in mind, to be used later.

I have Riyad to thank for so many things. And I am not the only one. When he dies in late 2003, his family in India is overwhelmed by the number of emails and phone calls they receive from men and women all over the world, telling them what a positive influence Riyad was in their lives. Whether it is advice regarding the collapse of my company, writing my recommendation letters for graduate school, or being there to share my exuberance at having met Q and later Z, it is him that I turn to, at every significant moment of my gay life. When I travel to America for the first time, to college hunt, Riyad voluntarily sets me up with his network of friends all over the country, so that I have a home in every city I visit. During that trip, I develop a strong relationship with Roy, Riyad's elder brother and the bond lasts till today. Once I see the lifestyle of Roy and his partner Alan in Atlanta, I have new role models that I want to emulate. They seem so normal, so comfortable in their domestic simplicity, cooking together, doing the dishes and shopping at Home Depot. Riyad senses this when I return and is often disparaging about me want to have a boring conformist hetero-normative life, but I think secretly, he is happy that I have chosen the Roy way over his.

Sometime in between, Riyad takes off for New York, to try and start a new life. It has been far too long since his last film and he is unwilling to make the compromises needed to survive in the cesspool of Bombay's film world. When he returns unsuccessful, the smile still remains but the spark seems to have dimmed. Yet, there is always an exciting project to keep him occupied—the big gay film that he will surely someday get funding for, the festivals and poster art exhibitions that he curates, the Condé Nast fashion shoot that he directs, the various avant-garde films he promotes, the parties and the glamour that are second nature to him.

During our conversations towards the end of his life, he cautions me to not make gayness the centre of my existence. It destroyed me, he says. Now people can't think of me in any other way. Don't bracket yourself, please. I can see that he is going through a bad phase, but he never volunteers information about his difficulties and I never ask. He is always guarded when we talk about his life; never completely honest with me—perhaps, in his mind, I have put him on a pedestal that he fears honesty would bring crashing down. So we continue with the charade—he is mentor, I am advisee and the roles can never change. I know that he believes in love but is scared of it; that his nonchalance and acerbic wit are a defense mechanism; that his nightly cruising and experiments with drugs are but a refuge to escape from the pain, loneliness and pangs of self-doubt that he is consumed by. But how do I say anything without upsetting the fragile status quo that we have built over the years?

I so badly want to show him a different life in Bombay—walks by the old Afghan Church, fresh plump paneer [cottage cheese] at Napean Sea Road, languid afternoons at the Jehangir art gallery, quiet evenings spent lounging on planter's chairs at the David Sassoon library, bus rides through crowded Dadar and Mahim on route number 1...but it is a wish that remains unfulfilled. Before I leave for the US, I gift him a heavy fountain pen, as I have once heard him complain in jest that there are no decent pens in his home to write with. I tell him that he should write his next film script with it. When he passes away, his mother tells me that just the night before, he had removed the pen from its case and was thinking of finally using it.

MODUS VIVENDI

And so we arrive...back to the future. Gay Bombay turned eight in September 2006, just as I returned to India and began finishing up this book. As part of my birthday wishes, I would like to offer some thoughts, ideas and suggestions that might be considered by the group as it plans its future. Perhaps these words might be able to generate a discussion that might then be extended beyond the scope of this book, into the online or offline spaces of Gay Bombay that I continue to inhabit.

For the Indian LBGT movement, it is clear that the battles need to be fought on multiple fronts and this is something we already see happening. Legally there are excellent groups like the Lawyer's Collective fighting against Article 377. Health wise, there is a lot is being done already (and the Humsafar Trust is doing stellar work in Bombay in this regard), but a lot more needs to be done, with regard to HIV especially. On the social front, identity based groups like Gay Bombay are providing spaces and opportunities for interaction in a manner that was unimaginable even five years ago.

I am in complete agreement with Gay Bombay's managing committee that their programs constitute activism too, only of a different kind. But I also think that it is inevitable that the group takes the next step and joins the political struggle purposefully. It must not sit out, indeed it cannot sit out, as the stakes are simply getting too large now; I sincerely feel that their active involvement would be a big boost to the movement.

As Cholan mentioned, the queer Indian movement is entering its crucial phase. The past few years have been spent in having discussions and debates among each other and in infrastructure building, but this has already been done and now it is time to speak to the bigots and take the case outside the ghetto. It is the time for lobbying—smartly and sensibly. Of course, this means that there will be repercussions. It would be foolish to think that increased visibility will not create the necessity for increased surveillance and increased disciplining action by the state. Conflict will arise and if, as Appadurai writes, this conflict will be resolved, 'not by academic fiat, but by negotiations...both civil and violent',[43] how can the Indian queer movement prepare for these negotiations? The remainder of this chapter aims at providing an answer to this question.

Throughout this book we have observed the differences between Gay Bombay and Humsafar that have crept up on different occasions. But these are not the only two groups within the larger movement that are jostling with each other—the movement is full of infighting and rivalries. As my respondent Vidwan observed—

VIDVAN: RIGHT NOW, THE QUEER WORLD IS BEING INCREASINGLY SPLIT IN INDIA ON GENDER LINES AS WELL AS ON ECONOMIC LINES. THERE SEEM TO BE DIFFERENT SPACES OPERATING FOR GAYS, LESBIANS, *HIJRAS* AND *KOTHIS,* INSTEAD OF A SINGLE SPACE FOR ALL QUEER PEOPLES. NOT THAT I DO NOT CONCEDE THE IMPORTANCE OF AN ALL-LESBIAN SPACE OR AN ALL-*KOTHI* SPACE, BUT, IT DOES SEEM, THAT THESE VARIED SPACES ARE INTERACTING VERY LITTLE AMONG EACH OTHER AND THIS IN-CREASES WITH THE ECONOMIC BARRIER BETWEEN MANY GAY AND *KOTHI* SPACES, AS WELL AS THE DIVIDE BETWEEN

GAY SPACES ON AN ECONOMIC BASIS AS WELL. INSTEAD OF BRIDGING THE GAP AND UNITING THE STRUGGLES, THE MOVEMENT SEEMS TO BE PROMOTING THE DIFFERENCES BETWEEN THESE VARIOUS GROUPS.

One way of reconciling these differences, as Bhudev told me, was to practice a 'politics of exclusion' and by that, he implied that the different sub–groups—all focus on their own constituencies, exclude each other from their plans and do not work towards a unified or common larger agenda. However, we both agreed that this could not really be a long-term solution. Another solution that Senthil discussed—was to continue to have separate social spaces for the different groups, but a unified political space—a common ground. I find this to be a problematic, but more appealing option.

It is my belief (and we have seen it play out in this book—for example, in the unity between Humsafar and Gay Bombay, despite their differences) that the divisions within the larger movement are not so insurmountable, nor are the issues so different that such a common ground cannot be reached. Perhaps we might be able to construct (to borrow a phrase from India's coalition politics of the past decade) a 'common minimum program' that could be agreed upon by all parties concerned? Coalitions like INFOSEM and 'Voices Against 377' exist as umbrella organizations for some activist groups—but their membership excludes unregistered amorphous entities like Gay Bombay. Perhaps, this common minimum programme might provide an opportunity for these entities to be actively involved in the political movement—given the constraints that they operate under. This would recognize that these social groups fulfill vital needs in the community at large and their activities are complementary to those of other activist organizations.

What might such a programme include? Here are some suggestions that I would like to put forward as considerations for its manifesto, should such a program ever materialize; I offer these with humility and with the sincere hope of making a constructive contribution towards the movement as it enters a crucial and exciting phase. I have gathered my thoughts under the rubric of *modus vivendi*, which stands for both a way of life and a negotiated settlement. I borrow the phrase and the spirit in which it is being used from an interview conducted with John Gray in the *New Perspectives Quarterly* Spring 2001 issue, whereby Gray advocates a *modus vivendi* approach to globalization that signifies a desire for 'commodious living'.[44] This approach incorporates the realization that neither extremism nor confrontation will work, accommodation is imperative and the key at every stage should be 'to openly work out conflicts'[45] and move ahead. Thus,—*modus vivendi*—or 'a negotiation between conflicting interests instead of an insistence on absolute rights'.[46]

Collaboration is the key of my *modus vivendi* approach and coalition is its defining organizational mechanism. Coalition politics does not mean that the member parties will agree on everything. It just means that there is consensus required to pursue a broad common minimum agenda. [As I read these points today, 12 years later, and in the context of all the changes that have taken place since then, this modus vivendi becomes more important than ever. We need to strive for equitable change within the queer movement. We need to build intersectional coalitions not just between queer groups but also between queer groups and other social justice collectives, such as those fighting anti-caste, or gender battles.]

(a) 'Strategic essentialism' + 'tactical pragmatism' = Unity within disparate queer activist groups

I am drawn to Gayatri Spivak's (1987) notion of 'strategic essentialism'— 'a strategic use of positivist essentialism in a scrupulously visible political interest'.[47] Spivak feels that essentialism (that is a certain essential meaning or property or quality that can be ascribed to something, say a word or a person or a race) is a trap, at the same time conceding that is impossible to be completely non-essential. She resolves the dilemma by pursuing 'strategic essentialism'—or self consciously essentializing in order to accomplish one's goals. Strategic essentialism advocates solidarity in the interest of action, to bring about real change.

Within the queer movement, it is easy to get caught up in infighting and identity politics and lose sight of the larger common objective that all sexual minorities are fighting against—for example, the repeal of Section 377. A strategic interventionist approach would recognize that gay, *kothi*, *hijra* and other identities are important on the ground and in people's lives, however reductionist they may appear to be theoretically. It would also recognize these identities as constructs—ways of seeing and being. It would further self-consciously define certain essential qualities of these identities if needed and reshape others, to achieve larger goals. Adopting strategic essentialism within a *modus vivendi* framework would mean maintaining separate LBGT subidentities, but tweaking them when needed and compromising on them, if the situation demands so.

The focus within the different groups should be on maintaining unity through what David Woolvine (2000) has called 'tactical pragmatism'— or the 'ability to distance [oneself] from [certain] organizations and from some of the goals or tactics of the organizations while at the same time supporting the organizations'.[48] We have seen in the previous chapter how Humsafar and Gay Bombay have worked together to schedule non-conflicting meetings on every alternative Sunday so as to allow cross attendance, how leaders of the groups post messages to each other's constituents complimenting them on good work done by them and so on. This model could be replicated by other LBGT organizations across the board, that are in similar relationships with each other. Events like the World Social Forum march in Mumbai in 2004 which had a large queer coalition—gays, lesbians, *hijras* and *kothis*, all marching together, or the annual Calcutta Pride march, or the organic strategic media visibility campaigns that accompany flashpoint events like the *Fire* film protests, or the letter writing campaign against Section 377, are all opportunities for and examples of strategic resistance and tactical pragmatism in action.

(b) Equitable change needs to be pursued

In order to be sustainable, change has to be equitable. Right now, the situation is far from so, but then, the LBGT community is only a reflection of the society and world in which it exists. In her essay 'Power Politics' Arundhati Roy writes of how the vast majority of poor Indians, whose lives have been devastated by India's government-led attempts at modernity, like damns and nuclear bombs, do not really count in the national imagination. There is a tiny convoy of people, she writes, moving towards a 'glittering destination somewhere near the top of the world', while a much larger one just melts away, 'into darkness'.[49] Amartya Sen is equally anguished at pointing out—'India has the dubious distinction of having both the largest number of poor in the world and also the largest middle class on earth…can we really live at peace with such massive contrasts?'[50] For Sen, the challenges of globalization and internal disparity in India are closely linked. He writes that unless the problems of poverty, inequality and social and economic exclusion are not addressed, the country will lose out of several benefits of participation in the process of globalization. This is as true for the Indian economy as it is for India's sexual minorities. It is imperative that members of social groups like Gay Bombay realize that upper middle class gay men in Bombay are not the only sexual minorities in the country and their needs are not the only needs around. Unless there is a genuine attempt being made at the pursuit of equitable change for all queer minorities, the problems of inequality and social exclusion within the queer movement will still remain at large, even if legal encumbrances like Section 377 are done away with. Seriously, what kind of a hollow empty victory will it be—if a few *gay* men are able to do their own thing—while their disenfranchised *hijra, kothi* and lesbian brothers and sisters languish, unheard and uncared for?

(c) *Small changes should be striven for, along with the big ones*

The larger political and health agendas should be pursued in tandem with smaller, ordinary day-to-day ones. So of course, Article 377 needs to go, but until then, it is equally valuable if say, an ad agency that has put up queer-insensitive billboard hoardings all over the city is sensitized enough to remove them and apologize for their insensitivity[51] or if the *Aravaani* transgender community of the south Indian state of Tamil Nadu is provided with ration cards.[52] On a smaller but equally significant level, it is imperative to acknowledge the courage of queer people who begin the process of coming out to their families and friends. All these small changes add up to a larger social transformation in mindsets and attitudes, without which any major legal or political victories will be shallow.

There are also many things that India's queer populations are in desperate and immediate need of beyond Section 377. To list just a few—counselling services, safe shelters, larger legal teams to analyze laws that impact their lives as well as to represent them in times of need, more targetted health services, a much wider and more sustained HIV prevention drive, creation of viable job opportunities for marginalized communities like *hijras* and so on. Efforts should be ongoing to fulfill these and other needs, with as much zeal as the efforts to change the law. In the words of Narrain (2004)—

> The premise of change with respect to sexuality is as much a change in societal mores as it is about legal change.... Since Section 377 is not purely a legal issue, the way we tackle it cannot be through the court room alone. One cannot expect judges to decide on Section 377 positively, if we have not started a process of public education about queer rights. If we want the courts to give us a decision like Lawrence versus Texas, then there is no way out of the difficult process of building a campaign based on queer visibility.[53]

(d) *The media should be co-opted and used in the process of building visibility*

We have seen in this book how the English media has served Gay Bombay's interests as an ambassador for gayness at large. My respondent Cholan echoed Narrain's words when he said that judges and politicians are also part of the world. They read the newspapers and watch television and can be as influenced from these as the general public. Thus, the media should be consciously co-opted and made a part of the larger queer struggle. Moral panic must not be allowed to be created at all cost by the bigots and if it occurs, it must be countered immediately and forcefully. The success enjoyed with the English media needs to be broad based further so as to include the vernacular media. Here is a wonderful step in this direction. The Chennai and Calcutta based NGO SAATHI has initiated the *SAATHII Rainbow Film Awards* for positive representation of LGBT people in Indian cinema. At the first such awards ceremony held in conjunction with Pride week in Calcutta in 2005, filmmaker Onir was honoured for his direction of the sensitive gay-themed *My Brother Nikhil*. The organizers plan to expand the reach of the Rainbow Awards to include other categories, following the example set by GLAAD (Gay and Lesbian Alliance Against Defamation) in the US.[54]

(e) *Indian queer histories and tradition should be emphasized*

I more or less agree with the hypothesis that once a certain visibility threshold is crossed and the battle for recognition and acceptance really enters the mainstream, it might lead to more pronounced homophobia.

We have seen through different incidents recounted earlier (such as the protests over the films *Fire* and *Girlfriend*) that the attack may well be framed as an overall attack on Westernization—being gay will be added into the 'well defined yet adaptable arsenal of "Western Evils"— divorce, drinking alcohol, eating meat, or drug abuse'. (Shah, 1993)[55]—as something that needs to be prevented from happening to the impressionable young men and women of the country. The Lucknow incident in 2006, already noted earlier in this book, where the police framed, victimized, arrested and then humiliated a group of gay men is an indication of the direction in which things could go. The police allegedly arrested one man who they had deduced was gay and forced him under torture, to call up some of his gay friends on his cellphone, telling them that he was ill and needed their help. When his friends reached him, they too were arrested, citing Section 377 as justification for the arrests and the police then called a press conference to declare that they had broken up a homosexual network and arrested men who were caught having sex in public. The impunity with which the police seem to have broken several human rights laws and their smugness that they were doing society a favour with their actions, is frightening.[56] There have also been several cases recorded of parents disowning or even legally disinheriting their children when they reveal their homosexuality to them.[57] Groups like the VHP and RSS are only too happy to jump on the 'anti-Indian culture' bandwagon at any given time, as their comments indicate.[58]

It is imperative therefore, to emphasize the localness and situatedness of India's queer sexual identities as a part of our *modus vivendi*. This might be done in three ways. First, it should be emphasized that gayness has a history in India and its own historical Indian traditions, (as documented in the books by authors like Ruth Vanita and Devdutt Pattanaik) as well as its own icons and heroes (as documented via events like Humsafar's Icons exhibition at WSF 2004 or Gay Bombay's visit to Bombay's National Gallery of Modern Art for the Bhuppen Khakar retrospective after the artist passed away in 2003). Second, contemporary traditions should be created for the community to increase and foster a community spirit. Gay Bombay's creative appropriations of *Bhishma Ashtami*[59] and pan Indian festivals like *Holi* celebrated by members of Gay Bombay and Humsafar are excellent examples of this ideal in practice. As Giddens writes, 'traditions are invented and reinvented'[60] constantly, according to the need of the hour. And finally, it should constantly be emphasized that queerness is not a threat to the strength of the family system in India. We have seen in this book what an important status my respondents assigned to family in their lives. A Gay Bombay event like the Parents' Meet unfailingly gathers the highest number of attendees—the one held in July 2006 for instance, had 103 participants (including nine parents).[61] Thus, every outreach effort should emphasize this inherent *Indianness* of queer individuals and their deep commitment to the institution of family and to *Indian* traditions. I contend that among the several reasons why *My Brother Nikhil* came and went along without much of a hullabaloo, as opposed to *Fire*, is that *Fire* threatened the family, while *My Brother Nikhil* was all about gaining acceptance by one's family. Like the mainstream blockbuster *Dilwale Dulhania Le Jayenge*[62] and all its clones of the 1990s, *My Brother Nikhil* implied that the child's happiness is not complete, unless his or her parents accept him completely. In this world, rebellion is futile; how can you rebel against tradition and your family? The right path lies in living your life the way you want to (so Nikhil did not give up being gay, or dump his boyfriend) but within the ambit of parental approval (or of constantly seeking it). I am certain that this suggestion will be attacked with accusations of pandering to ideals of hetero-normativity and assimilation tendencies—and I happily plead guilty to these charges. Within this *modus vivendi* orbit, I feel that this is a small price to pay and the issues at stake are much larger.

(f) *The west should not be vilified*

I am in agreement with Jackson that queer resistance 'must always be locally modulated. In one place, the dominant form of resistance may be street marches and agitation for law reform, in another place, the most important form of resistance may be avoiding arranged marriage' (Jackson, 2000).[63] Clearly, a Western style agenda is unsuitable for India, but at the same time, one should realize that *the West* is not the enemy of the Indian LBGT movement.

Vanita critically notes that 'it is usually those who have already obtained most of their basic civil rights and liberties in first world environments who object to the use of these terms in third world contexts'.[64] (These are, of course, the same people who have no qualms in accepting Western grant money!). The West has been a very good source of information for the gay community in India. Lots of queer health and political programmes operational in India are funded by Western agencies—for example, Lawyers Collective and the Humsafar Trust.

Thus, I feel that travelling to and fro and appreciating the positive aspects of Western style activism, need not necessitate replicating its institutions or practices. We should learn from these, of course, but freely adapt them to our needs. For instance, copying Gay Pride might not be such a good idea for all cities at this point, but having an institution like Fenway from Boston help out with HIV counselling and related services might be significant and relevant.

(g) *There should a realization that change is not just coming in from the West but also from other parts of the world*

One can and indeed, must find inspiration from non-western societies. For example, South Africa's new constitution, adopted on 10 December 1996, had an express non-discrimination clause against homosexuals, making it the first country in the world to do so (Narrain, 2004).[65] Fiji (2005) and Hong Kong (2006) have recently decriminalized same-sex acts between consenting adults. Examples like these are wonderful not just as models to emulate, but also to counter the notion that any progress made in terms of queer rights in India would indicate a tendency towards *aping the west*.

(h) *Ideas for change can also be found from within other Indian/ Asian cultural contexts*

Perhaps, the leaders of the Indian gay movement might wish to study the rise of Dalit politics within the Indian democratic system, especially the rise of the politician Mayawati and her Bahujan Samaj Party in Uttar Pradesh. By establishing themselves as stakeholders in the political process, the party has been able to effect social changes that would not have been possible otherwise.[66] There have been several emails posted on the politically conscious Lbgt-India Yahoo! Group that have explored this idea in detail. There have also been suggestions of learning from and furthering ties with the women's movement. Another idea proposed has been to study the models formed by *hijra* societies in India, as well as other Asian transgender societies and then adopt these for the larger queer population. Here is an excerpt from a message sent by Ashok Row Kavi to the Lbgt-India list that fleshes out this idea—

> The paradox of *hijras* or transgender is that on one hand they are the most visible of the sexual minorities under the LGBTs umbrella and yet they are the most marginalized of our brethren by the patriarchal ordered hetero-normative society. They live on a razor's edge all the time. However, I must give you an instance. Some years ago when I went to attend an Amnesty International conference in Australia, I was invited for an Australian Transgendered Conference in Syndey. What I saw was a pervasive fear of hetero-normative mainstream society. Violence was so purposeful, wilful and direct that many trans could not even walk down streets, sometimes even in gay areas, without being beaten up, killed or in some way harmed or hurt in all of Australia. Just north in Philippines or Indonesia, Bakhla or Waria were not just accepted as a 'third sex' but were organizing actively and were nearly as empowered as our *kothi* or *hijra* groups. And there was enough evidence that they were the most empowered of the LGBT populace. So what does that tell us? That trans seem to have such a huge cultural source of energy in different cultural settings. From here we can proceed a bit further. What and how do we use current cultural constructs and see them for what they are. I think the case of Familia was the best example. She was empowered by education to take matters in hand. Her erudite knowledge of English and the way she deployed it were constant indicators to me that we needed to emulate her and follow her example. One important fact about *hijras* is they were big bankers in the old days. They were also the repository of cuisine; I learnt my Hyderabad *dum-biryanis* from a *hijra* who worked in the Nizam's kitchens there! Is it possible to put the two together to start something new? Yes! We are getting there with some of those talents. In Mumbai, a little under 40 per cent of the people are single and have to depend on eating houses or dining rooms to keep body and soul together. Why not fill that niche using *hijra* skills and then open non-financial banking organizations? If you want, you can visit us in Mumbai to have this explained by one of our directors who is a financial manager of our credit society.
>
> Once a credit society goes over say rupees one crore, you have a massive interest accruing which becomes a capital base in itself. Invested in straight sound and safe government bonds, the interest alone becomes capital for micro-credit. The rest will depend on how well they manage the money. I firmly believe that there is no hope in heterosexual society; everything

they do is geared to serve the social units of biological family. We need to set up our own *gharanas* like the *hijras* have done, start off banking and credit societies and get a parallel social support system going that is more oriented towards our own culture. Trying to challenge hetero-normative society is no use because they will never accept us. Take that for granted and start from there. Though they are not our enemies, they are not friends either. Each minority has social resources like peers, heritage and tradition to buttress support for the younger generation. We have none and each generation evolves its own traditions.[67]

(i) *The diaspora, the closeted and non-queer identified groups should be co-opted in the struggle*

The queer and non-queer diaspora should be co-opted and strategically used and this is already happening to some extent. Remember that *Trikone* began in 1986, before *Bombay Dost*; the *Khush*-List was started before Gay Bombay; Indians marched in New York pride for many years before Calcutta pride... A lot of the success of the activist work in India has been due to the beneficial interaction of the movement with the Indian queer diaspora.

This Indian diaspora at large, are now imagined as part of *Pravasya Bharat*—non-resident Indians, or NRIs, that the central and state governments are so eager to pursue.[68] While a chunk of these NRIs might be considered *Hindutva*-oriented (and perhaps homophobic, although I do see that making this connection is rather facile), there are also others who are not. A strategy of outing Indian politicians and business leaders with regressive views will certainly need the co-operation of the Indian diaspora. India's penal code that permits the victimization of its sexual minorities is definitely shameful and the progressive world that India is so desperate to be a part of given its recent economic success, often mandates human right compliance as a prerequisite of membership. I believe that sustained lobbying by the diaspora will surely contribute to the progress being made on the ground in the home country—although I am aware this will again be hugely problematic as the idea of India and what con-stitute Indianness is perhaps played out with greater intensity within the diaspora. Still, it is something that needs to be done.

I strongly feel that closeted gay men should not be shunned. I dis-agree with my respondent Bhudev's contention that real activism is only on the ground and not in cyberspace; I think that real activism happens everywhere—offline as well as online, including social spaces like Gay Bombay. I find Nachiket's comments in this context to be crucial—activism is not just about awareness, but also about change and while activists on the ground bring about awareness, change can be brought about by everyone, including closeted queer people in positions of power. So it is important to co-opt the closeted and make them feel they are part of the community. Here I emphasize—that there is a difference between co-opting someone and endorsing someone—in coalition politics, you often work together with those whose policies or ideologies you disagree with, in the interest of the larger common minimum program agreed upon by everyone. What is important is doing whatever is necessary so as to keep the *modus vivendi* going.

I disagree with my respondent Rahim (in the context of passport princesses who remain closeted at home but go abroad to live their gay lives) that a gay man from Bombay dancing on the streets of Boston would not make a difference to the movement in India. Images circulate globally today and what is happening on the streets of Boston is shown on television screens in Bombay. Thus, when a news channel like NDTV covers Boston pride (as it did in 2004) and interviews the queer Indian men and women dancing on the streets, it *does* have an impact on opinions in India.

Non-queer identified groups and individuals when co-opted into the struggle can be powerful allies. We have seen the impact of a few high profile heterosexually identified individuals like Amartya Sen and Soli Sorabjee when their voices are added to Vikram Seth's letter. Groups like Voices Against 377—the Delhi based coalition of Women's Rights, Children's Rights, Human Rights and Queer Rights groups are another significant step in this regard. As Bhan and Narrain write, groups like 'Voices present[s] a forum that cannot be dismissed easily...'[69] as they frame queer issues in the public eye as not just queer issues, but also human right, women or children's issues.

(j) HIV needs to be battled much more strongly

The threat of HIV cannot be emphasized enough.[70] The potential catastrophe is far too large and the efforts being done to combat it are far too little. Fear and loathing within the queer sub-groups, including Gay

Bombay, must give way to a pragmatic approach of developing HIV education, prevention and management programmes. The battle against HIV is multi-pronged, with attention needing to be paid to education and awareness, provision for adequate medication and treatment to patients and treating patients with dignity. Queer people are discriminated against on a regular basis on all these counts. Consider this story from the Lbgt-India Yahoo! list—

> One transgender named Kokila, age 32, was suffering from abdominal pain and was admitted in Female Surgical Emergency Ward at G.H. Pondicherry [in the south Indian state of Tamil Nadu]. She was advised to have an operation. It was also found that she was HIV positive. The nurses attending on Kokila asked her to lift her saree to show her 'sex organ'—if male or female. Then, she was allowed to sleep on the floor. She asked a blanket for her use and was scolded as—'Transgender like you, can do without any comfort'. And the doctor threw the case sheet in her face and also threw her out of the room cursing her and warning her never to step again into G.H.[71]

In the above case, the transgender community in Tamil Nadu immediately took out a protest rally, met the state's chief minister and had action taken against the offending nurse.[72]

PARTING THOUGHTS

Throughout this book I have harped on the glocal, or the working of the process of globalization within a context that is peculiarly Indian. While wrapping up, I find that it is two of these *peculiarly Indian* traits that provide me with inspiration as I dream of the future of Gay Bombay and the larger Indian queer community. The first of these traits is fortitude—'the intrinsic Indian propensity for not losing hope' and 'the resilience that comes from being continuously exposed to adversity' (Varma, 2004).[73] Nothing fazes a Bombayite. Whether the city is almost drowned in torrential rains and floods, or bombed on multiple occasions with terrorist attacks, its citizens pick themselves and each other up and move on ahead, purposefully. Indeed, as Varma reiterates—

For the vast majority of Indians, life is a daily challenge. Even for a middle class family, very little can be taken for granted—schooling, water, electricity, medical care, higher education, housing—everything is a struggle. And yet, the miracle is that everyone seems to be getting by and in fact, planning for more.... The deprivations in India and the social callousness which ignores them is condemnable. But the Indian is the ultimate stoic. Indeed, the real Indian rope trick is the persistence of hope in the most hopeless of circumstances. (Varma, 2004)[74]

The second of these traits is adaptability. As Khilnani (2001) writes—

What is 'distinctively Indian' is 'a capacity…an ability to improvise, a kind of cunningness at historical survival, a knack for being able to respond to any question that may be asked. In the musical forms of India, as in its literary traditions, it is not fixity—the dogma of the singular text—that is valued, but rather the skill of improvisation and variation'.[75]

It is so difficult to just *physically* be gay in a place like Bombay. For someone coming for a party in a South Bombay pub from faraway Thane, the bone crushing train ride, the sweat bath and the time it takes to reach the party venue are all issues to be factored in—plus of course, an alibi for one's absence to the family waiting at home. Participants at Gay Bombay events overcome these logistical encumbrances with a ferocious vivacity that I find energizing. Changes are not just limited to those that dance at parties or fight for the abolition of 377. Conversations are being had by many other gay guys, with their friends, family members and colleagues at work. Situations are managed, whether at work or at home and spaces are being eked out for relationships, sex and love.

I am excited and scared as I look towards the future. The fears are not unfounded; however, neither is the excitement. If Indianness is something that grows out of imagination, then this imagination can also be *reimagined* to include gayness—and I see daily instances of this re-imagination occurring all around me. Take my own life for example and my relationship with my ex-boyfriend Z and his parents that I wrote about at the beginning of this book. Z did not have to come out to his parents—they brought up the issue with him sensitively and then followed it up with a reassuring dinner with me, where they comforted the two of us that they were supportive of our relationship and just wanted us to be happy. Or take the cases of gay marriages, commitment ceremonies and anniversary celebrations that keep on taking place in India, despite the laws being what they are. The daily newspapers are full of inspiring stories. In a tribal village in Orissa, two girls get married to each other in a traditional ceremony, in the presence of their family.[76] Another village in Assam votes for lesbian rights.[77] There are innumerable stories of hope and validation. *Time Out* magazine's gay columnist AllyGator writes about attending the 25th anniversary celebration of one such gay couple, where—

> Parsi queens rubbed shoulders with Parsi aunties. Gay couples with straight families. Strident gay activists with determinedly closeted gay men. People had come from all over the country and even from abroad.[78]

I feel inspired by the small acts of institutional change that are taking place with regularity. For example, applicants for a new passport can now fill in one of three options on their application form—*M*, *F* and *E* (for eunuch). (In an attempt to recognize the *hijras* as a separate category, the government seems to have erroneously followed the popular convention of categorizing *hijras* as eunuchs in this regard). Likewise, the Indian Ministry of External Affairs has made it possible to change one's sex in one's passports on the production of a sworn affidavit and a medical certificate from the hospital where the person has undergone treatment—implying that gender reconstructive surgery is not illegal in India. It is also possible to change one's sex on the electoral roll and on one's PAN card (Permanent Account Number card, used as an identification card and for taxation purposes).[79] NACO or the National Aids Control Organization[80]—a division of the Government of India's Health and Family Welfare ministry works with the Humsafar Trust and other organizations working with MSM regularly on intervention projects; NACO's officials continuously show their support to the organization— for example, Dr Prasada Rao, the head of NACO inaugurated Humsafar's Voluntary testing centre in June 1999. Similarly, the city's hospitals like Sion, Cooper and Jaslok all co-operate with Humsafar with regard to HIV counselling and referral. More significantly, as noted earlier, NACO has filed an affidavit in court supporting the demand to scrap Section 377, on the grounds that the presence of the section is an impediment to HIV prevention work in the country[81] and at the National AIDS Council convened by the Prime Minister in the annex of the Indian parliament on 16 February 2006; Ashok Row Kavi reported receiving encouraging signs from the ministers present.[82]

I am inspired by the market-led forces of globalization, even as I recognize their inherent flaws and weaknesses. As Khilnani writes—'if choice is an axiom of the market, it is hard to see how it can be excluded from the realm of culture and identity'.[83] The changing demographics of India will play a key role in how these choices will be exercised; soon, power will shift from the *pre-independence* and *Midnight's Children* age cohorts, to the emergent cohorts of *liberalization's children* and the *millennium children* who, 'God willing, could be a generation...markedly different because they are shaped by an India of plenty, well integrated with and respected by the world'[84] (Bijapurkar, 2005). Bijapurkar, a marketing expert, has observed [1995] an attitudinal transformation to 'freedom of choice' and survival of the fittest' as a new way of living, a liberalization of the mind that create[s] a new type of Indian culture—which, importantly does not subsume these changes or allow itself to be subsumed by them, but rather accommodates them creatively.[85] I am hopeful that this sense of integration and adroitness at managing plurality will translate into a respect for sexual minorities as well.

Indeed, I truly believe that society can and *does* change. As Giddens writes—'Society only has form and that form only has effects on people, in so far as structure is produced and reproduced in what people do'.[86] Thus, individual acts of resistance all add up to influence changes to the larger social structure. I like Bollywood style happy endings...endings that fill one with hope and the possibility of something magical.... And so, if there is one feeling I want to conclude this book with, it is with a belief that yes, tomorrow, we—Gay Bombay and the Indian queer movement at large—*will* be able to create a better society; a world where, even though it sounds terribly mushy, 'the only important thing is love and where everyone is welcome and included within that love' (Wilhelm, 2004).[87]

Notes

1. Devdutt Pattanaik, *The Man Who was a Woman and Other Queer Tales from Hindu Lore* (New York: Harrington Park Press, 2002), p. 113.

2. Thomas Babington Macaulay's, 'Minute of 2 February 1835 on Indian Education', as cited in Pawan Varma, *The Great Indian Middle Class* (New Delhi: Penguin/Viking, 1998), p. 2. The entire text of the minute and other writings of Macaulay may be found in *Macaulay, Prose and Poetry*, selected by G.M. Young (Cambridge MA: Harvard University Press, 1957).

3. Devesh Kapur, 'The Causes and Consequences of India's IT Boom', in *India Review* (Taylor and Francis, April 2002), Vol. 1(2), p. 7.

4. Pawan Varma, (1998), op. cit., p. 115.

5. Ibid, p. 116.

6. Ibid, p. 117.

7. Peter Jackson, 'Pre-gay, Post-queer: Thai Perspectives on Proliferating Gender/Sex Diversity in Asia', in Gerard Sullivan and Peter A. Jackson (Eds), *Gay and Lesbian Asia: Culture, Identity, Community* (New York: Harrington Park Press, 2000), p. 4.

8. Sunil Khilnani, 'Many Wrinkles in History', *Outlook Magazine*, 20 August 2001, as quoted in Pawan Varma, *Being Indian* (New Delhi: Penguin/Viking, 2004), p. 160. Article accessible online—http://www.outlookindia.com/full.asp?fodname=20010820&fname e=Sunil+Kilnani+%28F%29&sid=1

9. Ibid.

10. Pawan Varma (2004), op. cit., pp. 149–150.

11. Arjun Appadurai, *Modernity at Large: Cultural Dimensions of Globalization* (Minneapolis: University of Minnesota Press, 1996), p. 10.

12. Pawan Varma (2004), op. cit., p. 158.

13. Arjun Appadurai (1996), op. cit., p. 4.

14. Paola Bacchetta, 'When the [Hindu] Nation Exiles its Queers', *Social Text* (Durham: Duke University Press, 1999), No. 61, p. 144.

15. Greg Booth, 'Pandits in the Movies: 'Contesting the Identity of Hindustani Classical Music and Musicians in the Hindi Popular Cinema', *Asian Music* (University of Texas Press, Winter/Spring 2005), Vol. 36(1), pp. 72–73.

16. *Adaab* is an Urdu greeting. Shaayiri is a form of Urdu poetry. *Achkan* and *Gharara* are traditional Muslim male and female costumes respectively. See Fareed Kazmi, *The Politics of India's Conventional Cinema: Imaging a Universe, Subverting a Multiverse* (Sage Publications: New Delhi 1999), p. 155, for an incisive reading of *Hum Aapke Hain Kaun* as a medium of Hindutva propaganda.

17. Michael Hardt and Antonio Negri, *Empire* (Cambridge, MA: Harvard University Press, 2000), p. 198.

18. From an article published in the *Organizer*—the mouthpiece of the Rashtriya Swayamsevak Sangh (National Brotherhood of volunteers)—the mammoth right wing organization that the BJP is the political wing of. The article, by V.P. Bhatia is titled 'Raise Tempers, Lacerate and Raise the Whirlwind: The Philosophy Behind Deepa Mehta's Kinky Film *Fire*' and appears in the *Organizer* issue dated 27 December 1998. Cited in Paola Bacchetta, op. cit., p. 153.

19. Unsigned, 'Shabana's Swear, Rabri's Roar, Teresa's Terror: The Three which Sustain Secularism', from *Organizer*, 10 January 1999. Cited in Paola Bacchetta, op. cit., p. 157.

20. V.P. Bhatia, op. cit., p. 153.
21. 'Same Sex Marriage Stumps PM', *Indiatimes.com* http://people.indiatimes.com/articleshow/996155.cms
22. Arjun Appadurai, (1996), op. cit., p. 47.
23. Ibid.
24. Peter Jackson, op. cit., p. 5.
25. Shivanada Khan, '*Kothis*, Gays and (other) MSM', October 2000, Naz Foundation International.
26. Ruth Vanita and Saleem Kidwai (Eds), *Same-Sex Love in India: Readings from Literature and History* (New York: Palgrave, 2001), p. 199.
27. A popular pretzel-shaped gooey syrupy Indian sweet.
28. Meaning a platter of assorted items (usually food).
29. Parents, Families & Friends of Lesbians & Gays, or PFLAG, is an American support group with more than 200,000 members. See their website—http://www.pflag.org
30. Thomas Blom Hansen, *Wages of Violence: Naming and Identity in Postcolonial Bombay*, (Princeton, NJ: Princeton University Press, 2001), p. 2.
31. Jeremy Seabrook, *Love in a Different Climate: Men Who have Sex with Men in India* (New York/London: Verso, 1999), p. 47.
32. In *Life Online: Researching Real Experience in Virtual Space* (Walnut Creek, CA: Altamira Press, 1998, p. 85), Annette Markham puts forth these three terms as frameworks for how users of computer mediated communication frame their experiences online. For Markham, these 'definitions fall along a continuum, from tool, to place, to way of being'.
33. Chris Berry and Fran Martin, 'Queer 'n' Asian On and Off the Net: The Role of Cyberspace in Queer Taiwan and Korea', in David Gauntlett (Ed.), *Web.Studies: Rewiring Media Studies for the Digital Age* (London: Arnold Publishers, 2000), p. 80.
34. Giuseppe Mantovani, *New Communication Environments from Everyday to Virtual* (London: Taylor & Francis, 1996), pp. 123–127; as cited in Berry and Martin op. cit., p. 78.
35. John Edward Campbell, *Getting It on Online: Cyberspace, Gay Male Sexuality, and Embodied Identity* (New York: Harrington Park Press, 2004), p. 12.
36. Arjun Appadurai (1996), op. cit., pp. 55–56.
37. A 'community of sentiment' is a group that 'begins to imagine and feel things together. Arjun Appadurai (1996) op. cit., p. 8. Appadurai first used the term in his essay 'Topographies of the Self: Praise and Emotion in Hindu India', in C.A. Lutz and L. Abu-Lughod (Eds), *Language and the Politics of Emotion* (Cambridge: Cambridge University Press, 1990).
38. John Edward Campbell (2004), op. cit., p. 109.
39. Shane Phelan (1994), Getting Specific: *Postmodern Lesbian Politics Minneapolis: University of Minnesota Press*, p. 87 paraphrased in Nikki Sullivan (2003), *A Critical Introduction to Queer Theory*, New York: New York University Press, p. 146.
40. Sara Ahmed and Anne-Marie Fortier (2003), 'Re-imagining Communities', *International Journal of Cultural Studies*, Vol. 6(3), p. 257.
41. Ahmed and Fortier, op. cit., p. 257.
42. Ibid.
43. Arjun Appadurai (1996), op. cit., p. 23.
44. John Gray, 'Modus Vivendi: Liberalism for the Coming Middle Ages', in *New Perspectives Quarterly* (Oxford; Malden, MA: Blackwell Publishers, 2001), Vol. 18(2). http://www.digitalnpq.org/archive/2001_spring/modus.html

45. Ibid.
46. Ibid.
47. Gayatri Spivak, *In Other Worlds: Essays in Cultural Politic* (New York: Methuen, 1987), p. 205.
48. David Woolwine, 'Community in Gay Male Experience and Discourse', *Journal of Homosexuality* (New York: Haworth Press, 2000), Vol. 38 (4), p. 16.
49. Fred Dallmayr, 'But on a Quiet Day...A Tribute to Arundhati Roy', *Logos 3.3* Summer 2004. http://www.logosjournal.com/issue_3.3/dallmayr.htm
50. Amartya Sen 'India: What Prospects?', *Indian Horizons* (New Delhi: Indian Council for Cultural Research, 1998), Vol. 45(3/4), p. 21.
51. This incident occurred in the first fortnight of June 2005. Rediffussion, an ad agency working for the client *DNA* (a Bombay city newspaper) had put up billboards all over the city with the text 'Same sex' and 'Safe sex' written below each other and a checking box right next to each option. As Alok wrote on the Gay Bombay mailing list, this was offensive because
    (a) people [might] believe that Same Sex and Safe Sex are two mutually exclusive activities. Therefore, same sex can never be safe. So apart from being 'Bad' same sex is a death wish;
    (b) it takes us back to old 80s western rhetoric that all Gay Men have HIV/AIDS or that HIV/AIDS only happens to Gay people;
    (c) it is indirectly stating that Homosexuality equals AIDS and of course all hetero-sexual sex is safe, so straight people should just chuck the use of condoms'. Sustained pressure by some Gay Bombay members, including a visit to the ad agency in question, led to the agency and the client, withdrawing the campaign and apologizing to the group privately. Source—postings to the Gay Bombay List by Alok 'Same Sex or Safe Sex—What's in your DNA?' (Dated 15 June 2005) and Vikram 'On DNA's Offensive Ads—Good News' (Dated 16 June 2005).
52. J. Malarvizhi, 'Move to give Transgendered Ration Cards Welcome', *The Hindu* 27 July 2006. http://www.hindu.com/2006/07/27/stories/2006072720080300.htm
53. Arvind Narrain, 'There are No Short Cuts to Queer Utopia: Sodomy, Law and Social Change', *Lines Magazine*, Vol. 2(4), February 2004. http://www.lines-magazine.org/Art_Feb04/Arvind.htm
54. Source—Posting to the Lbgt-India Yahoo! Group 'Re: saying thanks: Rainbow awards' by Lramkrishnan2004, dated 30 December 2005.
    Also see—'On the Wings of a Rainbow—Film Fest, Music Video, Awards and a March to Mark Gay Pride Week', *The Telegraph* (Calcutta, India), 21 June 2005. http://www.telegraphindia.com/1050621/asp/calcutta/story_4893049.asp
55. Nayan Shah, 'Sexuality, Identity and the Uses of History', in Ratti Rakesh (Ed.), *A Lotus of Another Color: An Unfolding of the South Asian Gay and Lesbian Experience* (Boston: Alyson Publications, 1993), p. 119.
56. See—Tarrannum Manjul and Sanjay Singh, 'All Gays Have United Against Us, Laughs UP Cop', *Indian Express*, 15 January 2006.
57. See for example—Marya Shakil, 'Why Parents, Children go to Court?' *IBNLive.com*, 6 July 2006. http://www.ibnlive.com/news/why-parents-children-go-to-court/14793-3.html
58. Ban on Gays Under Review—'Delhi HC to Decide on Validity of Law Against Homo-sexuality', *The Telegraph* (Calcutta, India) 4 February 2006. http://www.telegraphindia.com/1060204/asp/frontpage/story_5804545.asp

In the article Rashtra Prakash, general secretary of the VHP has this to say about homosexuality—

'We see it as an attack on Indian culture and value system. These people are influenced by free societies in the West but they forget that they live in India'.

59. Bhishma-*ashtami* is a day of funeral offerings in many Hindu temples and Brahmin households to Bhishma, the legendary warrior hero of the epic Mahabharata, who died childless on the battlefield. In 2004, Gay Bombay decided to appropriate this ritual by dedicating 'one GB meeting a year to remember gay friends who are no longer with us. A kind of an "all souls day"'. The agenda was to—

(a) Remember some our friends who have moved on and of our personal views about our death

(b) Buy food that our friends would have liked…[and]

(c) Share that food with a street child
(Source—posting by zoxlnc on the Gay Bombay Yahoo! Group 'Bhishma-ashtami and Dead Gay Men' dated 28 January 2004).

60. Anthony Giddens, (Revised edition) *Runaway World: How Globalization is Reshaping Our Lives* (New York: Routledge, 2002 [2000]), p. 40.

61. Source—Message post to the *Khush*-List Yahoo! Group by Vgd67 '5th Gay Bombay Parents and Relatives Meet' dated 3 August 2006.

62. *Dilwale Dulhania Le Jayenge* ('The Brave-Hearted Will Take the Bride'), released in 1995, is considered one of Bollywood's biggest films and the defining Bollywood film of the 1990s—with its astute blend of ritzy foreign locations and 'Indian' family values. For more about the film and its impact, read the book *Dilwale Dulhania Le Jayenge* by Anupama Chopra (London: British Film Institute, 2003).

63. Peter Jackson, op. cit., p. 21.

64. Vanita Ruth (Ed.), *Queering India: Same-sex Love and Eroticism in Indian Culture and Society* (London; New York: Routledge, 2002), p. 5.

65. Arvind Narrain, *Queer: Despised Sexuality, Law and Legal Change* (Bangalore: Books For Change, 2004), p. 26.

66. The suggestion of drawing inspiration from and enlisting the support of the *Dalit* and women's movements was discussed with me by Bhudev during our conversations. It has been raised more recently on the Lbgt-India Yahoo! Group. See correspondence between Vijai Sai and queernls on 14 April 2005.

67. Ashok Row Kavi posted this message to the Lbgt-India Yahoo! Group on 17 November 2004.

68. *Pravasya Bharat* stands for the Indian diaspora. For an excellent reading of Bollywood as cultural propaganda manipulated by the central government in their bid to woo the *Pravasya Bharatiyas* (non resident Indians), see Aswin Punthabedkar 'Bollywood in the Indian-American Diaspora: Mediating a Transitive Logic of Cultural Citizenship' in *International Journal of Cultural Studies* (Sage Publications, 2005), Vol. 8(2), pp. 1–173.

69. Gautam Bhan and Arvind Narrain, *Because I Have a Voice: Queer Polics in India* (New Delhi: Yoda Press, 2006), Introduction, pp. 9–10.

70. 'India Surpasses South Africa with Largest AIDS Population', *FoxNews.com*, 31 May 2006. http://www.foxnews.com/story/0,2933,197569,00.html

71. Source—Message posted to the INFOSEM Yahoo! Group 'Rally among Discrimination of Transgender Kokila', by Snegyitham dated 27 October 2006.

72. Ibid.

73. Pawan Varma, (2004), op. cit., pp. 15–16.
74. Ibid, p. 205.
75. Sunil Khilnani 2001, op. cit.
76. See—Satyanarayan Pattnaik, 'Two Orissa Girls Defy Norms, Get Married', *Times of India*, 5 November 2006. http://timesofindia.indiatimes.com/articleshow/322874.cms
77. See—Rahul Karmakar, 'Ballot Statement with Same Sex Love', *Hindustan Times*, 8 April 2006. http://www.hindustantimes.com/news/181_1669963,001302200004.htm
78. AllyGator, 'Queer I: Happy Together', *Time Out Mumbai* (October 2005).
79. Government of India instructions for filling up passports are available on the website—http://www.passport.nic.in/ The form required to be filled up is titled 'Form No. 2' [Application for Miscellaneous Services on Indian passports]. The instructions for filling up this form, which mention the requirements of the affidavit and the medical certificate, are available on the website http://www.passport.nic.in/ To change one's sex in the Electoral Roll, one is required to approach the office of the Electoral Commission and make an application in Form 8. This form is available on the website of the Election Commission of India, http://eci.gov.in/Forms/FORM8A.pdf

    To change one's sex on the Permanent Account Number, one has to make the required application form titled 'Request For New PAN Card Or/And Changes Or Correction In PAN Data' and submit it along with documents in support. This form is available at—http://incometaxindia.gov.in/Archive/ChangeForm.PDF

    (Source—Message posting from Vivek Divan on the Lbgt-India mailing list 'On recognition of 'Eunuchs' and Gender Reassignment Surgery' dated 5 March 2005).
80. The official NACO website—http://www.nacoonline.org/ is a comprehensive source for up to date facts and figures relating to HIV in India.
81. See—'Govt's AIDS Cell Pushes to Legalise Homosexuality', *Times of India*, 20 July 2006. http://timesofindia.indiatimes.com/articleshow/1779097.cms
82. Source—Message posting from Ashok Row Kavi on the Lgbt-India Yahoo! Group ('Thoughts on future strategies on 377 in the Delhi High Court') dated 18 February 2006.
83. Sunil Khilnani, 'Many Wrinkles in History' Outlook Magazine, 20 August 2001, http://www.outlookindia.com/full.asp?fodname=20010820&fname=Sunil+Kilnani+%28F%29&sid=1
84. Rama Bijapurkar, 'Strategic Marketing Key to Customer Insight', *Focus Magazine* (Bombay: Central Bank of India, January 2005), p. 12. http://www.centralbankofindia.co.in/home/Focusnew/Pdf/CBI_Jan%20final%2009-16.pdf
85. See Rama Bijapurkar, Virginia Valentine and Monty Alexander, 'Charting the Cultural Future of Markets,' paper delivered at the European Society for Market Research Annual Congress at Davos (September), in ESOMAR 47th Congress Handbook (Amsterdam, 1995), pp. 143–161; cited in David Page and William Crawley, *Satellites Over South Asia* (London: Sage Publications, 2000), p. 141.
86. Anthony Giddens and Christopher Pierson, Conversations with Anthony Giddens: Making Sense of Modernity (Oxford: Polity Press, 1998), p. 77 quoted in Gauntlett, David (2002), *Media, Gender and Identity: An Introduction*, (London and New York: Routledge, 2002), pp. 94–95.
87. Amara Das Wilhelm, *Tritiya-Prakriti: People of the Third Sex* (Xlibris Corporation, 2004), p. xxi.

9

The Future Queer Histories That Must Be Written

*A Conversation between Parmesh Shahani and Dhiren Borisa**

P: Dhiren, thank you so much for having this conversation for the special anniversary edition of *Gay Bombay*.

D: Thank you for giving me this opportunity. On my way here, I was reminded about how I stumbled upon the book *Gay Bombay*. As a shy small-town boy in the big bad city of Delhi, I had come to seek a future and a refuge for my queerness—a word that I later learnt and am still learning. Among the several parallelly laid bookshelves at a distant dark end of the JNU library where I was studying, my eyes sparkled at the sight of the word 'gay' next to a 'city' that I had never been to, but knew of, through Bollywood and fashion—Bombay. There were several books on the subject of queerness here but not many that my closeted self could readily relate to. Nobody knew of my sexuality then, so I sneakily picked that book up (I could not dare issue it and proudly wander in the campus with that word too visible) and hid at some other corner—a place I would later hide and read this book. I had hidden it among other books which would train me to think of geography and places in particular, and often disciplining ways, and ways I have been since then trying to undo, as to queer it. It showed up in years later when I would do my doctoral research at the same university on queerness and city. Not Bombay but Delhi. When I was exploring my sexuality in the 1990s and in my early 20s, I was introduced to the Yahoo chat rooms, and the

* Assistant Professor at O. P. Jindal Global University.

excitement and the fantastic world that it allowed you to create. Your book spoke of similar worlds but of different times and possibilities and of people, and I think this conversation is interesting because it takes us to a decade after that and in the process many places that we both might have inhabited, loved and despised.

P: Let's talk about the prehistory of the queer Internet. How did my book influence your work?

D: It's interesting because queerness and technology have such an exciting relationship. And this book explores it so beautifully. There are so many similarities between what you do, and I did in my work. The very ways in which we write because we use the memoir. We undo the rigidity of ethnography by saying, 'I am going to tell my story and you will have to listen to it.' That itself is a moment of pride and queerness. That's how we queer the very idea of doing and writing about our lives. And that was very helpful. Like *Gay Bombay*...a list of this, and then for me to have my first interaction in Yahoo chat rooms and people asking 'asl' and I was like what is 'asl'.

P: Asl and 'have place'. That's the second question.

D: 'Have place' still continues. (chuckles)

P: Yes, have place continues. Even on Grindr...

D: Yes! Indeed. Not in similar sense of a place to mean the spatial possibility of a sexcapade (as on Grindr on any of these apps), what is interesting with *Gay Bombay* is that it is Bombay. The place. That located-ness of it. But it's still not limited to Bombay. It's global.

P: I write about how all these places come about because of a dialectic. I mean it's Gay Bombay, it's Indian queerness but how is it formed because of network of influences and possibilities. *Gay Bombay* built upon not just the work of say a *Bombay Dost* or Humsafar Trust or based on the dial-up Internet of VSNL but also magazines like *Trikone* that came out of San Francisco and South Asian queer networks like the Khush list. For large parts of time on the *Gay Bombay* and other lists, more than half the people were diasporic queers, more attached to the idea of Bombay as this imaginary homeland which they felt happier in than maybe the physical queer world they were living in whether London or San Francisco. I actually wanted to end this book with you because I really look up to you and your dissertation work which we hope is going to come out soon as a book. Scholars like you are in a sense the legacy that I was hopefully trying to create when I wrote *Gay Bombay*. Then there were very few queer books in Indian voices in terms of academia. There was literature but there were very few academic works on queerness.

I am actually very happy to see how you have taken this intersectionality of technology and sexuality into a new direction with your work, I wanted to ask you since you remember the time of chat rooms: what you feel has changed and how we imagine and articulate queerness today digitally since my times. I really feel like a veteran and in the foreword of this book I write how when *Gay Bombay* came out first it was an ethnography and anthropology, and now it belongs to the history section. You are now doing the queer anthropology today so what do you think has changed since those days in terms of how we express ourselves online?

D: I think a lot has changed and still a lot is very similar. In the sense the very question of access still remains, despite over time we know new kinds of bodies have entered these spaces often on contested terms. When you talked about how *Gay Bombay* came up, you said that the people you were writing about were mostly diaspora, people who were everywhere in the world, had access, had resources, could go anywhere, mostly men. I write about my first time in my PhD, when I got to know someone in the Yahoo chat room. They would tell me that they stayed in these cities that you speak of, around the world—Delhi, Bombay, London, San Francisco. At the same time, I was in love with this boy who was rich, upper caste. This boy would tell me, 'I could take you home' because you know you do not look lower caste. That I was meritorious, smart and popular in school and spoke so eloquently—traits that certain privileged bodies were entitled to.

P: ...and you still loved him?

D: Love is so flawed in that sense. We desire what kills us. He was studying in Delhi and I could not even imagine coming out of my home town. He took me for the first time to a cybercafé. This underground basement.

He said let me show you something. He opened Yahoo messenger and pointed, 'See, this is like Delhi Gay chat rooms and here we can talk to random people.' It was like some ₹50–₹60 for half an hour and from the background I came from, I did not have that luxury. So I would save money, go to the café but be very scared of leaving a browser history. When I talk about the intersections of technology and queerness, and many other social axes I struggle with, this is what I mean—survival, of desires and selves. What the Internet was allowing me to do was an attempt at undoing certain kinds of histories and recreating myself in that. Because if I was there at that point of history in those spaces, I was automatically assumed to be upper caste and upper class. Similar to how my then lover thought he could take me home because I didn't look lower caste.

It was on this random chat room that somebody asked me, 'what's your PR id?' and I was like what the hell is this? I thought and stupidly so that isn't it 'public relations'? Waiting only to be illuminated by someone who would introduce me to this portal, PlanetRomeo. I was asked to 'Go there, make an account.' That space itself, so fraught with anxiety, even if you want to be there, belong there, you are manufacturing so much. You know that you might not even meet that person you are talking to. Unlike today. Because not everybody was saying the truth, in that not saying the 'truth', everybody was saying the truth. A truth that could hold fantasy of the self more than the assigned identifications of the 'normal' world. Today there's a lot of conversation around what is real ID and what is fake ID. Why aren't you showing your picture and who gets to show their pictures? I feel that earlier it was very stationary in the sense that the cybercafé was a very located place bound entity and you had to go there and then randomly chat with people. The mobility that technology has allowed you in terms of smartphones that you can move around everywhere has changed the very grammar of this interaction but also made queerness available as a very thin archive.

We might not be bothered about location today (similar to the yesteryears of gay loneliness—not to say that we are not lonely anymore—I would differ and say we are all the more) but we still need place. Where will the act happen? Where is sex going to take place? Where are we going to meet?

P: You said that you think earlier was thick and now it's thin archive. That's one distinction?

D: I would not say there can be this neatness through which you can say that thick or thin but in times of this speed in which it happens today. I have interviewed a lot of people and people would say that we used to keep a phone book, this list of people that we have met. They would change three buses to go from Patparganj to Gurgaon to meet this person they randomly met on the Internet. Today even 1 km seems too far. That instant nature of the conversation, that hastiness with which you are practising that haptic geography. So fast we open Tinder on our smartphones, swipe like left, right—spells out the anxiety in our desires. I have some 700 matches right now and I have not talked to 90 per cent of them.

P: This is Dhiren swag! 700 matches, wow! So that's one of the changes, yes yet materially nothing has changed. Body still desires, body still needs a place....

D: Yes, the body still has some located-ness. What the Internet did for me and what it does for a lot of people is that it allows you a possibility to become something. Even today. A lot of people I interview, because I work at the intersection of caste and class, and religion, there's lot of anxiety around the location, gender, its presentation and I know a lot of lower caste people whom I have interviewed, including me, would use an upper caste surname in those spaces. On Facebook, there are a lot of people still who do not have access to Grindr. Because you need smartphone that materially is not easy for a lot of people or to have data pack and to continuously recharge the data pack. Or this flawed distinction between social and sexual, networking and dating that they would not want to be on something that claims to be a gay dating app and avoid certain risks. That you call oneself 'Top' and not 'Gay' has many stories to say and so much in how desire works. The Internet allows you to adopt names, even in those Yahoo chat rooms. A lot of people use upper caste surnames. There's one person who uses Karan Singhania and it's interesting. I asked him why Karan Singhania and he was like... *Ekta Kapoor ka serial nahi dekha kya?* (haven't you watched Ekta Kapoor's serial?)...all these Singhania and Mr Bajaj and Mr Basu people are a bit more affluent. They live in big bungalows, have multiple cars outside, and wear sleeping robes. Today it's all about the visuals. On Yahoo chat room, it was not about the visuals because you were happy that somebody was there, and somebody was chatting with you and somebody shared a similar kind of anxiety. Even on my Facebook fake account, I do not have a picture, I have like five random male models from *Gladrags* Manhunt that I have kept there. You know if you are called Karan Singhania or like what I call myself, Sanidhya Sharma, despite me not having the picture, people are going to talk to me. You realize that even though technology allows you anonymity, allows you possibility to become something and recreate yourself and open up a world of possibility, it collapses and it is a thin paste of fulcrum which is built through caste, class and other social privileges. The access of desire is itself going to be through that. That has not changed. It is still just gay men. I remember in JNU a few lesbians asked us, 'you have Grindr and PlanetRomeo; can you search something for us?' And then we found something called *Findher* and you had to pay to download that. It wasn't very useful.

P: Now, there's Bumble, na.

D: I think, more than Grindr, more than Facebook, now a lot of sex is happening on TikTok. We shifted from Grindr to Tinder because Tinder allowed you more anonymity. You could identify as straight and still be there and nobody is going to judge you for being present on a particular platform.

P: If someone catches you on Tinder, you can say I have said I like both men and women, and I'm interested in them as friends! It's all about the friendship….

D: Totally! Friendship is such an interesting idiom of sexuality, especially in India. It has helped so many of us survive our desires. Akhil Katyal writes about it so beautifully in *Doubleness of Sexuality*. The language of *masti, lat, aadat, shauq, dosti* and *baazi*. We all have had *best* friends and we have all been doing *laundebaazi*.

From TikTok to Instagram…all the gym boys with millions of followers, all ready to sleep, all excited and titillated by this idea and a lot of them might project themselves like Facebook people used to do...*you know I am top I am not gay.* That distinction between top and gay. I could be top Bombay, not gay Bombay. That same language is now on Instagram. You sneak into people's DM and chat with them and everybody is up for sexual pleasures.

P: You know, while doing this anniversary edition, I chopped out bits of the book. While I did that, I was struck by what you have told me about how caste is so obvious in this book by its non-existence. I don't write about it. I am not conscious about it in my own life, in my memoir bits and none of my interviewees raise that. It is a function of whom we are talking to and who I'm interviewing at that time and my own positioning 15 years ago where because of my privilege it didn't occur to me that this should be something I ask my interviewers about or that comes up in that conversation.

D: And as you said it is beautiful that you didn't have to ask. The structure of caste is so insidious. So every day. Despite not asking, it is already there by its absence. Like day before yesterday, in the Culture Lab panel discussion which you were moderating, I said caste is not a lower caste people's problem. Let's stop pushing it on lower castes and say deal with it.

P: Yet, 15 years later, in *Queeristan*, the book I'm doing now, caste consciousness is there in every line of the book. This is also a function of my growth over the years through friends like you, and the fact that the world has changed, and people are talking more and more about caste whether through the lens of intersectionality or by talking about caste alone. Your work and our friendship have been fundamental to me in unpacking some of this. I just wanted your thoughts on caste and queerness through your work and also through the work people are doing now which is rich and exciting.

D: Clearly, there is a lot of conversation around caste now, especially I see sociologists and anthropologists doing anthologies on caste. There is a historical erasure of lower caste people in university spaces. Activists have said it enough, it is not academy, it is an Agrahara. It has always been an Agrahara. Why *Gay Bombay* is manifestation of that Agrahara is because you network with people who are like you, you take people out on dates who look like you, who dress like you, and therefore for me, in terms of queerness and caste, there has been a lot to do with aesthetics and performance. To exist. To fit in. To survive. Not just performance through a fake account and fake name but how do I look, how do I dress because I know that the mike will come to me if I raise my hand only when I look a particular way. I should look academic, I should look serious, I should look worthy of asking a question. But the very fact, and I say it with hurt and pain, that it needed a Dalit boy to die in a university and create a furore, for people to talk about it, oblivious that people have been dying for centuries in universities and schools. Like my grandmother didn't want me to come to Delhi or any other city, she clearly said that when our people go out, they are killed. We are not going to lose more lives. For me, the conversation of caste is the question that our lives are not dispensable and not worth any of your politics and your writing and the ways in which you articulate. Today, everybody wants to write about caste and queerness. If you find a bundle of Dalit queer people, wow, your paper is going to be accepted in any international conference and you know that comes at such a huge cost of visibility. I get a lot of hate messages on Grindr, but not as many as our friend Vqueeram gets because there it becomes the question of gender, how you are gender nonconforming....

P: And celebrating this nonconformity with sauciness, humour, pleasure...

D: Vqueeram keeps changing what he keeps on doing...the name they keep is the last slang or slur they were subjected to on these platforms. So they would be called like Sixer or sick, so they would call themselves sixy—I'm sick and sexy...or *randi* or slut.... All those words and we know all these terms have a gendered history of controlling women's sexuality and femininity. For me, I get hits on Grindr because my Instagram is linked to it with nice and sexy pictures. I have taken efforts to curate it. Well, I don't, Vqueeram does it! My Instagram description reads 'awkward Dalit queer' and people who go to those pictures in Instagram, who like those pictures, then comment why do you have to mention 'Dalit'. Often,

I use 'D' as my profile name because my name is Dhiren, but people ask me, 'Have you written it to say Dalit'?

P: Who is doing the asking?

D: Random faceless profiles. They say horrible things, start abusing, threaten and, because I always try to engage and explain, they would block me. See how our presence, like Rohit's presence, in universities makes the university so anxious? These spaces, which you were saying, which build through cohort of access, when we pass, if I do not say anything, when I look as dandy as possible, as fag that I can be and as sassy, nobody cares. The moment I speak out, we speak out, then there is a problem.

P: As we saw in the documentary *Please Mind the Gap* yesterday at our event, queer upper caste people say thakur so casually, and novels like Anuja Chauhan's *Those Pricey Thakur Girls* can have a caste title and it will not be an issue but if we would say 'Those Pricey Dalit Girls' then I am sure everyone would raise an issue.

D: Yes, why are you bringing caste? Like caste only comes when Dalit people bring it and say that we are Dalit—now the caste has come!

P: Does this come in queer Dalit places as well? Is this, I mean, and I want to talk about the queer movement as well as I have been part of this in Bombay and as part of many organizing efforts and we have had, whether it's the pride organizing, it is very challenging for people who are trying to build nuanced conversation places or where one can talk about multiple identities.

D: I think both the sides of politically positioning are fraught with unrest from anxiety. In anti-caste spaces, people are anxious, which was true for women's movement also. Right? 'Don't bring any lesbian.'

P: Maya Sharma wrote about how for many years they excluded even talking about lesbians in the feminist movement.

D: Yes, they said if you want to come, come as a woman. Don't come as a lesbian woman, or a bisexual woman, because then you are dividing the movement. I don't blame the anti-caste movement for this because they are somehow trying to manage and survive themselves. It's very difficult to keep hold of everybody but I also see a lot of things changing. At least, at JNU where I studied, there is a flourishing student group called 'BAPSA' or Birsa Ambedkar Phule Students' Association. JNU is all about politics and wants to be the most progressive bastion in the world. But I have seen the 'Left' being more arrogant in saying you know we know the solutions. Straight people would come and teach gay people how to be gay or what it is to be queer? I am like 'what audacity'! And on the other hand, BAPSA people would come and say, 'you know we are trying to learn, can you tell us?' The very difference in the way you approach something, an issue or problem, says a lot in terms of what is possible. I feel the anti-caste movement is actually opening up to this and opening up queerness also in the process.

P: To its true and immense possibilities, right? In terms of what queerness can be…

D: And what queerness can do to the anti-caste movement as well. Being in a university when you are not destined to be in a university is itself a queer act. You are surviving in a university which was designed for you to collapse. Just being able to be here is beautiful. I'll tell you this incident in Bombay. I was going back after an event and this conversation was happening on Grindr, a faceless profile, who asked, 'oh why do you have to talk about Dalit?' I said, 'but it's there, caste determines desirability, whom you desire, how you desire, etc. Haven't you seen so many profiles called Hot Jats, top Gujjar 8 inches, what are these profiles? Phallocentric? How certain caste identities get to flaunt their caste location by saying that you are not talking by caste, but you have rationalized that body to look like that. When I say Jat and Gujjar, you imagine a hyper-masculine, hot dude with a 9-inch penis and that's all what you desire. When I say Dalit or somebody writes Chamar, can somebody write that? Or do this?'

I am trying to explain the distinction and he says, 'oh, I think I understand your thing.' Let me give you a solution. He says, 'Lord Vishnu in Bhagwad Gita writes…everybody can enter my temple. From Brahman, Kshatriya, Vaishya, Sudra, Ati Sudra…anybody can enter my temple.' And I am like, but our fight is not to enter your temple. It is for dignity and self-respect which are two different things. Stop making it all about yourself.

P: Did that conversation go anywhere?

D: No. I think both anti-caste and queer spaces have to do a lot of learning and unlearning. It comes through engagement and also by identifying the terms of this engagement. Are you using certain bodies as tools to learn or just tools to dissect and exploit them? In queer spaces, often one has to make oneself vulnerable at the risk of losing one's desirability. I have been thrown out in the middle of sex in a conversation when they figured out my location and politics. I have spoken this that how easy it is to come out as queer because queer is fashionable. But it is very difficult to come out as a lower caste, and when you happen to be both and many such things. Also not able-bodied, or you live in a small village in some remote part, where technology has not entered and probably they do not have enough money to buy a copy of *Gay Bombay*—you don't learn about what's happening and what fancy possibilities await outside, it is very difficult. How does one put oneself there as a body, but a body that also desires in both spaces? I am not giving any respite to any spaces. It is a continuous self-flagellation, and continuously making yourself available for violence and sometimes you feel it's necessary.

P: Akhil Kang wrote how the queer movement is really indebted to Ambedkar on the basis of which all these cases could be fought, in whether this was in 2001, 2009, certainly 2018 but how the queer movement doesn't really remember that or acknowledge that or celebrate that. I would say as part of this unlearning and learning process, also just relooking at wherever our queer rights come from and how they are so deeply rooted to the ideals on which this country boils, at least the modern vision of this country was imagined, I think would be a useful place.

D: But even within the frame of the constitution, the realm of law where we as queer people have been obsessed with getting our rights from, forgetting our lives is not just law, our lives are beyond law, they existed before 377...it has always been like that. We have been fabulous; we have been trying to make room for ourselves and live. We need to acknowledge the fact that in 2013 when the Supreme Court said get lost and in 2018 when suddenly they said let's embrace each other, that movement of transition is also about how you put across your case. In the 2018 verdict, who were the petitioners? You remove sex workers, you remove trans people? A number of people were harassed by police through 377 and we know rarely privileged gay men were harassed through that. If you go to cruising areas, the *kothis*, the trans people, the people who do not have the language of gay, people who do not know what queer means, people who cannot ride the day out, sometimes police catches you and asks for a blowjob and they have to—and they will do it. These are the people being harassed. Then there were the petitions which IIT students were filing. These IIT students are assets to our country, national pride, that they are the future. They represent caste merit. They are respectable citizens. A five-star hotelier who wants to marry his French husband. So you actually fought and won this case on the back of privileges and respectability, and in that moment, you made queer a possibility only for certain people, imagining that trickle-down economics will work without structurally doing anything about it. Very good! That 377 went away but what did it do materially for people? Did it transform people's lives? Maybe some people found it more confident to share about their lives, to talk to their parents, that now they feel it's easier. For many, they are back to their jobs, they don't even know about this law. Every time I go home, I switch on Grindr and trust me right now here in Delhi, if I open Grindr, I might find 100 people in the vicinity of 3 km and the farthest is 7 km in Rohini. In South Delhi, within 500 m, there are 100 people. In my home town, I will have to travel to a neighbouring village; maybe I see people till Vadodara or Udaipur… like the closest person it shows me is in Udaipur which is another 90 or 100 km away from where I live.

P: It's like going back to Yahoo chat.

D: Yes. They say, 'Oh will you come to my village? Are you taking a train via Falna, do you want to meet me? I stay in this village near Falna.' And most of them are married. Young, married people, right? Might not articulate as gay, because gay comes from the language that comes from a particular burden and history. But a practice in bisexuality or as Akhil Katiyal will say the doubleness of the lives through the doubleness of these spaces, of how Internet technology, queerness allows them this possible realm where they can be. Now that realm is beyond law. That realm is negotiated through social structures which have always and will continue to defy our desires on sexuality. Why those people we interview are upper caste people is not an accident, it is structural. And the solution can only come, and we can look at Ambedkar and think about it, through the Constitution by saying that it is not an accident. As Rohith Vemula wrote in the last letter: 'it is the probably the only thing I'll write and that my birth is my fatal accident.' What he says is structural and then probably we need structural remedies than these cosmetic surgeries we are trying to push for with the law. I'm sure the next big thing is gay marriage. There's already a petition.

P: A lot of the work I do in corporate world is on widening possibilities of inclusion and I'm struck as we are having this conversation, it's been relatively easy to get companies and I am saying this because I serve in the diversity council of my company, and while I have tried, it's been much easier to get mine and other companies to do queer inclusion and LGBTQ inclusion but I have raised the issue of caste and the answer I got was that we don't want to talk about caste.

D: Yes, we don't discriminate, and it doesn't exist. It isn't part of our hiring policy but inadvertently everybody you hire comes from a particular community.

P: I have spoken to other diversity heads in other companies, all of who are working on many facets of diversity and they all have said that it is easier to get their companies to talk about able-bodiedness, mental health, and gender and sexuality are now very fashionable but no one wants to talk about caste and they cite various reasons. Like if we stop asking people on forms, then how do we measure, but I think fundamentally there is this discomfort to talk about it and yet when you look all around the table at any corporate interaction you recognize how it's so much privileged.

Gay Bombay, by its very name as I declared in the book 15 years ago, was researched at a place in a particular time within this online offline community called Gay Bombay which consisted of mostly men and 15 years later, we still find there is not much, certainly way less, I would say about LBT. How do we create more? I guess part of it is structural, how do we get more women into networks of creating or how do we empower queer women or trans men to tell more of their stories? These two things are very absent in *Gay Bombay*. The presence and absence of caste and zero women in this book. How do we create the next generation of queer scholars?

D: There is a big gap that in both *Gay Bombay* and my research that we do not talk about women. We talk from our own subject's position and that also cites our privilege because that makes access to certain places and vocabulary to write about much easier. It is capitalism, neoliberal economy, it's how structurally men have access to material resources. I don't know about Bombay but in Delhi, there are gay parties 4 days in a week and multiple parties happen in the same night. If you go to all these spaces, all you would see gay and bisexual men or men who have sex with men. You would hardly see women and Trans* folks. Women would come with their gay friends, hardly 4–5, dancing in a circle and then go. And then you realize why you can't have LBT party spaces because it's not economical. The questions come down to who has money? Who has resources? And in whom should I invest? If I write about lesbians apart from people who fetishize lesbians erotically and bunch of queer women who have been expressing, articulating, resisting burden of the society, nobody is going to buy those books. So publisher is going to think if it is worth an investment to even publish it, but you know, gay men are everywhere.

P: Even within the movement, some years ago as part of the Mumbai pride organizing, the pride organizing committee decided that the closing party would be an LBT party. There was so much hatred within the gay community saying why is it LBT, why are you excluding gay men, and the gay men were so outraged that they threw a rival party because they just couldn't take that for one year after so many years of doing pride, it was an LBT party. And the LBT party was not excluding gay men, it was just saying it is LBT, if you are a gay man, make a friend with someone who is LBT and come for the party. It was inclusion. It made me realize how gay men are really acting like straight men, within patriarchy...

D: I think those moments are very important because otherwise we are staying in a cocoon thinking that oh, it's all about us. We need to acknowledge our own set of privileges through which we are able to exercise and access these spaces. Queering then because you are talking about queering the future is to rework this very logic, that logic of desirability which is right now manifested through neoliberal capitalism. Our spaces cannot continue to function with this lopsided amnesia of sorts where you forget who all are part of this community.

P: And it is always either/or!

D: Yes, why not everybody? In school, I used to go for interschool competition and there was this all women's school and this girl who would participate in debate competitions against me. She would always come and chat with me because I was this femme boy. I would not say anything to her but she would tell me, 'Do you see that girl, I have a crush on her?' and things like that and I felt like...it's nice...so maybe what I am having is also fine. And the last I heard about her, it's strange because she never said she was a lesbian, she said she liked that girl, so pretty...that she committed suicide on the day of her marriage. And I didn't know. Everybody said that the family had a narrative, but I was perhaps the only person she confided in, knowing that her story would perhaps never be shared.

P: So is there a queer future in which all of us can have our rights? And I come back to this conflict within the movement that is reminding me in what I wrote back 15 years in the book which still exists. But I come back to the first time when we met. And you are very kind for forgiving me for my stupidity at that time because you understood how I was brainwashed by the society to think of that narrative, but you remember how we argued at the Mingle Summit.

D: Because I'm shy and I don't speak up. I was like I am not going to say anything. I am going to speak up. It was the only moment in the entire two-day thing that I spoke because I thought now I have to. I can't keep quiet.

P: I had been arguing at that time very stupidly that queer people can…

D: You showed that *Dostana* clip…

P: I still show that *Dostana* clip but I show that now in a very different context and I said why can't we be like everyone else to win our rights and at that time for me it seemed perfectly okay to argue that we needed to squash all our other identities just to win this legal recognition but as you told me that day and over the past years I have understood that what kind of freedom is it if some of us have won rights but others haven't.

D: In the clip, it is about how the mother will accept if you be that daughter-in-law kind of image that you present…for a lot of queer people they are materially compelled to get married, women especially, and you have no escape from what kind of future they are fitting in, they are trying to fit in their best. That are still not surviving. While in the cab coming to the SAGE office, I was continuously chatting with this man from Himachal. He was telling me, 'I'm getting married next week. You think I will be able to do fine?' And in that very moment rather than giving him huge academic lecture on you know marriage is a heteronormative patriarchal institution that we need to get rid of it, I knew, this trope of choice people keep on flaunting does not exist. I'm sure if that person had a choice, he would have navigated through it. I know a lot of people who have survived, and they have survived through their doubleness. Ismat Chughtai writes about doubleness in 'Lihaf', and therefore actually the queer movement is more indebted to women than they think about. The spaces that have been created of LBT people even in cities like Delhi, the capital, are all of privileged women and people with access. One has to create an alternate space when the structure denies you space. Trans and women bodies are easily treated as available to exercise power that they started creating these small parties, but you have to be in those networks, they happen in houses. But the questions are where are these houses located? Who has this house? Who has this house big enough to host people in? And, therefore, people who would feel comfortable to be in those spaces are also particular kind of people, people who 15 years earlier could be part of this book. These are the people who go to these places. I know a queer woman, a *safai karamchari* (cleaner), Dalit women, who like going to dance parties. I know a trans man activist who goes with them to these parties because they won't go alone. I have to think many times how I'm looking, what I'm wearing, when I go out. I have been denied entry in Kitty Su multiple times. Kitty Su is a gay-friendly space but do I have ₹800 for a pint of beer? Once a friend told me that often on dance floors in these parties he would dance alone. But to dance alone, you also need some kind of confidence and alcohol has helped people for longest period of time, however ephemeral it might be. On one such night, possibly his first at this fancy night club, he decided to go grab a beer. He had been to a few other parties where a pint of beer is max ₹300. He approaches the bartender and buys a pint and only after handing over the card for payment realizes it costs ₹800 here. When you only get certain small amount to survive in this big city from parents who hardly earn anything unlike many bodies who comfortably own these spaces, it's a big deal. He took that beer and he couldn't even drink that beer, he just sat in a corner and felt sad. Now, that's what queerness is, that's what that Gay Bombay list was, that's what Yahoo chat rooms were, or Grindr or Instagram is; it gives you a brief moment of pleasure but at a heavy cost, because that space you think it is going to give you happiness and pleasure is going to collapse anytime, and you will collapse with it.

About the Author

Parmesh Shahani is Vice President at Godrej Industries Ltd and the founder of the award-winning Godrej India Culture Lab which sparks conversations and collaborations about the changing face of contemporary India. Parmesh is a passionate advocate for LGBTQ inclusion in corporate India and has guided many of the country's leading companies on their inclusion journeys. He is a member of the FICCI taskforce on diversity and inclusion, and a board member of Khoj International Artists' Association.

Parmesh holds an MS in Comparative Media Studies from Massachusetts Institute of Technology (MIT). He has been a TED Senior Fellow, a Yale World Fellow and a World Economic Forum Young Global Leader.

This is an updated edition of his first book *Gay Bombay: Globalization, Love and (Be)Longing in Contemporary India*, which was originally published by SAGE Publications in 2008. His second book *Queeristan: LGBTQ Inclusion at the Indian Workplace* is slated for publication in 2020.

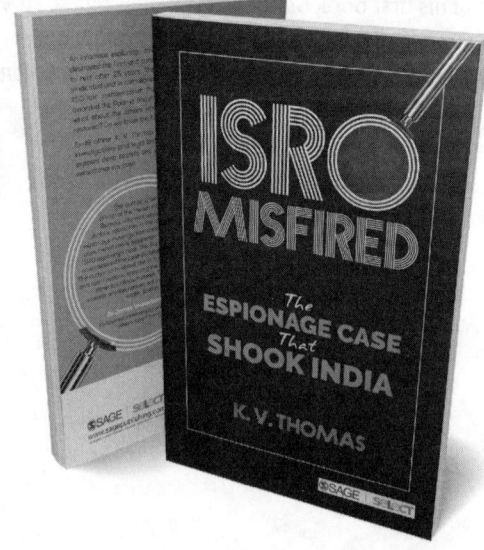